Philosophical Musings

Thirteen Questions That Provide
A Topical
Introduction to Philosophy

By
Glenn Rogers, Ph.D.

Simpson & Brook, Publishers
Abilene, Texas

Table of Contents

Preface

My first exposure to philosophy came when I was an undergraduate student in the early 1970s. I attended a three-night debate on the existence of God. That's all it took. I was hooked. It would be many years before I studied philosophy in any formal way (I was already committed to a different academic and career path), but when I finally began formal philosophical studies, I realized that philosophy was what I should have been doing all along. After earning the degree I needed, I became a philosophy professor for several years. I'm retired now, but when I was teaching, I realized that students were not always as enthusiastic about the discipline as I was. That's too bad. My hope is that in this introductory text I can impart to students an appreciation for the value of philosophy and the skills it helps one develop.

An ancient Hebrew philosopher, perhaps Solomon, said, *of the making of many books there is no end*. He was right. The world is filled with tens of millions of books on all sorts of subjects. Thousands of them are about philosophy and hundreds of those qualify as introductory philosophy texts. So why write another one? Why write a book entitled:

Philosophical Musings: Thirteen Questions That Provide A Topical Introduction To Philosophy? First, because I love to write. Second, because I know something about the subject. And third, (and this is the most important reason) because even though nearly all of what I say in this book will be similar to what you might read in another topical introduction to philosophy, it will not be identical. Some of what I say will be different˙ (perhaps very different—depending on who the other authors are), and all of it will be said differently. No two philosophers are going to explain things in exactly the same way. My hope is that the way I explain things as I answer the thirteen philosophical questions we're going to consider will interest students and help them see the value (and pleasure) of learning to think like a philosopher.

Glenn Rogers, Ph.D.
Abilene, Texas
2018

Introduction

A few years ago in my Introduction to Philosophy class one of my students (a young lady) emailed me. She explained that she had taken philosophy because she was about to graduate and needed one more humanities course. My Introduction to Philosophy course fit her schedule, so she took it. She explained that she hadn't really understood what philosophy was. She thought it was something that had to do with odd or weird questions that weren't very important or practical. Now, however (at the time she was emailing me, a little over half way through the course), she realized that philosophy was *real* (her word) and an important discipline that mattered, that it was something that you could do something with. Her note was not a very eloquent statement but I knew what she meant. It made me smile. She was right. Philosophy is real. It is important. And it is something you can use... it is eminently practical.

Perhaps you will see how important and practical philosophy can be if you pause to consider the thirteen questions we will be considering in this course. Turn to the Table of Contents and read the chapter titles. Really. Stop reading this page and go to the Table of Contents and read the chapter titles. Okay, the first three, *How Did Philosophy*

Begin, How Did Philosophy Develop, and *Why Study Philosophy,* may not sound all that interesting—even though they are. But they are important and will help you get a handle on the subject. The rest of the chapters might sound more interesting. For instance, the question under consideration in Chapter 4 is, *What can be known?* Philosophically, this has to do with what is referred to as *epistemology*, the study of knowledge—of what can be known and how can it be known. Did you ever "know" something only to find out later that you didn't really know it after all? Maybe you thought you knew what you needed to know for a test. Turned out you didn't. Or maybe you thought you knew something about someone or some situation or event. But later you realized that you were wrong. If you were wrong about it, you didn't really know it in the first place, did you? You can't "know" something that is not true. You can believe it. But you can't know it. What's the difference between knowing something and believing something? We'll talk about that more in Chapter 4. For now, let's just say that whatever the difference is between belief and knowledge, it's huge. Or maybe you thought you knew something that can't really be known. What kinds of things can be known and what kinds of things can't be known? How would one know the difference between them, and if a thing can be known, how does one come to know what can be known? We live our lives based on what we know, or sometimes based on what we think we know. Could it be that the difference between those two (what we know and what we think we know) is important? As it turns out, epistemological considerations are important to everyday life.

The question discussed in Chapter 5, *Why Is There Something Rather Than Nothing*, is also an important question. Have you ever asked yourself that question? Most people haven't. Why not? It seems like a foundational question. Three-year olds are good at asking "Why?" questions. Their minds are awakening to the world and they

9

want to know the reasons for things. So they ask: Why? Why? Why? That's the reason for this question—why is there something rather than nothing? We need to understand things. The cosmos is a reality that we experience every moment of our lives. Why does it exist? Why is that an important question? Because the answer provides us with insight into the origins and purposes of the things that exist— which happens to include us. We are part of the something that exists. So asking about why something exists includes asking why we exist. Why do we exist? Do we have purpose? What could it be? That's an interesting and important question. And it happens to be one that philosophers have spent a good deal of time considering.

Then there's the really big question of Chapter 6, *Does God Exist*? According to a Gallup Poll taken in 2011, 92% of the American people believe in God.[1] That's a lot of people. There are not as many atheists in our society as there used to be. I wonder, though, how many of those 92% would be able to provide good reasons (sound rational arguments) for why they believe in God. How many of them could claim to "know" that God exists and provide sound evidence for their knowledge? Some people claim that one cannot "know" but only believe that God exists. Is that true? Or is it possible to demonstrate rationally that God exists? That's the question that we will discuss in Chapter 6.

---

[1] Gallup, "*More than 9 in 10 Americans Continue to Believe in God.*"
[2] In this section on the pre-Socratic philosophers we can only highlight a few of the more prominent thinkers.
[3] O'Grady provides a nice overview of Thales and what he thought. "Thales of Miletus (c. 620 BCE--c. 546 BCE)," *Internet Encyclopedia of Philosophy*.
[4] Couprie, provides a nice overview of Anaximander in his material, "Anaximander (c.610—546 BCE)," in *Internet Encyclopedia of Philosophy*.
[5] Melchert, *Philosophical Conversations*, 12-13.
[6] Marias, *History of Philosophy*, 15.
[7] Huffman provides a good overview of Pythagoras in "Pythagoras," in *Stanford Encyclopedia of Philosophy*.
[8] Guthrie, *The Greek Philosophers From Thales to Aristotle*, 33-42.

In Chapter 7 we take up the obvious follow-up question, *What is God like*? If God exists, as most Americans believe, what is he like? We usually refer to God as a *he*. Is God a *he*? Is God embodied like we are? Or is God an immaterial being? How does he exist? Has God always existed? What qualities or characteristics make God God?

In Chapter 8 we ask one of the oldest and most challenging questions: *Why is there evil in the world*? Since most of us believe in the existence of God, and since we believe that God is good and kind and loving, and that he is all-powerful, why does he allow evil to fill the world? If God created the world, why did he create it in such a way that evil is present and people suffer? Questions about evil, about the relationship between good and evil, and about which is stronger are some of the oldest questions humans have asked. We will consider some of these questions in Chapter 8.

In Chapter 9, we turn our attention to human nature, asking, *What kind of beings are humans*? The answer is not as obvious as some might think. In a psychology class, for instance (depending on the point of view of the professor), you might be told that a human being is a just a physical thing, a body, a brain and a point of view. You might hear the same thing in some philosophy courses. Is that what a human being is—a body, a brain, and a point of view? If that is the case, what happens when brain waves cease to be present? If you are just the physical manifestation of brain waves, what happens to you when those brain waves cease to exist? You would cease to exist. But is that really the case? Are you just a bunch of fancy physical machinery with a point of view? Or is there more to you than your physical brain and body? There are some philosophers, past and present, who believe that the real you is an immaterial mind, an embodied mind to be sure, but an immaterial mind nonetheless, that will survive the death of the physical body. So which is it? When your body dies do you cease to exist or does the immaterial mind that is the real you, the essence of you, continue to live? These are some of the questions we will consider in Chapter 9.

Chapter 10 has to do with questions related to free will: *Are we really free to choose*? Some philosophers argue that we are not free to choose, that we are mechanistically determined and that the appearance of free will is merely an illusion. Is that true? Are we merely biological units doing what we are programmed to do? Or are we embodied minds that are self-determined? If we are mechanistically determined, are we responsible for what we do? Can we be held accountable for things we do if we have no choice? It seems like the idea of being mechanistically determined calls into question our entire justice system. But if we are free to choose, what kind of choices do we make? Do the kinds of choices we make have anything to do with the kinds of beings humans are? These are the kinds of questions that will be considered in Chapter 10.

The question under consideration in Chapter 11 is, *What is the purpose of life*? Is there a purpose? If the cosmos and everything in it is just the coincidental results of a cosmic explosion, there is no purpose for anything, for purpose can only exist in relation to consciousness, rationality, and intentionality. The coincidental results of a cosmic explosion, even if consciousness, rationality and intentionality eventually evolved, do not and cannot have purpose. Humans, then, as part of that accidental or coincidental result have no purpose. The question is, was that cosmic explosion, the Big Bang, accidental (random, unguided) or intentional (planned, guided)? This is the basic question. But once we get past it, if we decide that the Big Bang was not random or unguided and that there must be some kind of purpose for human existence, we are still stuck with trying to figure out what it is. Is it to be happy? Is it to achieve some level of excellence? Is it to become what we can become? Why are we here? What is our purpose in life?

The question in Chapter 12 is, *Is There Life After Death*? The discussion of Chapter 9 will have introduced some of the issues or questions related to this very specific and ancient question. Are you just your body or are you something more? If you are something more, what happens to you when your body dies? This is a very important question. My wife hates bugs, especially spiders. So a couple times a year I get out the sprayer, fill it with insecticide and spray around the outside of the house and in the basement. What happens when you spray insecticide on a bug (or when you step on one)? It dies. Then what? Then nothing. It's just dead. It no longer exists. Is that the way it is for us? When we die, is that it? The end? Some philosophical positions dictate that that is the case. But is it? Is death the end, or is it merely a transition to another phase of life, in a continuous existence that will never end? These are the questions of Chapter 12.

The question asked and answered in Chapter 13 is, *How should human beings live*? This question is important from two different points of view. If life does have a purpose and if there is life after physical death, then it seems that how we live is an important consideration. But even if those concerns are considered irrelevant, since living involves interaction with other people, and since our actions during those interactions with others can cause either pleasure or pain, how we live as we interact with others remains an important consideration. So, how should people live? How do we determine what is right or wrong or good or bad? How can we figure out what is the right thing to do in a given set of circumstances? Or maybe that is the wrong approach. Maybe we just need to work on being good people because good people usually do the right thing. But then we have to decide what constitutes being a good person. Chapter 13 will consider these kinds of questions and provide some basic guidelines for moral thinking and acting.

So there you are. Thirteen questions that will not only be interesting to consider but that will, as we consider them, serve as an introduction to philosophy. These are the kinds of questions that are at the very heart of philosophical inquiry. They are the most important questions the human mind can contemplate. As we consider them, you will be introduced to some of the greatest philosophers (thinkers) who have ever lived, men who asked and tried to answer the most challenging and perplexing questions facing humankind. As we discuss and think about these questions, you will be exposed to different ways (systems) of thinking and living. Some will make sense to you, some will not; some you will embrace, some you will reject. That's what the philosophical process is about: thinking and discussing, considering new ideas, analyzing arguments, examining evidence, evaluating implications—all part of an ongoing dialectical process designed to reveal truth, to reveal what is really the case, so you will have the knowledge and wisdom necessary to examine life and live well. Philosophy is ultimately and immanently practical because it is, in the end, if it is done well, about living well—at least, that's what Socrates advocated. And I think he was right.

Chapter 1
How Did Philosophy Begin?

The word philosophy is derived from two Greek words *philio*, one of the Greek words for love, and *sophia*, the Greek word for wisdom. Philosophy is the love of wisdom. The ancient philosopher-mystic, Pythagoras, may have been the first thinker to use the word.

What does it mean to be a philosopher, to be a lover of wisdom? It does not necessarily mean that one has wisdom, but that one sees the importance of wisdom, wants to have wisdom, and, therefore, dedicates his or her life to the search for wisdom. But what is wisdom? Ancient philosophers thought wisdom was insight, understanding and knowledge about the world and how it works. They wanted to know the truth about things, the way things really were. There had been lots of old stories told over and over, stories written by the ancient Greek poets Hesiod and Homer (who may have written between the middle of the 8th century and the middle of the 7th century BCE), about gods and the world and people and what was most important in life and how one ought to live. Most people accepted those stories without thinking too much about them. The world was what it was, and day-to-day living took up most of their time. Who had

15

time to worry about where the world came from, how it was made or formed, whether or not things really were the way they appeared to be? Most people just didn't think about those sorts of things. And for those who did occasionally think about them, the old stories seemed to provide all the information they needed. But in the late 7th and early 6th centuries BCE, a group of thinkers became disenchanted and dissatisfied with the old stories. They began to think critically and analytically about the cosmos, the world, and the nature of reality. These thinkers, the first philosophers (today they are referred to as *pre-Socratics* because chronologically they preceded Socrates) wanted to understand the truth about the way things really are. They wanted knowledge and insight. They wanted wisdom. They believed that if they thought about things long enough, they could figure things out and know what the truth is.

Basically this is how philosophy began. But to really understand how philosophy came to be what it is, we need a little more detail.

Thales [2]

Aristotle said that *Thales* was the first philosopher. Thales was from the city of Miletus, on the coast of Asia Minor, across the Aegean Sea from Greece. As near as scholars can figure, Thales lived between 620 and 546 BCE. He was interested in nature—the world, what things are made of, how things work. Because of his interest in nature, Thales might be referred to as a *natural philosopher*. In his study of nature, he felt that it was important to identify the primary or elemental *substance*, that is, *that which all other things depend on for their existence and which does not*

---

[2] In this section on the pre-Socratic philosophers we can only highlight a few of the more prominent thinkers.

depend on anything else for its existence. For Thales, the elemental substance upon which everything else depended was water.[3] Why would Thales say water was the primary substance? Humans and animals need water to live. Plants need water to sprout and grow. Life depends on water. Where there is no water, there is no life. So Thales concluded that water was what everything else depended on for its existence. Water was *The One*, the primary thing. Was Thales right? Well, it turns out that he was not right. Water is not the primary or elemental substance. But whether or not he was right is not really the point. The point is that someone came along and said that when it comes to understanding our world, we need to stop depending on old stories that don't make good sense. We need to think critically and analytically and figure things out. Even if Thales got it wrong, he was trying to get it right. He was thinking, asking, analyzing, trying to figure things out in a logical, rational manner. At that time, that way of approaching things was brand new. No one had done that before. Thales was a revolutionary thinker. We owe a lot to him. All that we have discovered, all that we now understand about how the world works, can, in a way, be traced back to Thales who believed that we can and should figure things out.

Anaximander

Following Thales was another thinker from Miletus, *Anaximander*, who probably lived between 612 and 546 BCE. Anaximander was about 10 years younger than Thales. Because they were from the same city, they likely knew each other and may have discussed their ideas with each other.

---

[3] O'Grady provides a nice overview of Thales and what he thought. "Thales of Miletus (c. 620 BCE--c. 546 BCE)," *Internet Encyclopedia of Philosophy*.

Like Thales, Anaximander wanted to think rationally and analytically about nature. He too, was a natural philosopher.[4] But he was not satisfied with Thales' suggestion that water was the elemental substance and should thus be referred to as *The One*. Instead Anaximander's reasoning (I suspect) ran something like this:

1. Whatever state of affairs we have, that is, whatever exists, came into being, it had a beginning.
2. Before that, there was another state of affairs that also had a beginning.
3. And before that, another that had a beginning, and so on.
4. But this kind of regression cannot go on forever—for then there is never "a beginning" but only a series of beginnings.
5. Therefore, there must be something that had no beginning, something that simply *is*.

That which had no beginning Anaximander called, The Infinite or The Boundless. And it is this Boundless, eternal in its movement, that is the source of the cosmos. Because the Boundless is infinite, it is not specifically anything, neither this nor that, for if it were a specific thing, it would be limited to that (to the nature and character of what it was) and would not, therefore, be limitless, not infinite. This Boundless, Anaximander reasoned, must be a swirling vortex, for the cosmos, which owes its existence to the Boundless, is a swirling vortex.[5] The Boundless was conceived of as divine in nature. Why? Because what else would something be (other than divine) if it was infinite, that is, if it had no beginning and no limits? For Anaximander, the Boundless (instead of water) was the elemental substance, that on which everything else was dependent. Was Anaximander right? Probably not entirely. But he was certainly on to something significant. He utilized rational

---

[4] Couprie, provides a nice overview of Anaximander in his material, "Anaximander (c.610—546 BCE)," in *Internet Encyclopedia of Philosophy*.

[5] Melchert, *Philosophical Conversations*, 12-13.

analysis and reached a conclusion. Even if we would not agree with him (entirely or in part) we must still give him credit for asking important questions and looking for an answer that made sense. Anaximander was another important pre-Socratic natural philosopher.

Anaximenes

A third important Milesian natural philosopher was *Anaximenes*, a student of Anaximander. Anaximenes lived in the second half of the 6th century BCE. And though Anaximander was his teacher, Anaximenes' approach was more like that of Thales, who had said that The One elemental substance was water. Instead of water, Anaximenes believed that air was the elemental substance. Anaximenes is important not only because he has an opinion about what the primary substance is (air—all things spring from it and upon death and decay return to it), but because he explains how all other things are generated from it—through the processes of condensation and *rarefication*. Rarefication, according to Anaximenes, is the process by which a thing is made less dense. Rarefied air is fire. But when air becomes more condensed (Anaximenes thought) it becomes clouds, water, land, rocks, and so forth, depending on its density.[6]

Again, whether or not Anaximenes was right is not the point. The point is that he was one of a small group of men that led the way into critical thinking. He wanted to make sense of the world using rational analysis. And even if his analysis was incorrect, he was making an effort, showing us in rough outline how the process must go.

---

[6] Marias, *History of Philosophy*, 15.

Pythagoras

The next crucial pre-Socratic philosopher was *Pythagoras*, who lived (probably) between 570 and 490 BCE. Pythagoras was not from Miletus. He came from the Isle of Samos (off the coast of modern Turkey) where he spent his early years before relocating to Croton, in Southern Italy, when he was 40 years old.[7] With Pythagoras and the school of thought that carried his name, *Pythagoreanism*, the focus of philosophy changed somewhat. While the Milesian school (i.e., the philosophers from Miletus, also known as the Ionians) had a scientific curiosity directed toward the natural world, a physical focus, Pythagoras and his followers had a metaphysical focus. They were, in effect, a mystical religious sect.[8] Pythagoras and his followers were deeply interested in issues like the immorality of the soul. They believed that the Universe was a living creature, one, eternal and divine. Humans, as part of this eternal oneness, were also eternal. During their physical lives, however, they were imprisoned in mortal bodies. They looked forward to the separation of the soul from the body (the soul getting rid of the body) so the soul could once again be part of the universal oneness, the cosmic whole that was the ultimate reality. The soul freeing itself from the material prison of the body involved a series of transmigrations (reincarnations). The soul would inhabit different bodies until the time came for the self (the individuated self identity) to be extinguished and reunited with the cosmic whole.[9]

There was a good deal more than this to Pythagoreansim but space does not permit a lengthier

---

[7] Huffman provides a good overview of Pythagoras in "Pythagoras," in *Stanford Encyclopedia of Philosophy*.

[8] Guthrie, *The Greek Philosophers From Thales to Aristotle*, 33-42.

[9] In this regard Pythagoreanism was similar to ancient Hindu and Buddhist theories of the soul/self and the goal, processes, and end result of life.

presentation. The reason Pythagoreanism is so significant is that it played a major role in the development of Plato's thinking. Since Plato influenced so many people, those who influenced Plato are of great significance. The point here is to note that ancient philosophy was not entirely physical in its orientation. Some was metaphysical. And eventually, for a considerable time, most of philosophy would be metaphysical in orientation. But we will get to that later.

Xenophanes

After Pythagoras and his metaphysical approach came *Xenophanes*, who was also interested in metaphysical concerns. Xenophanes was from Colophon, in Asia Minor. Scholars cannot provide specific dates for Xenophanes' birth and death. It is known that he came after Pythagoras and before Heraclitus, which would put him in the late 6th and early 5th centuries BCE. He was a philosopher-poet, though some would say a philosophically-minded poet,[10] a subtle though not unimportant distinction. Xenophanes would travel about reciting poetry, mostly his own. One of his noteworthy contributions was his criticism of the anthropomorphic nature of Greek religion, that is, the Greek tendency to *create the gods in the image of man*, to conceive of divine beings as if they were human, with human characteristics and natures. Specifically, Xenophanes said:

> The Ethiopians make their gods snub-nosed and black; the Thracians make theirs gray-eyed and red-haired… and if oxen and horses and lions had hands, and could draw with their hands and do what man can do, horses would draw their gods in the shape of

---

[10] Lesher, "Xenophanes," *Stanford Encyclopedia of Philosophy*.

horses, and oxen in the shape of oxen, each giving the gods bodies similar to their own.[11]

If Xenophanes does not appreciate the general Greek conception of the divine, how does he conceive of God? Xenophanes explains that there is:

> ...one god, greatest among gods and men, in no way similar to mortals either in body or mind. He sees all over, thinks all over, hears all over. He remains always in the same place, without moving; nor is it fitting that he should come and go, first to one place and then to another. But without toil, he sets all things in motion by the thought of his mind.[12]

These are very significant insights for a philosophically-minded poet. It is interesting how similar Xenophanes' insights into the divine are to those of the ancient Hebrews, whose ideas about God (*Yahweh*) are expressed metaphorically in the Old Testament Scriptures.

The reason for including Xenophanes in this brief overview of the pre-Socratics is not so much to point out the conclusions he reached concerning the divine nature, but to highlight another individual who deviated from the normal way of thinking. Xenophanes did not accept the standard explanations regarding the gods—Greek or otherwise. He thought critically, analytically, regarding foundational metaphysical concepts and reached conclusions that were far different from those of the people around him who were not engaged in rational analysis.

---

[11] Melchert (15) provides the Diels-Kranz (DK) references for these quotes from Xenophanes—DK 21 B 16 *IEGP* 52.
[12] As referenced by Melchert, 15, DK 21 B 23-25, *IEGP*, 53

Heraclitus

Heraclitus lived in the early 6th and late 5th centuries. Whether he should be placed before or after Parmenides has been questioned over the centuries, beginning with Plato, who believed that Heraclitus wrote after Parmenides. The present scholarly consensus, however, is that that he wrote before Parmenides.[13] Heraclitus was from the city of Ephesus, in Asia Minor. It is thought that he was from a royal family and in line to rule the city.

Heraclitus' writing is somewhat obscure and difficult to understand. In fact, the Greeks referred to him as *Heraclitus the Obscure.*[14] Both Plato and Aristotle accused Heraclitus of contradicting himself.[15] This may be the case because Heraclitus was attempting to move beyond simple physical theory into the realm of the metaphysical and did not have a clear conception of what he was trying to express. Heraclitus did not think highly of the intellectual skills of the average person, suggesting that most people sleepwalk their way through life, blissfully unaware of what's going on around them.[16] I think he may have been right about that.

One of the foundational ideas of Heraclitus' thinking has to do with what is described as *the one and the many.* What Heraclitus observed is that the world is made up of many individual things, but that all things (the many) are held together and function as one whole. The cosmos is many, but it is, at the same time, one. It is in constant motion, always changing, but it remains the same. One of his examples is a river. The river and the water in the river are not the same. The water in the river is constantly changing. In this sense, you cannot step into the same river twice,

---

13 Graham, "Heraclitus (fl. c.500 BCE)," *Internet Encyclopedia of Philosophy.*
14 Marias, *History of Philosophy*, 27.
15 Graham, "Heraclitus."
16 Graham, "Heraclitus."

because the water that was the river a moment ago is now different water. So, in one sense it is a different river, but not really. It is the same river. It is the same and different at the same time. The world is in constant flux. And the world consists of opposites, or things in opposition—the riverbed and the water of the river, for instance. They exist in opposition to each other. But the riverbed and the water together are the river. And the river, that is many and is in constant flux, is one. For Heraclitus, this is an example of how all of reality works.

But what holds all things together so the many can be one? Heraclitus used the Greek word *logos* to define/describe that which provides the basic structure or pattern of the cosmos. The word *logos* is challenging to translate into English because of the range of meaning it carries. The basic meaning of *logos* is *word, discourse* or *message*. But it is also used to identify the thought or rationale that underlies a message or an idea that is being expressed. So it also refers to logic or reason, wisdom, and even to the pattern or structure of an argument or discourse. It can mean word, message, logic, reason, wisdom, and pattern or structure. Heraclitus seems to be using *logos* to refer to the underlying structure or pattern of the cosmos, a pattern that is logical, rational, rooted in wisdom.[17] He is suggesting that the many are the one because there is a *logos*, an underlying pattern or structure, to the cosmos that holds all things together. In fact, Heraclitus says that *all things come into being in accordance with this logos*.[18] What is this *logos*? Heraclitus identifies it as fire. But is he referring to literal fire, saying that the elemental substance of the cosmos is fire? Probably not. Heraclitus is likely using fire metaphorically to describe the *logos* not only as powerful, but as eternal and therefore

---

17 Melchert, "Philosophical Conversations," 20-21.
18 Ibid.

divine.[19] Is this logos Zeus? Heraclitus seems to say, yes and no. From one point of view, since the *logos* is divine in nature it can be linked with the gods. Yet the *logos,* as Heraclitus conceives of it, is superior to the gods as the Greeks conceived of them—mortal, lustful, petty and so forth. The *logos* is something that is more and better than the Greek gods.

Again, the accuracy of Heraclitus' cosmology is not the point. He was trying to understand the physical and metaphysical nature of reality on the basis of rational analysis. For this, he is to be applauded.

Parmenides

Parmenides of Elea, considered by some to be the most significant of all the pre-Socratic philosophers, was active in the early 5th century BCE, born perhaps between 510 and 515. Like Pythagoras, Xenophanes, and Heraclitus, Parmenides was interested in more than physical explanations of nature. He was also interested in things that fall under the category of what came to be known as metaphysics. Like Heraclitus, Parmenides, is somewhat obscure and difficult to understand. It is clear, however, that he differed from Heraclitus in a significant way. Where Heraclitus stressed the One and the many, Parmenides stressed only the One.

Parmenides wrote a poem called *On Nature*, in which a goddess instructs him regarding two ways—the way of truth and the way of opinion, which is not truth at all. Most people follow the way of opinion, accepting what appears to be the case. Parmenides, however, as the poem suggests, is following the way of truth, using reason to figure out how

---

[19] Melchert, 19.

things really are, regardless of how they appear to be.[20] What was this truth revealed by reason? It was that there is only one universal, unchanging reality.[21] That which exists has always existed. For Parmenides there could never have been a time when nothing at all existed. If that were the case, then nothing would exist now, for *"from nothing comes nothing."* Therefore, for Parmenides, that which exists has always existed.[22] And it exists without change. How can this be? Parmenides' thinking here is not easy to follow but we must try to grasp it.

That the One is an unchanging reality begins with the concept of existence. That which exists, *is*. That which does not exist *is not*. That which *is not* cannot become that which *is*, and that which *is* cannot become that which *is not*. An apple exists and it cannot stop being an apple and become an orange. The color blue exists and cannot stop being blue and become red. A cat exists and cannot stop existing as a cat and become a dog. Neither can that which exists simply cease to exist. An *is* cannot become an *is not*.

Parmenides was arguing that things *appear* to change—it looks like the cat dies and ceases to exist. Most people accept what *appears* to be so. But when one applies reason to the concern, it is clear that change is not possible. Neither is a multiplicity of things. It looks like there are lots of things that exist separately and at various times. But that cannot be, according to Parmenides. What there is must exist

---

[20] Some have suggested that Parmenides' preference for the rational over the empirical places him at the beginning of the rationalist school of thought.

[21] See Guthrie, *The Greek Philosophers*, 46-52.

[22] The principle, *from nothing comes nothing*, is an important idea and I will use it later to develop an argument similar to Parmenides', that something has always existed. The question is, what is it that has always existed? Parmenides believed that that which exists (the cosmos) is that which has always existed. I think he was wrong. But my argument will come later. For now we must stay focused on Parmenides.

all at once, because what *is*, is. There cannot be things that come into and go out of existence. There is simply that which exists and it exists, therefore, as a single existent, as a unified whole, or as One, that which *is*.

Was Parmenides right? Not entirely. But at least he made an effort to think about and explain the nature of reality. And that's what is important. He entered into the philosophical conversation and made a contribution.

Democritus

Parmenides' philosophy was not only a contribution but something of a challenge. A number of thinkers who came after him attempted to respond to his argument. One such attempt may have been the atomistic theory of *Democritus*, who was probably born in 460 BCE. Cornford suggests that Atomism represents the culmination of pre-Socratic attempts to explain the cosmos from a naturalistic perspective.[23] How does Atomism seek to do this? At the foundation of Atomism is the idea that things exist. Things, of course, must be made of something. What are things made of? The question is not what is the specific material a specific thing is made of, but the more general question regarding all things and the primary or elemental substance of which all things consist. What is it that all things are made of? What is the elemental substance that exists in the cosmos? Democritus advocated what he had learned from his teacher, Leucippus—that all things are made of tiny atoms, so small that they cannot be seen. These atoms are the elemental substance. They are physical in nature. They are all that exists. They are the building blocks of all other things. Therefore, all that exists is a physical or material substance. Reality is entirely physical or material in nature. Atomism is

---

23 Cornford, *Before and After Socrates*, 20-21.

a *physicalist* theory, proposing that there are no kinds of things other than physical things.[24]

Was Democritus right? I'm pretty sure he was not and later on I will explain why. But for now the point is that, like those who preceded him, he was thinking, reasoning, and participating in the philosophical conversation. He was another who believed that reason must be exalted above myth in the pursuit of understanding and insight, of knowledge and wisdom.

The early philosophers who set the Greeks on the path of rational inquiry laid the foundation for the development of not only western science but a good deal of western culture in general. Their confidence in the human intellect for contemplation, investigation, analysis, and discovery, and their first faltering steps along the path of philosophy changed the world. We owe them a debt of gratitude. However, their efforts, valiant as they were, were not entirely satisfying. Something important was missing. In the early 5th century (BCE) a new intellectual wind began to blow that would change the course of philosophy, sharpening its focus, targeting a new subject of inquiry.

Summary

The word philosophy is derived from two Greek words *philio*, one of the Greek words for love, and *sophia*, the Greek word for wisdom. Philosophy is the love of wisdom. The ancient philosopher-mystic, Pythagoras, may have been the first thinker to use the word. Ancient philosophers thought wisdom (philosophy) had to do with insight, understanding and knowledge about the world and

---

[24] Berryman ("Democritus," in *Stanford Encyclopedia of Philosophy*) offers a more thorough overview of Democritus and Atomism than I can offer in the space I have.

28

how it works. They wanted to know the truth about things, the way things really were. There had been lots of old stories floating around, stories written by the ancient Greek poets Hesiod and Homer (who may have written between the middle of the 8th century and the middle of the 7th century BCE) about gods and the world and people and what was most important in life and how one ought to live. Most people accepted those stories without thinking too much about them. But in the late 7th and early 6th centuries BCE, a group of thinkers became disenchanted and dissatisfied with the old stories. They began to think critically and analytically about the cosmos, the world, and the nature of reality. These thinkers, the first philosophers (today they are referred to as *pre-Socratics* because chronologically they preceded Socrates), wanted to understand the truth about the way things really are. They wanted knowledge and insight. They wanted wisdom. They believed that if they thought about things long enough, they could figure things out and know what the truth is. This was the beginning of philosophy.

Thought and Discussion Questions

1. Discuss the merit of Thales' idea that there must be a One of some kind.
2. Discuss Xenophanes' observations about what he considered to be the true nature of God.
3. Discuss Parmenides' observation that from nothing comes nothing. What are the implications of this insight?
4. Discuss why the pre-Socratics are important even though much (though not all) of what they thought proved to be inaccurate or poorly conceived.
5. Which of the pre-Socratics is most interesting to you? Explain why.

Chapter 2
How Did Philosophy Develop?

Philosophy was born out of a need to understand the nature of the world we live in. The first philosophers wanted to develop a view of the world rooted in a rational analysis of the cosmos. Their question was, *what is the true nature of reality? What is really true about the world and how it works?* A lot of thought went into the answers to those basic questions, and a lot of different answers were generated. From one point of view, the years between Thales and Democritus were fruitful, yielding important results—the establishing of the rationalistic process. But for the average man in his day-to-day struggles, what the pre-Socratic philosophers were offering did not appear to be very helpful and was therefore not very appealing. The average person (if they were even aware of philosophical thought) was left to wonder: Is the elemental substance water, air or fire? Does it really matter one way or the other? Is Heraclitus right? Are all things constantly in flux? Or is Parmenides right? Is change merely an illusion? Is the world what it appears to be? Or is it something entirely different from what I experience (or seem to experience) on a daily basis? Or is Democritus right? Are atoms all that exist? Is there nothing beyond the realm of the physical? It is easy to see how the average person, the farmer, the merchant, the soldier, might wonder whether this new way of thinking, this *philosophy stuff*, offered anything useful.

Along with this concern about the usefulness of natural philosophy there were a number of other cultural and political realities that contributed to the refocusing of philosophical interests and inquiry. These included: 1) the social structures that had evolved in Greece—the Greek *polis*, that is, the city-state: Athens, Corinth, Sparta, and others, 2) the war with Persia, and 3) the development of democracy and the needs associated with it.

For much of the 6th century, Athens had been ruled by a series of leaders called tyrants (meaning bosses—originally the term tyrant did not have the negative connotation it has now). However, there had been alliances, betrayals and intrigue (as there often is in politics), and the Athenians had gotten tired of all of it. They rebelled and established a democratic form of government based on a constitution. They realized they were doing something new and special and hoped it would serve as a model for other peoples. The power was not in the hands of a few select individuals but in the hands of the people, a citizenship of equals (of course in their context "equals" meant male Athenian citizens).[25] The new democracy was a vast improvement over what they'd had, but the new political structure necessitated an educated, sophisticated citizenry capable of engaging in a direct democracy in a responsible, effective manner.

---

[25] Taking a few moments to read a speech given by Pericles to honor Athens' fallen soldiers will provide important insights into the social and political life of Athens in the middle of the 5th century BCE. A copy is available online at:
http://www.sammustafa.com/Resources/Thucydides.pdf

The war with Persia had taken a toll on Athens economically and socially. Sparta and Athens (often at war between themselves) had worked together to defeat the Persians, though Athens had carried most of the burden. Much of Athens had been destroyed and needed to be rebuilt. Under the leadership of Pericles, Athens became wealthy and powerful, the premier Greek city-state. Athens was a beautiful city with a large, wealthy population. But being wealthy and powerful and involved in a new kind of government and in a different kind of social structure (democracy is a social reality as well as a political one) generated a new focus. While the natural philosophers had been trying to figure out how the physical world worked, people were becoming aware of themselves as part of the world. Understanding the world included understanding people. Where the philosophical focus had been on an explanation of the physical world (*physis*, nature), the focus gradually began to shift to matters related to human endeavors, becoming humanistic rather than naturalistic in orientation. [26] From this social, economic, and political context, a new group of people rose to prominence: *the Sophists*.

The Sophists

The Sophists were itinerant teachers who offered to teach students for a fee. The name Sophist was based on the Greek word *sophos*, meaning wise. The Sophists were (supposedly) wise men. For a fee, they would teach (impart wisdom to) the sons of wealthy Greek families, teaching them how to become *arête*,[27] an excellent person.

---

[26] Guthrie, *The Greek Philosophers*, 63-66.
[27] The Greek word *arête* is often translated with the English world virtue. But our English word virtue carries ideas that were not part of the concept contained in *arête* and does not suggest the concepts to

32

One prominent Sophist was *Protagoras*. According to Plato, in his dialog entitled *Protagoras*, Protagoras offered to teach his students how to: 1) properly manage their affairs, 2) run their households, 3) manage public affairs, and 4) make an effective contribution to the affairs of the city in both word and deed.[28] In accomplishing these four goals, he would be leading his students toward *arête* which would, in turn, result in *eudaimonia*, a life that could be described as thriving or flourishing—a good, satisfying, happy life.

Based on this brief explanation, the Sophists sound like good guys doing good things. Actually, their methods generated a lot of concern. There was discussion among Greek thinkers regarding the relationship between *physis*, which means nature, and *nomos*, which means law, custom or convention. For some, *nomos* appeared to be in opposition to *physis*. For instance, on the human level *physis*, or nature, involves certain drives, the sex drive, for instance. Yet many of a society's *nomos* (laws or conventions) are aimed at controlling those drives. Some thinkers suggested that *nomos* (in the since of social norms or rules) were unjust because they circumvented *physis*.

Such discussions may be interesting when they occur at the theoretical level between intellectuals or academics. But in a real life day-to-day application they call into question the social norms of a group of people. If a society's norms are unjust, should they be abandoned? If they were,

---

our minds that *arête* suggested to the Greek mind. *Arête* had to do with being an excellent person, with achieving a level of excellence in who one was by what one did. Each individual had his own *arête*. There was the *arête* of the soldier, of the brick mason, of the merchant, of the farmer, of the politician, and so forth. Whatever a person was, he had an *arête* to achieve, an excellence at being who and what he was. To achieve *arête* was essential in achieving *eudaimonia*, often translated happiness, but better translated thriving or flourishing. To achieve *eudaimonia* one had to achieve *arête*.

[28] Plato, *Protagoras*, 318d-319a.

how would society maintain order? The Sophist, *Antiphon,* argued that what is just according to *nomos* may not be just according to *physis.*[29] This would not have been a popular idea, especially among those concerned with maintaining social order.

The Sophists also held what were considered problematic views related to truth and knowledge. They advocated philosophical *skepticism,*[30] claiming that either: 1) objective truth does not exist, or that, 2) if it does, the human mind cannot know it, so it is irrelevant. Either way, the inevitable result of skepticism is cultural and moral relativity—that there is no absolute right or wrong, that people make up right and wrong (as they see it) as occasions arise. Perhaps the best example of this is the comment made by Protagoras, "Of all things, the measure is man." Turn that around and you have, *man is the measure of all things*, which is another way of saying that there is no absolute truth or morality. Humans, in their own different contexts and circumstances, decide what is right and wrong. This, of course, was (and remains) a highly questionable proposition that is hotly debated, especially among ethicists.

The relativism of the Sophists came through quite clearly in their attitude and teaching concerning the goal of *rhetoric*, that is, of public speaking. The Sophists taught their students the art of persuasive presentation. As an exercise, students were required to be able to argue either side of an issue, either for or against, persuasively. The goal of a good

---

[29] Duke, "The Sophists (Ancient Greek)," the *Internet Encyclopedia of Philosophy*.

[30] A healthy dose of normal everyday skepticism (not simply believing everything you hear but expecting proof) can be useful. But philosophical skepticism is the belief that objective truth does not exist, or that if it does, it cannot be known (conceived) by the human mind. Philosophical skepticism has been considered unfounded, foolish, and dangerous by most philosophers (except for those few who embrace it) since ancient times.

presentation, as far as the Sophists were concerned, was to get people to agree with you. When they spoke before the people, as all male citizens would do at some point, the goal was to sway the crowd and get them to follow you. Discovering the truth of a proposition or the rightness of a position was not the point. The point was to present the argument in such a way that it sounded right. The Sophists taught their students how to *make the weaker argument appear to be the stronger argument*. Why would they do that? Because they did not believe in an objective truth. And if there is no truth, no absolute right or wrong, then the point of discussion and presentation is simply to get people to agree with and follow you. This way of thinking was also problematic for many people in Athens, people who believed that objective truth existed and could be discovered and understood.

The Sophists were part of an important transition in the focus of Greek philosophy. Their relativistic approach, however, did not sit well with many people and was one of the things that contributed to what became the most decisive paradigmatic shift in ancient philosophy, a refocusing effort led by Socrates, one of the greatest philosophers of all time.

Socrates

When Socrates (469-399 BCE) was young, he read and studied the work of the philosophers who came before him. Even as a young man, he was truly a lover of wisdom and hoped to gain important insights into life. But Socrates was disappointed with the work of those previous generations. Most of it consisted simply of different attempts to explain the nature of the physical cosmos and had little to do with what Socrates considered the important concerns of human life: understanding oneself and how one lives a good life, which required that one had insights into such things as goodness, justice, knowledge, truth, morality and so forth. For Socrates, insights into the workings of the physical cosmos were not very helpful when compared to insights about how to be a better person, how to live a better life, how to, as he put it, *care for one's soul*.

Socrates wanted to focus on different concerns than previous generations of philosophers had focused on. He was also very much opposed to the thinking of the Sophists, especially their relativism. Socrates believed in objective truth and wanted to discover it. Good and evil were real, not just matters of opinion. Justice and injustice were real, not just matters of opinion. Socrates saw the relativism of the Sophists for what it was—without rational foundation and philosophically dangerous. Demonstrating the error of relativism (philosophically defeating it) became one of his purposes in life. His other purpose, his philosophical goal, was to help people understand the absolute necessity of caring for one's soul, of paying proper attention to the development of insights regarding how to live well, how to be the best person one could be.

For Socrates, living well was rooted in two basic things: knowledge of good and evil, and knowledge of oneself. This presupposes that good and evil actually exist and that the human mind can distinguish between the two. It also presupposes that there is a *self* to be known. Cornford refers to what Socrates *discovered*: "Socrates' discovery was that the true self is not the body but the soul. And by the soul he meant the seat of that faculty of insight which can know good from evil and infallibly choose the good. Self-knowledge implies the recognition of this true self."[31]

Above the entrance to the temple of Apollo in Delphi was the inscription: *Know Thyself.* Socrates believed that this was of the utmost importance. But how does one gain this introspective insight? Socrates liked to say, *"Virtue is*

---

[31] Cornford, *Before and After Socrates,* 50-51.

Knowledge", at least that is the way it is often translated. But the English word virtue is misleading. Basically, what Socrates said was *arête is gnosis. Gnosis* is knowledge. But what is *arête*? *Arête* meant goodness or excellence. Marias points out that as Socrates meant it, it was to be applied personally, as in what is good or excellent for each individual.[32] For the ancient Greeks, each person had his own *arête*, his own goodness or excellence that he should strive for. To be the best person one could be, one had to have insight into his own true self so he could know what his *arête* (his excellence) ought to be. The soldier ought to be an excellent soldier, the merchant an excellent merchant. What is involved in being an excellent soldier, or an excellent merchant? What is good and right for a merchant—or a teacher, or a politician, or a brick mason, or a fisherman? The answer for each will involve some general things (being honest, true, just, courageous, and so forth) and some specific things related to what one does in life. For Socrates, the care of one's soul involved inquiries into these important concerns, asking what is good, what is just? And then making personal application—am I good, am I just? How can I be the best person I can be? For Socrates, this was the essence of philosophy. For this reason he is considered to be the father of *Moral Philosophy*, the branch of philosophy also known as *Ethics*.

Socrates was very good at what he did, so good, in fact, that it cost him his life. The Oracle at Delphi, thought to be the voice (spokesperson) of Apollo, had said that Socrates had more wisdom than all others. Socrates found this to be unbelievable and set out to find one among the Athenians who had more wisdom than he. His methodology was simple: he would question people throughout the city, asking questions that required wisdom to answer, and eventually he would find someone who possessed more wisdom than he.

---

[32] Marias, *History of Philosophy*, 40.

So he went about the city day after day starting conversations, looking for a truly wise person. The problem was, he couldn't find one. It turned out that the people who thought themselves wise were not. And in the course of Socrates' questions, it became apparent to everyone listening to the conversations that those who considered themselves wise were not. Socrates often made people feel completely inadequate. You can't do that too many times (especially to proud powerful people) before you make a number of dangerous enemies. That's what Socrates did. Eventually charges were brought against him. He was accused of not honoring the city's gods and of corrupting the youth. Without a doubt, these were false charges designed to shut Socrates up. There was a trial. Socrates defended himself (though perhaps not as vigorously as he could have), was found guilty and sentenced to death.[33] He died in 399 BCE, one of the most important and influential philosophers who ever lived.

Socrates is so significant in the development of Greek philosophy that all the philosophers who came before him are referred to simply as *Pre-Socrates*, that is, as those who came before Socrates. He is also significant because he was the teacher of *Plato*, perhaps the most significant philosopher (or one of the two most significant philosophers, depending on one's philosophical leanings) of all time.

Plato

Plato (429-347 BCE) was one of Socrates' students and perhaps the most important philosopher of all time. The British philosopher, Alfred North Whitehead, famously said, "The safest general characterization of the European philosophical tradition is that it consists of a series of

---

[33] You can read about the trial in Plato's dialog entitled *Apology*.

footnotes to Plato."[34] In other words, Plato asked and answered all the important questions. Those who came after him, whether they agree with him or not, must respond to and deal with what Plato said.

Guthrie's chapter on Plato begins as follows:

> We shall probably understand Plato's philosophy best if we regard him as working in the first place under the influence of two related motives. He wished first of all to take up Socrates' task at the point where Socrates had to leave it, to consolidate his master's teaching and defend it against inevitable questioning. But he was not acting solely from motives of personal affection or respect. It fitted in with his second motive, which was to defend, and to render worth defending, the idea of the city-state as an independent political, economic, and social unit. For it was by accepting and developing Socrates' challenge to the Sophists that Plato thought this wider aim could be most successfully accomplished.[35]

To what is Guthrie referring? Two things. One is Plato's desire to hold up the Greek *polis*, the city-state, as the ideal form of sociopolitical structure. This is the subject of Plato's famous work, *Republic*. The other is his desire to honor and support his teacher, Socrates. Why would Plato be concerned about sociopolitical issues? For one, he was a citizen of Athens, and he loved his city and his people. He wanted what was best for all concerned. Plato had grown up in the context of the Peloponnesian War (the ongoing struggle between Athens and Sparta) and had seen how it had ravaged the social and moral fiber of the city. The glory that had characterized Athens in the past had faded, and the

---

[34] Whitehead, *Process and Reality: An Essay in Cosmology*, 39.
[35] Guthrie, *The Greek Philosophers From Thales To Aristotle*, 81.

whole concept of the Greek city-state appeared to be in jeopardy. It could be jettisoned and replaced by a different system, or it could be reestablished and reinvigorated. Plato very much wanted to reestablish and reinvigorate the city-state, structuring it in such a way that it could be all that it was capable of being. For that to happen, the city-state (the *polis*) would have to be structured and governed in very specific ways. And those who governed would have to be pure lovers of wisdom—philosopher-kings, who would know the right thing to do and do it simply because it was the wise and right thing to do. Plato's *Republic*, considered by many to be his greatest achievement, is his presentation of the necessary structure and governing of the Greek city-state.

But Plato's concern for the sociopolitical state of his beloved Athens also included the concerns and perspectives of his teacher, Socrates. If Athens (or any other city-state) was to achieve social and political excellence, the people of the city (the individuals who were the city) would have to achieve personal excellence; they would have to achieve their own personal *arête*. How was that to be accomplished? They would have to care for their souls. They would have to focus their energies on those things that were truly important—the condition of the soul rather than on material concerns. So, as part of a larger sociopolitical agenda, Plato was very interested in supporting and sustaining Socrates' focus on the care of the soul.

What Socrates had suggested (that the *psyche*, the soul, was more important than the body, the spiritual more important than the material) was a radical idea. It would require a good deal of argument to demonstrate and support such an idea. As Plato analyzes the situation, he sees that Socrates' beliefs were rooted in an assumption: that things such as justice, goodness, courage and so forth really exist separate from specific instances of each. For instance, one might observe justice being carried out in that a poor man received equal treatment under the law—a judgment was rightly given in favor of a poor man. Justice was done. This is a specific example of justice. Yet for Socrates, and for Plato, for justice to be possible in the activities of men, justice itself, as a real thing, as an absolute, must exist. The same is true of goodness, courage, and so forth. But do they exist? That was one of the questions Plato knew he would have to address.[36]

Another question had to do with the relative importance of the *psyche* (the soul) in relation to the body. The Greek perception was that at death, when the body died, the *psyche*, now homeless, "slipped out into a pale and shadowy existence without mind or strength."[37] If, as Socrates (and Plato) believed, the *psyche* is the seat of the moral and intellectual faculties, Plato would have to spend considerable time arguing this point. He did. Much of Plato's writing has to do with the moral philosophy that was the focus of his teacher, Socrates.

But Plato had yet another interest, one that transcended Socrates' focus on moral philosophy. Like the pre-Socratics before him, Plato was also interested in the nature of cosmic reality. But unlike the pre-Socratics, Plato's view of the world included both physical and metaphysical perspectives. There was the physical world experienced and known by the physical senses, and there was the world of ideas, an immaterial realm experienced and known rationally. If justice really existed as a real thing, as an absolute, where did it exist? If beauty really existed as a real, absolute thing, where did it exist? Where did that which was really real exist? Contemplating these questions, especially in light of the competing philosophies of Heraclitus and Parmenides, is what led Plato to his theory of *ideas* (also referred to as his

---

[36] Guthrie, *The Greek Philosophers*, 81-100, includes a more expansive discussion of Plato's options and motivations, including how the philosophies of Heraclitus and Parmenides factored into what Plato did and how he went about doing it.
[37] Guthrie, 87.

theory of *forms*). For whatever exists in the physical world, the individual things that can be experienced by the senses, there is a perfect idea of that thing (a form or pattern of that thing) in the immaterial realm, the realm that can only be known by the mind. The physical entities experienced by the senses are copies (less than perfect copies) of the perfect nonphysical idea of those things. Think of it like this, if you wanted to paint a picture, a landscape for instance, you would have to have an idea in your head of what you wanted your landscape to look like. Based on the idea in your head you paint the picture. When you are done you are happy with the painting, but you admit that it is not exactly what you pictured in your mind. It is very close, but not exact. It is, you might say, a less than perfect replica of the image (the idea) you had in your head. Your idea was flawless. What you produced on canvas was not quite flawless. This is analogous to what Plato had in mind. For everything there is, there is a perfect idea of that thing, not in your mind or mine, but in the realm of ideas. Does such a realm exist? Plato thought it did.

Plato's theory of ideas (or forms) is his most controversial. Aristotle eventually came to disagree with Plato (his teacher) regarding the theory.[38] But even if Plato was wrong in the details, he was right about the need to understand the dualistic nature of reality, the material and the immaterial, a point he illustrated well in his parable of the cave.[39] Not all philosophers agree with Plato that reality is dualistic in nature. Many embrace the idea of physicalism, the idea that only physical things exist. That is a question we shall explore in more detail in Chapters 5 and 9. As far as Plato was concerned, reality was dualistic in nature,

---

[38] Earlier in his philosophical career, Aristotle embraced Plato's theory of Forms. Only later in life, after careful analysis and consideration did he reject the theory. Cornford, *Before and After Socrates*, 85.
[39] Plato's parable of the cave appears in *Republic*, Bk. 7.

comprised of the material and the immaterial.[40] It was Plato's philosophy, a combination of the interests of the pre-Socratics in natural philosophy and Socrates' interest in moral philosophy, that put philosophy in general on the path it has been on since. And if there was another philosopher as influential as Plato in clarifying the subject and task of philosophy, it was Plato's brilliant student Aristotle.

Aristotle

Aristotle (384-322 BCE), a brilliant young man whose father was a medical doctor in the court of the Macedonian king, came to study at Plato's Academy when he was seventeen years old. Aristotle remained at the Academy, first as a student, then as a teacher, for the next twenty years. Concerning Aristotle's time at the Academy and his relationship with Plato, Cornford notes that, "No young student has ever been subject to the dominance of a more overpowering personality."[41] If Cornford is right, given Aristotle's own brilliance, Plato was indeed in a class by himself. Yet because Aristotle's own intellect was quite formidable, he could and did think for himself. And even though he became and remained a Platonist, he did not agree with his master on all counts.

Cornford provides a comparison between the two great men that helps us understand the fundamental differences between the two philosophers:

---

[40] Many introductory discussions about Plato will focus attention on his theory of forms as if that theory defines his philosophy. It does not. It is only one small feature of the philosophical paradigm so broad and deep that every philosopher since Plato has been obliged to consider and deal with his thinking. To discuss Plato's theory of forms as if it defined his philosophy is to fail to grasp the depth and breadth of his thinking.

[41] Cornford, *Before and After Socrates*, 85.

Aristotle never ceased to reverence his master; and the founder of the Lyceum had no reason to envy the contemporary heads of the Academy. At the root of this antagonism [between Aristotle and Plato] lies a fundamental incompatibility of temperament; and a philosopher's temperament has more to do with the shaping of his philosophy than he would care to acknowledge, even if he were aware of the fact. Plato was (in the language of modern psychology) an introvert; and his philosophy is, in the end, a philosophy of withdrawal from the world of common experience. Platonism distrusts and condemns the senses. The eyes and ears are not, for the Platonist, windows of the soul, opening upon reality. The soul sees best when these windows are closed and she holds silent converse with herself in the citadel of thought. The native bent of Aristotle's mind was in the other direction, towards the study of empirical fact. His impulse was to explore the whole field of experience with insatiable curiosity. It is not hard to understand that a born man of science should have felt some measure of hardly conscious irritation at having been so long held in thrall by a philosopher whose thought, however magnificent, was radically uncongenial.[42]

But even though it is obvious that the two men were of a different sort and that there were some areas of disagreement between Plato and Aristotle, virtually every philosopher who knows much about Aristotle agrees that he remained a Platonist throughout his life, that the underlying foundation of his philosophy was the same as that of both

---

[42] Cornford, 86-87.

44

Socrates and Plato, namely, that life is *teleological*[43] in nature, that is, that it has a goal or purpose, an end result to be achieved, which is *human becoming*, people aspiring to become, to grow into the best versions of themselves, to achieve *arête*, realizing their full potential as human beings. This underlying foundation provided a unifying theme for the three philosophers so that even if there are some differences in some of the details of the systems they proposed, they have the same end result in mind: human becoming. It is not uncommon to find material that suggests that Aristotle was a *materialist*, that he accepted the Atomist view that only material substance exists. This is simply not true. Aristotle was a Platonist, not a materialist. He absolutely believed in an immaterial reality. His work *Metaphysics* makes this perfectly clear.

So what did Aristotle propose? Heraclitus had suggested that since the world is in constant flux, certain knowledge of anything is impossible. What a thing was a moment ago it is not now and what it is now it will not be a moment from now. Thus, we cannot know what a thing is. Aristotle, however, proposed that while the world appears to be in constant flux (and in fact on one level may be), there are certain underlying principles or elements of the world that do not change, and upon analysis and contemplation reveal truths that can be ascertained. Thus, real, certain knowledge is possible. Therefore, Aristotle advocated the careful and thorough study of all there is. Study nature and life in all its forms and manifestations to understand as much as can be understood.

As Aristotle engaged in this amazingly broad spectrum of inquiry, he observed that there is not only ordered progress occurring in nature (seeds germinate and

---

[43] Socrates did not explicitly discuss the teleological nature of life the way Aristotle did. But it is clear that he believed life had a purpose and that life's purpose is to become, which happens in the context of achieving *arête*.

grow into plants that produce seeds that germinate and grow into plants that produce seeds and so on), but that there is a goal or purpose toward which all things are directed. Thus, he developed a *teleological*[44] view of the cosmos and of life. All things are moving toward a goal or an end result.

The impact of Aristotle's teleological view can be seen most clearly in his books *Metaphysics* and *Nicomachean Ethics*. It is in *Nicomachean Ethics* where the influences of Socrates and Plato (and Aristotle's agreement with them) come through most clearly as Aristotle undertakes an in-depth study of moral philosophy, asking essentially, *what kind of a person ought one to be?* The conclusion he reaches is essentially the same conclusion Socrates and Plato had reached.

What are we to make, then, of the differences between Aristotle and Plato? What was the essence of the disagreement, and what did it mean for Greek philosophy? The basic difference between Plato and Aristotle (aside from Aristotle's interest in empirical research as the foundation for his natural philosophy and Plato's complete lack of interest in empirical research) was that Plato believed that objects in the world were copies of perfect immaterial forms (ideas) that existed outside the physical world. Aristotle believed that objects in the physical world are what they are and that there are no immaterial forms. Substance (what things are made of) and form (the form they have) combine to generate things, and things are simply what they are. The two philosophers had a basic *ontological* disagreement, ontology being the study of the nature of being, of existence. Two of the greatest minds in philosophy had a different point of view regarding ontology. It is not as big a deal as some try to make it. Aside from their ontological differences they were in basic

---

[44] From the Greek *telos*, meaning complete, mature, having reached its end. A ripe piece of fruit is *telos*, in that it has matured, reached it end. It is ready to be eaten and enjoyed.

agreement about the goal of life, becoming, and of philosophy, the pursuit and acquisition of a sure and certain knowledge while in the process of becoming.

Philosophy then, shaped by the three greatest philosophers of the ages, Socrates, Plato, and Aristotle, was directed toward gaining sure and certain insights (knowledge) about the nature of reality and how life ought to be lived. Reality was considered to be dualistic in nature, consisting of the material and the immaterial, and the goal of life was to become, to achieve *arête*, which would allow one to live a happy, fulfilling life.[45]

Philosophy After The Greeks

Things didn't change an awful lot, philosophically speaking, until the 3rd century CE, when a philosopher name Plotinus reworked some of Plato's philosophy, creating what is known as *Neoplatonism*. Platonism and Neoplatonism then became influential in the thinking of the 5th century philosopher-theologian, St. Augustine, whose writing provides the foundation for a good deal of Christian theology.

In the work of Augustine, western philosophy acquired a definite Christian articulation. Judeo-Christian and Classical Greek thinking were combined to generate a new hybrid philosophy, at least for philosophers who also happened to be Christians. This new articulation, on the philosophical side, was essentially Platonic until the 13th century and the work of St. Thomas Aquinas, who took advantage of the recent rediscovery and translation of Aristotle's work. As Augustine incorporated Platonic and Neoplatonic thinking into his Christian perspective, so Aquinas incorporated Aristotelian perspectives into his

---

[45] See Rogers, *21st Century Ethics: An Introduction to Moral Philosophy*, Chapter 2, Greek Moral Philosophy.

thinking, generating a large body of theological philosophy or philosophical theology, whichever your prefer, that shaped western philosophy for a couple hundred years.

The next major shift in western philosophy came at the beginning of what is referred to as the modern era. René Descartes is considered the father of modern philosophy because: 1) he abandoned traditional Aristotelian methods and conclusions in favor of a new method of his own design, and 2) he espoused and promoted the new mechanistic approach to the sciences.[46] Descartes was a dualist and a theist who presented arguments designed to demonstrate God's existence.

Not everyone at the dawn of the new age shared Descartes' beliefs. One who did not was Thomas Hobbes. Hobbes proposed that instead of working out of a dualistic paradigm, a materialistic paradigm should be assumed and embraced and that philosophy and science be done from that perspective.[47] Unfortunately many people accepted his idea and philosophy was set on a different path than it had been on for almost 2000 years, a path that either ignored or denied the existence of God and an immaterial reality. Thus Nietzsche, writing in the late 19th century, could remind his readers that (metaphorically speaking) *we have killed God.*

It is worth noting that when Hobbes (and others) suggested (and academics and intellectuals embraced his suggestion) that a materialistic paradigm be assumed, it was just that—an assumption. There was (and is) no positive evidence for rejecting a dualistic paradigm (that is, the idea that reality is comprised of both material and immaterial features) including the existence of God. Materialists argue that there is no evidence for the existence of God and the dualistic nature of reality. There may be little empirical

---

[46] Skirry provides a nice overview of Descartes: "René Descartes (1596-1650): Overview," in *Internet Encyclopedia of Philosophy.*
[47] This development will be discussed in more detail in Chapter 9.

evidence, but there is plenty of rational evidence. There is only one positive argument that can be made against the existence of God (the Problem of Evil) and that argument can and has been answered.[48] The assumption of a materialist paradigm (that only physical things exist) at the beginning of the modern era was an arbitrary and unwarranted step that resulted in relativistic thinking that has, in the opinion of many, damaged western society (morally speaking) in significant ways. Unfortunately a discussion of how it has damaged western society is beyond the scope of this introductory discussion. A study of contemporary ethical dilemmas, however, brings the damage into clear focus.

Summary

The pre-Socratics took a bold step away from the accepted notions about nature and in the process created and gave us what we call philosophy. But philosophy did not remain what it was in those early stages. The study of nature inevitably led to a consideration of human life and its purpose. The Sophists, itinerant teachers of wisdom, claimed to be able to teach young men how to live wisely, managing their affairs and participating in Greek society in appropriate and helpful ways. Yet the Sophists were philosophical skeptics, denying the existence of objective truth, embracing, therefore, moral relativism. Socrates stood firmly opposed to the Sophists, affirming the existence of objective truth and focusing the philosophic conversation on a fundamental moral question: what kind of a person ought one to be?

Socrates' student, Plato, perhaps the greatest philosopher of all time, fully supported his master's focus and purpose but added his own as well. In addition to moral

---

[48] See Rogers, *Proof of God?: Inquiries into the Philosophy of Religion, A Concise Introduction*, 195-218.

philosophy, Plato was interested in natural and sociopolitical philosophy, combining the three foci into what one might describe as a philosophical *grand unified theory* that was matched (if indeed it was) only by the work of his student, Aristotle, the other philosopher for the ages.

Plato and Aristotle had a fundamental ontological disagreement. Plato believed that objects in the world were copies of perfect immaterial forms or ideas that existed outside the physical world. Aristotle believed that objects in the physical world are what they are and that there are no immaterial forms. Things are what they are. Aside from this difference, which some philosophers blow way out of proportion, the two men agreed on the nature and purpose of philosophy and of life.

Philosophy continued on the path set by Socrates, Plato and Aristotle until the beginning of the modern era, when, without evidence or justifiable reason, the academics and intellectuals of the day (philosophers and scientists) assumed and embraced a materialistic paradigm. Philosophy hasn't been the same since.

Thought And Discussion Questions

1. Explain why Socrates and Plato were opposed to the teaching of the Sophists.
2. Discuss the significance of Socrates belief that moral philosophy was more important than physics.
3. Identify and discuss the philosophical differences between Plato and Aristotle.
4. Discuss the idea of life being teleological and the goal of life being human becoming.
5. Discuss the significance of the fact that all three of the most important and influential philosophers of all time each believed that moral philosophy (ethics) was essential to doing philosophy.

Chapter 3
Why Study Philosophy?

Now that we have some basic idea of what philosophy is, the next obvious question is, *why study it?* There are two basic answers: 1) because insight is better than ignorance, and 2) because, as Socrates observed, *the unexamined life is not worth living.* But to understand the full import of what these two statements mean will require some additional discussion and thought.

Because Insight Is Better Than Ignorance

The Utilitarian philosopher John Stuart Mill famously said, "It is better to be a human being dissatisfied than a pig satisfied; better to be Socrates dissatisfied than a fool satisfied."[49] In the context of his argument, he was reminding his readers that humans, as higher order beings, have

---

[49] Mill, *Utilitarianism*, Ch. 2.

capacities for both pleasure and pain that surpass those of animals, and that those enhanced capacities are an advantage. It is better to be a human dissatisfied than a pig satisfied. I think most people would agree with Mill on that point. But then Mill also said that it is better to be Socrates dissatisfied than a fool satisfied. That comparison is not between animals and humans, but between wise and foolish people. Mill is saying that it is better to be wise than foolish, better to be insightful than ignorant. One reason to study philosophy is that it helps us figure out which questions to ask. And knowing what to ask and how to ask it is essential if any significant answers are to be discovered.

Asking The Right Questions

From one point of view, philosophy is about asking and answering questions. But asking and answering questions is only a meaningful activity if the questions being asked are the right questions. One of the advantages of being over 2,500 years down the road from the beginning of philosophy is that philosophers have figured out what some of the important questions are.

Most of the time our minds are occupied with questions that are not ultimately important. What should I wear today? What should I eat for lunch? What should I watch on T.V.? Should I go to a movie tonight? Should I go out with this person? What kind of car should I buy? Should I take a psychology class or a sociology class? We do need to think about such things. Life consists of lots of unimportant little things that need to be considered. But for some people, these kinds of little, unimportant things are *all* they think about. That's not good. Studying philosophy reminds us that there are important questions to be considered.

What are some of these important questions?

Is there a God?

What is God like?

Does ultimate, objective truth exist?

What can be known and how?

What constitutes proof or evidence?

Is reality monistic or dualistic?

What is really real?

Are things that can be experienced by the senses the only things that really matter?

Is there life after death?

Do good and evil really exist, or do we just call some things good and some things evil?

What makes a human being different from an animal?

When is a human being a human being?

Are humans self-determined; are we really free to choose?

Do humans have rights?

If humans have rights, isn't it immoral to deny them those rights?

Do animals have rights?

Should humans be allowed to determine when and how they die?

In what ways are parents and children morally obligated to each other?

Is it moral to clone human beings?

Is capital punishment moral?

Is it moral for some people to be rich and others to be poor?

Does a woman have the right to decide to terminate the life of the child growing inside her?

Does equal opportunity demand equal responsibility and vice versa?

Is it moral for the government to treat one group of people differently than another?

What does it mean to be a good person?

How does one become a good person?

Does life have meaning?

Is there a purpose for human existence?

These are just some of the important questions philosophers have asked over the centuries and are the kinds of questions that need to be asked and answered by each person. Why? Because wrestling with questions such as these brings an intellectual and emotional dynamic to life, a richness and intensity that cannot exist if one's mind is only occupied with the banality of day-to-day existence. And even if after contemplating such questions we experience some level of frustration because the answers do not come easily or quickly, we still have Mill's conclusion to comfort us— *better to be Socrates dissatisfied than a fool satisfied.* At least we will have thought; at least we will have considered. And in those processes alone there is insight and enlightenment.

Answering The Questions Rationally

Studying philosophy helps us ask questions of cosmic significance, which all by itself is helpful. But studying philosophy also helps us learn how to answer those important questions in a rational manner. All normal people are capable of cognitive processing, of thinking. But thinking and *thinking well* are not the same things. Thinking well, thinking analytically, often referred to as *critical thinking*, is a skill that must be learned. In his book on critical thinking, Alec Fisher[50] draws an analogy between learning to play the game of basketball and learning to think well. He tells the story of his eleven-year-old daughter wanting to learn to play basketball. The gist of his analogy is this: you can hand just about anyone a basketball and tell them to bounce it a few times and then try to throw it at the backboard and get it to go through that little hoop. They may do something that approximates dribbling the ball and then toss it up and

---

[50] Fisher, *Critical Thinking: An Introduction*, 5-6.

through the hoop, making a basket. Technically then, from one point of view, they can say, *"Look, I'm playing basketball."* Well, yes, maybe. But not really. At least not in the way athletes who have been taught how to play basketball and who have spent years honing their skills play basketball. To play basketball well, you have to be taught how to play and you have to practice. Thinking is like that. Just about anyone can think. But thinking well is a learned skill that requires practice. Studying philosophy helps students develop the critical thinking skills they need to approach philosophical questions appropriately, answering the questions rationally and logically.

For instance, in the Platonic dialog entitled *Euthyphro,*[51] Plato has Socrates engage a young man named Euthyphro in a conversation about piety, that is, about what is right and good. In the course of the conversation, Socrates discovers that the enthusiastic young Euthyphro is prosecuting a man for manslaughter—a noble thing to be doing. But Socrates is shocked to find that the man Euthyphro is prosecuting is his own father. Socrates has never heard of such a thing. Can a son prosecuting his own father be pious, that is, is it the right thing to do? Euthyphro believes it is. But Socrates understands that in order to make such a determination one would need to know what the "right thing to do" is. One would need a definition of "right", as in "the right thing to do"[52] before one could really know if a specific action is right or the right thing to do. So Socrates asks Euthyphro for a definition of piety, of right or of rightness. What Socrates wants is a definition that is the essential idea of rightness, so that he can grasp it in his mind and apply it as a measure against an action or activity to see if it is, in fact, right. If Socrates knows what rightness is, then

---

[51] Plato, *Euthyphro.*
[52] In the actual dialog the word they use is the word *pious*, as in *what is piety?* and *what is the pious thing to do?* For my purposes here I prefer the word "right," as in what is the right thing to do?

he can know whether or not any act he observes is right. One can ask this same question about other basic concepts—What is good? What is evil? What is just?—so that one can apply the measure to what one is observing and determine the goodness, evilness, or justness of what he is observing. So Socrates asks Euthyphro to explain the essence of rightness so that Socrates can use that definition to determine whether or not a thing is right. Euthyphro's reply is that what he is doing, prosecuting his father, is right. Socrates considers Euthyphro's answer and responds that Euthyphro has not provided a definition but an example, and that an example of a thing is not the essential definition of that thing. Euthyphro is taken aback but recovers nicely and tries but fails again. He has to try four times before he finally comes up with a definition that comes close to a working definition of rightness. Then, of course, Socrates asks him another question that he cannot answer, and Euthyphro, becoming painfully aware of his ignorance and lack of insight, abruptly excuses himself and hurries off leaving Socrates standing there by himself.

What's the point? It is simple: you can't determine what is right or wrong, for example, if you don't know what "right" is and if you don't know what "wrong" is. What is the essence of rightness? What is the essence of wrongness? You can't possibly know what is right and what is wrong if you don't first know what the essence of rightness is and what the essence of wrongness is.

What do you think the essence of rightness is? Think about it a moment. Don't give an example of doing a right thing. Come up with an essential definition of right or rightness. Or, if you prefer, use justice or goodness or some other concept. Give it a try. The task is more difficult than you might think.

According to Aristotle, one of the most important things Socrates did as a philosopher was to demonstrate this very point—the importance of definitions. All good critical

56

thinking begins with definition. We cannot engage in rational analysis until we are clear about what we are considering. We can't know what we're talking about until we know what we're talking about! This is one of the basic lessons of philosophy. Philosophy students must learn to begin discussions by defining clearly and thoroughly what is being discussed. How can one arrive at a rational conclusion if one is not clear on what is being considered? Many times, like Euthyphro, we think we know what we are discussing when we do not.

But defining terms and using precise terminology is only one aspect of the rational process. Another is being logically consistent, which is part of making sound arguments for the positions one advocates.[53] What do you believe? Why do you believe it? Everyone can answer the first question. Few can answer the second, at least as far as a logical, rational answer is concerned. In the ethics classes I teach, I tell students that I am delighted that they have opinions about contemporary moral dilemmas. But I have a rule for the class: no one gets to express an opinion without having a valid and sound argument in support of it. I'm happy to hear what students believe as long as they can articulate a sound argument for why they believe it. I am constantly amazed how many students cannot make even a simple argument for what they believe. One young woman even complained to me in a paper she wrote, saying she did not understand why she needed to have reasons for what she believed. Her position was that if she believed a thing that should be enough. She should not have to give reasons for why she believed it. Sadly, this is how many people live their lives today—in a cognitive void.

---

[53] I'm not attempting to discuss the entire process of critical thinking here but merely pointing out a few aspects of a significant and complex process as an illustration of how the study of philosophy aids in the development of good critical thinking.

One semester in my ethics class, we were discussing the morality or immorality of abortion. Some in the class took the position that abortion is immoral because it involves the killing of a human being—a human being in the fetal stage of development, but a human being nonetheless. One man in the class objected, saying that abortion did not involve killing a human being because the fetus is not a person. I asked him why he thought a fetus is not a person. He said, "*It just isn't.*" "Why not," I asked. "Because it just isn't." "But why isn't it? What are your reasons for believing that the fetus is not a living human person?" He said, "Because it isn't." At that point I was getting a little frustrated and said, "So you don't have any reasons that you can explain. You have an opinion but no reasons for holding that opinion. You can make an *assertion* but not an *argument*." At that point he had no further response. He just sat there looking at me.

The reason you need rational reasons for believing what you believe is that you, as a human being, are a rational being. Rational beings think and behave rationally—at least they ought to. The study of philosophy helps you think rationally about life's most important questions. It helps you work your way through the complex maze that is life so that when someone asks you why you embrace a given position, you can provide him or her with a rational answer, an answer that makes sense. For instance, if someone asks, *Why do you embrace X?* You should be able to respond, *I believe X because of 1, 2, and 3* (1, 2, and 3 being sound arguments). Studying philosophy helps you learn how to do that.

But that process can be more challenging than you might think. It is not just about making arguments to support your positions, but about making *sound* arguments to support your positions. What is a *sound* argument? A sound argument is one: 1) in which the terms are clear and unambiguous, 2) in which the premises are true, 3) in which the conclusion logically flows from the premises, and 4) where the structure of the argument does not involve a logical contradiction or a logical fallacy. For example, consider the following argument, presented in a syllogistic form:

Premise 1:   It is either raining or it is not raining
Premise 2   It is not raining
Conclusion: Therefore, it is raining

This is a structurally valid argument. The terms are clear and unambiguous, the premises are true (assuming that it is, in fact, not raining—we can look outside and check to see), and the conclusion flows logically from the premises. Those features of the argument are valid. But the conclusion is clearly not true. If it is not raining, it can't be raining. The conclusion involves a logical contradiction, thereby violating the law of non-contradiction, that is, that an argument cannot be sound if it involves a logical contradiction. Therefore it is not a *sound* argument. It may be constructed in a valid manner, but it is not a sound argument.

In this example it is fairly obvious that something is wrong with this argument. It can't be not raining and raining at the same time. But many unsound arguments are not so obvious. Studying philosophy helps you develop the skills you need to critique arguments so you can identify problems in the arguments others make as well as construct your own sound arguments.

Studying philosophy provides you with an opportunity to figure things out, to become an enlightened, insightful person, so that you can be more like Socrates than the fool Mill mentioned. Another reason for studying philosophy is, as Socrates himself said, "The unexamined life is not worth living,"[54]

---

[54] Plato, *Apology*, (38).

Because The Unexamined Life Is Not Worth Living

The study of philosophy ought not be an impersonal academic process—what did Plato think about this or that, what did Kant think about this or that—but a personal dynamic, introspective process—how does what I have learned from Socrates and Aristotle change my life?

For Socrates, philosophy was not something one studied, but something one did. The distinction may appear small at first glance, but it is huge. One can study history, but one cannot, in the strict sense, do history. Philosophy is something one can do. It is possible, however, to study philosophy and not do philosophy. Socrates, Plato, and Aristotle would be very disappointed to meet a person and discover that he or she was studying but not doing philosophy. What is the difference between studying and doing philosophy? Studying philosophy is just learning about what philosophers, ancient and modern, have said about different philosophical issues. It is an interesting study. But actually doing philosophy requires that as you learn what others have said, you enter into the philosophical conversation as a participant. Doing philosophy requires that you engage in critical thinking and analysis and develop your own point of view (about whatever subject is being considered), discussing what you believe and why. And the most important part of the process is the personal introspection that connects what you believe with how you live. This is the part that was so important for Socrates. This is what he meant when he referred to the care of your soul.

For Socrates, doing philosophy meant thinking about the purpose of life. It meant figuring out what was most important in life. It meant putting all of one's energies into becoming the best person one could become, achieving personal excellence, which was the only way to be happy and satisfied in life. To do this, one had to engage in personal introspection, one had to "examine" his or her life. For

Socrates, not doing so was foolish. That's what he meant when he said: *the unexamined life is not worth living.*

To understand this idea more thoroughly, I have chosen two readings, one from Plato and one from Aristotle, that have to do with examining one's life, paying attention to who and what one is with an eye to becoming an excellent person. The first is Plato's dialog, *Apology*, which is his account of the trial of Socrates. It is during his trial that Socrates makes his famous comment: *the unexamined life is not worth living.*

Apology
by
Plato

How you, O Athenians, have been affected by my accusers, I cannot tell; but I know that they almost made me forget who I was—so persuasively did they speak; and yet they have hardly uttered a word of truth. But of the many falsehoods told by them, there was one which quite amazed me;—I mean when they said that you should be upon your guard and not allow yourselves to be deceived by the force of my eloquence. To say this, when they were certain to be detected as soon as I opened my lips and proved myself to be anything but a great speaker, did indeed appear to me most shameless—unless by the force of eloquence they mean the force of truth; for if such is their meaning, I admit that I am eloquent. But in how different a way from theirs! Well, as I was saying, they have scarcely spoken the truth at all; but from me you shall hear the whole truth: not, however, delivered after their manner in a set oration duly ornamented with words and phrases. No, by heaven! but I shall use the words and arguments which occur to me at the moment; for I am confident in the justice

61

of my cause (Or, I am certain that I am right in taking this course.): at my time of life I ought not to be appearing before you, O men of Athens, in the character of a juvenile orator—let no one expect it of me. And I must beg of you to grant me a favour:—If I defend myself in my accustomed manner, and you hear me using the words which I have been in the habit of using in the agora, at the tables of the money-changers, or anywhere else, I would ask you not to be surprised, and not to interrupt me on this account. For I am more than seventy years of age, and appearing now for the first time in a court of law, I am quite a stranger to the language of the place; and therefore I would have you regard me as if I were really a stranger, whom you would excuse if he spoke in his native tongue, and after the fashion of his country:—Am I making an unfair request of you? Never mind the manner, which may or may not be good; but think only of the truth of my words, and give heed to that: let the speaker speak truly and the judge decide justly.

And first, I have to reply to the older charges and to my first accusers, and then I will go on to the later ones. For of old I have had many accusers, who have accused me falsely to you during many years; and I am more afraid of them than of Anytus and his associates, who are dangerous, too, in their own way. But far more dangerous are the others, who began when you were children, and took possession of your minds with their falsehoods, telling of one Socrates, a wise man, who speculated about the heaven above, and searched into the earth beneath, and made the worse appear the better cause. The disseminators of this tale are the accusers whom I dread; for their hearers are apt to fancy that such enquirers do not believe in the existence of the gods. And they are many, and their charges against me are of ancient date, and they were made by them in the days when you were more impressible than you are now—in childhood, or it may have been in youth—and the cause when heard went by default, for there was none to answer. And hardest of all, I do not know and cannot tell the names of my accusers; unless in the chance case of a Comic poet. All who from envy and malice have persuaded you—some of them having first convinced themselves—all this class of men are most difficult to deal with; for I cannot have them up here, and cross-examine them, and therefore I must simply fight with shadows in my own defence, and argue when there is no one who answers. I will ask you then to assume with me, as I was saying, that my opponents are of two kinds; one recent, the other ancient: and I hope that you will see the propriety of my answering the latter first, for these accusations you heard long before the others, and much oftener.

Well, then, I must make my defence, and endeavour to clear away in a short time, a slander which has lasted a long time. May I succeed, if to succeed be for my good and yours, or likely to avail me in my cause! The task is not an easy one; I quite understand the nature of it. And so leaving the event with God, in obedience to the law I will now make my defence.

I will begin at the beginning, and ask what is the accusation which has given rise to the slander of me, and in fact has encouraged Meletus to proof this charge against me. Well, what do the slanderers say? They shall be my prosecutors, and I will sum up their words in an affidavit: 'Socrates is an evil-doer, and a curious person, who searches into things under the earth and in heaven, and he makes the worse appear the better cause; and he teaches the aforesaid

63

doctrines to others.' Such is the nature of the accusation: it is just what you have yourselves seen in the comedy of Aristophanes (Aristoph., Clouds.), who has introduced a man whom he calls Socrates, going about and saying that he walks in air, and talking a deal of nonsense concerning matters of which I do not pretend to know either much or little—not that I mean to speak disparagingly of any one who is a student of natural philosophy. I should be very sorry if Meletus could bring so grave a charge against me. But the simple truth is, O Athenians, that I have nothing to do with physical speculations. Very many of those here present are witnesses to the truth of this, and to them I appeal. Speak then, you who have heard me, and tell your neighbours whether any of you have ever known me hold forth in few words or in many upon such matters . . . You hear their answer. And from what they say of this part of the charge you will be able to judge of the truth of the rest.

As little foundation is there for the report that I am a teacher, and take money; this accusation has no more truth in it than the other. Although, if a man were really able to instruct mankind, to receive money for giving instruction would, in my opinion, be an honour to him. There is Gorgias of Leontium, and Prodicus of Ceos, and Hippias of Elis, who go the round of the cities, and are able to persuade the young men to leave their own citizens by whom they might be taught for nothing, and come to them whom they not only pay, but are thankful if they may be allowed to pay them. There is at this time a Parian philosopher residing in Athens, of whom I have heard; and I came to hear of him in this way:—I came across a man who has spent a world of money on the Sophists, Callias, the son of Hipponicus, and knowing that he had sons, I asked him: 'Callias,' I

64

*said, 'if your two sons were foals or calves, there
would be no difficulty in finding some one to put over
them; we should hire a trainer of horses, or a farmer
probably, who would improve and perfect them in
their own proper virtue and excellence; but as they
are human beings, whom are you thinking of placing
over them? Is there any one who understands human
and political virtue? You must have thought about the
matter, for you have sons; is there any one?' 'There
is,' he said. 'Who is he?' said I; 'and of what
country? and what does he charge?' 'Evenus the
Parian,' he replied; 'he is the man, and his charge is
five minae.' Happy is Evenus, I said to myself, if he
really has this wisdom, and teaches at such a
moderate charge. Had I the same, I should have been
very proud and conceited; but the truth is that I have
no knowledge of the kind.*

*I dare say, Athenians, that some one among you
will reply, 'Yes, Socrates, but what is the origin of
these accusations which are brought against you;
there must have been something strange which you
have been doing? All these rumours and this talk
about you would never have arisen if you had been
like other men: tell us, then, what is the cause of them,
for we should be sorry to judge hastily of you.' Now I
regard this as a fair challenge, and I will endeavour
to explain to you the reason why I am called wise and
have such an evil fame. Please to attend then. And
although some of you may think that I am joking, I
declare that I will tell you the entire truth. Men of
Athens, this reputation of mine has come of a certain
sort of wisdom which I possess. If you ask me what
kind of wisdom, I reply, wisdom such as may perhaps
be attained by man, for to that extent I am inclined to
believe that I am wise; whereas the persons of whom
I was speaking have a superhuman wisdom which I*

may fail to describe, because I have it not myself; and he who says that I have, speaks falsely, and is taking away my character. And here, O men of Athens, I must beg you not to interrupt me, even if I seem to say something extravagant. For the word which I will speak is not mine. I will refer you to a witness who is worthy of credit; that witness shall be the God of Delphi—he will tell you about my wisdom, if I have any, and of what sort it is. You must have known Chaerephon; he was early a friend of mine, and also a friend of yours, for he shared in the recent exile of the people, and returned with you. Well, Chaerephon, as you know, was very impetuous in all his doings, and he went to Delphi and boldly asked the oracle to tell him whether—as I was saying, I must beg you not to interrupt—he asked the oracle to tell him whether anyone was wiser than I was, and the Pythian prophetess answered, that there was no man wiser. Chaerephon is dead himself; but his brother, who is in court, will confirm the truth of what I am saying.

Why do I mention this? Because I am going to explain to you why I have such an evil name. When I heard the answer, I said to myself, What can the god mean? and what is the interpretation of his riddle? for I know that I have no wisdom, small or great. What then can he mean when he says that I am the wisest of men? And yet he is a god, and cannot lie; that would be against his nature. After long consideration, I thought of a method of trying the question. I reflected that if I could only find a man wiser than myself, then I might go to the god with a refutation in my hand. I should say to him, 'Here is a man who is wiser than I am; but you said that I was the wisest.' Accordingly I went to one who had the reputation of wisdom, and observed him—his name I need not mention; he was a politician whom I

66

selected for examination—and the result was as follows: When I began to talk with him, I could not help thinking that he was not really wise, although he was thought wise by many, and still wiser by himself; and thereupon I tried to explain to him that he thought himself wise, but was not really wise; and the consequence was that he hated me, and his enmity was shared by several who were present and heard me. So I left him, saying to myself, as I went away: Well, although I do not suppose that either of us knows anything really beautiful and good, I am better off than he is,—for he knows nothing, and thinks that he knows; I neither know nor think that I know. In this latter particular, then, I seem to have slightly the advantage of him. Then I went to another who had still higher pretensions to wisdom, and my conclusion was exactly the same. Whereupon I made another enemy of him, and of many others besides him.

Then I went to one man after another, being not unconscious of the enmity which I provoked, and I lamented and feared this: but necessity was laid upon me,—the word of God, I thought, ought to be considered first. And I said to myself, Go I must to all who appear to know, and find out the meaning of the oracle. And I swear to you, Athenians, by the dog I swear!—for I must tell you the truth—the result of my mission was just this: I found that the men most in repute were all but the most foolish; and that others less esteemed were really wiser and better. I will tell you the tale of my wanderings and of the 'Herculean' labours, as I may call them, which I endured only to find at last the oracle irrefutable. After the politicians, I went to the poets; tragic, dithyrambic, and all sorts. And there, I said to myself, you will be instantly detected; now you will find out that you are more ignorant than they are. Accordingly, I took them some of the most elaborate passages in their own writings, and asked what was the meaning of them—thinking that they would teach me something. Will you believe me? I am almost ashamed to confess the truth, but I must say that there is hardly a person present who would not have talked better about their poetry than they did themselves. Then I knew that not by wisdom do poets write poetry, but by a sort of genius and inspiration; they are like diviners or soothsayers who also say many fine things, but do not understand the meaning of them. The poets appeared to me to be much in the same case; and I further observed that upon the strength of their poetry they believed themselves to be the wisest of men in other things in which they were not wise. So I departed, conceiving myself to be superior to them for the same reason that I was superior to the politicians.

At last I went to the artisans. I was conscious that I knew nothing at all, as I may say, and I was sure that they knew many fine things; and here I was not mistaken, for they did know many things of which I was ignorant, and in this they certainly were wiser than I was. But I observed that even the good artisans fell into the same error as the poets;—because they were good workmen they thought that they also knew all sorts of high matters, and this defect in them overshadowed their wisdom; and therefore I asked myself on behalf of the oracle, whether I would like to be as I was, neither having their knowledge nor their ignorance, or like them in both; and I made answer to myself and to the oracle that I was better off as I was.

This inquisition has led to my having many enemies of the worst and most dangerous kind, and has given occasion also to many calumnies. And I am called wise, for my hearers always imagine that I myself possess the wisdom which I find wanting in others: but the truth is, O men of Athens, that God only is wise; and by his answer he intends to show that the wisdom of men is worth little or nothing; he is not speaking of Socrates, he is only using my name by way of illustration, as if he said, He, O men, is the wisest, who, like Socrates, knows that his wisdom is in truth worth nothing. And so I go about the world, obedient to the god, and search and make enquiry into the wisdom of any one, whether citizen or stranger, who appears to be wise; and if he is not wise, then in vindication of the oracle I show him that he is not wise; and my occupation quite absorbs me, and I have no time to give either to any public matter of interest or to any concern of my own, but I am in utter poverty by reason of my devotion to the god.

There is another thing:—young men of the richer classes, who have not much to do, come about me of their own accord; they like to hear the pretenders examined, and they often imitate me, and proceed to examine others; there are plenty of persons, as they quickly discover, who think that they know something, but really know little or nothing; and then those who are examined by them instead of being angry with themselves are angry with me: This confounded Socrates, they say; this villainous misleader of youth!— and then if somebody asks them, Why, what evil does he practise or teach? they do not know, and cannot tell; but in order that they may not appear to be at a loss, they repeat the ready-made charges which are used against all philosophers about teaching things up in the clouds and under the earth, and having no gods, and making the worse appear the better cause; for they do not like to confess that their pretence of knowledge has been detected— which is the truth; and as they are numerous and ambitious and energetic, and are drawn up in battle array and have persuasive tongues, they have filled your ears with their loud and inveterate calumnies. And this is the reason why my three accusers, Meletus and Anytus and Lycon, have set upon me; Meletus, who has a quarrel with me on behalf of the poets; Anytus, on behalf of the craftsmen and politicians; Lycon, on behalf of the rhetoricians: and as I said at the beginning, I cannot expect to get rid of such a mass of calumny all in a moment. And this, O men of Athens, is the truth and the whole truth; I have concealed nothing, I have dissembled nothing. And yet, I know that my plainness of speech makes them hate me, and what is their hatred but a proof that I am speaking the truth?—Hence has arisen the prejudice against me; and this is the reason of it, as you will find out either in this or in any future enquiry.

I have said enough in my defence against the first class of my accusers; I turn to the second class. They are headed by Meletus, that good man and true lover of his country, as he calls himself. Against these, too, I must try to make a defence:—Let their affidavit be read: it contains something of this kind: It says that Socrates is a doer of evil, who corrupts the youth; and who does not believe in the gods of the state, but has other new divinities of his own. Such is the charge; and now let us examine the particular counts. He says that I am a doer of evil, and corrupt the youth; but I say, O men of Athens, that Meletus is a doer of evil, in that he pretends to be in earnest when he is only in jest, and is so eager to bring men to trial from a pretended zeal and interest about matters in which he really never had the smallest interest. And the truth of this I will endeavour to prove to you.

Come hither, Meletus, and let me ask a question of you. You think a great deal about the improvement of youth?

Yes, I do.

Tell the judges, then, who is their improver; for you must know, as you have taken the pains to discover their corrupter, and are citing and accusing me before them. Speak, then, and tell the judges who their improver is.— Observe, Meletus, that you are silent, and have nothing to say. But is not this rather disgraceful, and a very considerable proof of what I was saying, that you have no interest in the matter? Speak up, friend, and tell us who their improver is.

The laws.

But that, my good sir, is not my meaning. I want to know who the person is, who, in the first place, knows the laws.

The judges, Socrates, who are present in court.

What, do you mean to say, Meletus, that they are able to instruct and improve youth?

Certainly they are.

What, all of them, or some only and not others?
All of them.
By the goddess Here, that is good news! There are plenty of improvers,

then. And what do you say of the audience,—do they improve them? Yes, they do.

And the senators?

Yes, the senators improve them.
But perhaps the members of the assembly corrupt them?—or do they too

improve them?

They improve them.
Then every Athenian improves and elevates them; all with the exception of

myself; and I alone am their corrupter? Is that what you affirm?

That is what I stoutly affirm.

I am very unfortunate if you are right. But suppose I ask you a question:

How about horses? Does one man do them harm and all the world good? Is not the exact opposite the truth? One man is able to do them good, or at least not many;—the trainer of horses, that is to say, does them good, and others who have to do with them rather injure them? Is not that true, Meletus, of horses, or of any other animals? Most assuredly it is; whether you and Anytus say yes or no. Happy indeed would be the condition of youth if they had one corrupter only, and all the rest of the world were their improvers. But you, Meletus, have sufficiently shown that you never had a thought about the young: your carelessness is seen in your not caring about the very things which you bring against me.

And now, Meletus, I will ask you another question—by Zeus I will: Which is better, to live among bad citizens, or among good ones? Answer, friend, I say; the question is one which may be easily answered. Do not the good do their neighbours good, and the bad do them evil?

Certainly.

And is there anyone who would rather be injured than benefited by those who live with him? Answer, my good friend, the law requires you to answer— does any one like to be injured?

Certainly not.

And when you accuse me of corrupting and deteriorating the youth, do you allege that I corrupt them intentionally or unintentionally?

Intentionally, I say.

But you have just admitted that the good do their neighbours good, and the evil do them evil. Now, is that a truth which your superior wisdom has recognized thus early in life, and am I, at my age, in such darkness and igno- rance as not to know that if a man with whom I have to live is corrupted by me, I am very likely to be harmed by him; and yet I corrupt him, and intentionally, too—so you say, although neither I nor any other human being is ever likely to be convinced by you. But either I do not corrupt them, or I corrupt them unintentionally; and on either view of the case you lie. If my offence is unintentional, the law has no cognizance of unintentional offences: you ought to have taken me privately, and warned and admonished me; for if I had been better advised, I should have left off doing what I only did unintentionally—no doubt I should; but you would have nothing to say to me and refused to teach me. And now you bring me up in this court, which is a place not of instruction, but of punishment.

It will be very clear to you, Athenians, as I was saying, that Meletus has no care at all, great or small, about the matter. But still I should like to know, Meletus, in what I am affirmed to corrupt the young. I suppose you mean, as I infer from your indictment, that I teach them not to acknowledge the gods which the state acknowledges, but some other new divinities or spiritual agencies in their stead. These are the lessons by which I corrupt the youth, as you say.

Yes, that I say emphatically.

Then, by the gods, Meletus, of whom we are speaking, tell me and the court, in somewhat plainer terms, what you mean! for I do not as yet understand whether you affirm that I teach other men to acknowledge some gods, and therefore that I do believe in gods, and am not an entire atheist—this you do not lay to my charge,—but only you say that they are not the same gods which the city recognizes—the charge is that they are different gods.

Or, do you mean that I am an atheist simply, and a teacher of atheism?

I mean the latter—that you are a complete atheist.

What an extraordinary statement! Why do you think so, Meletus? Do you mean that I do not believe in the godhead of the sun or moon, like other men? I assure you, judges, that he does not: for he says that the sun is stone,

and the moon earth.

Friend Meletus, you think that you are accusing Anaxagoras: and you have but a bad opinion of the judges, if you fancy them illiterate to such a degree as not to know that these doctrines are found in the books of Anaxagoras the Clazomenian, which are full of them. And so, forsooth, the youth are said to be taught them by Socrates, when there are not unfrequently exhibitions of them at the theatre *(Probably in allusion to Aristophanes who caricatured, and to Euripides who borrowed the notions of Anaxagoras, as well as to other dramatic poets.)* (price of admission one drachma at the most); and they might pay their money, and laugh at Socrates if he pretends to father these extraordinary views. And so, Meletus, you really think that I do not believe in any god?

I swear by Zeus that you believe absolutely in none at all.

Nobody will believe you, Meletus, and I am pretty sure that you do not believe yourself. I cannot help thinking, men of Athens, that Meletus is reckless and impudent, and that he has written this indictment in a spirit of mere wantonness and youthful bravado. Has he not compounded a riddle, thinking to try me? He said to himself:—I shall see whether the wise Socrates will discover my facetious contradiction, or whether I shall be able to deceive him and the rest of them. For he certainly does appear to me to contradict himself in the indictment as much as if he said that Socrates is guilty of not believing in the gods, and yet of believing in them—but this is not like a person who is in earnest.

I should like you, O men of Athens, to join me in examining what I conceive to be his inconsistency; and do you, Meletus, answer. And I must remind the audience of my request that they would not make a disturbance if I speak in my accustomed manner:

Did ever man, Meletus, believe in the existence of human things, and not of human beings? ... I wish, men of Athens, that he would answer, and not be always trying to get up an interruption. Did ever any man believe in horsemanship, and not in horses? or in flute-playing, and not in flute-players? No, my friend; I will answer to you and to the court, as you refuse to answer for yourself. There is no man who ever did. But now please to answer the next question: Can a man believe in spiritual and divine agencies, and not in spirits or demigods?

He cannot.

How lucky I am to have extracted that answer, by the assistance of the court! But then you swear in the indictment that I teach and believe in divine or spiritual agencies (new or old, no matter for that); at any rate, I believe in spiritual agencies,—so you say and swear in the affidavit; and yet if I believe in divine beings, how can I help believing in spirits or demigods;—must I not? To be sure I must; and therefore I may assume that your silence gives consent. Now what are spirits or demigods? Are they not either gods or the sons of gods?

Certainly they are.

But this is what I call the facetious riddle invented by you: the demigods or spirits are gods, and you say

75

first that I do not believe in gods, and then again that I do believe in gods; that is, if I believe in demigods. For if the demigods are the illegitimate sons of gods, whether by the nymphs or by any other mothers, of whom they are said to be the sons—what human being will ever believe that there are no gods if they are the sons of gods? You might as well affirm the existence of mules, and deny that of horses and asses. Such nonsense, Meletus, could only have been intended by you to make trial of me. You have put this into the indictment because you had nothing real of which to accuse me. But no one who has a particle of understanding will ever be convinced by you that the same men can believe in divine and superhuman things, and yet not believe that there are gods and demigods and heroes.

I have said enough in answer to the charge of Meletus: any elaborate defence is unnecessary, but I know only too well how many are the enmities which I have incurred, and this is what will be my destruction if I am destroyed;—not Meletus, nor yet Anytus, but the envy and detraction of the world, which has been the death of many good men, and will probably be the death of many more; there is no danger of my being the last of them.

Some one will say: And are you not ashamed, Socrates, of a course of life which is likely to bring you to an untimely end? To him I may fairly answer: There you are mistaken: a man who is good for anything ought not to calculate the chance of living or dying; he ought only to consider whether in doing anything he is doing right or wrong—acting the part of a good man or of a bad. Whereas, upon your view, the heroes who fell at Troy were not good for much, and the son of Thetis above all, who altogether despised danger in comparison with disgrace; and when he was so eager to slay Hector, his goddess mother said to him, that if he avenged his companion Patroclus, and slew Hector, he would die himself— 'Fate,' she said, in these or the like words, 'waits for you next after Hector;' he, receiving this warning, utterly despised danger and death, and instead of fearing them, feared rather to live in dishonour, and not to avenge his friend. 'Let me die forthwith,' he replies, 'and be avenged of my enemy, rather than abide here by the beaked ships, a laughing-stock and a burden of the earth.' Had Achilles any thought of death and danger? For wherever a man's place is, whether the place which he has chosen or that in which he has been placed by a commander, there he ought to remain in the hour of danger; he should not think of death or of anything but of disgrace. And this, O men of Athens, is a true saying.

Strange, indeed, would be my conduct, O men of Athens, if I who, when I was ordered by the generals whom you chose to command me at Potidaea and Amphipolis and Delium, remained where they placed me, like any other man, facing death—if now, when, as I conceive and imagine, God orders me to fulfil the philosopher's mission of searching into myself and other men, I were to desert my post through fear of death, or any other fear; that would indeed be strange, and I might justly be arraigned in court for denying the existence of the gods, if I disobeyed the oracle because I was afraid of death, fancying that I was wise when I was not wise. For the fear of death is indeed the pretence of wisdom, and not real wisdom, being a pretence of knowing the unknown; and no one knows whether death, which men in their fear apprehend to be the greatest evil, may not be the greatest good. Is not this ignorance of a disgraceful sort, the ignorance which is the conceit that a man

*knows what he does not know? And in this respect
only I believe myself to differ from men in general,
and may perhaps claim to be wiser than they are:—
that whereas I know but little of the world below, I do
not suppose that I know: but I do know that injustice
and disobedience to a better, whether God or man, is
evil and dishonourable, and I will never fear or avoid
a possible good rather than a certain evil. And
therefore if you let me go now, and are not convinced
by Anytus, who said that since I had been prosecuted
I must be put to death; (or if not that I ought never to
have been prosecuted at all); and that if I escape now,
your sons will all be utterly ruined by listening to my
words—if you say to me, Socrates, this time we will
not mind Anytus, and you shall be let off, but upon
one condition, that you are not to enquire and
speculate in this way any more, and that if you are
caught doing so again you shall die;—if this was the
condition on which you let me go, I should reply:
Men of Athens, I honour and love you; but I shall
obey God rather than you, and while I have life and
strength I shall never cease from the practice and
teaching of philosophy, exhorting any one whom I
meet and saying to him after my manner: You, my
friend,—a citizen of the great and mighty and wise
city of Athens,—are you not ashamed of heaping up
the greatest amount of money and honour and
reputation, and caring so little about wisdom and
truth and the greatest improvement of the soul, which
you never regard or heed at all? And if the person
with whom I am arguing, says: Yes, but I do care;
then I do not leave him or let him go at once; but I
proceed to interrogate and examine and cross-
examine him, and if I think that he has no virtue in
him, but only says that he has, I reproach him with
undervaluing the greater, and overvaluing the less.*

*And I shall repeat the same words to every one whom
I meet, young and old, citizen and alien, but
especially to the citizens, inasmuch as they are my
brethren. For know that this is the command of God;
and I believe that no greater good has ever happened
in the state than my service to the God. For I do
nothing but go about persuading you all, old and
young alike, not to take thought for your persons or
your properties, but first and chiefly to care about the
greatest improvement of the soul. I tell you that virtue
is not given by money, but that from virtue comes
money and every other good of man, public as well as
private. This is my teaching, and if this is the doctrine
which corrupts the youth, I am a mischievous person.
But if any one says that this is not my teaching, he is
speaking an untruth. Wherefore, O men of Athens, I
say to you, do as Anytus bids or not as Anytus bids,
and either acquit me or not; but whichever you do,
understand that I shall never alter my ways, not even
if I have to die many times.*

   *Men of Athens, do not interrupt, but hear me; there
was an understanding between us that you should
hear me to the end: I have something more to say, at
which you may be inclined to cry out; but I believe
that to hear me will be good for you, and therefore I
beg that you will not cry out. I would have you know,
that if you kill such an one as I am, you will injure
yourselves more than you will injure me. Nothing will
injure me, not Meletus nor yet Anytus—they cannot,
for a bad man is not permitted to injure a better than
himself. I do not deny that Anytus may, perhaps, kill
him, or drive him into exile, or deprive him of civil
rights; and he may imagine, and others may imagine,
that he is inflicting a great injury upon him: but there
I do not agree. For the evil of doing as he is doing—*

the evil of unjustly taking away the life of another—is greater far.

And now, Athenians, I am not going to argue for my own sake, as you may think, but for yours, that you may not sin against the God by condemning me, who am his gift to you. For if you kill me you will not easily find a successor to me, who, if I may use such a ludicrous figure of speech, am a sort of gadfly, given to the state by God; and the state is a great and noble steed who is tardy in his motions owing to his very size, and requires to be stirred into life. I am that gadfly which God has attached to the state, and all day long and in all places am always fastening upon you, arousing and persuading and reproaching you. You will not easily find another like me, and therefore I would advise you to spare me. I dare say that you may feel out of temper (like a person who is suddenly awakened from sleep), and you think that you might easily strike me dead as Anytus advises, and then you would sleep on for the remainder of your lives, unless God in his care of you sent you another gadfly. When I say that I am given to you by God, the proof of my mission is this:—if I had been like other men, I should not have neglected all my own concerns or patiently seen the neglect of them during all these years, and have been doing yours, coming to you individually like a father or elder brother, exhorting you to regard virtue; such conduct, I say, would be unlike human nature. If I had gained anything, or if my exhortations had been paid, there would have been some sense in my doing so; but now, as you will perceive, not even the impudence of my accusers dares to say that I have ever exacted or sought pay of any one; of that they have no witness. And I have a sufficient witness to the truth of what I say—my poverty.

Some one may wonder why I go about in private giving advice and busying myself with the concerns of others, but do not venture to come forward in public and advise the state. I will tell you why. You have heard me speak at sundry times and in divers places of an oracle or sign which comes to me, and is the divinity which Meletus ridicules in the indictment. This sign, which is a kind of voice, first began to come to me when I was a child; it always forbids but never commands me to do anything which I am going to do. This is what deters me from being a politician. And rightly, as I think. For I am certain, O men of Athens, that if I had engaged in politics, I should have perished long ago, and done no good either to you or to myself. And do not be offended at my telling you the truth: for the truth is, that no man who goes to war with you or any other multitude, honestly striving against the many lawless and unrighteous deeds which are done in a state, will save his life; he who will fight for the right, if he would live even for a brief space, must have a private station and not a public one.

I can give you convincing evidence of what I say, not words only, but what you value far more—actions. Let me relate to you a passage of my own life which will prove to you that I should never have yielded to injustice from any fear of death, and that 'as I should have refused to yield' I must have died at once. I will tell you a tale of the courts, not very interesting perhaps, but nevertheless true. The only office of state which I ever held, O men of Athens, was that of senator: the tribe Antiochis, which is my tribe, had the presidency at the trial of the generals who had not taken up the bodies of the slain after the battle of Arginusae; and you proposed to try them in a body, contrary to law, as you all thought afterwards; but at

*the time I was the only one of the Prytanes who was
opposed to the illegality, and I gave my vote against
you; and when the orators threatened to impeach and
arrest me, and you called and shouted, I made up my
mind that I would run the risk, having law and justice
with me, rather than take part in your injustice
because I feared imprisonment and death. This
happened in the days of the democracy. But when the
oligarchy of the Thirty was in power, they sent for me
and four others into the rotunda, and bade us bring
Leon the Salaminian from Salamis, as they wanted to
put him to death. This was a specimen of the sort of
commands which they were always giving with the
view of implicating as many as possible in their
crimes; and then I showed, not in word only but in
deed, that, if I may be allowed to use such an
expression, I cared not a straw for death, and that my
great and only care was lest I should do an
unrighteous or unholy thing. For the strong arm of
that oppressive power did not frighten me into doing
wrong; and when we came out of the rotunda the
other four went to Salamis and fetched Leon, but I
went quietly home. For which I might have lost my
life, had not the power of the Thirty shortly
afterwards come to an end. And many will witness to
my words.*

*Now do you really imagine that I could have
survived all these years, if I had led a public life,
supposing that like a good man I had always
maintained the right and had made justice, as I ought,
the first thing? No indeed, men of Athens, neither I
nor any other man. But I have been always the same
in all my actions, public as well as private, and never
have I yielded any base compliance to those who are
slanderously termed my disciples, or to any other.
Not that I have any regular disciples. But if any one*

likes to come and hear me while I am pursuing my mission, whether he be young or old, he is not excluded. Nor do I converse only with those who pay; but any one, whether he be rich or poor, may ask and answer me and listen to my words; and whether he turns out to be a bad man or a good one, neither result can be justly imputed to me; for I never taught or professed to teach him anything. And if any one says that he has ever learned or heard anything from me in private which all the world has not heard, let me tell you that he is lying.

But I shall be asked, Why do people delight in continually conversing with you? I have told you already, Athenians, the whole truth about this matter: they like to hear the cross-examination of the pretenders to wisdom; there is amusement in it. Now this duty of cross-examining other men has been imposed upon me by God; and has been signified to me by oracles, visions, and in every way in which the will of divine power was ever intimated to any one. This is true, O Athenians, or, if not true, would be soon refuted. If I am or have been corrupting the youth, those of them who are now grown up and have become sensible that I gave them bad advice in the days of their youth should come forward as accusers, and take their revenge; or if they do not like to come themselves, some of their relatives, fathers, brothers, or other kinsmen, should say what evil their families have suffered at my hands. Now is their time. Many of them I see in the court. There is Crito, who is of the same age and of the same deme with myself, and there is Critobulus his son, whom I also see. Then again there is Lysanias of Sphettus, who is the father of Aeschines—he is present; and also there is Antiphon of Cephisus, who is the father of Epigenes; and there are the brothers of several who have

associated with me. There is Nicostratus the son of
Theosdotides, and the brother of Theodotus (now
Theodotus himself is dead, and therefore he, at any
rate, will not seek to stop him); and there is Paralus
the son of Demodocus, who had a brother Theages;
and Adeimantus the son of Ariston, whose brother
Plato is present; and Aeantodorus, who is the brother
of Apollodorus, whom I also see. I might mention a
great many others, some of whom Meletus should
have produced as witnesses in the course of his
speech; and let him still produce them, if he has
forgotten—I will make way for him. And let him say,
if he has any testimony of the sort which he can
produce. Nay, Athenians, the very opposite is the
truth. For all these are ready to witness on behalf of
the corrupter, of the injurer of their kindred, as
Meletus and Anytus call me; not the corrupted youth
only—there might have been a motive for that—but
their uncorrupted elder relatives. Why should they
too support me with their testimony? Why, indeed,
except for the sake of truth and justice, and because
they know that I am speaking the truth, and that
Meletus is a liar.

Well, Athenians, this and the like of this is all the
defence which I have to offer. Yet a word more.
Perhaps there may be some one who is offended at
me, when he calls to mind how he himself on a
similar, or even a less serious occasion, prayed and
entreated the judges with many tears, and how he
produced his children in court, which was a moving
spectacle, together with a host of relations and
friends; whereas I, who am probably in danger of my
life, will do none of these things. The contrast may
occur to his mind, and he may be set against me, and
vote in anger because he is displeased at me on this
account. Now if there be such a person among you,—

84

mind, I do not say that there is,—to him I may fairly reply: My friend, I am a man, and like other men, a creature of flesh and blood, and not 'of wood or stone,' as Homer says; and I have a family, yes, and sons, O Athenians, three in number, one almost a man, and two others who are still young; and yet I will not bring any of them hither in order to petition you for an acquittal. And why not? Not from any self-assertion or want of respect for you. Whether I am or am not afraid of death is another question, of which I will not now speak. But, having regard to public opinion, I feel that such conduct would be discreditable to myself, and to you, and to the whole state. One who has reached my years, and who has a name for wisdom, ought not to demean himself. Whether this opinion of me be deserved or not, at any rate the world has decided that Socrates is in some way superior to other men. And if those among you who are said to be superior in wisdom and courage, and any other virtue, demean themselves in this way, how shameful is their conduct! I have seen men of reputation, when they have been condemned, behaving in the strangest manner: they seemed to fancy that they were going to suffer something dreadful if they died, and that they could be immortal if you only allowed them to live; and I think that such are a dishonour to the state, and that any stranger coming in would have said of them that the most eminent men of Athens, to whom the Athenians themselves give honour and command, are no better than women. And I say that these things ought not to be done by those of us who have a reputation; and if they are done, you ought not to permit them; you ought rather to show that you are far more disposed to condemn the man who gets up a doleful scene and makes the city ridiculous, than him who holds his peace.

But, setting aside the question of public opinion, there seems to be some- thing wrong in asking a favour of a judge, and thus procuring an acquittal, instead of informing and convincing him. For his duty is, not to make a present of justice, but to give judgment; and he has sworn that he will judge according to the laws, and not according to his own good pleasure; and we ought not to encourage you, nor should you allow yourselves to be encouraged, in this habit of perjury—there can be no piety in that. Do not then require me to do what I consider dishonourable and impious and wrong, especially now, when I am being tried for impiety on the indictment of Meletus. For if, O men of Athens, by force of persuasion and entreaty I could overpower your oaths, then I should be teaching you to believe that there are no gods, and in defending should simply convict myself of the charge of not believing in them. But that is not so—far otherwise. For I do believe that there are gods, and in a sense higher than that in which any of my accusers believe in them. And to you and to God I commit my cause, to be determined by you as is best for you and me.

***

There are many reasons why I am not grieved, O men of Athens, at the vote of condemnation. I expected it, and am only surprised that the votes are so nearly equal; for I had thought that the majority against me would have been far larger; but now, had thirty votes gone over to the other side, I should have been acquitted. And I may say, I think, that I have escaped Meletus. I may say more; for without the assistance of Anytus and Lycon, any one may see that he would not have had a fifth part of the votes, as the law requires, in which case he would have incurred a fine of a thousand drachmae.

And so he proposes death as the penalty. And what shall I propose on my part, O men of Athens? Clearly that which is my due. And what is my due? What return shall be made to the man who has never had the wit to be idle during his whole life; but has been careless of what the many care for—wealth, and family interests, and military offices, and speaking in the assembly, and magistracies, and plots, and parties. Reflecting that I was really too honest a man to be a politician and live, I did not go where I could do no good to you or to myself; but where I could do the greatest good privately to every one of you, thither I went, and sought to persuade every man among you that he must look to himself, and seek virtue and wisdom before he looks to his private interests, and look to the state before he looks to the interests of the state; and that this should be the order which he observes in all his actions. What shall be done to such an one? Doubtless some good thing, O men of Athens, if he has his reward; and the good should be of a kind suitable to him. What would be a reward suitable to a poor man who is your benefactor, and who desires leisure that he may instruct you? There can be no reward so fitting as maintenance in the Prytaneum, O men of Athens, a reward which he deserves far more than the citizen who has won the prize at Olympia in the horse or chariot race, whether the chariots were drawn by two horses or by many. For I am in want, and he has enough; and he only gives you the appearance of happiness, and I give you the reality. And if I am to estimate the penalty fairly, I should say that maintenance in the Prytaneum is the just return.

Perhaps you think that I am braving you in what I am saying now, as in what I said before about the tears and prayers. But this is not so. I speak rather because I am convinced that I never intentionally wronged any one, although I cannot convince you— the time has been too short; if there were a law at Athens, as there is in other cities, that a capital cause should not be decided in one day, then I believe that I should have convinced you. But I cannot in a moment refute great slanders; and, as I am convinced that I never wronged another, I will assuredly not wrong myself. I will not say of myself that I deserve any evil, or propose any penalty. Why should I? because I am afraid of the penalty of death which Meletus proposes? When I do not know whether death is a good or an evil, why should I propose a penalty which would certainly be an evil? Shall I say imprisonment? And why should I live in prison, and be the slave of the magistrates of the year—of the Eleven? Or shall the penalty be a fine, and imprisonment until the fine is paid? There is the same objection. I should have to lie in prison, for money I have none, and cannot pay. And if I say exile (and this may possibly be the penalty which you will affix), I must indeed be blinded by the love of life, if I am so irrational as to expect that when you, who are my own citizens, cannot endure my discourses and words, and have found them so grievous and odious that you will have no more of them, others are likely to endure me. No indeed, men of Athens, that is not very likely. And what a life should I lead, at my age, wandering from city to city, ever changing my place of exile, and always being driven out! For I am quite sure that wherever I go, there, as here, the young men will flock to me; and if I drive them away, their elders will drive me out at their request; and if I let them come, their fathers and friends will drive me out for their sakes. Some one will say: Yes, Socrates, but cannot you hold your tongue, and then you may go into a foreign city, and no one will interfere with you? Now I have great difficulty in making you understand my answer to this. For if I tell you that to do as you say would be a disobedience to the God, and therefore that I cannot hold my tongue, you will not believe that I am serious; and if I say again that daily to discourse about virtue, and of those other things about which you hear me examining myself and others, is the greatest good of man, and that the unexamined life is not worth living, you are still less likely to believe me. Yet I say what is true, although a thing of which it is hard for me to persuade you. Also, I have never been accustomed to think that I deserve to suffer any harm. Had I money I might have estimated the offence at what I was able to pay, and not have been much the worse. But I have none, and therefore I must ask you to proportion the fine to my means. Well, perhaps I could afford a mina, and therefore I propose that penalty: Plato, Crito, Critobulus, and Apollodorus, my friends here, bid me say thirty minae, and they will be the sureties. Let thirty minae be the penalty; for which sum they will be ample security to you.

***

Not much time will be gained, O Athenians, in return for the evil name which you will get from the detractors of the city, who will say that you killed Socrates, a wise man; for they will call me wise, even although I am not wise, when they want to reproach you. If you had waited a little while, your desire would have been fulfilled in the course of nature. For I am far advanced in years, as you may perceive, and not far from death. I am speaking now not to all of you, but only to those who have condemned me to death. And I have another thing to say to them: you think that I was convicted because I had no words of the sort which would have procured my acquittal—I mean, if I had thought fit to leave nothing undone or unsaid. Not so; the deficiency which led to my conviction was not of words—certainly not. But I had not the boldness or impudence or inclination to address you as you would have liked me to do, weeping and wailing and lamenting, and saying and doing many things which you have been accustomed to hear from others, and which, as I maintain, are unworthy of me. I thought at the time that I ought not to do anything common or mean when in danger: nor do I now repent of the style of my defence; I would rather die having spoken after my manner, than speak in your manner and live. For neither in war nor yet at law ought I or any man to use every way of escaping death. Often in battle there can be no doubt that if a man will throw away his arms, and fall on his knees before his pursuers, he may escape death; and in other dangers there are other ways of escaping death, if a man is willing to say and do anything. The difficulty, my friends, is not to avoid death, but to avoid unrighteousness; for that runs faster than death. I am old and move slowly, and the slower runner has overtaken me, and my accusers are keen and quick, and the faster runner, who is unrighteousness, has overtaken them. And now I depart hence condemned by you to suffer the penalty of death,—they too go their ways condemned by the truth to suffer the penalty of villainy and wrong; and I must abide by my award—let them abide by theirs. I suppose that these things may be regarded as fated,—and I think that they are well.

And now, O men who have condemned me, I would fain prophesy to you; for I am about to die, and in the hour of death men are gifted with prophetic power. And I prophesy to you who are my murderers, that immediately after my departure punishment far heavier than you have inflicted on me will surely await you. Me you have killed because you wanted to escape the accuser, and not to give an account of your lives. But that will not be as you suppose: far otherwise. For I say that there will be more accusers of you than there are now; accusers whom hitherto I have restrained: and as they are younger they will be more inconsiderate with you, and you will be more offended at them. If you think that by killing men you can prevent some one from censuring your evil lives, you are mistaken; that is not a way of escape which is either possible or honourable; the easiest and the noblest way is not to be disabling others, but to be improving yourselves. This is the prophecy which I utter before my departure to the judges who have condemned me.

Friends, who would have acquitted me, I would like also to talk with you about the thing which has come to pass, while the magistrates are busy, and before I go to the place at which I must die. Stay then a little, for we may as well talk with one another while there is time. You are my friends, and I should like to show you the meaning of this event which has happened to me. O my judges—for you I may truly call judges—I should like to tell you of a wonderful circumstance. Hitherto the divine faculty of which the internal oracle is the source has constantly been in the habit of opposing me even about trifles, if I was going to make a slip or error in any matter; and now as you see there has come upon me that which may be thought, and is generally believed to be, the last and

91

worst evil. But the oracle made no sign of opposition, either when I was leaving my house in the morning, or when I was on my way to the court, or while I was speaking, at anything which I was going to say; and yet I have often been stopped in the middle of a speech, but now in nothing I either said or did touching the matter in hand has the oracle opposed me. What do I take to be the explanation of this silence? I will tell you. It is an intimation that what has happened to me is a good, and that those of us who think that death is an evil are in error. For the customary sign would surely have opposed me had I been going to evil and not to good.

Let us reflect in another way, and we shall see that there is great reason to hope that death is a good; for one of two things—either death is a state of nothingness and utter unconsciousness, or, as men say, there is a change and migration of the soul from this world to another. Now if you suppose that there is no consciousness, but a sleep like the sleep of him who is undisturbed even by dreams, death will be an unspeakable gain. For if a person were to select the night in which his sleep was undisturbed even by dreams, and were to compare with this the other days and nights of his life, and then were to tell us how many days and nights he had passed in the course of his life better and more pleasantly than this one, I think that any man, I will not say a private man, but even the great king will not find many such days or nights, when compared with the others. Now if death be of such a nature, I say that to die is gain; for eternity is then only a single night. But if death is the journey to another place, and there, as men say, all the dead abide, what good, O my friends and judges, can be greater than this? If indeed when the pilgrim arrives in the world below, he is delivered from the

*professors of justice in this world, and finds the true
judges who are said to give judgment there, Minos
and Rhadamanthus and Aeacus and Triptolemus, and
other sons of God who were righteous in their own
life, that pilgrimage will be worth making. What
would not a man give if he might converse with
Orpheus and Musaeus and Hesiod and Homer? Nay,
if this be true, let me die again and again. I myself,
too, shall have a wonderful interest in there meeting
and conversing with Palamedes, and Ajax the son of
Telamon, and any other ancient hero who has
suffered death through an unjust judgment; and there
will be no small pleasure, as I think, in comparing my
own sufferings with theirs. Above all, I shall then be
able to continue my search into true and false
knowledge; as in this world, so also in the next; and I
shall find out who is wise, and who pretends to be
wise, and is not. What would not a man give, O
judges, to be able to examine the leader of the great
Trojan expedition; or Odysseus or Sisyphus, or
numberless others, men and women too! What infinite
delight would there be in conversing with them and
asking them questions! In another world they do not
put a man to death for asking questions: assuredly
not. For besides being happier than we are, they will
be immortal, if what is said is true.*

*Wherefore, O judges, be of good cheer about
death, and know of a certainty, that no evil can
happen to a good man, either in life or after death.
He and his are not neglected by the gods; nor has my
own approaching end happened by mere chance. But
I see clearly that the time had arrived when it was
better for me to die and be released from trouble;
wherefore the oracle gave no sign. For which reason,
also, I am not angry with my condemners, or with my
accusers; they have done me no harm, although they*

did not mean to do me any good; and for this I may gently blame them.

Still I have a favour to ask of them. When my sons are grown up, I would ask you, O my friends, to punish them; and I would have you trouble them, as I have troubled you, if they seem to care about riches, or anything, more than about virtue; or if they pretend to be something when they are really nothing,—then reprove them, as I have reproved you, for not caring about that for which they ought to care, and thinking that they are something when they are really nothing. And if you do this, both I and my sons will have received justice at your hands.

The hour of departure has arrived, and we go our ways—I to die, and you to live. Which is better God only knows.

The second reading is from Aristotle's *Nicomachean Ethics* (book 2) where Aristotle discusses the Virtues he believes enhance a person's life.

Nicomachean Ethics
Book 2
By Aristotle

1

Virtue, then, being of two kinds, intellectual and moral, intellectual virtue in the main owes both its birth and its growth to teaching (for which reason it requires experience and time), while moral virtue comes about as a result of habit, whence also its name (ethike) is one that is formed by a slight variation from the word ethos (habit). From this it is also plain that none of the moral virtues arises in us by nature; for nothing that exists by nature can form a habit contrary to its nature. For instance the stone which by nature moves downwards cannot be habituated to move upwards, not even if one tries to train it by throwing it up ten thousand times; nor can fire be habituated to move downwards, nor can anything else that by nature behaves in one way be trained to behave in another. Neither by nature, then, nor contrary to nature do the virtues arise in us; rather we are adapted by nature to receive them, and are made perfect by habit.

Again, of all the things that come to us by nature we first acquire the potentiality and later exhibit the activity (this is plain in the case of the senses; for it was not by often seeing or often hearing that we got these senses, but on the contrary we had them before we used them, and did not come to have them by using them); but the virtues we get by first exercising them, as also happens in the case of the arts as well. For the things we have to learn before we can do them, we learn by doing them, e.g. men become builders by building and lyreplayers by playing the lyre; so too we become just by doing just acts, temperate by doing temperate acts, brave by doing brave acts.

This is confirmed by what happens in states; for legislators make the citizens good by forming habits in them, and this is the wish of every legislator, and those who do not effect it miss their mark, and it is in this that a good constitution differs from a bad one.

Again, it is from the same causes and by the same means that every virtue is both produced and destroyed, and similarly every art; for it is from playing the lyre that both good and bad lyre-players are produced. And the corresponding statement is true of builders and of all the rest; men will be good or bad builders as a result of building well or badly.

For if this were not so, there would have been no need of a teacher, but all men would have been born good or bad at their craft. This, then, is the case with the virtues also; by doing the acts that we do in our transactions with other men we become just or unjust, and by doing the acts that we do in the presence of danger, and being habituated to feel fear or confidence, we become brave or cowardly. The same is true of appetites and feelings of anger; some men become temperate and good-tempered, others self-indulgent and irascible, by behaving in one way or the other in the appropriate circumstances. Thus, in one word, states of character arise out of like activities. This is why the activities we exhibit must be of a certain kind; it is because the states of character correspond to the differences between these. It makes no small difference, then, whether we form habits of one kind or of another from our very youth; it makes a very great difference, or rather all the difference.

2

Since, then, the present inquiry does not aim at theoretical knowledge like the others (for we are inquiring not in order to know what virtue is, but in order to become good, since otherwise our inquiry would have been of no use), we must examine the nature of actions, namely how we ought to do them; for these determine also the nature of the states of character that are produced, as we have said. Now, that we must act according to the right rule is a common principle and must be assumed-it will be discussed later, i.e. both what the right rule is, and how it is related to the other virtues. But this must be agreed upon beforehand, that the whole account of matters of conduct must be given in outline and not precisely, as we said at the very beginning that the

96

accounts we demand must be in accordance with the subject-matter; matters concerned with conduct and questions of what is good for us have no fixity, any more than matters of health. The general account being of this nature, the account of particular cases is yet more lacking in exactness; for they do not fall under any art or precept but the agents themselves must in each case consider what is appropriate to the occasion, as happens also in the art of medicine or of navigation.

But though our present account is of this nature we must give what help we can. First, then, let us consider this, that it is the nature of such things to be destroyed by defect and excess, as we see in the case of strength and of health (for to gain light on things imperceptible we must use the evidence of sensible things); both excessive and defective exercise destroys the strength, and similarly drink or food which is above or below a certain amount destroys the health, while that which is proportionate both produces and increases and preserves it. So too is it, then, in the case of temperance and courage and the other virtues. For the man who flies from and fears everything and does not stand his ground against anything becomes a coward, and the man who fears nothing at all but goes to meet every danger becomes rash; and similarly the man who indulges in every pleasure and abstains from none becomes self-indulgent, while the man who shuns every pleasure, as boors do, becomes in a way insensible; temperance and courage, then, are destroyed by excess and defect, and preserved by the mean.

But not only are the sources and causes of their origination and growth the same as those of their destruction, but also the sphere of their actualization will be the same; for this is also true of the things which are more evident to sense, e.g. of strength; it is produced by taking much food and undergoing much exertion, and it is the strong man that will be most able to do these things. So too is it with the virtues; by abstaining from pleasures we become temperate, and it is when we have become so that we are most able to abstain from them; and similarly too in the case of courage; for by being habituated to despise things that are terrible and to stand our ground against them we become brave, and it is when we have become so that we shall be most able to stand our ground against them.

3

We must take as a sign of states of character the pleasure or pain that ensues on acts; for the man who abstains from bodily pleasures and delights in this very fact is temperate, while the man who is annoyed at it is self-indulgent, and he who stands his ground against things that are terrible and delights in this or at least is not pained is brave, while the man who is pained is a coward. For moral excellence is concerned with pleasures and pains; it is on account of the pleasure that we do bad things, and on account of the pain that we abstain from noble ones. Hence we ought to have been brought up in a particular way from our very youth, as Plato says, so as both to delight in and to be pained by the things that we ought; for this is the right education.

Again, if the virtues are concerned with actions and passions, and every passion and every action is accompanied by pleasure and pain, for this reason also virtue will be concerned with pleasures and pains. This is indicated also by the fact that punishment is inflicted by these means; for it is a kind of cure, and it is the nature of cures to be effected by contraries.

Again, as we said but lately, every state of soul has a nature relative to and concerned with the kind of things by which it tends to be made worse or better; but it is by reason of pleasures and pains that men become bad, by pursuing and avoiding these- either the pleasures and pains they ought not or when they ought not or as they ought not, or by going wrong in one of the other similar ways that may be distinguished. Hence men even define the virtues as certain states of impassivity and rest; not well, however, because they speak absolutely, and do not say 'as one ought' and 'as one ought not' and 'when one ought or ought not', and the other things that may be added. We assume, then, that this kind of excellence tends to do what is best with regard to pleasures and pains, and vice does the contrary.

The following facts also may show us that virtue and vice are concerned with these same things. There being three objects of choice and three of avoidance, the noble, the advantageous, the pleasant, and their contraries, the base, the injurious, the painful, about all of these the good man tends to go right and the bad man to go wrong, and especially about pleasure; for this is common to the animals, and also it accompanies all objects of choice; for even the noble and the advantageous appear pleasant.

Again, it has grown up with us all from our infancy; this is why it is difficult to rub off this passion, engrained as it is in our life. And we measure even our actions, some of us more and others less, by the rule of pleasure and pain. For this reason, then, our whole inquiry must be about these; for to feel delight and pain rightly or wrongly has no small effect on our actions.

Again, it is harder to fight with pleasure than with

anger, to use Heraclitus' phrase', but both art and virtue are always concerned with what is harder; for even the good is better when it is harder. Therefore for this reason also the whole concern both of virtue and of political science is with pleasures and pains; for the man who uses these well will be good, he who uses them badly bad.

That virtue, then, is concerned with pleasures and pains, and that by the acts from which it arises it is both increased and, if they are done differently, destroyed, and that the acts from which it arose are those in which it actualizes itself- let this be taken as said.

4

The question might be asked,; what we mean by saying that we must become just by doing just acts, and temperate by doing temperate acts; for if men do just and temperate acts, they are already just and temperate, exactly as, if they do what is in accordance with the laws of grammar and of music, they are grammarians and musicians.

Or is this not true even of the arts? It is possible to do something that is in accordance with the laws of grammar, either by chance or at the suggestion of another. A man will be a grammarian, then, only when he has both done something grammatical and done it grammatically; and this means doing it in accordance with the grammatical knowledge in himself.

Again, the case of the arts and that of the virtues are not similar; for the products of the arts have their goodness in themselves, so that it is enough that they should have a certain character, but if the acts that are in accordance with the virtues have themselves a certain character it does not follow that they are done

100

*justly or temperately. The agent also must be in a
certain condition when he does them; in the first
place he must have knowledge, secondly he must
choose the acts, and choose them for their own sakes,
and thirdly his action must proceed from a firm and
unchangeable character. These are not reckoned in
as conditions of the possession of the arts, except the
bare knowledge; but as a condition of the possession
of the virtues knowledge has little or no weight, while
the other conditions count not for a little but for
everything, i.e. the very conditions which result from
often doing just and temperate acts.*

*Actions, then, are called just and temperate when
they are such as the just or the temperate man would
do; but it is not the man who does these that is just
and temperate, but the man who also does them as
just and temperate men do them. It is well said, then,
that it is by doing just acts that the just man is
produced, and by doing temperate acts the temperate
man; without doing these no one would have even a
prospect of becoming good.*

*But most people do not do these, but take refuge in
theory and think they are being philosophers and will
become good in this way, behaving somewhat like
patients who listen attentively to their doctors, but do
none of the things they are ordered to do. As the
latter will not be made well in body by such a course
of treatment, the former will not be made well in soul
by such a course of philosophy.*

5

*Next we must consider what virtue is. Since things
that are found in the soul are of three kinds- passions,
faculties, states of character, virtue must be one of
these. By passions I mean appetite, anger, fear,
confidence, envy, joy, friendly feeling, hatred, longing,*

101

*emulation, pity, and in general the feelings that are
accompanied by pleasure or pain; by faculties the
things in virtue of which we are said to be capable of
feeling these, e.g. of becoming angry or being pained
or feeling pity; by states of character the things in
virtue of which we stand well or badly with reference
to the passions, e.g. with reference to anger we stand
badly if we feel it violently or too weakly, and well if
we feel it moderately; and similarly with reference to
the other passions.*

*Now neither the virtues nor the vices are passions,
because we are not called good or bad on the ground
of our passions, but are so called on the ground of
our virtues and our vices, and because we are neither
praised nor blamed for our passions (for the man
who feels fear or anger is not praised, nor is the man
who simply feels anger blamed, but the man who feels
it in a certain way), but for our virtues and our vices
we are praised or blamed.*

*Again, we feel anger and fear without choice, but
the virtues are modes of choice or involve choice.
Further, in respect of the passions we are said to be
moved, but in respect of the virtues and the vices we
are said not to be moved but to be disposed in a
particular way.*

*For these reasons also they are not faculties; for we
are neither called good nor bad, nor praised nor
blamed, for the simple capacity of feeling the
passions; again, we have the faculties by nature, but
we are not made good or bad by nature; we have
spoken of this before. If, then, the virtues are neither
passions nor faculties, all that remains is that they
should be states of character.*

*Thus we have stated what virtue is in respect of its
genus.*

6

*We must, however, not only describe virtue as a
state of character, but also say what sort of state it is.
We may remark, then, that every virtue or excellence
both brings into good condition the thing of which it
is the excellence and makes the work of that thing be
done well; e.g. the excellence of the eye makes both
the eye and its work good; for it is by the excellence
of the eye that we see well. Similarly the excellence of
the horse makes a horse both good in itself and good
at running and at carrying its rider and at awaiting
the attack of the enemy. Therefore, if this is true in
every case, the virtue of man also will be the state of
character which makes a man good and which makes
him do his own work well.*

*How this is to happen we have stated already, but it
will be made plain also by the following
consideration of the specific nature of virtue. In
everything that is continuous and divisible it is
possible to take more, less, or an equal amount, and
that either in terms of the thing itself or relatively to
us; and the equal is an intermediate between excess
and defect. By the intermediate in the object I mean
that which is equidistant from each of the extremes,
which is one and the same for all men; by the
intermediate relatively to us that which is neither too
much nor too little- and this is not one, nor the same
for all. For instance, if ten is many and two is few, six
is the intermediate, taken in terms of the object; for it
exceeds and is exceeded by an equal amount; this is
intermediate according to arithmetical proportion.
But the intermediate relatively to us is not to be taken
so; if ten pounds are too much for a particular person
to eat and two too little, it does not follow that the
trainer will order six pounds; for this also is perhaps
too much for the person who is to take it, or too little-*

too little for Milo, too much for the beginner in athletic exercises. The same is true of running and wrestling. Thus a master of any art avoids excess and defect, but seeks the intermediate and chooses this- the intermediate not in the object but relatively to us.

If it is thus, then, that every art does its work well- by looking to the intermediate and judgling its works by this standard (so that we often say of good works of art that it is not possible either to take away or to add anything, implying that excess and defect destroy the goodness of works of art, while the mean preserves it; and good artists, as we say, look to this in their work), and if, further, virtue is more exact and better than any art, as nature also is, then virtue must have the quality of aiming at the intermediate. I mean moral virtue; for it is this that is concerned with passions and actions, and in these there is excess, defect, and the intermediate. For instance, both fear and confidence and appetite and anger and pity and in general pleasure and pain may be felt both too much and too little, and in both cases not well; but to feel them at the right times, with reference to the right objects, towards the right people, with the right motive, and in the right way, is what is both intermediate and best, and this is characteristic of virtue. Similarly with regard to actions also there is excess, defect, and the intermediate. Now virtue is concerned with passions and actions, in which excess is a form of failure, and so is defect, while the intermediate is praised and is a form of success; and being praised and being successful are both characteristics of virtue. Therefore virtue is a kind of mean, since, as we have seen, it aims at what is intermediate.

Again, it is possible to fail in many ways (for evil belongs to the class of the unlimited, as the

Pythagoreans conjectured, and good to that of the limited), while to succeed is possible only in one way (for which reason also one is easy and the other difficult- to miss the mark easy, to hit it difficult); for these reasons also, then, excess and defect are characteristic of vice, and the mean of virtue;

For men are good in but one way, but bad in many.

Virtue, then, is a state of character concerned with choice, lying in a mean, i.e. the mean relative to us, this being determined by a rational principle, and by that principle by which the man of practical wisdom would determine it. Now it is a mean between two vices, that which depends on excess and that which depends on defect; and again it is a mean because the vices respectively fall short of or exceed what is right in both passions and actions, while virtue both finds and chooses that which is intermediate. Hence in respect of its substance and the definition which states its essence virtue is a mean, with regard to what is best and right an extreme.

But not every action nor every passion admits of a mean; for some have names that already imply badness, e.g. spite, shamelessness, envy, and in the case of actions adultery, theft, murder; for all of these and suchlike things imply by their names that they are themselves bad, and not the excesses or deficiencies of them. It is not possible, then, ever to be right with regard to them; one must always be wrong. Nor does goodness or badness with regard to such things depend on committing adultery with the right woman, at the right time, and in the right way, but simply to do any of them is to go wrong. It would be equally absurd, then, to expect that in unjust, cowardly, and voluptuous action there should be a mean, an excess, and a deficiency; for at that rate there would be a mean of excess and of deficiency, an excess of excess,

105

and a deficiency of deficiency. But as there is no
excess and deficiency of temperance and courage
because what is intermediate is in a sense an extreme,
so too of the actions we have mentioned there is no
mean nor any excess and deficiency, but however
they are done they are wrong; for in general there is
neither a mean of excess and deficiency, nor excess
and deficiency of a mean.

7

   We must, however, not only make this general
statement, but also apply it to the individual facts.
For among statements about conduct those which are
general apply more widely, but those which are
particular are more genuine, since conduct has to do
with individual cases, and our statements must
harmonize with the facts in these cases. We may take
these cases from our table. With regard to feelings of
fear and confidence courage is the mean; of the
people who exceed, he who exceeds in fearlessness
has no name (many of the states have no name), while
the man who exceeds in confidence is rash, and he
who exceeds in fear and falls short in confidence is a
coward. With regard to pleasures and pains- not all
of them, and not so much with regard to the pains-
the mean is temperance, the excess self-indulgence.
Persons deficient with regard to the pleasures are not
often found; hence such persons also have received
no name. But let us call them 'insensible'.
   With regard to giving and taking of money the mean
is liberality, the excess and the defect prodigality and
meanness. In these actions people exceed and fall
short in contrary ways; the prodigal exceeds in
spending and falls short in taking, while the mean
man exceeds in taking and falls short in spending. (At
present we are giving a mere outline or summary,

and are satisfied with this; later these states will be more exactly determined.) With regard to money there are also other dispositions- a mean, magnificence (for the magnificent man differs from the liberal man; the former deals with large sums, the latter with small ones), an excess, tastelessness and vulgarity, and a deficiency, niggardliness; these differ from the states opposed to liberality, and the mode of their difference will be stated later. With regard to honour and dishonour the mean is proper pride, the excess is known as a sort of 'empty vanity', and the deficiency is undue humility; and as we said liberality was related to magnificence, differing from it by dealing with small sums, so there is a state similarly related to proper pride, being concerned with small honours while that is concerned with great. For it is possible to desire honour as one ought, and more than one ought, and less, and the man who exceeds in his desires is called ambitious, the man who falls short unambitious, while the intermediate person has no name. The dispositions also are nameless, except that that of the ambitious man is called ambition. Hence the people who are at the extremes lay claim to the middle place; and we ourselves sometimes call the intermediate person ambitious and sometimes unambitious, and sometimes praise the ambitious man and sometimes the unambitious. The reason of our doing this will be stated in what follows; but now let us speak of the remaining states according to the method which has been indicated.

With regard to anger also there is an excess, a deficiency, and a mean. Although they can scarcely be said to have names, yet since we call the intermediate person good-tempered let us call the mean good temper; of the persons at the extremes let the one who exceeds be called irascible, and his vice irascibility, and the man who falls short an inirascible sort of person, and the deficiency inirascibility.

There are also three other means, which have a certain likeness to one another, but differ from one another: for they are all concerned with intercourse in words and actions, but differ in that one is concerned with truth in this sphere, the other two with pleasantness; and of this one kind is exhibited in giving amusement, the other in all the circumstances of life. We must therefore speak of these too, that we may the better see that in all things the mean is praise-worthy, and the extremes neither praiseworthy nor right, but worthy of blame. Now most of these states also have no names, but we must try, as in the other cases, to invent names ourselves so that we may be clear and easy to follow. With regard to truth, then, the intermediate is a truthful sort of person and the mean may be called truthfulness, while the pretence which exaggerates is boastfulness and the person characterized by it a boaster, and that which understates is mock modesty and the person characterized by it mock-modest. With regard to pleasantness in the giving of amusement the intermediate person is ready-witted and the disposition ready wit, the excess is buffoonery and the person characterized by it a buffoon, while the man who falls short is a sort of boor and his state is boorishness. With regard to the remaining kind of pleasantness, that which is exhibited in life in general, the man who is pleasant in the right way is friendly and the mean is friendliness, while the man who exceeds is an obsequious person if he has no end in view, a flatterer if he is aiming at his own advantage, and the man who falls short and is unpleasant in all circumstances is a quarrelsome and surly sort of person.

There are also means in the passions and concerned with the passions; since shame is not a virtue, and yet praise is extended to the modest man. For even in these matters one man is said to be intermediate, and another to exceed, as for instance the bashful man who is ashamed of everything; while he who falls short or is not ashamed of anything at all is shameless, and the intermediate person is modest. Righteous indignation is a mean between envy and spite, and these states are concerned with the pain and pleasure that are felt at the fortunes of our neighbours; the man who is characterized by righteous indignation is pained at undeserved good fortune, the envious man, going beyond him, is pained at all good fortune, and the spiteful man falls so far short of being pained that he even rejoices. But these states there will be an opportunity of describing elsewhere; with regard to justice, since it has not one simple meaning, we shall, after describing the other states, distinguish its two kinds and say how each of them is a mean; and similarly we shall treat also of the rational virtues.

8

There are three kinds of disposition, then, two of them vices, involving excess and deficiency respectively, and one a virtue, viz. the mean, and all are in a sense opposed to all; for the extreme states are contrary both to the intermediate state and to each other, and the intermediate to the extremes; as the equal is greater relatively to the less, less relatively to the greater, so the middle states are excessive relatively to the deficiencies, deficient relatively to the excesses, both in passions and in actions. For the brave man appears rash relatively to the coward, and cowardly relatively to the rash man; and similarly the temperate man appears self-indulgent relatively to the insensible man, insensible relatively to the self-indulgent, and the liberal man prodigal relatively to the mean man, mean relatively to the prodigal. Hence also the people at the extremes push the intermediate man each over to the other, and the brave man is called rash by the coward, cowardly by the rash man, and correspondingly in the other cases.

These states being thus opposed to one another, the greatest contrariety is that of the extremes to each other, rather than to the intermediate; for these are further from each other than from the intermediate, as the great is further from the small and the small from the great than both are from the equal. Again, to the intermediate some extremes show a certain likeness, as that of rashness to courage and that of prodigality to liberality; but the extremes show the greatest unlikeness to each other; now contraries are defined as the things that are furthest from each other, so that things that are further apart are more contrary.

To the mean in some cases the deficiency, in some the excess is more opposed; e.g. it is not rashness, which is an excess, but cowardice, which is a deficiency, that is more opposed to courage, and not insensibility, which is a deficiency, but self-indulgence, which is an excess, that is more opposed to temperance. This happens from two reasons, one being drawn from the thing itself; for because one extreme is nearer and liker to the intermediate, we oppose not this but rather its contrary to the intermediate. E.g. since rashness is thought liker and nearer to courage, and cowardice more unlike, we oppose rather the latter to courage; for things that

110

*are further from the intermediate are thought more
contrary to it. This, then, is one cause, drawn from
the thing itself; another is drawn from ourselves; for
the things to which we ourselves more naturally tend
seem more contrary to the intermediate. For instance,
we ourselves tend more naturally to pleasures, and
hence are more easily carried away towards self-
indulgence than towards propriety. We describe as
contrary to the mean, then, rather the directions in
which we more often go to great lengths; and
therefore self-indulgence, which is an excess, is the
more contrary to temperance.*

9

*That moral virtue is a mean, then, and in what
sense it is so, and that it is a mean between two vices,
the one involving excess, the other deficiency, and
that it is such because its character is to aim at what
is intermediate in passions and in actions, has been
sufficiently stated. Hence also it is no easy task to be
good. For in everything it is no easy task to find the
middle, e.g. to find the middle of a circle is not for
every one but for him who knows; so, too, any one
can get angry- that is easy- or give or spend money;
but to do this to the right person, to the right extent,
at the right time, with the right motive, and in the
right way, that is not for every one, nor is it easy;
wherefore goodness is both rare and laudable and
noble.*

*Hence he who aims at the intermediate must first
depart from what is the more contrary to it, as
Calypso advises-*

Hold the ship out beyond that surf and spray.

*For of the extremes one is more erroneous, one less
so; therefore, since to hit the mean is hard in the
extreme, we must as a second best, as people say,*

111

take the least of the evils; and this will be done best in the way we describe. But we must consider the things towards which we ourselves also are easily carried away; for some of us tend to one thing, some to another; and this will be recognizable from the pleasure and the pain we feel. We must drag ourselves away to the contrary extreme; for we shall get into the intermediate state by drawing well away from error, as people do in straightening sticks that are bent.

Now in everything the pleasant or pleasure is most to be guarded against; for we do not judge it impartially. We ought, then, to feel towards pleasure as the elders of the people felt towards Helen, and in all circumstances repeat their saying; for if we dismiss pleasure thus we are less likely to go astray. It is by doing this, then, (to sum the matter up) that we shall best be able to hit the mean.

But this is no doubt difficult, and especially in individual cases; for or is not easy to determine both how and with whom and on what provocation and how long one should be angry; for we too sometimes praise those who fall short and call them good-tempered, but sometimes we praise those who get angry and call them manly. The man, however, who deviates little from goodness is not blamed, whether he do so in the direction of the more or of the less, but only the man who deviates more widely; for he does not fail to be noticed. But up to what point and to what extent a man must deviate before he becomes blameworthy it is not easy to determine by reasoning, any more than anything else that is perceived by the senses; such things depend on particular facts, and the decision rests with perception. So much, then, is plain, that the intermediate state is in all things to be praised, but that we must incline sometimes towards

112

*the excess, sometimes towards the deficiency; for so
shall we most easily hit the mean and what is right.*

For the ancient Greeks, philosophy was not just an academic exercise. It was the thoughtful process of living life wisely. Why study philosophy? Because insight is better than ignorance, and because the unexamined life is not worth living.

Summary

The Utilitarian philosopher John Stuart Mill famously said, "It is better to be a human being dissatisfied than a pig satisfied; better to be Socrates dissatisfied than a fool satisfied." In the context of his argument, he was reminding his readers that humans, as higher order beings, have capacities for both pleasure and pain that surpass those of animals, and that those enhanced capacities are an advantage. It is better to be a human dissatisfied than a pig satisfied. I think most people would agree with Mill on that point. But then Mill also said that it is better to be Socrates dissatisfied than a fool satisfied. That comparison is not between animals and humans, but between wise and foolish people. Mill is saying that it is better to be wise than foolish, better to be insightful than ignorant. One reason to study philosophy is that it provides us with some insights that help us figure out which questions to ask.

From one point of view, philosophy is about asking and answering questions. But asking and answering questions is only a meaningful activity if the questions being asked are the right questions. One of the advantages of being over 2,500 years down the road from the beginning of philosophy is that philosophers have figured out what the important questions are.

Studying philosophy also helps us learn how to answer those important questions in a rational manner. All normal people are capable of cognitive processing, of thinking. But thinking and *thinking well* are not the same things. Thinking well, thinking analytically, often referred to as *critical thinking*, is a skill that must be learned. In his book on critical thinking, Alec Fisher draws an analogy between learning to play the game of basketball and learning to think well. He tells the story of his eleven-year-old daughter wanting to learn to play basketball. The gist of his analogy is this: you can hand just about anyone a basketball and tell them to bounce it a few times and then try to throw it up and get it to go through that little hoop. They may do something that approximates dribbling the ball and then toss it up and through the hoop, making a basket. Technically then, from one point of view, they can say, "Look, I'm playing basketball." Well, yes, maybe. But not actually. At least not in the way athletes who have been taught how to play basketball and who have spent years honing their skills play basketball. To play basketball well you have to be taught how to play and you have to practice. Thinking is like that. Just about anyone can think. But thinking well is a learned skill that requires practice. Studying philosophy helps students develop the critical thinking skills they need to approach life's most important questions appropriately, answering the questions rationally and logically.

But philosophy is more than just asking and answering questions. If done well, as Socrates, Plato, and Aristotle did it, it involves introspection and growth. It includes a process of becoming.

Thought And Discussion Questions

1. Select three questions from Rogers' list of important philosophical questions (in this chapter) and explain why you think those three questions are important.

2. Discuss Rogers' idea that it is necessary to have rational reasons for what you believe, reasons that you can explain to people.

3. Explain what you think Socrates meant by his comment: *the unexamined life is not worth living.*

4. From Aristotle's list of virtues, select the one you think is most important and explain why.

5. If someone asked you, *why study philosophy,* how would you answer them?

Chapter 4
What Can Be Known?

I had oatmeal for breakfast this morning. As I am writing this, it was about an hour and a half ago, and I distinctly remember the experience. I *know* I had oatmeal for breakfast. Yesterday afternoon I taught my World Religions course to students on five different campuses using the college's teleconferencing system. I distinctly remember doing it and the students at the various locations also remember the experience. Also, those students handed in written assignments that I have already received. So I *know* I taught my World Religions class yesterday. Additionally, I also *know* that I taught my Introduction to Philosophy course yesterday. I remember doing it.

When I was a kid in school, I learned that the sun is 93 million miles from the earth. So I *know* that, too. I know that my wife loves me—we've been married for over 30 years and there's lots of good evidence that she stays with me not because she has to but because she wants to. So I *know* she loves me. I also *know* that atoms exist, that God

116

exists, and that this afternoon when I get into my truck to drive home it will start and convey me comfortably the one mile I have to drive from campus to my house. I *know* that since today is the 30th day of the month that the college has processed my paycheck and deposited it into my bank account. I *know* that tomorrow the sun will rise and that I will teach my Critical Thinking course. I also know that all brothers are male and that no bachelors are married. I don't need to do research to be sure; I'm already sure. I *know* these things are true.

I *know* lots of stuff. But do I really? Do I *know* these things? Or do I merely *believe* these things, or hope them? What is the difference between believing something and knowing it? Can you believe something and not know it? Can you know something and not believe it? How do you know when you know something? How do you know when someone else knows something? What is knowledge? Where does knowledge come from? How does one get knowledge? These are the kinds of questions that are part of the philosophical specialty known as *Epistemology*—the study of knowledge.

What Is Knowledge

We have lots of beliefs. We believe that the earth is round and that 7+3=10. We believe that the sun will come up tomorrow and that democracy is the best form of government. We believe that eating a salad is healthier than eating a cheeseburger and that medical science will discover a cure for cancer. Can any of these things be known rather than simply believed? What is it to know something? What is knowledge? Philosophers usually say that knowledge is *true justified belief*. What does that mean?

117

Belief

Beliefs are ideas that we accept and embrace. We *believe* them—which means we believe they are true. It is true, I believe, that my wife loves me. It is true, I believe, that my truck was manufactured by Ford Motor Company. It is true, I believe, that my shoe size is 11 D. I believe that all these things, along with tens of thousands of other beliefs I hold, are true. But some of them could turn out to be not true. Truth is not a condition for belief. Truth is a condition for knowledge. I can *believe* something that is not true, but I cannot *know* something that is not true. For a thing to be *known* it must be true. How could one possibly know something that is not true? For instance, how can one know that 2+2=5 when it does not? You can believe it does, but you cannot know it does when it doesn't. You cannot know that which is not true. Thus, truth is a condition of knowledge. There can only be knowledge where there is truth. If truth does not exist, neither does knowledge.

True Beliefs

How can I know whether or not my beliefs are true? I have to investigate, test, and analyze. In some cases, depending on the belief under consideration, I will engage in empirical research. Suppose I believe that a heavier object (a book, for example), if released from my hand, will fall to the ground (the floor of my office) faster than a lighter object (a cough drop, for example). I can conduct a simple experiment. I can hold a book in one hand (waist-high) and a cough drop (still in the wrapper of course) in the other and then release them simultaneously and observe the results. When I do, I discover that I was mistaken. The two objects, one considerably heavier than the other, fall at the same rate of descent, hitting the floor at the same time. What I believed to

118

be true turned out to be false.

If a belief I want to analyze is not subject to empirical analysis, in other words, if I can't do physical experiments to discover the truth about that belief, I can still engage in rational analysis. Let's say, for instance, that I believe that there could never have been a time when absolutely nothing existed. I can't travel back in time to observe if there was a time when nothing existed, so how can I test my belief to see whether or not it is true? I can utilize rational inquiry. It is a long-recognized truth that *from nothing comes nothing.*[55] Based on this truism (a self-evident truth) I can reason as follows: Since something exists now, it is necessary that something has always existed because something cannot come from nothing. Since something exists now, something has always existed. I can know this with certainty by means of rational analysis just as I can know that all brothers are male and that there are no married bachelors. No empirical evidence is required for this knowledge to be ascertained. Thus, many of the beliefs I hold can be tested, either empirically or rationally, to determine whether or not they are true.

Note that I said *many* of my beliefs can be tested to determine whether or not they are true. Why only many of them? Why not all of them? Because not everything that can be believed is either true or false. For instance, I might believe that Angelina Jolie is the most beautiful woman on the planet. Someone else might believe Scarlett Johansson is the most beautiful. How could it be decided that Angelina (or Scarlett) is truly the most beautiful? It could not. Why not? Because beauty is not the kind of a thing that can be either true or false. Beauty is a value judgment. Some people believe that modern art is intriguing. I find it boring and often silly. Is it true that modern art is intriguing or is it true

---

[55] The ancient Greek philosopher, Parmenides (born around 510 BCE), may have been the first to write down this truism.

119

that it is boring and often silly? Neither. Because the appeal of modern art is a relative value that cannot be either true or false. Many of our beliefs, then, must remain just that— beliefs (or opinions). They can never achieve the status of knowledge. But some things can. We can know this to be true and that to be false. Knowledge is available because truth exists.

Justified True Beliefs

Suppose we examine our beliefs and find that they are true. Is the discovery or confirmation that our belief is true enough for that belief to qualify as knowledge? An epistemologist would say, no. Why? Because for a belief to qualify as knowledge, we must be *justified* (or warranted) in believing it. Not only must a belief be true to qualify as knowledge, we must have good reasons (valid, justifiable reasons) for believing it. Knowledge is not only true belief, it is true *justified* belief. What constitutes *justification*? When am I *justified* (or warranted) in believing that A is true or that A is false? In 1963 Edmund Gettier published a short but influential article that illustrates some of the challenges related to epistemic justification.[56] The scenario he described goes roughly as follows. Suppose one of the clocks on campus that usually keeps accurate time stops one night at 11:56. Suppose that the next day (about 12 hours later) a professor happens to be passing by the room that clock is in and sees that is says it is 11:56. In fact it is not 11:56, it is 12:13, but the professor does not know that. Believing the clock is accurate, the professor forms the belief that it is 11:56. Is the professor justified in his belief? Obviously, he thinks he is. But in fact (in my opinion), since the clock is

---

[56] Truncellito provides a brief overview of the problem in his article, "Epistemology," in *Internet Encyclopedia of Philosophy*.

not working and since it is not 11:56, the professor is not justified in his belief, even though he thinks he is. Just as truth is a condition for knowledge (you can't know that which is not true), valid justification is also essential for knowledge. Valid justification cannot grow out of inaccurate information.

But suppose a different scenario occurs. Suppose that when the professor is passing by the broken clock it just happens to be 11:56. He forms the belief that it is 11:56, a belief that turns out to be a true belief, on the basis of information that by an amazing coincidence turns out to be accurate—by accident, but accurate nonetheless. Is his true belief justified? I do not think so, because the clock upon which he based his belief was not functioning. It just happened, by coincidence, to be correct because the professor passed by it exactly 12 hours after it stopped running. An inaccurate clock (or any other kind of inaccurate information) cannot be the basis for a justified belief. Whatever is going to serve as a justification so that a true belief qualifies as knowledge must be an accurate fact or a valid rational argument. Anything that is wrong, inaccurate, invalid, or unsound cannot serve as epistemic justification.

Theories of Justification

There are two basic theories about how epistemic justification works. One is *foundationalism*; the other is *coherentism*.

Foundationalism

Foundationalism argues that justified beliefs are like a building. There is a foundation and a superstructure. The foundation of the building (the building of our justified beliefs) is comprised of *basic beliefs* for which we need no additional justification. For instance, I know that I exist. Like Descartes, I am aware of myself thinking. I think about all sorts of things. Right now I'm thinking about what I'm writing. I can only do that if I exist as a thinking entity. I'm thinking, so I know I exist. I need no further justification for that belief. Even if I were the only entity, the only thinking mind that existed and that there were no other people for me to interact with, I would still know that I existed. Belief in my own existence is basic; it is justified, it needs no further justification than my awareness of my existence. I also know that I had oatmeal for breakfast this morning. I experienced it and remember it. I need no further justification for my belief that I had oatmeal this morning. These and many other basic beliefs I hold serve as the foundation for the rest of the building, the superstructure of my additional *non-basic* beliefs. Non-basic beliefs are those beliefs that I hold that are not *basic*, that require additional justification, justification that can be traced back to my basic beliefs.

How can a non-basic belief be justified on the basis of a basic belief? Suppose, for instance, that I buy a bookcase that comes in pieces in a box and has to be assembled. Suppose also that I have never assembled anything like this before. Yet I believe that I will be able to assemble the bookcase (a non-basic belief). Why would I believe that? In what way am I justified in believing that I will be successful in putting the bookcase together? My non-basic belief that I can assemble the bookcase is based on my belief that I am a rational being who can figure things out. Why would I believe that I am a rational being? My belief that I am a rational being grows out of and depends on my basic belief that I exist as a thinking being. But I don't just think. I engage in high-level abstract conceptualization. I can think in ways animals cannot. I can discover logical and mathematical principles. I can contemplate good and evil, justice and oppression. I am a rational being. And as a rational being, I can figure things out. Because I can figure things out, I believe I will be able to figure out how to assemble the bookcase. My non-basic belief follows a chain of reasoning backward to my basic belief and is ultimately justified because of my basic belief. Therefore, I am justified in believing I can assemble the bookcase. This is an example of how the theory of foundationalism works.

Coherentism

As noted above, an alternative theory regarding epistemic justification is *coherentism*. Coherentism holds that rather than thinking of epistemic justification as a building where the superstructure must be built on the foundation, a more apt metaphor is that epistemic justification involves a web of interrelated factors. Foundationalists seek to justify beliefs on the basis of a linear process, beginning with a true belief and working backward in a straight line to the basic belief that provides justification for non-basic beliefs. Coherentists, however, claim that: 1) it is unwarranted for foundationalists to simply assume that knowledge is based on that sort of linear relationship, and 2) that ultimately foundationalism fails because it provides no basis for the justification of what they (foundationalists) call basic beliefs. Coherentists claim that basic beliefs do not exist—at least they are not justified. Instead, coherentists insist that justification must be based on the holistic interrelationship of beliefs. Justified knowledge grows out of an interconnected web where beliefs are justified because of their linkage to other justified beliefs. Of course foundationalists would ask, what justifies all those interconnected justified beliefs? It sounds as if all those interconnected beliefs that justify each other ultimately have nothing to justify them. Perhaps this is why most epistemologists prefer foundationalism over coherentism.[57]

It appears to me that foundationalism makes more sense. However, one of the dangers of foundationalism is claiming too many basic beliefs that need no justification. Caution must be exercised, and the list of basic beliefs must, by the very nature of things, remain a short list. It is far too easy to say, "I just know that X is true and do not, therefore, need further justification." That temptation must be avoided. There can only be a few truly basic beliefs.

Objective Truth

What does the field of epistemology say about the existence of objective truth? I think it says quite a bit. The fact that there are epistemologists who aim at describing the nature and limits of knowledge implies that knowledge (true justified belief) is possible, which means that truth exists. True justified belief can only exist where truth exists. And truth, by its very nature, is objective. There is no such thing as a subjective truth. There is subjective opinion; but truth is not subjective. You will remember that the ancient Sophists embraced skepticism, claiming that objective truth did not exist, or that if it did exist, the human mind was not capable of comprehending it, rendering it, therefore, irrelevant at best. Those who reject objective truth reject it along with all universals, claiming that all things are subjective and perspectival (that all things depend simply on one's perspective). It does not seem to occur to them that such a claim is a universal (and objective) claim and that in making it they are contradicting themselves. The claim that objective

---

[57] Time and space (and the fact that this is an introductory course) do not permit a more extensive discussion of issues such as internalism vs. externalism and other epistemic considerations. Dancy provides a nice overview of this complex field in his article, "*Epistemology, Problems of*," in The Oxford Companion To Philosophy.

truth does not exist is an objective claim that they insist is true. How can it be true that there is no objective truth if there is no objective truth?

Those who hold that there is no objective truth (or that we cannot know what it is) deny that knowledge is possible. None of our beliefs, therefore, can be justified. Thus, instead of holding true justified beliefs, what we have are simply subjective opinions. This becomes especially problematic in the field of moral philosophy. Is it the case that when it comes to that which is moral or immoral, all we have is social or personal opinion? Is everything subjective and absolutely relative? While some insist that this is the case, I align myself with Socrates, Plato, Aristotle, Kant, and a host of others who believe that moral absolutes exist and can be ascertained by the rational human mind.

But how do we know objective truth exists? By a combination of two things: reason and experience. For instance, as discussed earlier, I know I exist. I am sitting at my computer thinking about myself thinking. I can't be thinking without the ability to think. And if I have the ability to think, then whatever else I might be (or might not be) I am at least a thinking being—which means I exist. I cannot simply be a character in some other being's imagined reality. The only being who could pull off something of that magnitude (creating an imaginary reality where I thought I existed but did not) would be God. And God, given what is required for God to be God, that he must be good and kind and benevolent, would not (nor have reason to) perpetrate such a ruse. I am not an imaginary character in a nonexistent reality. I am thinking about myself thinking because I am a thinking being. Therefore, I exist.[58] I am an objective reality.

_____

[58] This, of course, was René Descartes' famous explanation of how he knew he existed and how he knew he was not being fooled into thinking he existed when he really did not. See Descartes, *Discourse on Methods*, Part 4, where Descartes recounts the events that gave

And as such I can think about other objective realities, such as mathematical realities. 2+2=4 is an objective reality. 2+2 is not 4 if I want it to be or think it is, or if you want it to be or think it is. 2+2 is 4 because it *is* 4. It is an objective reality, an objective truth. And it is an objective truth that can be comprehended (known) by the human mind.

We can experience other sorts of objective truth—the physical laws of the cosmos, for instance, that function with absolute regularity. For example, if you add vinegar to baking soda you get the same result every time. Not some of the time, not most of the time. Every time. Why? Because objective reality exists.

David Hume (1711-1776), a philosopher of the early modern period, was not convinced that we could ascertain much in the way of objective truth from an observation of the cosmos. For instance, he argued that what appears to be cause and effect cannot be *known* to be cause and effect. For Hume, what appears to be a cause is simply an event that precedes another event, thought to be the effect. He illustrated his point using billiard balls. One ball hits a second ball and the second ball moves. Hume argues that we say that the first ball hitting the second ball *caused* the movement of the second. But he insists that we can't know that. All we can know is that we observe one event preceding another. We cannot know that one event caused the other.[59] Hume would argue that it would not matter how many times we observed the events (even if we observe the cue ball hitting the 5 ball and the 5 ball going into the corner pocket 100,000 times), we could still not know that the cue ball *caused* the 5 ball to go into the corner pocket. I believe, however, that Hume was quite mistaken and that observation (especially many multiple observations) allow for sound

rise to perhaps the most famous philosophical saying of all time— Cogito Ergo Sum... *I think, therefore, I am.*

[59] Hume, *An Essay Concerning Human Understanding*, Chapter VII, Section II.

inductive reasoning regarding causal relationships.

One of the things Hume was trying to accomplish was to help us understand that we may not *know* as much as we think we know. In this respect he was correct. Genuine knowledge, true justified belief, is not easy to come by. However, in his eagerness to make his case, he appears to have gone too far. He comes off as something of a skeptic, putting genuine knowledge of many things out of reach. In this, he was mistaken. Objective truth exists and is available to the human mind. We can observe, experience, and use reason to achieve genuine knowledge (true justified belief).

Empiricism vs. Rationalism

I have already said that knowledge can be achieved by both experience and the use of reason. But to understand the nature of those two different paths to knowledge we need to discuss two different approaches (theories) regarding how we come to know that which can be known. Those two different approaches are *empiricism* and *rationalism*.

Empiricism, in its most radical form, is the idea that knowledge is only available where empirical evidence is available, empirical evidence being sensory experience. Whatever can be experienced by the physical senses can be known. That which is not available to be examined physically, that which cannot be experienced by the senses, cannot be known. A less radical form of empiricism holds that knowledge of matters of fact (as opposed to knowledge of the logical relations of concepts, such as mathematical concepts) is based on experience. For the moment I want to focus on the more radical form—that that which actually qualifies as knowledge is only available where empirical evidence is available—that you can only know that which is available as sensory experience.[60] Initially, empiricism was a reaction against the belief that ideas exist in the mind at birth before sensory experience puts them there. Some early empiricists, Locke, Hume, and others, pointed out the problems related to that sort of an assumption. Clearly, when it comes to knowledge about the physical world, it is experiencing the physical world that makes knowledge of it possible. What I mean is that we can know what a strawberry tastes like only by eating a strawberry. We can know how refreshing a drink of cool water can be only by drinking cool water when we are hot and thirsty. In these and thousands of other ways, knowledge of the physical world comes by experiencing the physical world. One would be hard pressed to find a contemporary philosopher who would disagree with this.

But there are some who advocate that one can *only* know that which can be experienced by the senses. I have had students in my Introduction to Philosophy course who have argued that epistemic justification must be empirical in nature, that is, that knowledge is only available by means of empirical verification. And there have been philosophers who have advocated this, namely, that lacking empirical verification one is left only with opinion, that no certainty is possible where there is nothing physical to examine. This position is problematic since clearly we can enjoy what is referred to as *a priori* certainty, that is, we can attain certainty (we can have knowledge) of things that are not physical and cannot be empirically verified, such as mathematical and logical concepts. Radical empiricism, that you can only know that which can be experienced by the senses, does not appear to be a plausible theory. But it's opposite, radical rationalism, is just as problematic.

Rationalism, in its most radical form, is the idea that

---

[60] For a good but brief overview of empiricism see Flew, "Empiricism," *A Dictionary of Philosophy.*

the physical senses cannot be trusted, and that knowledge is the product not of sensory experience but of rational reflection. The most radical form of rationalism argues that humans are born with innate ideas (knowledge) already in the mind. Additional knowledge would then be achieved by means of a rational process that does not include empirical data.

The problem with this form of radical rationalism is that there is not really any way to show that innate ideas are present in the mind at birth. Also, it is difficult to argue that one could know what a strawberry tastes like without having ever tasted a strawberry, that is, without having the physical experience of taste.

Throughout the centuries, especially since the 1600s, philosophy has been divided into two epistemological camps: the rationalists and the empiricists. The tension between rationalism and empiricism can be traced all the way back to Plato and Aristotle. Plato was a rationalist, focused on concerns that would later be identified as metaphysical, that is, concerns associated with things not part of the physical aspect of reality but with the non-physical, or the immaterial. Plato, like his teacher Socrates, was not very interested in the physical world. But Plato's student, Aristotle, whose father was a medical doctor, was very interested in the physical world, which required a detailed analysis of physical (empirical) data. Aristotle was empirically-oriented. It would be inaccurate, however, to describe Aristotle as a strict empiricist. Aristotle did not argue that knowledge is only available on the basis of empirical investigation. Aristotle believed, along with Socrates and Plato, that rational analysis could lead to knowledge regarding immaterial things. For instance, in reading Aristotle's material regarding the necessity of an unmoved mover, it is clear that he believed his logical process had resulted in certainty. He *knew* there was an unmoved mover because reason had led him to that conclusion. So in one sense Aristotle was an empiricist, and

129

in another he was a rationalist.

Most (though not all) philosophers between Aristotle and John Locke could be described as rationalists. They were focused on metaphysics rather than physics. For them, knowledge was the result of an *a priori* rational process, that is, a process of thinking critically about things rather than experiencing those things. Since much of what they thought about could not be experienced in any physical way, the need for empirical verification was simply not a concern. But as thinking began to change during the Renaissance and new ideas, new perspectives, and new methodologies emerged, so did a new curiosity about knowledge—what is it and how one gets it.

The British philosopher, John Locke, is normally credited with being the father of empiricism, at least as far as western philosophy is concerned. Rationalists had claimed that people are born with innate ideas present in the mind. Locke disagreed, arguing that the mind is a *tabula rasa*, a blank slate, that gets filled up as it experiences the world via the human sensory apparatus. We start with nothing in our minds and impressions are formed and ideas generated (we gain knowledge) as we experience the world we live in. Locke was followed by a number of British philosophers (besides Locke, Hume is probably the best known of the British empiricists) who maintained this same basic position: that knowledge is the result of sensory experience.

As noted above, empiricists argued that one could only have knowledge of those things that could be studied physically. On the other side of the issue, rationalists distrusted sensory perception, insisting that knowledge could only be achieved through a strictly rational process. Each school of thought believed that knowledge of reality, that is, of how things really are, was possible. But each believed it was achieved through a different process. Philosophy was divided into these two epistemological camps until Immanuel

Kant published his work, *Critique of Pure Reason*,[61] which effectively ended the dispute between rationalists and empiricists, taking epistemology in a new direction by pointing out the limitations of the human mind. Kant pointed out that the human mind can only experience and imagine within a given set of parameters. For Kant, there is the world we experience, the *phenomenal* world, and the world as it really is, the *noumenal* world. The world as it really is appears to us the way it does because of the way the human mind is constructed. Our eyes see as they are designed to see; our ears hear as they are designed to hear and so forth. Our mind receives sensory input and then processes it. The incoming sensory data is received, organized, categorized, and understood as it is because of the way the human mind works. We do not see all there is to see; we do not hear all there is to hear. We do not experience reality in any complete or absolute sense, and our rational analyses of the incomplete sensory data we receive is constrained by the structure and capacity of the human mind. For Kant, the phenomenal world is what it is because of the way our physical senses and our minds work. If our senses and our minds worked differently, our perception of the world would be different. The noumenal world, the world as it really is, is not as we perceive.[62]

That being the case, where does that leave us epistemologically? How can we have knowledge of reality? Instead of an either/or approach, either rationally or empirically, Kant argued that the two methods of knowing

---

[61] Kant, *Critique of Pure Reason*, 1781.

[62] Whether or not Kant was right or the extent to which he was correct remains a matter of debate. Assuming he was basically correct in his identifying of the phenomenal and noumenal worlds and that our perception of what it is is different from what really is, one must ask, *how different is our perception of how the world is from how the world really is?* However, one must then wonder if that is a question that can be answered.

131

must be blended. The physical world must be studied empirically. The data gathered from empirical studies must then be analyzed in a rational manner. The result is knowledge of the phenomenal world, the world as we experience it. Kant was arguing that there are limits to what we can know and how we come to know it. Neither rationalism nor empiricism, in Kant's view, provides us with knowledge of the noumenal world.

Kant's work was monumental. His impact on epistemology is still felt today. But his intentions, I believe, are often misunderstood. In *Critique of Pure Reason,* he seems to be saying that knowledge of the noumenal world (reality as it really is—metaphysical knowledge) is unavailable. This would include knowledge about things such as God, values, morals and so forth. In other of his writings, however, he argues that one can be certain of God's existence. In his *Critique of Practical Reason,* Kant presents a rationalistic argument for the existence of God in which he concludes that God is necessary.[63] To understand Kant, it is crucial to be familiar with all his work not just *Critique of Pure Reason.* In that work, he does discuss the challenges of knowledge of the noumenal world. However, based on his other writings, he clearly believed that a rationalistic approach could provide one with knowledge of the metaphysical realities.

What, then, does all this add up to? Epistemologically, it is not a matter of either rationalism or empiricism. To have knowledge of our world requires both. The physical world can only be understood by gathering physical data and evaluating it. The process is both empirical and rational. But there are features of reality that are not physical. For those features, empirical data is not available. Where physical data

---

[63] For a detailed analysis of Kant's argument for the existence of God see Rogers, *Proof of God? Inquiries in the Philosophy of Religion, A Concise Introduction,* 110-113.

is not available, rational reflection is appropriate and sufficient. We can understand the nature of things, arriving at knowledge (true justified belief) by careful critical analysis. Some of the time our critical analysis will include empirical data, and some of the time it will involve only rational analysis. When we carry out the process of inquiry correctly, using all the tools at our disposal, the result will be justified true belief. The result will be knowledge.

Summary

We know lots of stuff. How do we know it? What does it mean *to know*? What is knowledge? What is belief? What is opinion? Are there substantive differences between belief, opinion, and knowledge? Knowledge is normally defined as true justified (warranted) belief. What does that mean? We have many beliefs, and they may be true or false. It is possible to believe something that is not true. But many of our beliefs are probably true. If our beliefs are true, do they constitute knowledge? Believing something, even if our belief is sincere and ardent, does not mean that we know it. How, then, do we come to know rather than merely believe?

That which we know must be true. You cannot know that which is not true. You cannot know that 2+2 equals 5 because 2+2 does not equal 5. That which is not true can be believed, but only that which is true can be known. Additionally, for a true belief to qualify as knowledge, it must be justified or warranted. There must be a valid, justifiable reason for why we believe what we believe. Beliefs can be justified in a number of ways. Coherentism and Foundationalism are two different theories of epistemic justification.

In the bigger picture of historical epistemology, two theories of achieving knowledge have divided philosophy: rationalism and empiricism. Kant's *Critique of Pure Reason*

133

(1781) settled that fundamental debate but raised additional epistemological questions that are still being discussed. Most philosophers today, however, will probably tell you that knowledge involves a blend of empirical analysis and rational reflection.

Thought and Discussion Questions

1. Discuss Gettier's illustration of the broken clock as it applies to epistemic justification.
2. Briefly compare and contrast Coherentism and Foundationalism.
3. Discuss your thinking on whether or not objective truth exists and is available to humans.
4. Briefly compare and contrast empiricism and rationalism.
5. Explain why empiricism cannot possibly be the only methodology used in arriving at knowledge of our world.

Chapter 5
Why Is There Something
Rather Than Nothing?

Why is there something rather than nothing? It is an odd question, isn't it? Who asks those kinds of questions? Who thinks like that? Philosophers. Specifically, the philosopher who asked this question was Leibniz, Gottfried Wilhelm Leibniz (1646-1716). Leibniz answered the question he asked, and his answer is complex and intriguing. I answer the question somewhat differently than did Leibniz. I think my answer is simpler and easier to follow. However, both answers, Leibniz's and mine, generate a number of additional questions that need to be considered, questions that have to do with the nature of reality. That's what this chapter is about.

So, why is there something rather than nothing? Because something has always existed. We understand and accept the principle articulated by Parmenides 2,500 years ago, that *from nothing comes nothing*. It is a simple but profound insight, a truism, self-evident and obvious. If there was ever a time when there was absolute nothingness—no thing of any sort at all—then nothingness would still be the case. Why? Because from nothing comes nothing. If there is nothingness, nothingness is all there will ever be. But we do not have nothingness. We have somethingness. Something exists. It is necessary, then, that something has always existed. The only way you can have something now is because there has always been something. So the answer to the question, *why is there something rather than nothing,* is, because something has always existed. And that something, whatever it is, is somehow responsible for the things that exist now.[64]

The obvious follow-up question, then, is, *what is it that has always existed?* This is a fundamental *metaphysical* question, metaphysical referring to those aspects of reality that are beyond the reach of the physical senses, the immaterial rather than the material. An empiricist, of course, would say that a question like, *what is it that has always existed,* cannot be answered because it is a *suprasensical* question, a question about things beyond the reach of the physical senses and therefore unknowable. I disagree. So would nearly all the philosophers before the modern era. They understood that rational reflection can provide answers that the senses cannot. The very fact that we can even get to the question, *what is it that has always existed,* provides evidence that rational reflection is epistemically valid because it is rational reflection that tells us that from nothing

---

[64] Someone may doubt this premise, that that which always existed is responsible for all else that exists. However, that which has always existed must be responsible for all else that now exists, for if it is not, then all else that exists (other than that always existing something) would have to be its own cause, which is a logical impossibility. Contingent things did not always exist. Even the cosmos itself is a contingent thing, coming into existence approximately 13.8 billion years ago. Contingent things must have a cause. By process of elimination then, that always existing something, whatever it was, must be the cause of all else that exists.

comes nothing, and that since we have something now, we know that something always existed. So the same rational reflection that brought us to the question, *what is it that has always existed*, can answer the question.

So what is the answer—what is it that has always existed? It appears that there are two possibilities or candidates for that which has always existed: *matter* or *mind*. Many of the ancient philosophers assumed that matter had always existed. Many today make that same assumption. Those who do would be identified as materialists or physicalists. But there are serious problems that arise if one takes the position that that which has always existed is matter. While I will deal with a larger range of issues related to this topic in Chapter 6, I will present enough material here to clarify the issue.

There are two serious problems with which physicalists have to contend. One is that astrophysicists now know that the universe did not always exist. It is now widely accepted that the cosmos came into existence about 14 billion years ago. Some would give a more precise date of 13.8 billion years ago. But why quibble over a couple hundred million years? Let's just round it up to 14 billion years. That's when the Big Bang occurred and all the matter and energy that is the cosmos came into being. The universe has not always existed. It is not eternal. It came into being at a given point in time. This generally accepted fact seems to me to make it difficult to claim that that which always existed is the physical matter of which the cosmos consists.

Suppose, however, that someone argued that that tiny piece of highly compacted matter, the singularity, that exploded (generating the Big Bang) had always existed. Such an idea is theoretically possible. Even though the universe has not always existed, it is theoretically possible that that which exploded, creating the universe, had always existed. The problem with that is this (it is the second difficulty I referred to above): *if matter is that which always existed, then one has to explain how non-conscious, non-thinking matter ultimately gave rise to conscious, thinking minds.* This is a serious obstacle for physicalists to overcome. How does that which is not conscious generate that which is conscious? How does that which does not think generate that which does think? The answer that is often given is: *Well, we can't explain exactly how it worked, but we know it did because here we are.* This is an unacceptable explanation because it is circular in nature, assuming that which needs to be demonstrated or proven. If one is going to argue that matter is that which has always existed and, therefore, that which gave rise to (or is the cause of) all that now exists, he is obligated to explain how matter generated consciousness and rationality. So far, no physicalist has been able to offer a coherent explanation.[65] In Chapter 6, I will offer a detailed argument about that which has always existed that will provide a coherent explanation. For now, however, the answer to the basic question of this chapter, *why is there something rather than nothing*, is because something has always existed and that something is the cause of all that exists now.

Existence And The Nature of Reality

Understanding the nature of reality is one of the major concerns of philosophy. There are a number of questions that epitomize this enterprise: *What is the ultimate source or cause of all that exists? What is the nature of reality? What is the nature of existence?* These questions (along with a host of others) are dealt with in the philosophical discipline referred to as *Metaphysics*. No one knows exactly when or under what circumstances the term came into use. Aristotle did not use it. But an editor who

---

[65] For additional comments see Rogers, *Proof of God?*, 51.

complied his works after he died described one of his books as *Metaphysics*, combining two Greek words, *meta*, meaning after or beyond, and *physis*, meaning nature. He was referring to the material Aristotle wrote after he had written extensively on natural phenomena. Today, metaphysics refers to considerations that are beyond the scope of physics, those things that are not subject to empirical verification.

What is really real? What is the really real like? Is reality limited to what we can experience with our physical senses? Is the reality we experience with our physical senses actual reality, or is it just the way we perceive it? Is our perception of reality all there is to reality? Could reality be different from my perception of it? Could reality be much bigger or more inclusive than I am able to perceive? Whatever reality is, what is my place in it? How do I exist as part of reality? What kind of a being am I? What does it mean to exist? The study of existence or being is referred to as *ontology*. It is the study of *being as being*, or technically, *being-qua-being*, focusing on the essential nature of being. What is it to exist? But when that question is considered, I must also ask the more personal question—what does it mean for me to exist? What does it mean that I exist? How do I exist? In what way do I exist?

How can I, or anyone else, live in any meaningful way if these sorts of questions are not asked? To answer them requires a basic framework for thinking about such matters. To lay out the options for a functional framework for thinking about reality, we can ask a very basic question: *Is this all there is?*

Is This All There Is

The question focuses attention on our physical experience of the cosmos. Many people assume that their physical experience of the cosmos represents a direct and complete experience of reality. They assume that all there is to the cosmos is the physical aspect they can experience with their physical senses. Plato did not make this assumption. He reasoned that there was more to reality than those parts that can be experienced with the senses. In Book 7 of *Republic*, he has his main character, Socrates, tell a story, a parable or allegory, about people held captive in a cave. The point of the story is not only that reality involves more than what we can physically experience, but that the really important aspect of reality is that part which is beyond physical experience. Think about reality from that point of view as you read Plato's parable of the cave. The parable appears in Book 7 of the dialog entitled, Republic. The parable occurs in the middle of an ongoing conversation between Socrates and Glaucon.

> *[**Socrates**] And now, I said, let me show in a figure how far our nature is enlightened or unenlightened: --Behold! human beings living in a underground cave, which has a mouth open towards the light and reaching all along the cave; here they have been from their childhood, and have their legs and necks chained so that they cannot move, and can only see before them, being prevented by the chains from turning round their heads. Above and behind them a fire is blazing at a distance, and between the fire and the prisoners there is a raised way; and you will see, if you look, a low wall built along the way, like the screen which marionette players have in front of them, over which they show the puppets.*
> *[**Glaucon**] I see.*
> *[**Socrates**] And do you see, I said, men passing along the wall carrying all sorts of vessels, and statues and figures of animals made of wood and stone and various materials, which appear over the wall? Some of them are talking, others silent.*
> *[**Glaucon**] You have shown me a strange image, and they are strange prisoners.*
> *[**Socrates**] Like ourselves, I replied; and they see*

*only their own shadows, or the shadows of one
another, which the fire throws on the opposite wall of
the cave?*

*[Glaucon] True, he said; how could they see
anything but the shadows if they were never allowed
to move their heads?*

*[Socrates] And of the objects which are being carried
in like manner they would only see the shadows?*

[Glaucon] Yes, he said.

*[Socrates] And if they were able to converse with one
another, would they not suppose that they were
naming what was actually before them?*

[Glaucon] Very true.

*[Socrates] And suppose further that the prison had
an echo which came from the other side, would they
not be sure to fancy when one of the passers-by spoke
that the voice which they heard came from the
passing shadow?*

[Glaucon] No question, he replied.

*[Socrates] To them, I said, the truth would be
literally nothing but the shadows of the images.*

[Glaucon] That is certain.

*[Socrates] And now look again, and see what will
naturally follow if the prisoners are released and
disabused of their error. At first, when any of them is
liberated and compelled suddenly to stand up and
turn his neck round and walk and look towards the
light, he will suffer sharp pains; the glare will
distress him, and he will be unable to see the realities
of which in his former state he had seen the shadows;
and then conceive some one saying to him, that what
he saw before was an illusion, but that now, when he
is approaching nearer to being and his eye is turned
towards more real existence, he has a clearer vision,
-what will be his reply? And you may further imagine
that his instructor is pointing to the objects as they
pass and requiring him to name them, -will he not be
perplexed? Will he not fancy that the shadows which
he formerly saw are truer than the objects which are
now shown to him?*

[Glaucon] Far truer.

[Socrates] And if he is compelled to look straight at

*the light, will he not have a pain in his eyes which
will make him turn away to take and take in the
objects of vision which he can see, and which he will
conceive to be in reality clearer than the things which
are now being shown to him?*

[Glaucon] True, he now.

*[Socrates] And suppose once more, that he is
reluctantly dragged up a steep and rugged ascent,
and held fast until he's forced into the presence of the
sun himself, is he not likely to be pained and
irritated? When he approaches the light his eyes will
be dazzled, and he will not be able to see anything at
all of what are now called realities.*

[Glaucon] Not all in a moment, he said.

*[Socrates] He will require to grow accustomed to the
sight of the upper world. And first he will see the
shadows best, next the reflections of men and other
objects in the water, and then the objects themselves;
then he will gaze upon the light of the moon and the
stars and the spangled heaven; and he will see the sky
and the stars by night better than the sun or the light
of the sun by day?*

[Glaucon] Certainly.

*[Socrates] Last of he will be able to see the sun, and
not mere reflections of him in the water, but he will
see him in his own proper place, and not in another;
and he will contemplate him as he is.*

[Glaucon] Certainly.

*[Socrates] He will then proceed to argue that this is
he who gives the season and the years, and is the
guardian of all that is in the visible world, and in a
certain way the cause of all things which he and his
fellows have been accustomed to behold?*

*[Glaucon] Clearly, he said, he would first see the sun
and then reason about him.*

*[Socrates] And when he remembered his old
habitation, and the wisdom of the cave and his fellow-
prisoners, do you not suppose that he would felicitate
himself on the change, and pity them?*

[Glaucon] Certainly, he would.

*[Socrates] And if they were in the habit of conferring
honors among themselves on those who were quickest*

*to observe the passing shadows and to remark which
of them went before, and which followed after, and
which were together; and who were therefore best
able to draw conclusions as to the future, do you
think that he would care for such honors and glories,
or envy the possessors of them? Would he not say
with Homer,* Better to be the poor servant of a poor
master, *and to endure anything, rather than think as
they do and live after their manner?*
*[Glaucon] Yes, he said, I think that he would rather
suffer anything than entertain these false notions and
live in this miserable manner.*
*[Socrates] Imagine once more, I said, such a one
coming suddenly out of the sun to be replaced in his
old situation; would he not be certain to have his eyes
full of darkness?*
[Glaucon] To be sure, he said.
*[Socrates] And if there were a contest, and he had to
compete in measuring the shadows with the prisoners
who had never moved out of the cave, while his sight
was still weak, and before his eyes had become steady
(and the time which would be needed to acquire this
new habit of sight might be very considerable) would
he not be ridiculous? Men would say of him that up
he went and down he came without his eyes; and that
it was better not even to think of ascending; and if
any one tried to loose another and lead him up to the
light, let them only catch the offender, and they would
put him to death.*
[Glaucon] No question, he said.
*[Socrates] This entire allegory, I said, you may now
append, dear Glaucon, to the previous argument; the
prison-house is the world of sight, the light of the fire
is the sun, and you will not misapprehend me if you
interpret the journey upwards to be the ascent of the
soul into the intellectual world according to my poor
belief, which, at your desire, I have expressed
whether rightly or wrongly God knows. But, whether
true or false, my opinion is that in the world of
knowledge the idea of good appears last of all, and is
seen only with an effort; and, when seen, is also
inferred to be the universal author of all things*

143

beautiful and right, parent of light and of the lord of light in this visible world, and the immediate source of reason and truth in the intellectual; and that this is the power upon which he who would act rationally, either in public or private life must have his eye fixed.

[Glaucon] I agree, he said, as far as I am able to understand you.

[Socrates] Moreover, I said, you must not wonder that those who attain to this beatific vision are unwilling to descend to human affairs; for their souls are ever hastening into the upper world where they desire to dwell; which desire of theirs is very natural, if our allegory may be trusted.

[Glaucon] Yes, very natural.

[Socrates] And is there anything surprising in one who passes from divine contemplations to the evil state of man, misbehaving himself in a ridiculous manner; if, while his eyes are blinking and before he has become accustomed to the surrounding darkness, he is compelled to fight in courts of law, or in other places, about the images or the shadows of images of justice, and is endeavoring to meet the conceptions of those who have never yet seen absolute justice?

[Glaucon] Anything but surprising, he replied.

[Socrates] Anyone who has common sense will remember that the bewilderments of the eyes are of two kinds, and arise from two causes, either from coming out of the light or from going into the light, which is true of the mind's eye, quite as much as of the bodily eye; and he who remembers this when he sees any one whose vision is perplexed and weak, will not be too ready to laugh; he will first ask whether that soul of man has come out of the brighter light, and is unable to see because unaccustomed to the dark, or having turned from darkness to the day is dazzled by excess of light. And he will count the one happy in his condition and state of being, and he will pity the other; or, if he have a mind to laugh at the soul which comes from below into the light, there will be more reason in this than in the laugh which greets him who returns from above out of the light into the cave.

144

[Glaucon] That, he said, is a very just distinction.
[Socrates] But then, if I am right, certain professors of education must be wrong when they say that they can put a knowledge into the soul which was not there before, like sight into blind eyes.
[Glaucon] They undoubtedly say this, he replied.
[Socrates] Whereas, our argument shows that the power and capacity of learning exists in the soul already; and that just as the eye was unable to turn from darkness to light without the whole body, so too the instrument of knowledge can only by the movement of the whole soul be turned from the world of becoming into that of being, and learn by degrees to endure the sight of being, and of the brightest and best of being, or in other words, of the good.
[Glaucon] Very true.
[Socrates] And must there not be some art which will effect conversion in the easiest and quickest manner; not implanting the faculty of sight, for that exists already, but has been turned in the wrong direction, and is looking away from the truth?
[Glaucon] Yes, he said, such an art may be presumed.
[Socrates] And whereas the other so-called virtues of the soul seem to be akin to bodily qualities, for even when they are not originally innate they can be implanted later by habit and exercise, the of wisdom more than anything else contains a divine element which always remains, and by this conversion is rendered useful and profitable; or, on the other hand, hurtful and useless. Did you never observe the narrow intelligence flashing from the keen eye of a clever rogue --how eager he is, how clearly his paltry soul sees the way to his end; he is the reverse of blind, but his keen eyesight is forced into the service of evil, and he is mischievous in proportion to his cleverness.
[Glaucon] Very true, he said.
[Socrates] But what if there had been a circumcision of such natures in the days of their youth; and they had been severed from those sensual pleasures, such as eating and drinking, which, like leaden weights, were attached to them at their birth, and which drag them down and turn the vision of their souls upon the

145

things that are below --if, I say, they had been
released from these impediments and turned in the
opposite direction, the very same faculty in them
would have seen the truth as keenly as they see what
their eyes are turned to now.
*[**Glaucon**] Very likely.*
*[**Socrates**] Yes, I said; and there is another thing*
which is likely. or rather a necessary inference from
what has preceded, that neither the uneducated and
uninformed of the truth, nor yet those who never
make an end of their education, will be able ministers
of State; not the former, because they have no single
aim of duty which is the rule of all their actions,
private as well as public; nor the latter, because they
will not act at all except upon compulsion, fancying
that they are already dwelling apart in the islands of
the blest.
*[**Glaucon**] Very true, he replied.*
*[**Socrates**] Then, I said, the business of us who are*
the founders of the State will be to compel the best
minds to attain that knowledge which we have
already shown to be the greatest of all-they must
continue to ascend until they arrive at the good; but
when they have ascended and seen enough we must
not allow them to do as they do now.
*[**Glaucon**] What do you mean?*
*[**Socrates**] I mean that they remain in the upper*
world: but this must not be allowed; they must be
made to descend again among the prisoners in the
cave, and partake of their labors and honors, whether
they are worth having or not.
*[**Glaucon**] But is not this unjust? he said; ought we to*
give them a worse life, when they might have a
better?
*[**Socrates**] You have again forgotten, my friend, I*
said, the intention of the legislator, who did not aim
at making any one class in the State happy above the
rest; the happiness was to be in the whole State, and
he held the citizens together by persuasion and
necessity, making them benefactors of the State, and
therefore benefactors of one another; to this end he
created them, not to please themselves, but to be his

146

instruments in binding up the State.
[Glaucon] True, he said, I had forgotten.
[Socrates] Observe, Glaucon, that there will be no injustice in compelling our philosophers to have a care and providence of others; we shall explain to them that in other States, men of their class are not obliged to share in the toils of politics: and this is reasonable, for they grow up at their own sweet will, and the government would rather not have them. Being self-taught, they cannot be expected to show any gratitude for a culture which they have never received. But we have brought you into the world to be rulers of the hive, kings of yourselves and of the other citizens, and have educated you far better and more perfectly than they have been educated, and you are better able to share in the double duty. Wherefore each of you, when his turn comes, must go down to the general underground abode, and get the habit of seeing in the dark. When you have acquired the habit, you will see ten thousand times better than the inhabitants of the cave, and you will know what the several images are, and what they represent, because you have seen the beautiful and just and good in their truth. And thus our State which is also yours will be a reality, and not a dream only, and will be administered in a spirit unlike that of other States, in which men fight with one another about shadows only and are distracted in the struggle for power, which in their eyes is a great good. Whereas the truth is that the State in which the rulers are most reluctant to govern is always the best and most quietly governed, and the State in which they are most eager, the worst.
[Glaucon] Quite true, he replied.
[Socrates] And will our pupils, when they hear this, refuse to take their turn at the toils of State, when they are allowed to spend the greater part of their time with one another in the heavenly light?
[Glaucon] Impossible, he answered; for they are just men, and the commands which we impose upon them are just; there can be no doubt that every one of them will take office as a stern necessity, and not after the fashion of our present rulers of State.

147

[Socrates] Yes, my friend, I said; and there lies the point. You must contrive for your future rulers another and a better life than that of a ruler, and then you may have a well-ordered State; for only in the State which offers this, will they rule who are truly rich, not in silver and gold, but in virtue and wisdom, which are the true blessings of life. Whereas if they go to the administration of public affairs, poor and hungering after the' own private advantage, thinking that hence they are to snatch the chief good, order there can never be; for they will be fighting about office, and the civil and domestic broils which thus arise will be the ruin of the rulers themselves and of the whole State.

[Glaucon] Most true, he replied.

[Socrates] And the only life which looks down upon the life of political ambition is that of true philosophy. Do you know of any other?

[Glaucon] Indeed, I do not, he said.

[Socrates] And those who govern ought not to be lovers of the task? For, if they are, there will be rival lovers, and they will fight.

[Glaucon] No question.

[Socrates] Who then are those whom we shall compel to be guardians? Surely they will be the men who are wisest about affairs of State, and by whom the State is best administered, and who at the same time have other honors and another and a better life than that of politics?

[Glaucon] They are the men, and I will choose them, he replied.

[Socrates] And now shall we consider in what way such guardians will be produced, and how they are to be brought from darkness to light, -- as some are said to have ascended from the world below to the gods?

[Glaucon] By all means, he replied.

[Socrates] The process, I said, is not the turning over of an oyster-shell, but the turning round of a soul passing from a day which is little better than night to

the true day of being, that is, the ascent from below,
which we affirm to be true philosophy?
[Glaucon] Quite so.[66]

What is Plato's point? His point is that if we think that reality is limited to those parts of it that we can experience with our physical senses, we are mistaken. For Plato, reality is composed of two substances,[67] the material and the immaterial, or the physical and the non-physical. The physical is encountered with the physical, that is, with the physical senses. The non-physical is encountered with the non-physical, that is, with the mind (note, the mind and the brain are not the same things). Thus Plato does not have a materialist view of reality, believing that only physical things exist. Instead, Plato's view of reality is *dualistic*—that reality is composed of at least two substances, one physical and one non-physical, or the material and the immaterial.

There are those, of course, who disagree with Plato. They ask for evidence of this non-physical aspect of reality. After all, if the non-physical cannot be encountered with the senses, how do we know it exists? That is a good question. Let us consider each position: *Physicalism* and *Dualism*.

---

[66] Plato, *Republic,* Book VII.

[67] I'm using the word *substance* here to refer to the most basic and elemental stuff that exists. A physical substance is the elemental stuff that physical objects are made of. Things that are composed of physical substance are located in space, have weight, shape, size, and so forth. We encounter them with our physical senses. In contrast, an immaterial or non-physical substance is an elemental substance that cannot be encountered with the senses. Immaterial or non-physical things have no shape, size, weight, and so forth. A bowling ball is a physical thing, a thought is an non-physical thing.

Physicalism

Physicalism[68] is the idea, generally speaking, that physical reality can be explained entirely in terms of physical phenomena. We live in a cause and effect universe. For every physical effect, there is a physical cause to account for it. Generally speaking, this is a satisfactory paradigm from which to examine the physical world. However, most physicalists (and materialists) believe that all that exists is physical space and the physical objects that exist in it. A rock, a tree, an eye, and a brain are examples of individual physical things that exist in a physical universe.

If one asked a physicalist or materialist to provide an argument that physical things are all that exist, the argument would be very simple. The argument is that the universe can be explained adequately in terms of physical phenomena. Since any additional explanation is unnecessary (Occam's Razor), it is the case that only physical phenomena, physical things and physical processes, exist.

Is this a satisfying argument? I'm not convinced it is. The argument hinges on the term *adequately*. What does it mean to explain the universe *adequately* on the basis of purely physical phenomena? What constitutes *adequately*, and from whose perspective?

For example, suppose a man is holding a ball in his hand and lets go of it. The ball falls to the ground. If the man then explains that gravity is the reason the ball fell to the

---

[68] For many philosophers the terms physicalism and materialism are synonymous, referring to the idea that all of reality can be explained in terms of physical phenomena—which is how I am using the terms here. However, within the technical literature the terms are not synonymous, and many physicists and philosophers have argued that materialism, as it was specifically defined, has been proven false and has been replaced by physicalism, a less dogmatic idea and term that can be adjusted to accommodate new discoveries at the sub-atomic level. Since this is an introductory text, however, it is not appropriate to go into the details of those controversies.

ground, I would accept his explanation as satisfactory or adequate. Gravity is a force that functions in the physical universe, and the explanation that a ball (or any other object) falls to the ground because gravity pulls it to the ground makes sense. Physical phenomena are easily explained in terms of physical causes.

But can all phenomena be explained on the basis of physical interactions? For instance, suppose I wake one morning to discover that during the night my dog, Max, had passed on. Max had been part of my life for nearly fifteen years, and I loved Max. I'm overwhelmed with powerful emotions. Grief stricken, I cry. How is that emotional reaction to be explained?

A physicalist would attempt to explain it in terms of purely physical interactions. I see the dead dog, and a physical reaction to the image on my retina results in electrical impulses in the brain. Chemicals are released into my bloodstream, and those physical interactions cause me to feel sad and cry. The emotions I feel are really just reactions to electrical impulses and chemical discharges. Emotions are really just physical reactions. The electrical impulses and the chemicals come first and the emotional response (in this case, crying) follow. Is this really a satisfying explanation of what emotions are and how they work? I do not think so. Why, for instance, would the image of a dead dog on my retina cause electrical impulses in my brain and the release of chemicals into my bloodstream that would cause me to feel sad and cry if there was not something about the dead dog that would generate the electrical impulses and the chemical release that resulted in sadness and crying? Why sadness and crying at the image of a dead dog on my retina? Why not joy and laughter? If emotions are just reactions to physical processes, what would generate emotionally appropriate responses, such as sadness and crying over the loss of my beloved Max, instead of emotionally inappropriate responses such as joy and laughter?

I believe the physicalists have the process reversed. First, I see my dead pet. Then, I feel the emotion (a real substantial manifestation of something we call feelings) that triggers a physical response. Generally speaking, emotions precede physical responses; they do not follow them. Emotions as feelings exist separately from the physical manifestations of them. Emotions are not just the result of physical processes. Emotions are real non-physical feelings we have. They cause physical responses. They are not the result of physical responses.

How do I know this? Because I am often aware of the presence of the emotion (sadness, for instance) before the physical manifestation (crying) is produced. I am not always aware of the presence of emotion before the physical response is manifested. But often I am. When am I not aware of the presence of the emotion before the response presents itself? When the emotion is very powerful. When something occurs that generates a very powerful emotional reaction, the physical response appears to occur simultaneously. How do I know it does not always occur simultaneously? Because sometimes I am aware of the emotion (sadness) before the physical reaction (crying) occurs. The presence of emotions cannot be adequately explained from a physicalist point of view.

Another example is consciousness. Philosophically, consciousness is awareness of experience. I am aware of sitting on my chair in my office typing on my computer keyboard. My chair is not aware of me sitting on it. It is not conscious. My office is not aware that I am in it. My computer keyboard is not aware that I am typing on it. But I am aware of all of this and more because I am a sentient being. I am conscious of experiencing different things.

How is consciousness to be explained? Physicalists explain consciousness (along with thought and emotion) as emerging from very complex interactions between the brain and the nervous system.

The problem with this explanation is that it is no explanation at all, at least not one that can be demonstrated or explained in any satisfactory way. It is merely an assertion, an article of physicalist faith that does not come with any evidence or data to back it up.

How do two non-conscious physical things, the brain (the brain is just an organ, no more conscious than a liver or a spleen) and a nervous system, produce consciousness? They cannot. Two physical things can produce a physical response. But consciousness is not merely a physical response. I know this (that consciousness is more than a physical response to a physical experience) because I am conscious of nonphysical experiences. I can experience the satisfaction of solving a rational conundrum that involves the identification of the relationship of one thing to another—of good for instance, in relation to justice. There is nothing physical that generates the relationship. It is a mental process beginning to end.

Obviously, something more than physical objects exist. A physicalist is likely to argue that the electrical impulses firing in the brain in relation to the "mental" processes involved in solving the problem are the physical "things" that constitute what we wrongly refer to as a non-physical mental process. However, that is merely an assertion that lacks support of any kind. Electrical impulses in the brain can be detected because they are indeed a physical manifestation. But to say that those electrical impulses *are* the thoughts and that no mental activity (in the sense of non-physical phenomena) is occurring is entirely unwarranted.

Just because a thing is not a physical object does not mean it does not exist. Concepts are not physical. But they exist. Numbers are not physical. The number 327 is not an object that exists somewhere. Does that mean that the mathematical entity of 327 does not exist and cannot be used in an equation? Of course not. The idea that the thoughts involved in any reasoning process are merely the electrical

153

impulses of the brain (that mental states are simply brain states) is rooted in an unwarranted assumption and is entirely without merit.

These examples of physicalist theory have to do with features of humanness (emotions and consciousness) that require explanation. What about the physicalist explanation of the presence of the earth as a place fit for the development of complex life? A physicalist explanation of how the earth came to be what it is is rooted in the idea of random chance. The Big Bang shot energy and matter (in various forms) in all directions, and bits and pieces of it (large bits and pieces but still bits and pieces) came together in different places in relation to other bits and pieces and different proportions, forming galaxies, solar systems, planets, moons, asteroids, and so forth. Some of the bits and pieces of the Big Bang were solid matter, some were gases and other types of chemical compounds. In a few places just the right blend of things came together so that complex life could develop. The earth just happened to be one of the places where the right blend of elements came together so complex life could develop. This is basically a physicalist explanation of how the earth came to be what it is.

Is this a satisfactory explanation? Lots of scientists and philosophers would say no. Why? Because, as plausible as it might sound on the surface, when one begins to calculate the odds of all the features, elements, and placements necessary for complex life to develop on earth coming together randomly, coincidentally, the odds are simply too great. Scientists have calculated the odds that everything necessary for the development of complex life to come together randomly would be one thousandth of one trillionth, or the same number could be expressed as one in one quadrillionth.[69] Written out mathematically, that would be:

---

[69] Rogers, *Proof of God?*, 79-84.

1, 000,000,000,000,000

To put this in terms that non-mathematicians (like me) can grasp, it is virtually impossible that everything necessary for the development of complex life on earth came together randomly. The physicalist answer that the earth is as it is because of random events is not scientifically sound. It is therefore an unsatisfactory explanation. A better explanation is dualism.

Dualism

What is Dualism? Basically, dualism says that reality is not composed of one substance that is physical in nature, but that there are at least two substances, one being physical or material and the other being non-physical or immaterial. The immaterial substance is usually identified as mind. What evidence is there that reality is dualistic in nature? The best and simplest evidence for the dualistic nature of reality is our awareness that mental events are different from physical things. Thoughts are not physical things. They are not extended, that is, they are not located in space. They have no physical form, no weight, no shape, no size. A thought is an immaterial thing.

It was René Descartes who helped us understand the immaterial nature of the mind. Descartes was born in 1596 into a family of means and received a first class Jesuit education. As a French gentleman, he had money and had no need to earn a living. In addition to financial security, Descartes had a hunger for knowledge and insight. He wanted not just to believe, but to know with certainty what was true. While he was living a life of contemplation, however, he needed something else to do. Gentlemen needed to be engaged in worthwhile efforts, so Descartes offered his services as an army officer to Prince Maurice of Orange. He may have been present at the battle of Prague in 1620. It was while in the military that Descartes experienced his philosophical epiphany that gave rise to probably the best known phrase in all of western philosophy: *cogito ergo sum,* I think, therefore, I am.

As Descartes tells the story, he was in Germany. He had been invited (probably because he was a French officer) to attend the coronation of the emperor. On his way back to his post, winter set in and delayed him. Since there was nothing of social interest to him in that particular location, he settled into his warm cabin to think about things that did interest him—philosophy.[70] As he thought, he decided that if he was to find the certainty he craved, if he was to have a rock-solid foundation upon which to build a complete system of thought and investigation, he would have to start from scratch, sweeping away all previously accepted notions, finding that one thing about which he could be absolutely certain, one thing that could not be questioned or doubted, one thing that could be the foundational thought upon which he could build his system. To do this, he would need a method, a system designed to assure he was approaching things systematically, that he was considering everything that needed to be considered, questioning everything that needed to be questioned. Parts two and three of his *Discourse On Method* provide an explanation of the method he settled on. It is in part four of his *Discourse* that Descartes explains the cognitive insight that became the foundation for modern Western philosophy.

As his narrative unfolds, Descartes explains that it became apparent to him that:

---

[70] Descartes, *Discourse On Method*, Part II.

... I ought to reject as absolutely false all opinions in regard to which I could suppose the least ground for doubt, in order to ascertain whether after that there remained aught in my belief that was wholly indubitable. Accordingly, seeing that our senses sometimes deceive us, I was willing to suppose that there existed nothing really such as they presented to us; and because some men err in reasoning, and fall into paralogisms, even on the simplest matters of geometry, I, conceived that I was as open to error as any other, rejected as false all the reasonings I had hitherto taken for demonstrations, and finally, when I considered that the very same thoughts (presentations) which we experience when awake may also be experienced when we are asleep, while there is at that time not one of them true, I supposed that all the objects (presentations) that had ever entered into my mind when awake, had in them no more truth than the illusions of my dreams. But immediately upon this I observed that, whilst I thus wished to think that all was false, it was absolutely necessary that I, who thus thought, should be somewhat; and as I observed that this truth, I think, therefore I am, (COGITO ERGO SUM), was so certain and of such evidence that no ground of doubt, however extravagant, could be alleged by the skeptics capable of shaking it, I concluded that I might, without scruple, accept it as the first principle of the philosophy of which I was in search.[71]

I think, therefore, I am. This was Descartes' rock-solid foundation, a reality that could not be doubted. Regardless of whatever else may be uncertain, that which

---

[71] Descartes, *Discourse on Method*, Part IV.

was absolutely certain was that he existed.[72] But *how* did he exist? What was he? This was the next question to be considered. Descartes elaborates:

> *In the next place, I attentively examined what I was and as I observed that I could suppose that I had no body, and that there was no world nor any place in which I might be; but that I could not therefore suppose that I was not; and that, on the contrary, from the very circumstances that I thought to doubt of the truth of other things, it most clearly and certainly followed that I was; while, on the other hand, if I had only ceased to think, although all the other objects which I had ever imagined had been in reality existent, I would have had no reason to believe that I existed; I thence concluded that I was a substance whose whole essence or nature consists only in thinking, and which, that it may exist, has need of no place, nor is dependent on any material thing; so that "I," that is to say, the mind by which I am what I am, is wholly distinct from the body, and is even more easily known than the latter, and is such, that although the latter were not, it would still continue to be all that it is.[73]*

Through his rigorous introspective *a priori* analysis Descartes concluded not only that he existed, but that he existed as a mind, a thinking substance not a material substance, a mind that is not dependent on anything material for its existence, including a body. Descartes appears to have

---

[72] The argument that one must exist in order to doubt that he exists was apparently first articulated by Augustine in *On Free Choice of the Will*, bk 2.3. Descartes borrowed it. He argued it, however, in a modern context using a rigorous *a priori* method that puts the argument in a different context than it had in Augustine's material.

[73] Descartes, *Discourse on Method*, Part IV.

158

been successful at this level. His analysis that he had to exist in order to wonder (and doubt) whether or not he existed was correct. Descartes then went on to conclude that the physical world also existed and that he had a physical body. However, he was more than and was different from his body. He was an immaterial thinking substance that could exist apart from his body. His essence, the real Descartes, was a mind being who was embodied."[74]

Most of Descartes' philosophy has been overturned. He was wrong about quite a few things. But his insight into the immaterial nature of conscious mind is a point that has not been overturned. Physicalists question his insights. But questioning something does not prove that it is not true.

An immaterial mind generates immaterial thoughts about both material and immaterial things. I can think about a baseball, and I can think about justice. I can think about a physical book, and I can think about the ideas (the immaterial concepts) contained in the book. I can pick up my mug and take a sip of hot tea, and I can imagine myself lounging on a tropical beach enjoying the sights. The two events, the sip of tea and the imaginary beach adventure, are different types of events, one physical and one mental. I can shoot a gun, and I can dream about shooting a gun. The two events are quite different, having a different feel, a different quality.

But perhaps the most important fact that demonstrates the dualistic nature of reality is that the mind can conceive of things that the brain cannot experience. If physical matter (or whatever quantum physicists want to call it these days) is all that exists, and if my brain has access to it only by means of my physical senses, then all that can get into my brain, and therefore all that can be in my brain (all that the brain can process), is data related to the physical world. My brain can

---

[74] This brief section on Descartes was borrowed from Rogers, *Proof of God?*, 144-148, and is used with permission.

deconstruct and reconstruct that data in many ways, creating combinations, some of which may not actually exist in the physical world. But all it has to work with is the physical data presented to it by my physical senses. For instance, the physical data my brain has to work with includes horses, horns, wings, lizards, and fire. From those physical things my brain can construct things (imagine things) that do not really exist in the physical world—unicorns and fire-breathing dragons. But all it can imaginatively create are things that are composites of physical reality—*unless there is something other than the brain that has access to a reality that is not physical*. And this is the case. My brain can process ideas that are not simply composites of physical reality because by means of my brain's linkage to the immaterial mind that is the essential me, my brain has access to an immaterial reality. In short, I know that reality is not only physical because I can conceive of things that cannot in any way be linked to the physical world. If there is no immaterial mind but only a physical brain, all the brain could "think" about would be physical stuff, aspects of physical reality deconstructed and reconstructed in many different ways but still just physical stuff. But that is clearly not the case. The immaterial mind can conceive of things that are not part of the physical universe. Like what? Things that are funny, for instance. That something is *funny* is an idea, not a physical thing. Funny does not occupy space in the physical universe. Neither do joy, sorrow, anger, fear, courage, beauty, or God. But all of those things are real things that impact our lives in significant ways. Therefore, reality cannot be composed only of physical stuff. Reality is dualistic in nature, consisting of physical and non-physical features.

If what I have argued is correct, why do so many scientists and philosophers embrace physicalism? Certainly not because there is any evidence or positive arguments that can be made demonstrating that physicalism is the paradigm most reflective of actual reality. It is embraced because over

160

a long period of time it became the accepted paradigm. I will examine the historical development of materialism and physicalism in more detail in Chapter 9.

Summary

A fundamental philosophical question is, *why is there something rather than nothing*? The answer is, because something has always existed and that something is the cause (is the ultimate source) of all else that exists. What is it that has always existed? There appear to be two possibilities. Let's call them matter (even though physicists don't like that name for it) and mind. That which has always existed is either physical stuff, or mental stuff, mind.

In asking and answering the question, *why is there something rather than nothing*, we are discussing *the nature of reality*. What is reality like? Of what does reality consist? There are two schools of thought: physicalist and dualist. Physicalists argue that reality consists of only one substance, physical matter, and that all events that occur can be explained in terms of physical interactions—physical stuff interacting with other physical stuff. Dualists argue that reality consists of (at least) two substances, one physical or material and one non-physical or immaterial, usually referred to as mind.

If one argues, as physicalists do, that physical matter is that which always existed and that which is the ultimate cause of all other things, one is obligated to explain how that which is non-conscious produced that which is conscious, how that which does not think produced that which does. Physicalists cannot explain this. If, however, as dualists argue, that which always existed in mind, which is by nature conscious, then that which is conscious and thinking is the ultimate cause of that which is conscious and thinking.

The problem that exists for physicalists does not exist

161

for dualists. Also, based on the mental experiences we all have, Dualism not only feels right logically, it makes more sense.

Reality is dualistic in nature and that which has always existed is mind.

Thought and Discussion Questions

1. Discuss Parmenides' assertion that *from nothing comes nothing* as it relates to Rogers' argument that if something exists now something has always existed.
2. Discuss and evaluate the physicalist position that only physical matter exists and that all events (physical and mental) can be explained on the basis of physical interactions.
3. Discuss and evaluate Rogers' argument regarding the limitation of brain processes as they relate to the processing of physical data—if there is only physical data, how can the brain think about things not associated with the physical world?
4. Discuss and evaluate the dualist position that reality consists of at least two substances, one physical and one non-physical. How does Rogers' argument about mental states and events support the dualist position?
5. Discuss your own view about the nature of reality and how your view provides insight into the question, *why is there something rather than nothing?*

Chapter 6
Does God Exist?

Philosophers ask a number of important and challenging questions. None are more important or challenging than this one: *Does God exist*? A related question is, *Can the existence of God be proven*? Neither question is new. About 3,000 years ago, an ancient Hebrew poet wrote, *"The fool has said in his heart, 'There is no God',"* (Psalm 14). He would have had no occasion to make such a comment if there were not people claiming that God does not exist.

Over the centuries, many people have either said emphatically that God does not exist or wondered whether or not he does. On the whole, more people have believed that God does exist than have believed that he does not. Of course, because some people believe that God exists does not mean that God does, in fact, exist. As we have discovered already, there is a difference between believing a thing is true and that thing being true. Is it possible to determine whether or not God exists? I believe it is. I believe it can be demonstrated rationally that God exists. Whether or not a given individual will accept the evidence provided (in the form of rational arguments) is another matter.[75]

Throughout the centuries, a number of arguments have been developed to demonstrate the existence of God. Without a doubt, some are better than others. What I want to do in this chapter is explain and present representative examples of the four kinds of arguments most often used to demonstrate that sound arguments can be made for the existence of God, and that it is, therefore, rational to believe in the existence of God.

Cosmological Argument

What is a cosmological argument? The word cosmological is from the Greek *cosmos*, their word for the universe. A cosmological argument is one that involves rational reflection on the presence of the cosmos. The cosmos exists. The obvious question is how does one account for its existence? How did it get here? A related question might be, why does the cosmos exist?

I have already discussed the idea that the cosmos exists because something has always existed. And I have said that that something was mind rather than matter. I did not, however, present a detailed argument to that effect. Now is the appropriate time to offer such an argument. A number of good cosmological arguments have been designed and offered over the centuries. Aquinas and Leibniz each offered their own versions of a cosmological argument. More recently Tom Morris and William Lane Craig have offered cosmological arguments of their own design.[76] Here is my

---

[75] I have addressed this issue in more detail in *Proof of God?* (22-26) and cannot take time to duplicate that discussion here.
[76] These arguments can be examined in Rogers, *Proof of God?*

cosmological argument.

I begin with the observation of Parmenides that from nothing comes nothing.[77]

1. If there was ever a time when nothing existed (i.e. when no thing at all existed), then nothing (no thing at all) would exist now— *for from nothing comes nothing.*

2. Something exists now—the cosmos.

3. Therefore, something (some kind of a thing) has always existed.

The question that grows out of this basic observation is, *what is the relationship between that which exists now and that which has always existed?*

4. Since there is no scientific or logical reason to believe that things simply pop into existence out of their own accord out of nothing, it must be the case that that which exists now (the cosmos) must have come from (i.e., somehow been produced by) that which always existed. There is a causal connection.

The question that emerges from this observation is, *what is it that has always existed?* There appear to be two options: a material substance or a non-material substance. Why limit the possibilities to either material or non-material substances? Because based on our observation and experience of the cosmos there are two and only two options available to us.

We experience material realities as part of the cosmos: material things—rocks and trees, dirt, air, water, animals, people, and so forth. We also experience features of reality that are part of the non-material or immaterial aspect of reality—thoughts, for instance. The material substance we can refer to simply as *matter*, the physical stuff physical things are made of. The immaterial substance associated with thoughts could be referred to as simply *immaterial*

---

[77] This material is borrowed from Rogers, *Proof of God?*

substance,[78] but that is rather cumbersome. Something more descriptive is in order. Thoughts are produced by the *mind*. We can, therefore, refer to this immaterial substance simply as *mind*.

Having clarified the terminology, we can make the next two crucial points:

5. Based on everything that can be experienced and known, either material stuff (matter) or mental stuff (mind) are the only options for substances that have always existed.

(If someone wishes to postulate additional substances I would ask, upon what basis? To say merely, *we do not know and cannot therefore assume that there is only matter and mind,* is insufficient, for it is not based on anything other than pure speculation. My assertion that either matter or mind are the only two options is rooted in empirical observation.)

6. That which has always existed, either a material substance or a mental substance, either matter or mind, is the source or cause of all other things that exist.

Which was it that served as the source (the cause) of all that now exists, matter or mind, a material substance or a mental substance? To answer that question we must examine the nature of the cosmos. When we look at the cosmos in broad scope, we note that there are non-living, non-conscious,

---

[78] When I use the term substance I have in mind the same basic idea as Descartes: a basic or simple substance that is not composed of something else. A chess piece carved from wood (say a knight) exists as a material object. The knight exists separate from the rook, the pawn, the bishop, and so forth. But the knight (and all the pieces, in fact) can only exist as the wood they are carved from exists. The knight is not a substance. It is a mode. It exists in (or as) a given form, made from something else. But a substance exists simply as itself, not as a thing made out of something else. Mind is a substance.

non-rational things, things made of a material substance. But we also note that the cosmos contains living, conscious, rational things, things associated with a mental substance. For the sake of brevity, let us focus attention on just one of these features: *consciousness.* Consciousness has to do with awareness and perception—mental processes, things related to the mind.

7. At least part of all that exists is consciousness.

This brings us to a crucial realization: we have a serious problem if we attempt to explain the presence of consciousness in the cosmos on the basis of non-consciousness. How does that which is not conscious give rise to that which is conscious? There is no satisfactory materialistic explanation (an explanation that is rooted in a materialistic paradigm) for the rise of consciousness. Richard Swinburne observes that, "given the scientific laws as we believe them to be, which operated to govern the inanimate world for the first nine of the first fifteen billion years of the time of the Big Bang, there is not the slightest grounds for supposing that conscious life would evolve." [79] David Chalmers also observes that, "No explanation given wholly in physical terms can ever account for the emergence of conscious experience."[80]

8. The existence of consciousness in the cosmos cannot be satisfactorily explained if that which has always existed and is the cause of all other things is non-conscious matter.

The argument here is based on the principle of sufficient reason. A frog, for example, is not a *sufficient reason* (a sufficiently powerful cause) for the existence of an automobile.

If you have two possible explanations for the existence of a thing (point 5) and one of the two

---

[79] Swinburne, *The Existence of God,* 201.
[80] Chalmers, *The Conscious Mind,* 93.

can be ruled out (because it is not sufficient), (point 8), the only possible explanation is the remaining one.

9. The existence of consciousness in the cosmos can only be satisfactorily explained if that which has always existed and which is the cause of all other things is a mental substance, a conscious mind.

10. Therefore, that which has always existed and is responsible for all else that exists is a mental substance, a conscious mind.

Let us now consider the ten-point argument without the additional or explanatory comments:

1. If there was ever a time when nothing existed (i.e. when no thing at all existed), then nothing (no thing at all) would exist now—*for from nothing comes nothing.*

2. Something exists now—the cosmos.

3. Therefore, something (some kind of a thing) has always existed.

4. The something that exists now (the cosmos) must have come from (somehow been produced by) that which always existed.

5. Based on everything we observe and experienced, either material stuff (matter) or mental stuff (mind) are the only options for substances that have always existed.

6. That which has always existed, either a material substance or a mental substance, either matter or mind, is the source or cause of all other things that exist.

7. At least part of all that exists is consciousness: awareness and perception.

8. The existence of consciousness in the cosmos cannot be satisfactorily explained if that which has always existed and is the cause of all other things that exist is non-conscious matter.

9. The existence of consciousness in the cosmos can only be satisfactorily explained if that which has always existed and which is the cause of all other things that exist is a mental substance, a conscious mind.

10. Therefore, that which has always existed and is responsible for all else that exists is a mental substance, a conscious mind.

There are many ways to construct a cosmological argument. Each, however, will begin with a basic observation—the cosmos exists—and will then proceed to explain how its presence can be accounted for in a rational, logical manner. I believe this particular cosmological argument is structured in such a way that it is both valid and sound.

Teleological Argument

The word teleological comes from the Greek word *telos*, which has to do with the idea of completion, as in the achievement of purpose. A piece of fruit that is ripe can be described as *telos* because it has completed its purpose, becoming ripe so it can be eaten. *Teleological*, then, is the study or thoughtful contemplation about the purpose of the cosmos. While cosmological arguments ask, where did the cosmos come from, teleological arguments ask, why is it here?

Teleological arguments are rooted in the idea that the design that can be observed in nature suggests that the cosmos is the product of intention and purpose, that it has a reason for existing, which suggests that an intelligent mind designed it rather than it being the product of simple random coincidence. Random chance is neither intentional nor purposeful. Only rationality can be intentional and purposeful. Teleological arguments are based on the idea that if intention and purpose can be identified in nature, they are evidence that the cosmos was not the product of random chance but of intelligent design. Designed for what? Designed for the development of complex life.

Some teleological arguments are based on the order that is apparent in nature. However, it is fairly obvious that in nature there is also a lot of chaotic disorder. For instance, forests and jungles do not grow in any kind of ordered pattern. The stars do not exist in any kind of ordered pattern. Teleological arguments based on the order that is occasionally apparent in nature do not appear to be sound arguments. However, teleological arguments rooted in the complexity of nature (technically called regularities of succession) are much more powerful and compelling arguments. If designed well, they can be both valid and sound. Here is an example of a teleological argument rooted in regularities of succession.[81]

> 1. If the development of complex life on earth is dependent on a vast number of extremely precise and complex natural interrelationships and interactions,
> 2. And if the likelihood of those interrelationships and interactions are so numerous that the likelihood of their occurring by chance is virtually non-existent,
> 3. Then it is logically justifiable to conclude that those extremely precise and complex natural interrelationships and interactions did not occur by chance but are the result of intelligent, intentional design.
> 4. Evidence in the fields of physics and chemistry suggests that complex life forms could not have developed on earth if the earth was not part of a system that is *anthropic* (life friendly) in nature. That is, if all the elements essential for the development of complex life were not present and "fine tuned" to the

---

[81] This argument is my own and is borrowed from *Proof of God*?

minutest degree, complex life could not have developed on earth.

For complex life to develop and thrive on any planet:[82]

(1) It must be in the right location in the galaxy and solar system. It must be the right distance from the source of heat so liquid water can be present. If the planet is too close to its star, water will evaporate; if it is too far away, water will freeze. If, for instance, the earth were only 5% closer to the sun, temperatures would rise to nearly 900 degrees. If it were 20% further away, carbon dioxide would form in the upper atmosphere generating the kinds of temperatures that occur on Mars.

(2) It must be in orbit around the right kind of star—not too hot or cold and the right size so that it generates the right amount of gravitational pull. For instance, if our sun were smaller it would have less gravitational pull. Planets would have to be closer to it to remain in orbit. But being closer would not allow for planetary rotation, which means that one side of the planet would always be dark. Our moon, for instance, because it is so close to earth, does not rotate, resulting in one side always being dark. Such a state is not conducive to the development of complex life.

(3) It must be in a planetary system containing a number of large planets to provide shielding from asteroid or meteor impact.

(4) It must have a moon large enough to provide a gravitational pull sufficient to keep the planet on

---

[82] The eight points in this section are gleaned from Gonzalez and Richards, *The Privileged Planet.*

its axis so it can rotate appropriately, keeping water circulating.

(5) It must be a planet where the crust is just the right thickness to allow for the movement of the tectonic plates, which is how the continents formed so that complex life could develop in different locations on the planet.

(6) It must be a planet with sufficient interior heat so that (in conjunction with axis rotation) it can generate a magnetic force sufficient to block the effects of solar winds.

(7) It must have an atmosphere with the right chemical makeup and balance to support life.

(8) It must have enough liquid water to dissolve and transport the chemicals necessary for life, and to absorb the heat of the sun to help control and maintain an appropriate temperature.

These are just eight of the simple and obvious things that even those of us who are not Astrobiologists can understand. What are the odds that all of the factors required for complex life to develop and thrive would come together in one place at the same time? Astrobiologists have calculated the odds to be one thousandth of one trillionth, or one in one quadrillionth. In equation form that would be:

$$\frac{1}{1,000,000,000,000,000}$$

Continuing on with the argument:

5. The evidence clearly suggests that the cosmos is anthropic in nature and that the odds of all the features necessary for the development of complex life on earth developing by mere happenstance are so great as to be virtually impossible.

6. Observation and experience suggest to us that the presence of complexity and purposefulness are the result of intelligent, intentional design rather than mere chance.

7. It is, therefore, based on observation and experience, logically justifiable to conclude that the anthropic nature of the cosmos is the result of intelligent design rather than mere happenstance.

For the sake of clarity and continuity, let us look at the argument set out without the scientific evidence inserted into it.

1. If the development of complex life on earth is dependent on a vast number of extremely precise and complex natural interrelationships and interactions,

2. And if the likelihood of those extremely precise and complex natural interrelationships and interactions are so numerous that the likelihood of their occurring by chance is virtually non-existent,

3. Then it is logically justifiable to conclude that those extremely precise and complex natural interrelationships and interactions did not occur by chance but are the result of intelligent, intentional design.

4. Evidence in the fields of physics and chemistry suggest that complex life forms could not have developed on earth if the earth was not part of a system that is *anthropic* (life friendly) in nature. That is, if all the elements essential for the development of complex life were not present and "fine tuned" to the minutest degree, complex life could not have developed on earth.

5. The evidence clearly suggests that the cosmos is anthropic in nature and that the odds of all the features necessary for the development of complex

life on earth developing by mere happenstance are so great as to be virtually impossible.

6. Observation and experience suggest to us that the presence of complexity and purposefulness are the result of intelligent, intentional design rather than mere chance.

7. It is, therefore, based on observation and experience, logically justifiable to conclude that the anthropic nature of the cosmos is the result of intelligent design rather than mere happenstance.

This argument is, I believe, not only scientifically accurate but is also valid and sound, demonstrating that an intelligent mind is responsible for the presence of the cosmos. Whether or not you agree, of course, is for you to decide.

Ontological Argument

Another kind of argument that is often used to demonstrate the existence of God is the ontological argument. Ontological arguments are entirely rationalistic. Unlike cosmological and teleological arguments, ontological arguments do not involve any kind of empirical observations. They involve only rational reflection. The word ontological comes from the word *ontology*, referring to the study of being or existence. It was first used by Immanuel Kant to describe arguments about the existence of God that are purely rational in nature.

Throughout the centuries a number of ontological arguments for the existence of God have been offered. Augustine, Anselm, Descartes and others have designed purely rationalistic arguments to demonstrate that God, does, in fact, exist. However, it is St. Anselm's argument that philosophers have found to be the most intriguing of the ontological arguments since Anselm (Archbishop of Canterbury) offered it in the late 11th century.

The argument is brief but complex, so you need to read the argument itself as well as a point-by-point analysis of it. Anselm's argument is presented in Chapter 2 of his small work entitled, *Proslogion*. It is presented in the form of a prayer to God.

Well then, Lord, you who give understanding to faith, grant me that I may understand, as much as you see fit, that you exist as we believe you to exist, and that you are what we believe you to be. Now we believe that you are something than which a greater cannot be conceived. Or can it be that a thing of such a nature does not exist, since "the fool has said in his heart, there is no God" (Ps. 14:1)? But surely, when this same fool hears what I am speaking about, namely, something-than-which-a-greater-cannot-be-conceived, he understands what he hears, and what he understands is in his mind, even if he does not understand that it actually exists. For it is one thing for an object to exist in the mind, and another thing to understand that an object actually exists. Thus, when a painter plans beforehand what he is going to execute, he has [the picture] in his mind, but he does not yet think that it actually exists because he has not yet executed it. However, when he has actually painted it, then he both has it in his mind and understands that it exists because he has now made it. Even the fool, then, is forced to agree that something-than-which-a-greater-cannot-be-conceived exists in the mind, since he understands this when he hears it, and whatever is understood is in the mind. And surely, that-than-which-a-greater-cannot-be-conceived cannot exist in the mind alone. For if it exists solely in the mind, it can be thought to exist in reality also, which is greater. If that-than-which-a-greater-cannot-be-conceived exists in the mind alone,

175

this same that-than-which-a-greater-cannot-be-conceived is that-than-which-a-greater-<u>can</u>-be conceived. But this is obviously impossible. Therefore there is absolutely no doubt that something-than-which-a-greater-cannot-be-conceived exists both in the mind and in reality.[83]

In order to critique Anselm's argument we will need to summarize and analyze it to be sure we understand exactly what Anselm is and is not arguing. Anselm argues that:

1. God is *that-than-which-a-greater-cannot-be-conceived.*

2. The fool says that there is no God (this "fool" who denies God's existence is referred to in Psalm 14:1).

    2a. However, even as he denies (and in order to deny) that God exists, he must have the idea of God in his mind.

3. It is one thing to exist in the mind and it is another to actually exist in reality.

    3a. For example, an artist may have in his mind the picture he intends to paint, but until he paints it, the scene exists only in his mind. When he paints it, then it exists in reality also.

4. Even the fool, then, must admit that a *that-than-which-a-greater-cannot-be-conceived* must exist at least in the mind, for that idea is in the fool's head when he says that such a being does not exist in reality.

5. But if a *that-than-which-a-greater-cannot-be-conceived* exists only in the mind, then it is not *that-than-which-a-greater-cannot-be-conceived*, for to actually exist in reality is greater than to exist only in the mind.

---

[83] Anselm, *St. Anselm's Proslogion*, 117.

6. To actually be a *that-than-which-a-greater-cannot-be-conceived* it must exist not only in the mind but in reality also.

7. It is not possible that a *that-than-which-a-greater-cannot-be-conceived* can exist in the mind and not exist also in reality.

8. Therefore, there can be no doubt that a *that-than-which-a-greater-cannot-be-conceived* exists both in the mind and in reality.

9. Thus, God exists.

Though this argument is almost 1,000 years old, philosophers still discuss it today, some arguing that it is a sound argument, others arguing that it is not. I believe it is sound. However, it can be tricky to get Anselm's point, so read it and think about it for a while (or maybe for a long time!) before making up your mind.

The Moral Argument

The moral argument for the existence of God seeks to demonstrate God's existence based on the presence of human morality. Animals are amoral creatures, humans are moral beings. Why? What is the difference between animals and humans, and how is that difference to be accounted for? The moral argument says, in effect, that the difference is God.

In his *Critique of Pure Reason*, Immanuel Kant argued that God's existence could not be proven using either the cosmological, teleological, or ontological arguments (a conclusion with which many philosophers disagree). However, in his *Critique of Practical Reason* Kant argued that God's existence (his *necessary* existence) could be

177

demonstrated on the basis of the moral argument.[84]

The moral argument for the existence of God can be summarized as follows:

A moral God who created moral people is the only satisfactory explanation for the presence of morality in the cosmos.

1. Just as the presence of consciousness in the cosmos can only be accounted for by the existence of an eternally-existing conscious mind that created other conscious minds, so the presence of morality in the cosmos can only be accounted for by an eternally-existing moral mind who created other moral minds.

1a. A monistic materialistic paradigm contains no mechanism for explaining the rise of morality out of egoistic amorality (as Hobbes argued) anymore than it does for explaining the rise of consciousness out of non-consciousness.

1b. But a dualistic "mind paradigm" explains the presence of morality by arguing that that which always existed and is responsible for all else that exists (including morality) is a self-determined moral mind.

1c. A self-determined mind is a moral mind in the sense that it makes moral choices.

2. Moral minds can only be produced by a previously existing moral mind.

3. It is necessary, therefore, that a moral mind exist to account for the presence of morality in the cosmos. That moral mind is normally referred to as God.[85]

A more extensive treatment of this topic is possible but is beyond the scope of this material. The idea, however, in the simplest terms, is that morality could not simply have

---

[84] A detailed analysis of Kant's argument is presented in Rogers, *Proof of God?*
[85] Borrowed from *Proof of God?*

evolved out of egoistic amorality, as Hobbes argued, anymore than consciousness could have simply evolved out of non-consciousness. To make such an assertion is utterly unwarranted.

Whether or not you agree with any or all of the arguments designed to demonstrate the existence of God is a matter for you to contemplate and determine. The point of this chapter has been to highlight the basic arguments that are used to argue for the existence of God. For every argument offered to demonstrate God's existence, counterarguments are offered. The subject has been of interest since the birth of philosophy and will continue to be argued as long as there are people to discuss the issue. As for me, I believe that God's existence can be rationally and logically demonstrated. It is, therefore, logical and rational to believe that God exists.

Summary

Philosophers ask a number of important and challenging questions. None are more important or challenging than this one: *Does God exist*? A related question is, *Can the existence of God be proven*? Neither question is new. Is it possible to determine whether or not God exists? I believe it is. I believe it can be demonstrated rationally that God exists. Whether or not a given individual will accept the evidence provided (in the form of rational arguments) is another matter.

The four basic arguments used to demonstrate that God exists are: the cosmological, teleological, ontological, and moral arguments. Each has been defined and explained and examples of each have been presented. I believe they do, in fact, demonstrate the existence of God. Each reader must decide whether or not he or she is convinced.

Thought and Discussion Questions

1. Evaluate the strengths and weaknesses of the cosmological argument and explain your views as to whether or not it is a sound argument.

2. Evaluate the strengths and weaknesses of the teleological argument and explain your views as to whether or not it is a sound argument.

3. Evaluate the strengths and weaknesses of the ontological argument and explain your views as to whether or not it is a sound argument.

4. Evaluate the strengths and weaknesses of the moral argument and explain your views as to whether or not it is a sound argument.

5. Explain your thinking regarding all four arguments combined. Do they present convincing evidence for the existence of God?

Chapter 7
What Is God Like?

If, in fact, God does exist, what is God like? What is entailed in being God? Unless God somehow reveals himself to us so we can experience him and discover what he is like, the only option open to us is *abductive reasoning* about God. Abductive reasoning is a reasoning process that examines the available evidence and, using inferential logic, reaches the best conclusion that can be reached based on the evidence one has. This chapter, then, in part, will consist in an exercise in abductive reasoning—looking at the available evidence and drawing inferences (hopefully warranted and logical inferences) about God. However, there are a few things to consider before we begin.

Thinking and Talking about God

In thinking and talking about God, we must recognize the rather severe limitations we have. Based on what we have

181

already argued, God has always existed and always will exist. God existed before anything else existed, such as time and space, which God somehow created. That means that God is infinite. God is not limited to any particular context. We, however, are finite and limited to a particular context. How can the finite ever fully understand that which is infinite? It cannot. Complete comprehension of God is simply beyond us. That's the first thing we must understand about God. Full comprehension of the divine is not within our reach.

The second thing we need to understand before we begin is that even talking about God in a meaningful way is going to be challenging. Language is a human communication convention. It is an arbitrary system of symbols that we use to think, understand, and communicate. Human language can go as far as the human mind can go and no further. If in our minds we cannot fully comprehend God, we will not be able to design language about God that adequately explains God in any real or accurate way. For instance, you may have noticed in this section so far I have not used personal pronouns (he or she) to refer to God. I have used the word God each time. Why? Because while we often refer to God has a he, God is not a *he,* for the word *he* refers to a male being or creature. But God, if he is a mind being and is not embodied in some way, is not and cannot be a male. Neither is God a female. God is not a physical being who needs to engage in physical reproduction so God is not a sexual being. God is neither male nor female and cannot, therefore, accurately be referred to as he or she. But calling God an *it* doesn't really work because the word it refers to an object and God is not an object. So if God is not a he or a she or an it, what is God? How do we refer to God? For simplicity sake let's say we can refer to God as a he. But we must be ever mindful that he is not really a "he."

The problem gets even more complicated when we try to describe God with other words. Some people are fond of saying God is great. But what, exactly, does that mean?

182

What is great? What does it mean to be great? Tony the Tiger says Sugar Frosted Flakes are *Great*! So in what way is God great? Is God like Sugar Frosted Flakes? Some might say Abraham Lincoln was a great man. So if Lincoln was great and God is great, does that make God like Lincoln or Lincoln like God, or are we trying to say something entirely different? If we say Socrates was wise and God is wise, in what ways are Socrates and God similar? Or are they similar at all? If we say God is a king (as the Bible says) is he really, literally, a king? The problem with talking about God using human language is a serious one, and we must keep in mind that whatever we say about God is problematic because of the infinite nature of God and the finite nature of the human mind and the language human minds use to think, understand, and communicate.

What we must do is remind ourselves that whatever we think about God is at best an approximation. We cannot fully understand God. However, we must not overreact and conclude that we cannot understand anything at all about God. That is not the case. We know an eternally-existing mind has always existed and that it is enormously powerful (we might say all-powerful) because it created the cosmos and set in motion the processes that would lead to all else that now exists. Since most people call this eternally-existing mind God (and refer to God as a "he"), we can say that we understand at least a couple of very significant things about God. He has always existed and he is very powerful. We do not really understand infinite, eternal existence because those things are beyond our frame of reference. But we are able to grasp the concept of infinity enough to identify it and explain (at least abstractly) what it is. So we understand a little bit about God. The point is to remember that we can understand a little about God, not a lot.

At this point it might be helpful to remember what Xenophanes said about God and human conceptions of God. He said:

> *The Ethiopians make their gods snub-nosed and black; the Thracians make theirs gray-eyed and red-haired... and if oxen and horses and lions had hands, and could draw with their hands and do what man can do, horses would draw their gods in the shape of horses, and oxen in the shape of oxen, each giving the gods bodies similar to their own.*[86]

If Xenophanes does not appreciate the general Greek conception of the divine, how does he conceive of God? He explained that there is:

> *...one god, greatest among gods and men, in no way similar to mortals either in body or mind. He sees all over, thinks all over, hears all over. He remains always in the same place, without moving; nor is it fitting that he should come and go, first to one place and then to another. But without toil, he sets all things in motion by the thought of his mind.*[87]

The point here is not to say that Xenophanes got it right—though I think much of his brief comment about the nature of God is correct. Rather, the point is that he pointed out a problem with the common conceptions of God and suggested that we think differently about God. One aspect of God's nature that needs careful consideration is that based on what we can infer about God (based on my cosmological

---

[86] Melchert (15) provides the Diels-Kranz (DK) references for these quotes from Xenophanes—DK 21 B 16 *IEGP* 52.
[87] As referenced by Melchert, 15, DK 21 B 23-25, *IEGP*, 53

argument in Chapter 6), God is an immaterial mind kind of a being. God is not embodied. God has no material form of any kind. He exists as a mind kind of a being, a being whose nature is thought or contemplation, or we could say, rationality. God's fundamental nature and activity is rationality. And that, as far as Aristotle was concerned, is the essence of life.

In *Metaphysics*, Bk. 12: Ch. 6, Aristotle concluded that, "we must assert that it is necessary that there should be an eternal unmovable substance." He continues his presentation about this unmoved mover and its nature through the rest of Chapter 6 and into Chapter 7, introducing the idea that this unmoved mover is necessary, that is, he must exist, and is a thought or a mind kind of being. This, for Aristotle, is the essence of life. He says, "And life also belongs to God; for the actuality of thought is life, and God is that actuality; and God's self-dependent actuality is life most good and eternal. We say therefore that God is a living being, eternal, most good, so that life and duration continuous and eternal belong to God; for this *is* God."[88]

Plato, as well, Aristotle's teacher, had some interesting ideas about God and God's nature. The following is an excerpt from Plato's dialog entitled *Timaeus*.

> **Timaeus** ...*Now everything that becomes or is created must of necessity be created by some cause, for without a cause nothing can be created. The work of the creator, whenever he looks to the unchangeable and fashions the form and nature of his work after an unchangeable pattern, must necessarily be made fair and perfect; but when he looks to the created only, and uses a created pattern, it is not fair or perfect. Was the heaven then or the world, whether called by this or by any other more appropriate name-assuming the name, I am asking a question which has to be asked at the beginning of an enquiry*

---

88 Aristotle, *Metaphysics*, Bk. 12: Ch. 7, 25.

about anything-was the world, I say, always in existence and without beginning? or created, and had it a beginning? Created, I reply, being visible and tangible and having a body, and therefore sensible; and all sensible things are apprehended by opinion and sense and are in a process of creation and created. Now that which is created must, as we affirm, of necessity be created by a cause. But the father and maker of all this universe is past finding out; and even if we found him, to tell of him to all men would be impossible. And there is still a question to be asked about him: Which of the patterns had the artificer in view when he made the world-the pattern of the unchangeable, or of that which is created? If the world be indeed fair and the artificer good, it is manifest that he must have looked to that which is eternal; but if what cannot be said without blasphemy is true, then to the created pattern. Every one will see that he must have looked to, the eternal; for the world is the fairest of creations and he is the best of causes. And having been created in this way, the world has been framed in the likeness of that which is apprehended by reason and mind and is unchangeable, and must therefore of necessity, if this is admitted, be a copy of something. Now it is all-important that the beginning of everything should be according to nature. And in speaking of the copy and the original we may assume that words are akin to the matter which they describe; when they relate to the lasting and permanent and intelligible, they ought to be lasting and unalterable, and, as far as their nature allows, irrefutable and immovable-nothing less. But when they express only the copy or likeness and not the eternal things themselves, they need only be likely and analogous to the real words. As being is to becoming, so is truth to belief. If then, Socrates, amid the many opinions about the gods and the generation of the universe, we are not able to give notions which are altogether and in every respect exact and consistent with one another, do not be surprised. Enough, if we adduce probabilities as likely as any others; for we must remember that I who

186

am the speaker, and you who are the judges, are only mortal men, and we ought to accept the tale which is probable and enquire no further.

Socrates *Excellent, Timaeus; and we will do precisely as you bid us. The prelude is charming, and is already accepted by us-may we beg of you to proceed to the strain?*

Timaeus *Let me tell you then why the creator made this world of generation. He was good, and the good can never have any jealousy of anything. And being free from jealousy, he desired that all things should be as like himself as they could be. This is in the truest sense the origin of creation and of the world, as we shall do well in believing on the testimony of wise men: God desired that all things should be good and nothing bad, so far as this was attainable. Wherefore also finding the whole visible sphere not at rest, but moving in an irregular and disorderly fashion, out of disorder he brought order, considering that this was in every way better than the other. Now the deeds of the best could never be or have been other than the fairest; and the creator, reflecting on the things which are by nature visible, found that no unintelligent creature taken as a whole was fairer than the intelligent taken as a whole; and that intelligence could not be present in anything which was devoid of soul. For which reason, when he was framing the universe, he put intelligence in soul, and soul in body, that he might be the creator of a work which was by nature fairest and best. Wherefore, using the language of probability, we may say that the world became a living creature truly endowed with soul and intelligence by the providence of God.*[89]

Plato considered God to be a transcendent being, rational, powerful, purposeful and intentional. God was the creative cause that brought the cosmos into existence, designed with a specific purpose in mind. It is important to

---

[89] Plato, *Timaeus*, 29c-30a.

understand that neither Plato nor Aristotle were influenced in any way by ancient Hebrew thinking about a transcendent creative God who had a specific purpose in mind. Plato and Aristotle arrived at their conceptions of God based on a rigorous process of rational reflection about reality, drawing inferences about God and his nature based on *a priori* and *a posteriori* processes, that is, upon rational reflection alone and upon rational reflection on their experiences of the physical world. When they did that, they concluded that God existed as an eternally-existing, thinking, creative being, completely good with a specific plan in mind for the world he created.

It is interesting that Plato very specifically identifies God's creative purpose or intention as *becoming*. In his view, God wanted his creation to become like him. Since he understood God as a rational being (evidenced by his purposefulness, his intentionality), it makes since to understand the becoming especially as it relates to humans, who are also rational beings. Could Plato be saying that God's purpose was (is) to create a context for human development so that humans can become like God? That seems to be, at least in part, what Plato was suggesting.

What does this have to do with God as an immaterial mind? Plato and Aristotle understood God to be different from the physical world he created. God was not a physical being, but an immaterial mind, a thinking being. And this is the argument I have made in Chapter 6 in my cosmological argument. That which always existed and which is responsible for all else that exists is not matter but mind, a substance whose essence is to think, to be rational.

Is God Like Us Or Are We Like God

Humans have a self-central focus. We tend to think of everything else as it relates to us. When I see someone who looks a little like me I think to myself, *he looks like me*. I do not think, *I look like him*. It is he who looks like me, not the other way around. Why? Because we are at the center of our gaze. Everything exists in relation to us. We do not exist in relation to everything else. A self-central focus puts us at the center of everything and causes us to interpret everything from that point of view. Even God does not escape this self-central perspective. Humans tend to think of God as being like them. This was Xenophanes' complaint. God ends up being anthropomorphized (conceived of in human terms) because we have a self-central focus.

Yet if God existed before we did, if God is infinite and we are finite, if God is the creator (regardless of what creative process he used) and we are the created, then it cannot be that God is like us. If there is any similarity between God and humans, it is we who are like God not God who is like us.

Logical Inferences About God's Nature[90]

The best place to begin drawing inferences about God's nature is with the cosmological argument. The cosmological argument I presented began with two possibilities for that which always existed: matter or mind. I argued that it is mind that has always existed and that that mind is responsible for everything else that exists. Since we know that the material cosmos (matter) came into existence approximately 13.8 billion years ago, it does not appear that matter always existed. Mind, therefore, must have always existed. Why? Because something cannot come from nothing. Something exists now, so something has always existed. It was not the matter that comprises the cosmos, for we know the cosmos began to exist. It also seems apparent, based on

---

[90] The material in this section is borrowed from Rogers, *Proof of God?*

189

empirical observation and rational reflection, that non-conscious matter could not have produced a conscious mind. That which is conscious can produce that which is not conscious (for example, when a fifth grader builds a birdhouse for a school project that which is conscious has produced that which is not conscious), but never has anyone seen, nor is there reason to believe, that that which is non-conscious can produce that which is conscious.[91]

What we can justifiably infer from this is that a thinking substance has always existed. Since something other than that eternally-existing, thinking substance exists now, it appears that we can also justifiably conclude that that eternally-existing mind is responsible for it. In other words, God created the universe. Although this is traditional theological language regarding God, it should not be assumed that I am advocating traditional theological perspectives regarding God. I simply find the language convenient. For instance, I refer to God as a *he* though I am aware that the eternally-existing mind is not a sexual being. The language, however, is familiar and comfortable. So we refer to God as a he and say that he created the universe. But one should not assume that traditional theological paradigms are at work here.

Based on the cosmological argument we can say:

1. that God has always existed

2. that God created the cosmos

From these two basic inferences, we can draw additional inferences regarding God.

3. If God is eternally-existing, he existed before space and time, for space and time exist because the cosmos exists.

---

[91] The suggestion that that which is non-conscious (matter) can produce that which is conscious (mind) is simply a desperate attempt on the part of materialists to avoid the obvious reality.

4. If God existed before space and time, which exist because of his creative activity, then God exists separate from space and time, outside those aspects of the material cosmos. God, therefore, is not affected by space and time the way beings and objects inside the space-time continuum are affected.

5. Though existing separate from and not impacted by the space-time continuum, God, having created the cosmos, can certainly interact with it, impacting it, manipulating it as any creator can interact with and impact what he has created.

6. Since God is not a material substance, but a mental substance, existing before any material substance existed, God is not extended, that is, is not embodied and does not have a form.

7. If God is not extended, he is not located in space, he does not exist in any one location or particular place. If he exists but is not located in space, then he simply exists, not here or there, but everywhere.

8. God, then (a non-extended thinking substance), may be described as *omnipresent*, that is, existing in all places simultaneously, inside and outside the time-space continuum. There isn't any place God isn't.

9. If God created all other things that exist, material things (matter) and non-material things (other minds) that exist within the time-space continuum, then he possesses *every power that it is logically possible to possess*, for otherwise how could he have created all other things?[92]

---

[92] While some would question this conclusion, I would respond by arguing that the concept of God (as argued in ontological arguments) must include omnipotence. Otherwise, God is merely a more powerful being than humans are. But the concept of an eternally-existing mind that is responsible for all else that exists simply must include the idea of omnipotence as surely as it includes the idea of

10. If God possesses every power that it is logically possible to possess then God can be described as *omnipotent*, that is, all-powerful, which can only mean able to do anything that can be done.

Some philosophers have scoffed at the idea of omnipotence, suggesting that the idea is non-sensical. To demonstrate their point they ask "can an omnipotent being create a rock so big that he can't lift it?" The problem here is that the question is rooted in a basic misunderstanding of the meaning of omnipotence. The term *all-powerful* is often used as a synonym for omnipotence and is thought to refer to being able to do anything. If one can do anything, he ought to be able to make a rock so big that he can't lift it. Of course if he can't lift it then he isn't all-powerful. And if he can lift it, then he couldn't make a rock so big that he couldn't lift it, which again means that he isn't all-powerful. So either way, whether he can't make a rock so big that he can't lift it or whether he can, he is not all-powerful. The problem is that the riddle involves a logical contradiction, which automatically invalidates it. All the riddle points out is that it is possible to conceive of a logical contradiction. It does not prove that omnipotence is a non-sensical concept. Omnipotence does not mean all-powerful in the sense of being able to do anything. Omnipotence refers to the power to do anything that can logically be done. Some things cannot be done. It is not possible, for instance, to make a round square, or a square triangle or a triangular circle. It is not possible to make a married bachelor. Omnipotence is not the power to do the impossible; it is the power to do anything that can be done. God, then, as the creator of the cosmos, can

---

omniscience. Otherwise we do not have "God" we have simply a superbeing.

be described as *omnipotent*, that is, as *possessing every power that it is logically possible to possess.*[93]

11. If God is the eternally-existing thinking substance who created all other things, including other thinking substances, then we can also reasonably infer that God knows that which can be known, that is, that he is *omniscient*.

In brief summation then, we can say, based on the cosmological argument I presented, that God is omnipresent, omnipotent, and omniscient. What else may we reasonable infer regarding his nature?

12. We may logically infer that God is *self-determined*. God, as the eternally-existing mind that created everything that exists, could not be anything less (or other) than self-determined, for nothing other than God existed that could have impacted him in any way to make him anything less than self-determined. God did and does whatever he wants. He is absolutely free to choose. His creative activity was by choice.

13. It may also be reasonably inferred that the eternally-existing mind that created the cosmos is a *rational mind*, since the cosmos created by that mind is a rational place that is home to other rational minds. An irrational mind could not have created a rational cosmos.

14. It may also be inferred that since God created the cosmos he is *creative*.

15. Based on the teleological argument, we may also reasonably infer that God is *intentional and purposeful* (which are functions of rationality). God had a specific purpose or goal in mind when he created the cosmos.

---

[93] Anthony Kenny, in *The God of the Philosophers*, 96, coined this phraseology to deal with this specific issue.

16. We may also infer that comprehending the eternally-existing infinite mind in any complete sense is beyond the abilities of finite minds.

What we may logically infer about God, then, is that he is: omnipresent, omnipotent, omniscient, self-determined, rational, creative, purposeful and intentional, infinite and therefore beyond our ability to fully comprehend.

These eight attributes represent only shallow insights into the nature of God, the child-like efforts of the finite trying to comprehend the infinite. They are *a posteriori* in nature because they are inferences based on cosmological and teleological arguments. Are they valid inferences? The inferences are valid: 1) if the arguments they are drawn from are valid, and 2) if the inference follows logically from the point it is rooted in. Take point 14 as an example: *It may also be inferred that since God created the cosmos he is creative.* God created, therefore, God is creative. The inference that God is creative grows out of the idea that God created the cosmos. That is a valid inference—if, in fact, God created the cosmos. Thus, point one above: if the argument the inference is based on is valid the inference can also be valid. Then, point two, does the inference flow from the point it is rooted in—in this case, God's creative activity? So, we can ask again, are the eight inferences valid? The reader will have to review the points and make up his or her own mind. I believe they are valid inferences.

Summary

If God exists, what is God like? We have some rather severe limitations related to that question. If God is the eternally-existing mind that is responsible for all else that exists, he is infinite. Since we are part of all that he created, we are finite. Can the finite ever hope to fully comprehend the infinite? Can the created fully understand the creator?

Probably not. But does acknowledging that mean that we cannot understand anything about God? No. We can understand some things about God. How? By using an abductive process of logical inferences. We can analyze the available evidence, clues left by God, that will allow us to draw inferences and reach some tentative conclusions about God.

One of the challenges of the process, however, is that thinking and talking about God using human language involves some inherent limitations that must be recognized and acknowledged. Human language is an arbitrary system of symbols used for thinking and communicating. Because humans invented and developed it, it is limited to the capacities of the finite human mind. Thus, thinking about and talking about those things that transcend the finite world is challenging. Human conceptions and communication about God will never be truly accurate because we do not possess language skills that allow us to accurately conceive of God.

Understanding the inherent limitations, when we begin to draw inferences about God, we see that God is omnipresent, omnipotent, omniscient, self-determined, rational, creative, purposeful and intentional, infinite and therefore beyond our ability to fully comprehend.

Thought and Discussion Questions

1. Discuss how and why human language is unable to facilitate complete or fully accurate insights about God. Provide examples.
2. Discuss the idea of God being self-determined. What are the implications?
3. Discuss the meaning of omnipotent—that it is not that God can do anything, but that God can do anything that can be done. What are the implications of this?

4. Discuss the idea of God being omnipresent. What are the implications of this?

5. Based on the cosmological, teleological, ontological and moral arguments, can you draw additional inferences about the nature of God? Explain.

Chapter 8
Why Is There Evil In The World?

In the Fall of 2012, Hurricane Sandy blew through the Northeastern United States killing 125 people, destroying more than 72,000 homes and businesses (in New Jersey alone) and doing a total of more than $62 billion in damage.[94] A few years earlier, Hurricane Katrina did even more damage to the Gulf region. There are earthquakes and tsunamis, fires and mudslides, floods, blizzards, tornadoes, pandemics, droughts and famines, volcanic eruptions, and diseases that maim, disable, disfigure, and kill. Why?

Every year there are 3.3 million reports of child abuse involving 6 million children. Five children die each day in the United States due to child abuse.[95] In December of 2012, a twenty-year-old man went into the Sandy Hook Elementary

---

[94] Huffington Post, Superstorm Sandy Deaths, Damage and the Magnitude.
[95] Childhelp: National child Abuse Statistics.

School and killed twenty young students (kindergartners and first-graders) and six adults.[96]

Beginning on April 6, 1994, Hutus began slaughtering the Tutsis in the African country of Rwanda. As the brutal killings continued, the world stood idly by and just watched the slaughter. Lasting 100 days, the Rwanda genocide left approximately 800,000 Tutsis and Hutu sympathizers dead.[97]

Husbands abuse wives, wives abuse husbands, parents abuse children, adult children abuse aging parents, children bully other children, humans abuse animals. People lie, cheat, steal, defraud, demoralize, molest and use other people to satisfy their own interests every day. Why?

People suffer. They suffer from all sorts of things for all sorts of reasons in all sorts of ways. Why? People are born and people die, and in between all sorts of bad stuff happens to an awful lot of them. Why? Why is there so much evil in the world, so much pain and suffering? That's part one of the question—why is there so much suffering in the world? Part two of the question complicates it considerably. If there is a God, who is supposed to be completely good and also omnipotent, who, presumably then, could rid the world of evil and suffering, why does he not do so? Or, to ask the question another way, why would God, if he exists and if he created the world, create one where evil was possible? Why wouldn't a good God create a good world? Philosophically, this is known as the problem of evil.

---

[96] CNN, *Sandy Hook shooting: What Happened?*
[97] Rosenberg, *Rwanda Genocide: A Short History of the Rwanda Genocide*

Natural And Moral Evil

When philosophers think about the "evil" people encounter in their world, they divide it into two basic categories: natural evil and moral evil. Natural evil has to do with natural events that result in animal and human suffering: a lightning strike that starts a fire that destroys forests or homes and perhaps kills animals and/or people. A fire started by a careless human (someone tossing a lit cigarette out of a moving car or truck) is not something that would be classified as a natural evil because the fire started by a careless human is not a natural event (not an act of nature) like a lightning strike. A tornado that destroys homes and perhaps kills people would be considered a natural evil. So would a hurricane, an earthquake, a flood (not caused by human stupidity), a volcanic eruption, a rogue wave in the ocean that capsizes a ship and other natural events that result in human and/or animal suffering. Natural evil is pain and suffering that comes as a result of natural events.

Moral evil is pain and suffering that occurs because of the choices humans make as they exercise their free will, choosing what they will or will not do.[98] Rape, molestation, bullying, stealing, murdering, defrauding, deceiving, brutalizing, terrorizing, traumatizing, dehumanizing, and many others are acts of moral evil, actions that self-determined humans engage in of their own free will.

The problem of evil makes extensive use of the words pain and suffering. Perhaps it is wise to think in more detail about different aspects of those words. Usually the words are used in the sense that pain is bad and suffering is bad; they are evil. Generally speaking it may be the case that pain and suffering are things we try to avoid. It may be the case that often they are described as "bad" because they are unpleasant.

---

[98] The subject of free will (self-determination) will be dealt with in detail in Chapter 10.

But are they evil? It does not take a great deal of reflection to see that pain is not always a bad thing (it may hurt, but it is not always bad, not always evil). The same is true for suffering. All suffering is not evil.

For instance, in March of 2011 (during spring break!), I suffered a heart attack. It hurt. There was pain involved. I had to undergo a triple bypass. It hurt. I suffered. Yet in retrospect the entire episode was not at all evil, but was a positive event. I had clogged arteries. The heart attack (that hurt) said, in effect, that there was a serious problem that needed immediate attention. I got the attention I needed and today I'm healthy and able to continue my teaching and writing. The pain of the heart attack turned out to be a good thing. That is not always the case, but in my case it was. So what is the point? While all pain may be unpleasant, not all pain is evil. While all suffering may be unpleasant, not all suffering is evil. Some pain and suffering generate good results and cannot, therefore, be described as evil. Unpleasant, yes. But evil? No. We need, therefore, to identify what kind of pain and suffering can rightly be identified as evil.

As the discussion has unfolded over the centuries, philosophers have tended to put pain and suffering into one of two categories: unjustified suffering and justified suffering. Unjustified suffering would be suffering that occurs without any *greater good* being realized. Justified suffering would be suffering that produces some good result, a good that, in the end, is greater than the pain required to produce it. The suffering I had to endure because of my triple bypass resulted in a greater good—my continued life and improved health. Therefore, that suffering was justified. The doctors who cut me open, operated, and then sewed me up again were not guilty of bad or evil behavior because what they did to me, in the end, resulted in something good and desirable. The pain they caused me was justified. When our sons were babies, we took them to the doctor to be vaccinated. The nurse poked

200

them with needles, causing them pain. They cried. But there was a greater good involved in the painful process—protecting them against dangerous diseases. The pain, therefore, that they suffered was justified and not evil. Surely, whether or not suffering results in a greater good is the determining factor in whether or not any specific case of suffering is justified. Suffering that results in a greater good cannot be evil because it produces a greater good. It may be unpleasant to endure, but the good it generates makes it worthwhile. This is a crucial concept in any serious discussion of the problem of evil.

When suffering involves no greater good, it can be considered evil. The question is, is there suffering that occurs in the world that does not generate a greater good of any kind and that cannot, therefore, be justified in any way? This, of course, is not an easy question to answer and not one likely to generate a consensus among philosophers. Still it is a crucial consideration in the problem of evil.

Yet another terminological concern in discussion of the problem of evil is the term omnipotent, often translated all-powerful. What, exactly, does the term omnipotent mean? If God is said to be omnipotent, does that mean he can do anything, as in anything at all, without any kind of restrictions or limitations? Some people say that that is what the term means, that God can do, quite literally, anything at all. There isn't anything God can't do. Yet many philosophers have pointed out (as I have already done in Chapter 7) that the idea of omnipotence must be limited to that which can actually be done. As an omnipotent being, God can do anything *that can be done*. But some things simply can't be done. Not even an omnipotent being can make a round square, or a circular triangle, or a married bachelor. Not even an omnipotent being can both exist and not exist at the same time. There are just some things that can't be done regardless of how much power one has. Some things are not subject to power. So when an argument about the presence of evil in the world makes reference to God being omnipotent, we must be aware of what, exactly, the word means and the inherent limitations associated with the concept.

Having discussed some of the terminological issues involved in discussing the problem of evil, let us now look at a couple of arguments that suggest that because evil exists in the world, God does not exist.

Mackie and Rowe on Evil[99]

J. L. Mackie (1917-1981) was an Australian philosopher who taught in New Zealand and England. His work on the atheistic side of the problem of evil is the most often quoted or referred to in contemporary philosophy. In considering what he calls the traditional problem of evil, Mackie says, "Here it can be shown, not that religious beliefs lack rational support, but that they are positively irrational."[100] Mackie goes on to explain:

> *The problem of evil, in the sense in which I shall be using the phrase, is a problem only for someone who believes that there is a God who is both omnipotent and wholly good. And it is a logical problem, the problem of clarifying and reconciling a number of beliefs...*
>
> *In its simplest form the problem is this: God is omnipotent; God is wholly good; and yet evil exists. There seems to be some contradiction between these three propositions, so that if any two of them were true the third would be false. But at the same time all*

---

[99] Borrowed from Rogers, *Proof of God?*
[100] Mackie, "Evil and Omnipotence," in *Mind Association*, Vol. 64, No. 254, (1955) pp. 200-212.

three are essential parts of most theological positions: the theologian, it seems, at once must adhere and cannot consistently adhere to all three.

While this represents the basics of the problem, Mackie realizes that additional propositions are needed to complete the argument and make the contradiction apparent. Thus, he continues:

However, the contradiction does not arise immediately; to show it we need some additional premises, or perhaps some quasi-logical rules connecting the terms "good," "evil," and "omnipotent." These additional principles are that good is opposed to evil, in such a way that a good thing always eliminates evil as far as it can, and that there are no limits to what an omnipotent thing can do. From these it follows that a good omnipotent thing eliminates evil completely, and then that propositions that a good thing exists, and that evil exists, are incompatible.[101]

To clarify, Mackie's argument can be set out in syllogistic form:

1. God [is said] to be omnipotent
2. God [is said] to be completely good (omnibenevolent)
3. There are no limits to what an omnipotent being can do
4. An omnipotent, omnibenevolent being eliminates evil as far as it can
5. Evil exists

---

[101] Mackie, "Evil and Omnipotence."

6. Therefore, an omnipotent, omnibenevolent being does not exist

Premises 1, 2, and 5 are true and valid premises that few people would disagree with. Premises 3 and 4, however, are problematic. Premise 3, there are no limits to what an omnipotent being can do, is simply wrong. It is an incorrect definition of omnipotence. Why? Because there are some things that are simply not subject to power. It does not matter how much power God has, not even God (an omnipotent being) can make a round square. That is simply not possible, not even for God. God cannot make a married bachelor; neither can he make a female brother. There are some things that by definition are simply not possible.[102] An omnipotent being cannot do that which is logically impossible, such as existing and not existing at the same time. For Mackie to suggest that there are no limits to what an omnipotent being can do is a mistake. Mackie knows, however, that this is one of two points that are crucial for his argument to be successful so he argues his case. But he is mistaken and argues in vain.

Premise 4, an omnipotent, omnibenevolent being eliminates evil as far as it can, is also mistaken. Whether or not an omnipotent, omnibenevolent being eliminates evil depends on that being's purpose and the greater good involved. Later in this chapter, I will argue that God has a purpose for humans that informed and guided the creative choices he made, resulting in the kind of a world we live in, and that the "evil" we experience is justified because of the greater good that can result by our encountering and coping with pain and suffering, our own and that of others. For the moment, however, we will have to be satisfied with my

---

[102] I was first introduced to this idea years ago in a book by Thomas Warren, *Have Atheists Proved There Is No God* (1972) in which he specifically addresses Mackie's arguments, 26-28.

assertion that Mackie is mistaken in his assertion that God would eliminate all evil if he could. Mackie has asserted this but has not argued his case. When I present my argument, rooted in the concepts of justified evil and the greater good, I will demonstrate that Mackie is mistaken in premise 4. I have, however, at this point demonstrated that Mackie is mistaken in his definition of omnipotence (premise 3), which makes his argument invalid and unsound. He has not presented a contradiction (because he has not made his case) and has not demonstrated that God does not exist.

William Rowe (born 1931) is Professor Emeritus of Philosophy at Purdue University. During his career, Rowe wrote several significant papers or books related to the philosophy of religion in general and specifically on the problem of evil. He is an authority on the subject.

Generally, Rowe agrees with Mackie's argument (the traditional argument) regarding the inconsistency involved in the existence of an omnipotent, omnibenevolent being and the existence of evil. He would agree with Mackie that the omnipotent being (who can do what he wants) would eliminate evil. Since evil exists, God cannot exist. The two concepts are simply incompatible for Rowe. The difference in the approach between Mackie and Rowe is that Rowe adds some material that Mackie does not. That additional material is what we will focus on.

Rowe acknowledges the possibility that some "evil" that might be experienced by humans (or animals) might be justified, depending on whether or not it is the cause of some greater good. What he argues is that there is some evil that is not justified because it does not lead to a greater good. It is, therefore, evil that God, if he existed, would eliminate. Since God does not eliminate it, God must not exist.

Rowe says:

Taking human and animal suffering as a clear instance of evil which occurs with great frequency in our world, the evidential form of the problem of evil can be stated in terms of the following argument for atheism.

1. There exist instances of intense suffering which an omnipotent, omniscient being could have prevented without thereby preventing the occurrence of any greater good.

2. An omniscient, wholly good being would prevent the occurrence of any intense suffering it could, unless it could not do so without thereby losing some greater good. Therefore,

3. There does not exist an omnipotent, omniscient, wholly good being.[103]

It is clear that Rowe's argument is a variation on Mackie's, with a subtle difference. Rowe believes that the slightly different way he presents the argument not only makes it valid and sound, but eliminates the theistic objection related to a possible greater good. What has he done to adjust the argument? He has: 1) acknowledged that a greater good can justify some evil, but 2) also argued that not all evil can be linked to a greater good. Therefore, he concludes that since unjustified evil exists, God does not.

To help his readers evaluate whether or not his premises are true and his argument sound, Rowe provides an example to be analyzed.

Suppose in some distant forest lightening strikes a dead tree, resulting in a forest fire. In the fire a fawn is trapped, horribly burned, and lies in terrible agony for several days before death relieves its suffering. So far as we can see, the fawn's intense suffering is pointless. Leading to no greater good. Could an

---

[103] Rowe, *Philosophy of Religion: An Introduction*, 99.

omnipotent, omniscient being have prevented the fawn's apparently pointless suffering? The answer is obvious, as even the theist will insist. An omnipotent, omniscient being could easily have prevented the fawn's intense suffering by quickly ending its life, rather than allowing the fawn to lie in terrible agony for several days. Since no greater good, so far as we can see, would have been lost had the fawn's intense suffering been prevented, doesn't it appear that premise 1 of the argument is true, that there do exist instances of intense suffering which an omnipotent, omniscient being could have prevented without thereby preventing the occurrence of any greater good?

Rowe asks what we can do with this example and acknowledges that we cannot *know* that there is no greater good that the fawn's suffering might accomplish. However, he argues, we have rational grounds for believing that the fawn's suffering is not connected to any greater good. His *rational grounds* are: since we can't see any greater good there isn't any. Therefore, he concludes, the fawn's suffering is pointless.

Rowe believes he has presented a sound argument that demonstrates that God does not exist. I believe Rowe has failed to make his case. There is no way of knowing or of having rational grounds for belief regarding premise 1. Therefore we cannot conclude that it is a valid premise. Premise 2 suffers from the similar weaknesses: first, we do not know what an omniscient, omnipotent, omnibenevolent being would do in relation to what we think of as suffering. For instance, things that a two year old thinks of as a horrible tragedy that results in deep suffering, a broken toy or not being able to go somewhere with an older sibling, we, as adults, might not consider a tragedy at all. Why would we assume that an omniscient, omnibenevolent being would

207

think as we do when it comes to what is and what is not horrible suffering? Second, the term *intense suffering* is a rather broad and therefore unclear term. How does intense suffering differ from regular suffering? What kind of suffering did my heart attack generate, intense or regular? Does Rowe's argument apply only where the suffering is intense and not regular? Third, he has not defined any *greater good* that might justify any *intense suffering*. Speaking in vague generalities is no way to make an argument.

Further, Rowe has committed an argumentative fallacy known as the *Argumentum Ad Misericordiam*, the appeal to pity. By using a beautiful, harmless young fawn (Bambie), who suffers horribly and pointlessly, he hopes to gain sympathy for his argument.

The biggest flaw, however, in Rowe's argument is that he assumes that if humans can't make sense of a thing, then it is senseless. If we can't see the justification we are looking for, then justification doesn't exist. It is a very arrogant point of view. Also, Rowe and others who argue from the atheistic perspective fail to provide an acceptable definition of what a greater good might be. How do we know whether or not there is a greater good being accomplished if we haven't defined what a greater good might be? Later in this chapter, when I present my theodicy (my explanation of God's justification for allowing pain and suffering), I will provide an explanation of the greater good I believe God has in mind.

A Teleological World

As noted already in Chapter 6, the English word *teleological* is rooted in the Greek word *telos*, which has to do with completion, maturity, reaching an end or goal. A piece of ripe fruit can be described as telos because it has achieved its purpose, it has ripened so it can be eaten and enjoyed. Because the idea of telos involves a goal or purpose, it also necessarily involves the idea of intention and design. A goal or a purpose is the product of intentional design, which can only exist where rationality exists. If, for instance, an apple ripening so it can be eaten and enjoyed is merely a happy coincidence, a purpose has not been achieved, a goal has not been reached. Instead, a happy accident has occurred. So here is the question: are apples ripening so they can be eaten and enjoyed, along with strawberries, bananas, peaches, watermelons, tomatoes, carrots, potatoes, onions, cucumbers, and all the other fruits and vegetables, happy accidents that we get to enjoy, or are they part of a larger system that was intentionally designed and produced to accomplish some goal or purpose? Is the world teleological, or is it coincidental? Was it designed with a specific purpose in mind, or did it just happen to come together in this manner, the product of random chance?

Teleological arguments, like those discussed in Chapter 6, are designed to argue and demonstrate that the world (the entire cosmos, which includes the planet earth) is not the result of blind random chance but is the product of intentional design. That is, it was conceived, designed, and implemented with a purpose in mind. There is a goal to be achieved. Whether or not teleological arguments demonstrate this is up to each person to consider and conclude. I believe they do. It is apparent to me that the world is teleological in nature. It has a purpose.

What purpose could the world have? How would one go about discovering such a purpose? Discovering the world's purpose would require the use of rational reflection, specifically abductive reasoning—reaching the best conclusion possible based on the available evidence. What evidence? The rationalistic evidence of cosmological arguments, for instance, and the physical evidence of teleological arguments. I have argued, for instance, that the eternally-existing mind created not only the material cosmos but also other minds, other conscious, rational, moral minds. He created them in or as part of the material cosmos he created. Why would he have done that? So those new minds might learn to develop their mental capacities, becoming fully developed or mature, rational, moral beings. Why put an immaterial mind into a material environment and into a physical body? Perhaps those new (baby) minds can best learn some of the lessons they must learn and develop the skills they need to develop in a material context. For instance, we put babies into cribs and playpens, confined areas from which they cannot escape and hurt themselves. Only when they are developed enough to go exploring do we allow them to go roaming around in a large, more complex environment. Perhaps the cosmos is our crib or playpen, a context area where we can develop until we are ready for a more complex environment.

A number of scientists have identified the world as *anthropic* in nature, that is, the world is life friendly. It is a place where complex human life can develop and thrive. The idea is intriguing. Out of all the possible ways the world could be, it is this way—anthropic, the perfect place for complex life to develop and thrive. Did that happen by mere chance? A growing number of scientists and philosophers believe that blind, random chance cannot account for the extreme complexity necessary for the development (and thriving) of complex life on planet Earth. Instead of random chance, intelligent design appears to be a better explanation for how the planet Earth came to be the way it is—anthropic in nature.

My point here is not to develop an argument for the teleological nature of the world (a brief teleological argument was offered in Chapter 6) but to explain the possibility and the process (abductive reasoning) for discovering whether or not the world is teleological in nature.

Many philosophers believe the cosmos is teleological

in nature. Plato was one who did. In his dialog, *Timaeus*, he wrote: (at this point in the dialog Timaeus is speaking)

> *... Now why did he who framed this whole universe of becoming frame it? Let us state the reason why: He was good, and one who is good can never become jealous of anything. And so, being free of jealousy, he wanted everything to become as much like himself as was possible. In fact, men of wisdom will tell you (and you couldn't do better than to accept their claim) that this, more than anything else, was the most preeminent reason for the origin of the world's coming to be.*[104]

For Plato, God had a goal in mind, a purpose, something he wanted to accomplish. Specifically, he wanted what he created to become like him—good. Personally, I would approach it somewhat differently. I would suggest that God created humans (other rational minds) so they could learn, grow and mature, achieving their potential as rational minds. To do so, they would need an environment that would allow for such intellectual and emotional growth and development. He created the cosmos as that environment. The cosmos, therefore, is teleological in nature because it was designed and created with a specific purpose in mind.

The Best Of All Possible Worlds

A philosopher who thought a great deal about the problem of evil was Gottfried Wilhelm Leibniz (1646-1716). His interest in the problem of evil is illustrated in the fact that the only book-length treatises he wrote, one at age 26

---

[104] Plato, *Timaeus*, 29 e.

(*Philosopher's Confessions*) and the other at 63 (*Theodicy*), were both dedicated to the topic.

In the 17th century, a group known as the Socinians advocated that the existence of God and of evil were not incompatible realities. There was evil in the world God created. They did, however, believe there was a problem if God created the world as he did *knowing* that there would be evil in it. They claimed, therefore, that God was not omniscient, that he did not know that the world would be filled with evil.[105] One of the problems Leibniz wanted to address was this one regarding God's creative decisions: did God create the world as he did knowing there would be evil in it? And if he did, what possible justification could there have been for doing so?

Since Leibniz wrote two books on the broad topic of the problem of evil, it is not possible that we go into detail regarding his arguments. There is, however, a nice summary of his position on the subject in his work entitled, *Monadology*. He says:

> Now as there is an infinite number of possible universes in the ideas of God, and as only one can exist, there must be a sufficient reason for God's choice, determining him to one rather than to another.
>
> And this reason can only be found in the fitness, or in the degrees of perfection, which these worlds contain, each possible world having the right to claim existence in proportion to the perfection which it involves.
>
> And it is this which causes the existence of the best, which God knows through his wisdom, chooses

---

[105] Murray, "Leibniz on the Problem of Evil," in *Stanford Encyclopedia of Philosophy*.

through his goodness, and produces through his power.[106]

What Leibniz is saying here is that God, in his wisdom, knew what the world would need to be like to accomplish the purposes he had in mind. Knowing what he wanted the world to accomplish, God, out of all the possible worlds he could have created, intentionally chose to create this one this way because it is the one that has just what it needs to accomplish his purposes. The world is as it is not by accident or because God had no clue as to what was going to happen, but because God, knowing how the world needed to be, made it so.

Leibniz's argument became known as *the best of all possible worlds* argument. While it generated thoughtful consideration in some, it generated outrage in others. One of the outraged was the French playwright, Voltaire. In a scathing response entitled *Candide*, Voltaire ridiculed the idea that the world as it is, with all the pain and suffering that goes on, could be considered the best of all possible worlds. The problem with Voltaire's response is that it is simply ridicule. There is no serious response in it, no arguments, no philosophy. The reason for that, of course, is simple: Voltaire was not a philosopher and not capable of a serious philosophical response, especially to a genius like Leibniz. Voltaire probably fancied himself a philosopher but produced nothing worthy of the designation, philosophy.

From a theistic point of view Leibniz's argument has merit. Aristotle viewed the world from a teleological perspective, believing the world had a purpose. Lots of thinkers between Aristotle and Leibniz viewed the world in the same way, as having a purpose or a goal toward which it was moving, or being designed with a specific purpose in mind. Leibniz was simply saying that, given God's purpose, he created the world in a specific way, including the things or

---

[106] Leibniz, *Monadology* 53-55.

features he knew it would need to have for his purpose to be achieved. The concept is logical and not difficult to grasp. The challenge comes in trying to understand how pain and suffering can be necessary for God's purpose to be achieved. In the next section, I will attempt to provide a rational explanation.[107]

Justified Evil

When atheists like Mackie and Rowe bring up the problem of evil, they do so in an affirmative manner, claiming that the presence of evil in the world demonstrates (proves) that God does not exist because if God existed evil would not exist. Evil and God, in their view, are mutually exclusive. If God existed, there would be no evil in the world. Since evil exists, God does not. They are not simply asking for an explanation (how does one account for the presence of evil in God's world); they are making an affirmative argument claiming that they can prove that God does not exist. They are obliged, therefore, to make their case, to present an argument that proves that God does not exist. Their case stands or falls on the idea that there is a contradiction between the idea of an omnipotent, omnibenevolent God and evil. They must prove the contradiction exists in order to make their case. If, however, it can be demonstrated that no such contradiction exists, that it is logically possible for an omnipotent, omnibenevolent God and evil to coexist, then atheists fail to make their case, fail to demonstrate that God does not exist. The point, then, of a theodicy is to demonstrate that there is no contradiction between the existence of God (as an omnipotent, omniscient, omnibenevolent being) and the existence of evil.

---

[107] This material on Leibniz was borrowed from Rogers, *Proof of God?*

214

One of the ideas that Leibniz included in his theodicy was the Principle of Sufficient Reason (PSR). Leibniz did not invent the idea. It has been around since the days of Aristotle, implicitly underlying his four causes. It is the idea that every *effect* must have a sufficient reason, a cause sufficient to generate that effect. Things don't just happen. There is always a cause. The world had a cause (a reason sufficient to bring it about), and the world being just as it is also had a sufficient reason. What could God's reason have been for creating the world as he did?

The title of this section is *Justified Evil*. How can the presence of evil in the world possibly be justified? It depends on what you mean by evil and what larger purpose might be involved. Might it lead to some greater good? What does God want to achieve for humankind? What does he want to achieve for each individual person? Whatever it is, does suffering play some vital role in whether or not that thing is achieved? Does suffering lead to some greater good in God's *teleotic* scheme for humankind? I believe it does. But for the reason to make sense, it is best to begin at the beginning and walk through the argument step by step.

> 1. If God is the cause of the cosmos, he is also the cause of the cosmos being (generally speaking) the way it is. If evil is present in the cosmos, either: 1) God caused or causes it, in which case he is directly responsible for the presence of evil in it, or 2) God allowed or allows it, in which case he is indirectly responsible for the evil present in it.
> 2. As the eternally-existing mind, God is rational, self-determined and moral (as well as omnipotent, omniscient, omnibenevolent and so forth). As such, God makes rational, intentional choices. If God is the source of all else that exists, nothing else (no thing and no other being) existed before he created it. Who or what, then, could have compelled God to create the

215

world in a given way? There was no one or no thing that could have compelled God. God chose to create the world as he did.

3. Part of his creative choice was to create other minds who were also rational, self-determined, and moral—people who make choices. Because people are self-aware and rational, they are also self-determined. You cannot have a self-aware, rational being who is not self-determined.[108]

4. This being the case, we must consider that it is humans who make choices that often result in suffering for themselves or others. Human free-will becomes an important factor in determining, at least in part, who is and who is not responsible for much of the evil in the world.

> 4a. Those who work out of a materialist paradigm often embrace some kind or level of determinism—that humans do not have free will but are mechanistically determined. Those who work out of a dualistic paradigm typically (though not always) embrace free-will.[109] Space does not permit a discussion of the differences between being mechanistically determined or being self-determined. I believe that humans are self-determined (and have explained why in a previous section) and will proceed on that basis.

---

[108] Please remember that earlier we defined rationality in such a way that it is more than merely thinking. Animals think and are aware of themselves. But they are not aware that they are aware and are not rational in the sense of making moral choices. They do not engage in high-level abstract thinking, contemplating concepts such as justice, goodness, and so forth. Only humans do this. Like God, we are rational, self-aware and, therefore, self-determined.

[109] I am not suggesting that all materialists are determinists and all dualists embrace free will. That may not the case. I am speaking in broad general terms.

4b. When people make choices of their own free will that result in pain and suffering for themselves or others, is God who created them as self-determined beings, responsible for the choices they make? I suggest that he is not. Part of being self-aware, rational, and self-determined is being responsible for the choices one makes. And if one is free to make a choice, one must: 1) have options to choose from, and 2) actually be free to choose from among the options he has.

4c. Mackie and Rowe both suggest that it would be possible for God to create people who were free to choose but who would always choose good and never evil. If he wanted to, they argue, God could have, in this way, eliminated much of the evil in the world evil.[110] The problem is that the suggestion involves a logical impossibility. A being that is created as a self-determined being but who can only choose good is not really self-determined, not really free to choose. Advocates of this position would likely say that the individual *can* choose evil but *will not* choose evil. Why not? What is it that God would have to withhold or put into a self-determined being so that that being *can but will not* ever choose evil instead of good? However, the only being that is self-determined but never chooses evil is God himself. Mackie and Rowe have suggested, whether they realize it or not, that God create other Gods equal to himself. Yet this is a logical impossibility because God is (among many other things) infinite and omniscient. When he creates

---

[110] Mackie, *Evil and Omnipotence,* 209, and Rowe, *Philosophy of Religion,* 97-98.

217

another mind, it cannot be equal to him.[111] It has not always existed. And without being infinite, the created mind cannot be omniscient. If a mind is not omniscient, it cannot always choose good and never evil, for some forms of evil can only be recognized by omniscience. A non-omniscient mind will, at least some of the time, choose evil by mistake because it does not recognize evil for what it is. What Mackie and Rowe have suggested is simply not possible. Therefore, since God cannot recreate (replicate) himself, his only other option would be for him to create a self-determined person who will only choose good and never evil. To do that, God would have to add or delete something that eliminates absolute freedom of choice, which would result in a being that is not self-determined.

4d. If God is omniscient, he knew before creating humans that if he created humans as self-determined beings, they would do evil and people would suffer. He is, therefore, responsible, at least indirectly, for the moral evil done freely by humans. It is certainly the case that God knew humans would sometimes cause pain and suffering. However, the most that God can be held responsible for is creating *the potential for evil* by creating self-aware, rational, and therefore, self-determined beings. He could not have created beings that were self-aware and rational who were not self-determined. Self-awareness and rationality add up to or result in self-

---

[111] One of the things that God cannot do, because it is logically impossible, is to create another being identical to himself, which is what a being would have to be to be omniscient. God cannot "create" an eternally-existing being that has the character traits of God, for if it did have those traits it would be God. God cannot create himself.

determination. God could have created some other kind of creatures (like chimpanzees or orangutans or human-looking automatons who were not free to make moral choices), but he chose to create minds that are self-aware and rational and therefore self-determined. In doing so, he created the potential for evil, but not evil itself.

4e. Why would God do that? Why create beings that could make choices that would result in pain and suffering for themselves and for others? At this point one can only surmise.[112] But if humans are very much like God (not identical, which is impossible, but very much like him), then humans have amazing potential. If humans are God's offspring, how much like God can humans become? If humans are infant minds that need to grow, learn and mature, achieving their potential as thinking substances (who one day may not need to be embodied to interact with other minds and with an environment), we must be free to make choices and learn from the mistakes we make. In making mistakes (even if we or others suffer because of them) there are lessons to be learned, character formation occurs. The learning of those lessons and the forming of character traits, which allow us to move along a growth trajectory (as individuals and as a species), is

---

[112] In other words, I am not claiming to know this or to be able to definitively argue this and subsequent points. My aim is to demonstrate that Mackie and Rowe are incorrect and that there is no contradiction between the propositions, *an omnipotent, omnibenevolent being exists,* and, *evil exists*; I do not need to prove anything. I just need to demonstrate that the two propositions are not contradictory. It is not illogical or contradictory that both God and evil exist. In demonstrating that, I demonstrate that Mackie and Rowe's arguments are invalid.

ultimately a good thing, part of the greater good God wants to accomplish.

4f. What kind of lessons are learned from pain and suffering? When we suffer, we learn what it feels like. When we see others suffering, we can develop character traits such as compassion, sympathy, empathy, and so forth. And we can learn to love, that is, to try to relieve pain and suffering. The highest form of love is a love that acts, that responds to need, that does what can be done, that finds a way to make a difference. Becoming people of compassion, sympathy, empathy, and love (among other things) are lessons that cannot be learned, traits that cannot be developed, without the presence of pain and suffering.

4g. Could not an omniscient God come up with some other way for humans to learn those kinds of things? Perhaps. But one thing we know about ourselves is that *the lessons we learn best are those we learn ourselves based on our own experience*. Perhaps God knows this about us, and perhaps learning these basic lessons or developing these crucial character traits is so important that the best way for the learning and development to occur is by experience. If that is the case and if God has our best interests at heart, he allows us to experience pain and suffering because as unpleasant as it is, ultimately it results in a greater good.

4h. Does the idea of "learning important lessons" or "developing crucial character traits" really provide adequate justification for the levels of pain and suffering we see in the world? From a materialistic perspective where biological life is all there is and death is the end of existence, probably not. But when one sees physical life only as one small, temporary aspect of a life that will never end, a life where learning, growth and achieving one's potential is the goal, then pain and suffering for a relatively brief time that lends itself to a greater good is justified.[113]

4i. How can pain and suffering be justified for innocent children? The same way it is justified for anyone else who is "innocent". The age of the innocent person (innocent meaning that the person did not bring the suffering on him or herself or do anything to deserve what is happening) is irrelevant.

5. While God may not be responsible for moral evil (because moral evil is the result of human self-determination), God created the cosmos in such a way that natural disasters cause a great deal of pain and suffering. God, therefore, is directly responsible for the evil that is referred to as natural evil. Can there be any justification for that?

5a. Yes. If greater good results from natural evil, then natural evil is justified.

5b. What greater good can result from natural evil? Just as moral evil can result in the learning of important lessons and the development of important character traits such as compassion, sympathy, empathy, love and so forth, natural evil can produce those same results as well as additional traits such as determination and ingenuity.

---

[113] If the physical stage of life is all there is to life (as materialists assume), then suffering during this life would be tragic. But since life is enduring, and since this stage of life is very brief, the *"tragedy"* of suffering can be viewed from a different perspective—it hurts, but the hurt is temporary and produces a greater good.

5c. God created a world where the environment is such that "natural disasters" may occur. Those events provide opportunities for analysis, critical and creative thinking, experiment and discovery (in addition to the traits enumerated above), all of which are crucial for development of humans as individuals and as a species.

6. The value of those lessons learned and traits developed provide justification for moral and natural evil because they produce a greater good in relation to God's teleotic scheme for humankind.[114]

Is my argument convincing? That is for you to decide. But I believe I have demonstrated that no contradiction exists between the propositions, *a good all-powerful God exists*, and *evil exists*. If no contradiction exists between those two propositions, then atheists have not proven, by utilizing the problem of evil, that God does not exist.

Summary

Bad things happen in the world. People suffer. If there is a God, who is supposed to be completely good and also omnipotent, who, presumably then, could rid the world of evil and suffering, why does he not do so? Or, to ask the question another way, why would God, if he exists and if he created the world, create one where evil was possible? Why wouldn't a good God create a good world? Philosophically, this is known as the problem of evil. It is an important question that philosophers and theologians have wrestled with for several thousand years.

Atheists argue that there is a contradiction between the propositions *a good, all-powerful God exists* and *evil*

---

[114] Borrowed from Rogers, *Proof of God?*

exists. Essentially they argue as follows: If a good, all-powerful God existed, he would eliminate evil. But evil exists. Therefore a good, all-powerful God does not exist. There is no question that evil exists. The problem with the reasoning of the argument is in the claim that a good, all-powerful God would eliminate evil.

What appears to be evil to us may not appear to be evil to God. Quite often those things that appear to be evil to children do not appear to be evil to adults. And even if something is truly evil, there could be legitimate reasons why God allows it to occur. One of those reasons is that humans have free will. As self-determined people we choose how we will behave. Often we choose to behave in ways that cause pain and suffering. But not all suffering (evil) is the result of human free will. Some of it is natural evil. Why would God allow such evil? Why would he allow any evil? Because there may be a greater good associated with it. Perhaps in coping with evil, we learn something important, something so important that it justifies the suffering that helps us learn the lesson. It has been argued that God is justified in allowing suffering to exist because of the greater good that comes from enduring it.

Thought and Discussion Questions

1. How serious is the problem of evil for you? Does it raise serious doubts for you as to the existence of God? Explain.
2. Explain the strengths and weaknesses of Mackie's argument as you see them.
3. Explain the strengths and weaknesses of Rowe's arguments as you see them.
4. Explain the strengths and weaknesses of Rogers' argument as you see them.
5. If there can be a greater good that justifies evil in the world, what do you think it is? Why?

Chapter 9
What Kind of Beings Are Humans?

What kind of beings are human beings? The fairly obvious answer is that we are physical beings. We exist in the space-time continuum as extended beings located in space with size, shape, weight and so forth. But is that all we are? Does our physical nature comprise the totality of our existence? Or is a human being something more than a physical body with a personal point of view? What it is to be human is a question philosophers have wrestled with for ages. What is it that constitutes humanness? One position is that the human being is just a physical organism. There is a body that is controlled by a brain and everything about being a human can be explained on the basis of the physical (electrical) operations going on between the brain and body. This position is generally referred to as *physicalism*.

Another position is that there is more to a human being than just the body and the brain that controls it. In addition to the brain, there is also an immaterial or non-physical mind that works in conjunction with the brain. It is the immaterial mind that does the thinking, the willing and deciding, using the brain to carry out the mind's (the person's) will. It is the immaterial mind that is the person. The body is the house the person lives in. This position is known as *dualism*.

In physicalism, the person is the physical unit, the body. In dualism, the person (the essence of the person, what the person really is) is the mind that interacts with its body.

The two positions are radically different, each with staggering implications. Is there evidence that might provide clues as to which position, physicalism or dualism, is correct?

Consciousness

One of the most obvious features of humanness that suggests that there is more to the human than simply the physical interactions of body and brain is consciousness. Moreland opens his discussion of consciousness with a quote from the 17th century philosopher, Leibniz. "It must be confessed, moreover, that perception and that which depends on it are inexplicable by mechanical causes."[115] Over three hundred years ago, Leibniz recognized the unique nature of consciousness and understood that attempts to explain it mechanistically were futile. Why? Because consciousness goes way beyond mere physical processes. In their comments on consciousness, Moreland and Craig note that, "It is virtually self-evident to most people that they are different from their bodies."[116] While there may be some who would argue that it is not at all self-evident that people are different from their bodies, many people (perhaps most) do share the

---

[115] Moreland, *Consciousness and the Existence of God*, 1.
[116] Moreland and Craig, *Philosophical Foundations for a Christian Worldview*, 228.

feeling that the real them, that which makes them who they are, their psyche and their will—that something that is distinctively and uniquely them—is something more than their physical body. There seems to be an interior us that though closely connected with the body somehow transcends the body. We are aware of our physical surroundings, of warm and cool temperatures, of dim or bright light, of being crowded or being isolated. We know whether or not we are hungry or thirsty, whether we are happy or sad, whether or not we are in pain. We are aware of all of these experiences. That's what consciousness is—awareness of having experiences. Some of our experiences are directly related to our physical nature: the feeling of warmth or coldness, a headache, seeing the color red when we look at a tomato or green when we look at a head of lettuce. Without a doubt, much of our consciousness has to do with our physical context and our physical bodies. We are physical beings living in a physical cosmos, so most of the experiences we are conscious of are associated with our physical nature and context.

But not all of our conscious experiences appear to be related to the physical world. Through our sensory apparatus we see things, smell things, hear things, taste things and feel things. Our five senses bring data from the physical world into our brain to be experienced and processed, categorized and stored. But then we also experience things that have nothing to do with sensory input, nothing to do with the data of the physical world that the brain receives and processes. We experience *conceptual reflection*, that is, we think about concepts such as justice. We experience *intentionality*, such as the intention of being a just person, a person who acts justly. We experience *the self* (the "I" or the "me"), that part of us that is uniquely us, most clearly in acts of the will. *I* will do this; *I* will not do that. We experience *mental content that is not in any way related to physical phenomena*, content that has nothing to do with sensory input. If everything is to

226

be explained in terms of physical processes, all mental content would have to be related to physical phenomena, because that is what the physical brain processes—sensory data. But all mental content is not related to sensory data. So something other than physical processes must be involved.[117]

Reflection on what consciousness is and what it entails reveals that there is more to the human being than just a body controlled by a brain. Humans are more than biological organisms. There is more to us than our physical bodies and physical processes. Physicalism, then, fails as a paradigm for explaining humanness. The alternative, Dualism, which suggests that humanness consists of both the material body and the immaterial mind, is preferable.

But as soon as one takes this position, a problem arises. The problem is known as the mind-body problem.

The Mind-Body Problem

What, exactly, is the mind-body problem? The mind-body problem has to do with questions that arise in trying to understand how a material body and an immaterial mind could interact. The most basic question is how can two fundamentally different kinds of substances, one material and one immaterial, interact with each other the way the mind and body (brain) apparently do. Related questions have to do with other complex issues such as understanding the nature of physical states (brain activity, for instance) versus mental states (thoughts, insights, flashes of inspiration), and whether or not and to what extent physical states generate mental

_____

117 Chalmers, in his book, *The Conscious Mind: In Search of a Fundamental Theory*, offers a number of detailed arguments that demonstrate that consciousness is not a product of (does not grow out of) physical phenomena and that conscious experience is not related only to sensory input. Consciousness cannot be reduced to or explained in terms of physical processes.

states and vice versa.[118] There is a great deal of philosophical material dedicated to the mind-body problem and no introductory text can deal with it in detail. In the sections below, I will provide an introductory discussion of these questions. To do that, however, we must understand materialism and physicalism—what they are and how they developed.

Materialism and Physicalism

In the simplest terms (as noted already in previous chapters), materialism is the idea that only material things exist. The cosmos consists of physical matter (objects composed of atoms and subatomic particles), and that is all that exists. Thus, it can be said that there is only one substance—physical matter. It may take many different forms (rocks, sand, trees, water, air, horses, people), but when it is broken down to its most basic elemental stuff, it is material in nature; it is physical matter. Thus, the word *materialism* refers to the idea that there is only one substance. And because there is only one substance, the idea of *monism* (that there is only one thing that exists or only one kind of a thing) can be applied as well. So *monistic materialism* is the idea that there is only one substance that exists and that that one substance is material in nature.

For all practical purposes, the word *physicalism* means the same thing as materialism, that only physical things exist. Technically, however, physicalism refers to the idea that everything can be explained in terms of physical processes. It involves a philosophical position, a hypothesis, that grew out of the positivism of the early 20th century and says the only explanations of phenomena that make sense are those that can be empirically verified. If only physical things

---

[118] Robinson, "Dualism," in *Stanford Encyclopedia of Philosophy.*

exist, then all interactions between physical things can be explained in terms of physical processes.[119] Physicalism is the paradigm that most contemporary scientists and philosophers embrace.

Physicalism is an interesting idea. There is a certain logic to it—assuming that only physical things exist. But not everyone agrees that only physical things exist. Neither Plato nor Aristotle were physicalists. Neither were the vast majority of philosophers before the modern era. How, then, did physicalism come to dominate scientific and philosophical thinking?

The Historical Development of Materialism and Physicalism

The ancient Greek Leucippus is credited with developing the original materialistic theory known as atomism, though we know of it through Democritus (4th century BCE), who was perhaps a student of Leucippus. Democritus argued that everything that exists is composed of matter that consists of tiny particles that cannot be seen. He called these particles *atoms*. This physical stuff, he claimed, was all that existed and all that had ever existed. Had he discovered any evidence that led him to this conclusion? No. It was a theory—and not a very popular one. Neither Plato nor Aristotle embraced it. Epicurus, however, did embrace it and made it part of his hedonistic system. *Atomism*, as the theory came to be called, was not a widely accepted mainstream theory in the ancient world. Most philosopher-scientists of that era embraced a dualistic paradigm. There were, however, a few materialists around.

The beginning of the Renaissance marked a new

---

[119] Stack, "Materialism," in *The Shorter Routledge Encyclopedia of Philosophy*, 633-635.

direction for thinking in Western Europe. One of the early forward thinking people of that time was Nicolaus Copernicus. In the early 1500s, Copernicus began toying with the idea of a heliocentric solar system. His work established him as a leader (perhaps the founder) of modern scientific methodology.[120] Other thinkers of the Renaissance who were dedicated to utilizing a scientific methodology were Johannes Kepler and Galileo Galilei. They understood that the physical world could only be understood by utilizing a thoroughgoing scientific methodology. And we can be thankful they did. Without them we'd still be living in the Dark Ages. However, what they understood as scientific methodology and what is being expressed today in the idea of scientific materialism are two very different things.

In the 17th century, Pierre Gassendi, a theist, "appreciated the scientific interpretation of nature,"[121] and advocated a scientific methodology. Serious thinkers had long since grown weary of explanations rooted in myth and tradition and wanted to do research, figuring things out using a scientific methodology. Gassendi advocated this, though he retained a dualist perspective, believing in the immortality of the soul and God as the creator of atoms as the elemental stuff of which the cosmos is constructed. The idea seemed like a good one to a number of important thinkers. Like the original ancient Greek philosophers, it seemed to them that the best way to understand the world was to cast aside the old explanations of how and why, and do research, looking for explanations that were rooted in logic, mathematics, and empirical verification. Gassendi was followed by Hobbes, who advocated the idea, that *the cosmos is matter in motion.*

Hobbes was followed by a host of others who adopted the same approach: researching, experimenting,

---

[120] Mcphee, *Physics: Everyday Science at the Speed of Light,* 35.
[121] Stack, "Materialism," in *The Shorter Routledge Encyclopedia of Philosophy,* 633-635

discovering, seeking to understand how the world worked by studying the world. There were no questions that could not be asked, no subject that could not be investigated, no long-held belief that could not be questioned. This new attitude toward scientific research paved the way for amazing scientific discoveries that have benefited humanity tremendously.

Once the new methodology was embraced, it did not take long for new ideas to begin emerging. In studies related to the brain, as early as 1770, Paul H.D. d'Holbach wrote his book, *The System of Nature*, in which he postulated that cognitive and emotive states could be reduced to or accounted for by internal changes within the brain.[122] This may have been one of the earliest expressions of the idea that mental states are really just brain states.

It is impossible to find fault with a method of investigation (that physical effects are generated by physical causes) that has generated so many important and helpful discoveries. Good things came from this reoriented view of how to study and understand the world. The work of Copernicus, Galileo, Newton, Einstein, and others was rooted in this naturalistic methodology. However, it is also important to notice that when Gassendi got this modern scientific movement going, he did so while retaining a dualistic perspective and belief in God. Others did the same. It was not necessary to reject God to study the world from a scientific cause and effect point of view. Yet eventually many thinkers did abandon belief in God, embracing a materialistic paradigm. The thinking that appeared to justify such a dramatic paradigm shift was rather simple. It came to be accepted that the presence and workings of the cosmos could be satisfactorily accounted for and explained in purely naturalistic terms without reference to God. God, therefore, at first became unnecessary. Eventually, however, for some,

---

[122] Ibid.

God became non-existent. Such a conclusion was unnecessary and unfortunate.

It must also be remembered that this embracing of a purely naturalistic (materialistic) perspective did not involve any scientific discovery or rational insight that suggested that a materialistic paradigm, rather than a dualistic paradigm, was more reflective of the ultimate cosmic reality. The decision to embrace a materialistic perspective—a paradigm that said physical effects have physical causes and we must seek to discover and understand them—was an arbitrary choice (to be sure) but not problematic in any way. In fact, it has yielded good results. But from that point a giant leap was then made that said *not only do we not need God to adequately explain things, God does not even exist*, a position that is highly questionable and utterly unwarranted. Today, materialists embrace the idea that only material things exist, which of course means that God does not exist.

If questioned about the validity of this paradigmatic perspective, materialists present a number of different arguments designed to demonstrate that their view of reality reflects what is really the case.

Arguments For Materialism

One argument in favor of a strong materialist view (that only physical things exist) is that humans are the result of a very long line of evolutionary developments or stages that began with single-cell organisms and ended (so far) with rational human beings. Atoms and electrical charges (non-living physical matter) generated simple living organisms (physical matter come to life) that began to evolve. Those organisms began to generate different forms, and once the process got started (non-living physical matter becoming living physical matter), it continued to produce ever more complex forms of living physical matter until the form of human was achieved. But even at that tremendous level of complexity (living matter that had become rational), you had physical matter that became living physical matter. There was never more or anything other than physical matter. Physical matter in different forms is all there has ever been.

This is an interesting story, and given the fact that there is an amazing amount of evidence that evolution has indeed occurred (which I do not doubt for a moment), the story is somewhat compelling. However, as an argument goes, it is based on unwarranted assumptions and assertions that have little actual evidence to support them. First is the underlying assumption that matter has always been around, that physical matter is that which always existed. This, of course, is not the case. The cosmos and the physical matter of which it is composed came into existence about 14 billion years ago as a result of the Big Bang. That matter has always existed is an assumption that the evidence does not support. A second questionable assumption is that once non-living matter did exist, it could, by itself (in an entirely random manner), spontaneously generate living matter. A third assumption is similar—that non-conscious matter could somehow give rise to conscious matter. The fourth assumption is that the idea of *conscious matter* does not contain an incoherent oxymoron. Matter is not conscious; minds are conscious.

The story that non-living, non-conscious matter randomly generated living, conscious matter, in addition to involving an incoherent oxymoron, is based on a number of other assumptions that are simply unwarranted. It is, therefore, an unsound and unsatisfactory argument that does not demonstrate that materialism is a perspective that reflects what is actually the case in the cosmos.

Another argument often put forward in support of materialism argues that, as we learn more and more about the brain, it is becoming clear that functions that in the past were attributed to the mind are really just functions of the brain.

233

Instead of mental states we have brain states. That is, everything thought and felt can be accounted for in a specific physiological function of the brain. There is no mind that works in conjunction with the brain; there is only the brain.

The argument is unsound because it is circular in nature. It assumes true that which needs to be proven true. Based on the assumption that there is no immaterial mind, physiological activity in the brain is assumed to be all there is to mental states. In other words, when we have a thought, a certain brain function occurs. It is assumed that that observable brain function is all there is to the thought. Based on that assumption, then, it is said that there is no mind separate from the brain that generated the thought. There is only the brain that registered an electrical impulse in conjunction with the thought. Or, put another way, because scientific equipment can only monitor the electrical impulse in the brain, the electrical impulse must be all there is. A thought or a feeling is just a little electrical blip in the brain. The argument is clearly circular and is, therefore, unsound, and of course, unconvincing.

Another argument often put forward in favor of a materialistic paradigm is that there is no evidence (meaning empirical evidence) that an immaterial mind is present or exists. In fact, there is no empirical evidence that anything immaterial exists. That is obviously the case. How could it be otherwise? How could anything immaterial generate a material presence, thus providing empirical evidence of its existence? Of course there is no empirical evidence for the existence of immaterial minds. That, however, does not mean that there is no evidence at all. There is rational evidence (in the form of rational arguments) that an immaterial reality, which includes immaterial minds, exists. This evidence will be considered in the next section.

Yet another argument in favor of adopting a materialist perspective has to do with the 1st and 2nd laws of thermodynamics. The 1st law of thermodynamics says that the total amount of energy and matter in the universe remains constant, merely changing from one form to another. This means that energy can be changed from one form to another, but not created or destroyed. The 2ⁿᵈ law of thermodynamics says that it is not possible for a process (of a closed system) to have as its only result the transfer of heat from a cooler body to a warmer body. This means that in that closed system with only a given amount of energy available, the system will seek equilibrium, with the warmer body being cooled and the cooler body becoming warmer.

I have heard more than one materialistic philosopher claim that if there is an immaterial mind present that exerts an influence on the brain that either one or both of these two laws are violated, which in their view is impossible. Therefore, immaterial minds do not exist. This, however, is simply not the case. An immaterial mind is not a force outside the physical cosmic system that creates energy within the system, thus violating the 1ˢᵗ law of thermodynamics. It is a force that merely manipulates the energy that already exists within the system, neither creating nor destroying the existing energy. The existence of immaterial minds interacting with material brains does not in any way violate the 1ˢᵗ law of thermodynamics. As for the 2ⁿᵈ law, there is nothing in it that would have anything to do with immaterial minds interacting with material brains. Referring to the 2ⁿᵈ law of thermodynamics in a discussion of the mind-body problem is a non sequitur. Thus, materialistic arguments that reference violations of the laws of thermodynamics are unsound and unconvincing.

What this all boils down to is that there are no arguments, no good reasons for adopting a materialistic perspective, denying the existence of an immaterial reality, which would include denying the existence of immaterial minds. It is one thing to suggest that the best way to understand the physical world is to look for physical causes of physical effects. That would appear to be (and has proven to have been) a very logical and helpful approach. It is quite another to say that only material things exist. It is entirely possible to be a thoroughgoing scientist utilizing a sound scientific method without embracing the extremist and unsupportable position that only material things exist. Materialism is, in my view, an extremist position that is unsupportable and does not reflect what is actually the case, that is, it does not provide an accurate picture of reality.

The Dualistic Alternative

If materialism is, as I have claimed, unsupportable and does not provide an adequate explanation of reality, what is the alternative? Dualism. What is Dualism? There are different kinds of dualism, different ways of explaining it. Since this is an introductory text, we cannot go too deeply into all the different forms dualism takes. The most basic form is known as *Cartesian Dualism*, linking it to the French philosopher René Descartes.

I briefly introduced Descartes and Dualism in Chapter 5 in our discussion of the question, *Why is there something rather than nothing?* It might be helpful to go back and read the sections of Descartes quoted there. In brief, Descartes was looking for a rock-solid foundation upon which he could build his philosophical system. He found it in his absolute certainly that he existed. He concluded, *"I think, therefore, I am."* But what kind of a being was the *I* that was thinking? It was *a thinking kind of a being*, a being whose essence was to think. Descartes realized that he was a mind. He *had* a body, but he *was* a mind. His essence was not to eat and drink, to sleep and move about. His essence was to think. Being physically embodied was essential to functioning in the physical world, but it did not define the kind of being he was. Mind was what he was, not body. This, in essence, is Cartesian Dualism.

For Descartes, the mind and body are not only

236

separate things, they are different kinds of things, different substances. The body was a material substance (physical matter), while the mind was an immaterial substance. But can that be right? Can human existence involve the interaction of two different substances? What arguments can be put forward to support such a view? There are three that I believe are effective in demonstrating that humans are indeed dualistic in nature: 1) the *inner mental life* argument, 2) the *intentionality* argument, and 3) the *metaphysical content* argument.

The inner mental life argument: The argument here is that the existence of a mental life that is qualitatively different from physical life demonstrates that there is something other than the physical present in the human being. We are not only aware, we are aware of being aware. I refer to this as second level awareness. It is a higher level of awareness than that present in animals. Additionally, we contemplate, we muse, we dream, we pretend, and we engage in abstract conceptualization, wrestling with difficult concepts or projecting ourselves into different situations and different places and times. We have very rich mental lives that are qualitatively different from our physical lives. Mental activity is quite different from physical activity, which means that the two things are in fact different kinds of things and not the same kind of things. The experiences that we get from sensory input, physical experiences of the physical world, are of a different sort than our mental experiences. As we experience each, we are aware of the differences between them. The differences cannot simply be ignored or explained away by saying that they are just a different kind of a physical experience such as the smell of something being different from the feel or sight of that same thing. Our different physical senses provide us with different experiences of our physical context. But mental experiences are of a fundamentally different sort. They are not just different kinds of physical experiences, they are completely

237

different kinds of experiences. It is one thing to think about being on a roller coaster, it is an entirely different thing to actually be on one. It is one thing to think about being in the ardent embrace of someone you love, it is quite another to actually experience such an embrace. It is one thing to think about having a special meal in a favorite restaurant, it is another to sit down in that restaurant and actually eat the food you anticipated eating. The qualitative differences between the physical and the mental suggest that the two are not at all the same, not just two different kinds of physical experiences, but two fundamentally different kinds of experiences. Mental life exists because there is an immaterial mind that exists separate from the physical body.[123]

The intentionality argument: The argument here is that the presence of intentionality as a feature of mental activity demonstrates that something qualitatively different from physical matter exists. It is not possible for physical matter, in any form, to be intentional.

What is intentionality? Basically, it is the ability to be intentional. It is my intention, my will, my desire, my plan, my goal, to finish writing this book. Given my past track record in writing books, I believe my intention will be realized. It is my intention to be the best professor I can be—an intention that requires constant monitoring. It is my intention that I be a good, moral person. I have many individual specific intentions because intentionality is one of

---

[123] Feser provides an example: water and H_2O are the same thing. Where you find one you find the other. They are qualitatively identical. Even if the "water" is in different forms—vapor, ice or liquid water—H_2O is still present. The point that Feser is making is that a thought, for example, and water are fundamentally different kinds of things. One can be present where the other is not because they are not the same things. If only physical things exist, then at some level the physical features of what makes a thing physical in nature will be present. But some things that exist do not have physical properties. They, cannot, therefore, be physical things. Feser, *Philosophy of the Mind: A Short Introduction*, 30.

the features of human rationality, of being a self-determined person. I can determine what I want to do; I can determine the kind of person I want to be. I have a will. Each time I make a decision, each time I decide what I want to do or do not want to do, I engage in an act of will that is the clearest and strongest expression of being me—a self-determined being, an individual with a will that has nothing to do with any physical aspect of who I am—my height, weight, skin color, heart rate, blood pressure, how fast my finger nails grow, how fast my hair is falling out, and so forth. Why is intentionality crucial in the discussion of the mind-body problem? Because humans are intentional beings but physical things are not intentional. A chair is not and cannot be intentional. Neither is a hammer, a desk, a tree, a rock, a kidney, a pancreas, a lung, or even a brain. Physical things (whether inanimate or animate) are not intentional. But human beings are intentional. It must be the case, then, that human beings are more than merely physical objects. To put the idea in syllogistic form we could say:

1. Nothing that is merely a physical object has the quality of intentionality
2. Humans have the quality of intentionality
3. Therefore, humans cannot be merely physical objects

This being the case, the presence of intentionality stands in the way of materialism being true.

The *metaphysical content* argument: The argument here is that the content of our minds (the kind of content) suggests that it is not the case that only physical things exist. This is a simple but extremely important argument. If only physical things exist (one of them being the human brain), and if our experience of those physical things occurs by means of sensory input, then all that can be in anyone's brain for processing would be the data that comes in via the physical senses, and all we could think about would be aspects of the physical world. Those things that could end up in the brain and about which we could think would be things we see, hear, smell, taste, and touch. But those are not the only kinds of things we can think about. We think about many things that are not part of the physical world. We think about things that are metaphysical in nature. Based on a materialistic paradigm (in other words, if materialism is true and only physical things exist), we would not be able to think about things that are not physical in nature. Some might object to this conclusion, pointing out that the brain is capable of what we call imagination. We can imagine all sorts of things. But it is not that simple. As data from the physical world comes into the brain via the physical senses, that data can be deconstructed and reconstructed (imaginatively) in many different ways. But if all there is for the brain to work with is physical data, all it can imagine is features of the physical reality organized differently. In the real world, horses, horns, wings, lizards, and fire exist. Unicorns and fire-breathing dragons do not exist. But the imaginative brain (if that is indeed what is doing the imagining) can deconstruct physical forms and reconstruct them, creating things that do not actually exist in the real world. The imaginative brain will be able to take a lizard and imagine it much larger than it is, add wings to it, and put fire in its throat and create a fire-breathing flying dragon, a thing that does not exist in the real world. But all the components of the dragon exist in the real world. The brain reorganized the data to imagine that which does not really exist. That kind of imagination would be possible if all there were is a physical brain processing physical data—imagination that is simply a deconstruction and reconstruction of physical data. But human thinking is not limited to those things that are merely reconstructions of physical data. The human *mind* can conceive of all sorts of things that are not in any way part of the physical cosmos, things (real things) that are not physical objects—humor, joy, equality, and rights, for example.

How is that possible? Because nonphysical things exist. And the mind, itself one of those immaterial realities, is aware of their existence and can contemplate those as well as other immaterial realities. Therefore, it is not the case that only physical things exist. Materialism is not true.

At this point the materialist will object, arguing that for there to be a mind separate from the brain, two different substances would have to interact with each other and that such a thing cannot be done. Such an assertion is an unwarranted assumption. How does the materialist know that two different substances, the material and the immaterial, cannot interact? In fact, I think they can, and we have examples of similar interactions in nature. For example, gravity is not a physical object. It is a force. The same is true of electromagnetism. Neither gravity nor electromagnetism is an object located in space with size, shape, form, color, and so forth. Yet they interact with objects that do have those characteristics. A force and an object are two fundamentally different kinds of things, yet they interact all the time. So the objection that an immaterial mind and a material brain could not interact is not a valid objection.

Dualists cannot explain exactly how the mind and the brain interact, but because we cannot explain how they interact does not mean they cannot. Two different substances interacting does not involve any kind of a contradiction or impossibility, as does the idea that non-conscious matter could produce a conscious entity.

Any argument that dualism is, in fact, a viable paradigm for explaining reality must ultimately be rooted in a larger cosmology of the type presented in earlier chapters. In brief, it would go something like this: something exists now, therefore something has always existed. What was it—*matter* or *mind*? *Matter* is not a viable answer, for (in addition to other concerns) non-conscious matter cannot produce conscious entities. The only answer to the question, what is it that has always existed, is *mind*. That eternally-existing mind—conscious, rational, and self-determined—gave rise to other minds that are also conscious, rational and self-determined. Thus, minds exist—immaterial minds that are embodied and interact intimately with the body associated with it. And it is the mind that makes humans, for the most part, what we are. We are also physical beings and that aspect of our being is crucial. But it is the mind that is the essence of the person, the mind that "houses" (for lack of a better term) the will and the personality that we live out in our physical body. So as we think in terms of our *human nature*, trying to understand ourselves (the kind of beings we are), much of what we observe has to do with our immaterial self.

Observations About Human Nature[124]

Based on what has been argued in this and preceding chapters, premises for discussing human nature are:

1. That the eternally-existing mind created the cosmos and other minds that are part of it.
2. That Descartes was right in identifying humans as embodied thinking substances.
3. That though there is a complex interaction between mind and body, the human being is most thoroughly identified with the mind rather than the body because it is the mind that thinks and chooses, that wills and determines, making us the unique individuals we are.

With these premises in place, what observations can be made regarding human nature (that is, those traits that are

---

[124] The material in this section is borrowed from Rogers, *Proof of God?*

common to all humans) and what conclusions can be reached based on those observations?

1. Human beings are *self-aware*. Not only are we aware, but we are aware of being aware—it is a level of awareness that transcends the awareness of animals. Human awareness is a *second-level* awareness. Some animals are aware to a certain extent. They are aware that they are individuated selves. Elephants, chimps, and some dogs can recognize themselves in a mirror. They know they are looking at themselves. We use to have two dogs, a Rottweiler named Megan and a German Shorthair Pointer named Gabby. They were very much part of our family. They even had their own Christmas stockings. Just like our boys, each dog knew which stocking was hers and that the toys inside were hers as well. They were each aware of being an individual creature. But they were not aware that they were aware. That is, they did not contemplate their self-hood, they did not conceive of themselves as beings in time who, because of being self-aware, made moral choices that mattered. Humans are not only aware, but are aware of being aware. They have a second-level kind of awareness. This is what I mean when I refer to humans as self-aware. It is part of what makes humans who and what we are. It is part of our shared nature.

2. Human beings are *self-determined*. We make moral choices. Self-awareness and self-determination go hand-in-hand—they are ontologically linked. A being who is aware of being aware is one who makes moral choices and who is responsible for those choices. The idea that one is a self-aware, mechanistically-determined being is an oxymoron. If a being is self-aware, that being is of necessity self-determined. There is a great deal of philosophical material dedicated to the discussion of whether or not humans are self-determined or mechanistically determined. If one assumes a monistic materialistic paradigm (that the cosmos, including people, is simply matter in motion... atoms bumping into other atoms), there is little reason to assume

anything beyond mechanistic determination. However, for those who proceed from a dualistic perspective, appreciating the reality of self-aware minds, there is also an acknowledgment and appreciation of self-determination. The choices we *appear* to be making, we are actually making and those choices matter.[125] Self-determination is part of our shared human nature, part of what makes us unique as humans.

3. Human beings are *rational*. Humans don't just think, we think at a very high level, engaging in abstract conceptualization. We think mathematically, logically, metaphysically and imaginatively:

a. Mathematically: both $6 + 6$ and $15 - 3 = 12$.

b. Logically: all brothers are male, no bachelors are married.

c. Metaphysically: how thick is the present?

d. Imaginatively: projecting ourselves into alternate realities of the space-time continuum—as Alice in Wonderland. We can be in different places (including different dimensions where different laws of physics are at work) at different times—past, present, or future.

Rationality is ontologically linked with self-awareness and self-determination. Where you find one, you find the others. Rationality is a trait humans share; it is part of our human nature.

4. Human beings are *capable of aesthetic appreciation and creation*. Humans think not only about what is needful and useful, but what is beautiful. As we identify beauty in nature we create and replicate it in artistic

---

[125] Making a detailed argument for self-determination is beyond the scope of this chapter. However, having argued that that which has always existed is a self-determined mind who created other minds is itself an argument for self-determination. Also, what I have said about the self-awareness and self-determination being ontologically linked is an argument (though not detailed) for self-determination.

and personal expressions, creating beautiful things and making ourselves beautiful. There are no examples in nature that animals do this. Aesthetic appreciation and creation is part of our unique shared human nature.

5. Human beings are *rationally relational*. Animals are relational. There are herd and pack animals that live in groups. There are animals that mate for life. There is a "relational nature" about them—in the loose sense of the term. But humans are *rationally* relational. We think about relationships and the basis for them. We relate to each other on the basis of shared concepts of morality, justice, goodness, beauty and truth. We do not relate (that is, interact with different kinds and levels of intimacy) simply for the purposes of procreation and protection (like animals) but because we are self-aware, self-determined, rational beings, interacting on the basis of those unique characteristics. This, too, is part of our shared human nature.

6. Human beings are *culture builders and users*. This is similar to but not identical with aesthetic appreciation. Humans create complex social structures and traditions along with material and technological artifacts that are part of how we live. Human culture is so complex that it is staggering. Try, as an adult, moving to a radically different culture (such as an American going to Nigeria, West Africa, for instance) and learning all the different aspects of that culture, including the underlying worldview assumptions that are part of it. It can take years of concerted effort to learn the culture of another people. Why is it so difficult? One reason is because of the level of complexity involved.

We do not create and use culture simply because we prefer to. We do so because as self-aware, self-determined, rationally relational beings, we must do so. We could not live without creating a cultural context in which to live morally, rationally, and relationally. Since we are moral, rational and relational we must have structures that allow us to live in those ways. To be a cultural kind of a being is part of our shared human nature.

7. Human beings are *embodied minds*. The idea here is more than just having a body. Animals have bodies. But humans are self-aware, self-determined, rational, relational minds that are embodied. Animals are embodied but do not have the additional characteristics that make humans human. Our self-aware, self-determined, rational, relational realities are what make us who and what we are. Those qualities, all activities of the mind, are what make us who we are. The *who we are* (the mind) is embodied. This does not negate the importance of the body. We are who we are in bodily form. We interact with other minds by means of our bodies. We experience the world we live in by means of our bodies. The body simply cannot be unimportant. But it is not the body in any significant way that determines who we are. It is our will, our choices that in the end determine who and what we are. Environment is important. Family and culture and our personal circumstances impact us in crucial ways. But still, there is a mind that thinks, a will that determines, and we are responsible for the choices we make. The body is part of who we are, but the essence of each person is the mind, that thinking substance that makes both you and me the unique individuals we are. To be a mind, a thinking substance that is embodied, is part of our human nature.

8. Human beings are *enduing minds*. The body will die, but the mind will live on, it will endure. That is a bold claim. How can such a claim be made? The previous seven things are more or less self-evident or at least readily available on the basis of some basic rational reflection. But how can one know that the immaterial mind is enduring? How do we know it survives the death of the body? To refer to the mind as being immaterial is simply another way of saying that it is not material, not made of physical matter. But to say what a thing isn't is not the same as saying what it is. To say that the immaterial mind is enduring is to make a

246

claim regarding its nature. Since the mind is immaterial, it is not an object that can be examined. How do we know it is enduring? I think the answer must be in thinking about the kinds of things the mind does. The mind thinks thoughts, conceives ideas, contemplates principles and concepts, none of which are subject to decay. Thoughts do not get old and die. Ideas do not decay. Principles and concepts are enduring. They may be forgotten or ignored, but they do not deteriorate, decay, or die. They are enduring. So are the minds that think them, conceive them and contemplate them. The thought that does not die comes from a mind that does not die. The concept that endures is contemplated by a mind that also endures. The immaterial mind thinks immaterial thoughts. This enduring nature is one of the traits shared among humans.

To review, humans are:

1. Self-aware
2. Self-determined
3. Rational
4. Capable of aesthetic appreciation and creation
5. Rationally relational
6. Culture builders and users
7. Embodied minds
8. Enduring minds

These eight things are traits that all humans share, things that make us unique as human beings. None of these things are true of any other species on earth, but they are true of humans. They represent our human nature. What can be said about humans based on these eight things? Probably a great deal, depending on who is making the observations. What I would like to suggest is that there is an interesting correlation between this list and the list of traits we inferred about God in Chapter 7. Among other things, I noted that God is self-determined, rational, and creative. So are humans.

There are probably other similarities as well. What are we seeing here? Could the sayings, *like father like son* and *the apple doesn't fall far from the tree* be applicable? If God did intentionally create us this way, and "this way" happens to involve a level of similarity with/to him, what are the implications of that for ontology and for human potential?

Summary

What kind of beings are human beings? The fairly obvious answer is that we are physical beings. We exist in the space-time continuum as extended beings located in space with size, shape, weight and so forth. But is that all we are? Does our physical nature comprise the totality of our existence? Or is a human being something more than a physical body with a personal point of view? For me, the evidence suggests that we are much more than a physical body with a personal point of view. We are an immaterial mind, a thinking substance that happens to be embodied. We are not a body; we are an embodied mind.

Of course such a statement gives rise to what is known in contemporary philosophy as the mind-body problem, which asks, in effect, if humans are composed to two different substances, how can those different substances interact? An associated question would be, what evidence is there that an immaterial mind, separate from the brain, exists?

Materialism is the position that only physical things exist. In the context of the mind-body problem, there is a brain and what we refer to as the mind is really just the brain—mind states are just brain states. Dualism is the position that reality is composed of at least two substances, one material and one immaterial. Minds are immaterial. What does the evidence suggest? For me, the evidence suggests that a dualistic perspective is reflective of reality.

248

Materialism is not.

Consciousness itself is evidence that an immaterial reality exists, for consciousness is not a physical object located in space, with weight, mass, shape, and so forth. Consciousness is immaterial and so are the minds that are conscious. Three additional arguments that demonstrate the immaterial minds exist include: 1) the *inner mental life* argument, 2) the *intentionality* argument, and 3) the *metaphysical content* argument.

Human beings are dualistic in nature with a number of identifiable traits. Humans are: self-aware, self-determined, rational, capable of aesthetic appreciation and creation, rationally relational, culture builders and users, embodied minds, and enduring minds.

Thought and Discussion Questions

1. Explain your thinking on how consciousness is involved in helping us understand the nature of human existence.
2. Define materialism and explain what you believe to be the strongest arguments in support of materialism.
3. Explain which of the arguments for a dualistic perspective on reality is in your opinion the strongest argument.
4. Explain what Rogers is talking about when he discusses the qualitative difference between physical and mental experiences.
5. Having read and thought about the material in this chapter, how would you answer the question, what kind of beings are human beings?

Chapter 10
Are We Really Free To Choose?

It is Saturday afternoon, and my wife and I have decided to go out to lunch. There is a nice restaurant nearby, and we decide to go there. On the way I think to myself, I should have a salad. I'm trying to watch my weight and cholesterol, so a salad is what I ought to have. But I really don't want a salad. I want a hamburger—a big one, with fries. We arrive at the restaurant and are seated and begin to scan the menu. The restaurant is one of those where healthy eating is encouraged, and next to each item on the menu the number of calories for that item is noted—a very annoying new marketing strategy. I see that the burger combo I'm interested in (a burger without fries just somehow seems wrong) contains a whopping 800 calories. That's discouraging. On the menu page opposite the burger combos are the salads. I can get a salad with a grilled chicken breast on it that's only 350 calories. That's what I should order and I know it. It is within my power to order it. But I don't want to. I'm hungry, and I want the burger and fries. So that's what I order. In weighing my options and deciding what to order for lunch, did I act freely? Was my choice an act of free will or was it somehow predetermined so that I did not really have a choice?

Monday afternoon I needed some cash; so I went to my credit union. It was cold and windy, so instead of using the automated teller machine outside, I went inside. I needed $100 and asked for it in $20s. The teller took a stack of bills out of her drawer and counted out five twenty-dollar bills. Except they were brand new bills and two of them stuck together. She did not notice as she counted them out. But I did. She laid $120 on the counter in from of me instead of $100. I knew she had made a mistake and that the $20 I would gain from her mistake would make her drawer $20 short at the end of her shift—a serious problem for her. So I said, "I think you need to count those out again. I think there's an extra twenty in there." An expression of doubt flashed across her face as she picked up the stack of bills and recounted them. I had been correct. There was an extra twenty in the stack. Though embarrassed she had made such a mistake, she thanked me. I smiled, thanked her, took my money and left. I did not have to point out her mistake. I could simply have taken the money and enjoyed my $20 gain. But I did not believe that to be the right thing to do. It would have been dishonest for me to gain from her honest mistake. So I decided to do the right thing and point out her mistake. Was my decision to point out her mistake and give back the extra $20 an act of free will? Or were my actions somehow predetermined (by previous events, cosmic causes) so that what appeared to be a choice to be made was in fact no choice at all but an action that I was compelled to carry out?

In these two examples of free will, or apparent free will, depending on your point of view, one situation involved a moral choice; the other did not. Whether I have a salad or a burger and fries for lunch is not a moral choice. It may be a choice that has some small impact on my weight and my

251

overall health, but it is not a moral choice. But the decision to keep or give back to $20 was a moral choice. Keeping the money that was not mine would have been immoral. So one example had to do with moral responsibility and moral accountability; the other did not. But each scenario has to do with the question of whether or not I was acting freely in the decision I made and the action I took. Do humans have free will, or are we somehow determined so that we have no choice but to do what we do?

Mechanistically Determined

Philosophically, the question is discussed in the context of *free will* versus *determinism*. Are our actions freely chosen, or are they determined? Free will is the belief or position that the free will that we appear to have we do, in fact, have. We are free to decide and act without outside forces determining our choices and actions. It is the position that, while there may be influences and predispositions that nudge us toward one choice or another, toward one behavior or another, ultimately humans remain free to choose in that they actually do have the ability to choose between alternatives (doing this or that). What they choose and what they do is freely chosen. Determinism is the belief or position that "all our mental states and acts, including choices and decisions, and all our actions are effects necessitated by preceding causes."[126] Determinism says that humans do not have free will, that the things we think and do we must think and do, and we have no choice in the matter. The cosmos is a cause and effect system, and every effect (including what a person thinks and does) has been caused by something that preceded it. The causal chain that produces

---

[126] Weatherford, "freedom and determinism, in *The Oxford Companion to Philosophy*, 313.

given effects in humans (as well as all other effects) began eons ago and continues to the present (and will continue into the future) causing the effects that occur in the cosmos.[127]

Those who work out of a deterministic paradigm usually embrace one of two positions in relation to free will: incompatibility and compatibility. Those who embrace incompatibility, referred to as incompatibilists, argue that determinism and free will are incompatible, and that humans, therefore, do not have free will. Choices appear to be free, but in reality they are not. Choices are made, but they are determined by prior causes, and whatever "choice" is made is the only "choice" that could have been made. Thus, the concepts of free will and determinism are incompatible.

Compatibilists, however, argue that the concepts of determinism and free will are compatible, depending on how one understands the idea of freedom. For compatibilists, to be free is "to be free from constraints of certain sorts."[128] What does that mean? It means that from a compatibilist point of view, freedom is not being physically or psychologically forced to do something. For example, this Saturday I might wash my truck and work in the yard, or I might take my wife to Sioux Falls to shop and enjoy a nice dinner. Since no one is going to force me to do either one of those two things, I am "free" to choose, argues the compatibilist. However, it must be remembered that this "freedom" exists within the context of larger causal events that determine the choice I will make. There is no immediate

---

[127] It needs to be clarified, however, that one can embrace the basic law of cause and effect without embracing determinism. For instance, temperatures below freezing may cause the water in the pipes in my house to freeze—the frozen water in the pipes being the effect, the below freezing temperatures being the cause. That cause and effect, however, need not be linked to any sort of cosmic determinism that precludes anyone's free will. Van Inwagen has made this point in his, *An Essay on free Will*, 3-4.

[128] Strawson, "Free Will," in *The Shorter Routledge Encyclopedia of Philosophy*, 287.

physical or psychological coercion, but causal events in the past determine the choice I will make. Compatibilists argue that the lack of any immediate physical or psychological coercion allows one to enjoy freedom of choice. Incompatibilists would respond by arguing that compatibilists are trying to have it both ways, embracing both determinism and free will, which to incompatibilists appears contradictory and therefore incoherent.

To get a good handle on determinism (whether compatibilist or incompatibilist), it needs to be understood that the concept of determinism is an idea that exists as part of a larger materialistic paradigm. In other words, those who embrace determinism are materialists, embracing the idea that only physical things exist—or at least some form of materialism or physicalism. It would be highly unlikely that you would ever encounter a dualist that embraces determinism.

A word about cause and effect: it is important to reiterate that one can be a thoroughgoing scientist, working from a cause and effect paradigm (that every physical effect is generated by a sufficient physical cause), and that one can study and understand the physical workings of the cosmos through scientific investigation without embracing the idea that only physical things exist. It is also possible to embrace the universal law of causation (that every physical effect is generated by a sufficient physical cause) without embracing determinism, and the idea that because there are physical causes for physical effects that all human actions are determined by physical causes and that humans, therefore, do not have free will. Living in a world where physical laws govern the workings of the physical world and having free will are not mutually exclusive. For example, I can choose to drive 55 mph or 70 mph. If I choose to drive 70 mph, the laws of physics say that it is going to require 315 feet to stop the vehicle. How fast I drive is up to me. How long it takes to stop the vehicle I'm driving at a given speed is up to the laws of physics. Physical laws and free will can work in conjunction with each other.

Another crucial question is: are there physical causes that can be identified that would determine how fast I drive? For instance, are there physical causes that make me drive at 55 mph or keep me from driving at 70 mph? I might, for instance, have been taught and embraced the idea that obeying the law is important and if, therefore, the speed limit is 55 mph I should not exceed that speed. That kind of a cause is not the kind of physical cause determinists have in mind when they argue that physical causes determine us. Driving 55 mph to avoid getting a speeding ticket would also not be the kind of physical cause determinists are looking for. So what kind of physical causes (that happened long ago) make me drive 55 mph or keep me from driving 70 mph? What physical causes determine my behavior? Compatibilist philosophers may respond by arguing that you can choose to drive whatever speed you want, but whatever speed you do choose to drive will have been the only choice you could have made, thus, arguing that free will and determinism are compatible. The problem, of course, is that if I could only have made the choice I did make, then I did not really have alternatives from which to select. I did not really have free will, did I? But even that response does not explain what physical causes determine whether I will drive 55 or 70. What are these physical causes that determine how fast I drive? I can't come up with what they might be. Can you?

What kinds of physical causes would determine the choices I make? Suppose I have a vitamin deficiency that causes me to crave a certain kind of food. Suppose I am going through a cafeteria line and a food that is rich in that vitamin is available. I might select that food because of my deficiency-induced craving. Those sorts of physical causes certainly are possible some of the time. But can there be a physical cause of that sort for all of the decisions and choices I make? That seems very unlikely. Being able to prove the contention that there are physical causes that determine each choice we make also seems unlikely. Providing some examples like the one I just gave (the craving for a certain kind of food) that demonstrates that sometimes some of our decisions and actions have physical causes does not demonstrate that such is the case all the time. The kind of proof that would be necessary to prove determinism is not going to be forthcoming. Determinism is a theory rooted in materialism waiting for some proof that it is true. Peter Van Inwagen has written a thorough analysis of determinism and free will (*An Essay on Free Will*) and demonstrated convincingly that the concepts of determinism and free will are incompatible. He has argued that we are, in fact, free to choose in the most meaningful way and are not determined by physical events.

Cognitively Self-determined

If our behaviors are not determined by physical events,[129] how do we explain the nature of human behavior? An option for explaining human behavior that is better than materialistic determinism is what might be called *cognitive self-determination*, or as it is usually called, *free will*.

Most of us believe we have free will. But do we? What reasons exist for believing that we do, in fact, have free will? There are four good reasons or arguments in favor of free will. The first is the fact that the actual positive arguments that can be made regarding the nature of reality

---

[129] It was my intention in the previous section to present arguments to demonstrate that the theory of determinism ought to be rejected. Van Inwagen has done that in more detail than I, and students can refer to his work for those arguments. In this section, however, I will offer arguments designed to demonstrate that we do, in fact, have free will, or that we are self-determined, and that since that is the case, it is clear that determinism ought to be rejected.

support a dualistic view of reality rather than a materialistic one. [130] Immaterial minds exist. [131] Because minds are immaterial they are not subject to the physical laws of cause and effect. The immaterial mind cannot be determined by the physical laws of the universe—because it is not a physical object. The physical brain can be, but the non-physical mind cannot. It is possible for the immaterial mind to interact with the brain, using the brain to accomplish its purposes. But having non-physical (and therefore non-rational) events "determining" the choices (acts of the will) of an immaterial mind is not possible. What kind of coercion could a physical thing (a physical cause) exert over an immaterial mind that would force that mind to make a specific decision or keep it from making a specific decision? An acorn falling to the ground might be covered over with dirt, germinate, and

---

[130] You will recall that all materialists can argue in favor of their paradigm is: 1) a negative argument, that there is no physical evidence that anything non-physical exists, and 2) a claim that the cosmos can be adequately explained without reference to anything immaterial. Therefore, they argue, one should adopt a materialistic paradigm. However, a number of arguments can be made in favor of a dualistic perspective. The weight of actual evidence (in the form of rational reflection) suggests that dualism ought to be adopted as a working paradigm. Readers are encouraged to review arguments presented in Chapters 5 and 9.

[131] I realize that those who reject dualism will reject this argument immediately on the basis (they would argue) that dualism cannot be proven. Therefore any argument based on dualism is without support. Of course, the exact same argument can be leveled against those who embrace materialism and make arguments based on their acceptance of materialism (i.e., those who begin with materialistic assumptions). Materialism cannot be proven, so any argument rooted in materialistic assumptions is automatically without foundation. To build an argument on the basis of either dualism or materialism, there must be a presumption of truth for the paradigmatic approach we are adopting. In other words, we are going to begin with either dualistic assumptions or with materialistic assumptions. I believe dualism provides a better explanation of the nature of reality.

sprout, resulting in a new oak tree. The effect is the new oak tree. The cause would be the acorn—a physical effect generated by a physical cause. What kind of physical cause could determine the choice a mind makes... so that that mind *would have to make and could only make* the choice generated by the cause. Even in the case of a physical craving (mentioned above), could not the mind override the craving and decide against the craving? Certainly it could. It is simply not the case that a physical cause can determine a mental response, eliminating the possibility of an alternate response.

A second argument in favor of free will is the *introspection* argument. This, in my opinion, is the most powerful argument in favor of free will. It is the idea that I am aware of my own internal states and I know that I am deliberating on alternatives and making choices, and that no one or no thing other than me is determining what choice I make. Just as I know whether or not I have a headache (or any other internal or mental state), I know whether or not I am deliberating on alternatives and making a choice that is in fact freely determined by me. The materialistic response to this introspective assertion is to say, "No, you don't. It seems like you are making a free choice but you are not." That sort of a response is similar to saying, "No, you don't have a headache. It may feel like you have a headache but you don't." That of course is rather foolish. No one is in a better position than me to determine whether or not I have a headache. Neither is anyone else in a better position than me to know whether or not I am, in fact, deliberating between possible alternatives and making a free choice.

For instance, suppose I'm in a fast food restaurant where they give me a cup and I select what kind of a drink I want from an automated soda dispenser. I might select a soda that has sugar in it or a diet soda that is sweetened with a zero calorie sugar substitute. I have alternatives, so I have to deliberate, weighing the options and making a choice. I like the taste of sugar. I like the surge of energy it provides. But I know that too much sugar is not good for me. So I have to choose between two options, each of which will have an impact on my body. Suppose I choose the diet soda. What physical events that occurred in the past determined my choice? What if the next time (let's say the very next day) I choose to consume the sugar? What past physical causes have required me to make a different choice this time than I made last time? Introspectively, I am aware that on each visit to the restaurant I had choices to make. One time I made one choice, the next time I made a different choice. I know that no past physical events are determining my choices because the kinds of choices I'm making are not the kinds of choices that a physical event could impact. What kind of past physical events would on Tuesday determine that I must select a diet soda and on Wednesday determine that I must select a drink with sugar in it? Or what physical events would determine that one time I must choose a cola and the next time choose root beer? Physical events simply do not have that kind of power over me so that I have no choice but to comply. Even strong cravings such as the craving for something sugary or something salty can be overridden by cognitive self-determination. I might like and want (have a craving for) the oily, salty French fries but decide not to eat them because they are not good for me. I can choose to indulge a craving or not to indulge the craving.

Consider another example. Suppose I am considering the arguments regarding the morality of euthanasia. I ask the basic question, *what makes an act moral or immoral*, and begin to evaluate the different kinds of euthanasia (active, passive, and so forth) and the positions that are advocated regarding each in an effort to work through the problem and reach a decision. Based on my analysis and reflections I decide that euthanasia, as long as there are some agreed upon guidelines to serve as a safeguard against abuse, is moral. What physical events could determine that I reach that conclusion and no other? None. The question is not, could there be physical events that influenced my thinking on the subject? Of course there could have been. Perhaps as a young man twenty years ago I had been part of a family squabble over the fate of an aunt who had been in an automobile accident and was in a persistent vegetative state. Some family members wanted to disconnect the machinery keeping her "alive," and some did not. Discussions were heated; accusations were made. A vote was called. As a young adult I voted, but was not really confident in my choice. So now, twenty years later, I want to study the issue and figure it out. Could the fact that I experienced those events somehow impact my reflections and subsequent decision? Certainly it could. It could *impact* my thinking. Could those events that occurred twenty years ago *determine* (limit) my cognitive processes so that I could arrive at only one decision and no other? No they could not. Why not? Because the cognitive processes of an immaterial mind cannot be controlled by mere physical events. They can be impacted but not controlled.

Introspectively, I am aware of alternatives I have. I consider the options and make choices. And I know that the kinds of mental processes I'm engaged in are not subject to the control of past physical events. Introspectively, I know that I am making choices that are, in fact, free of outside control. *I* am choosing.[132]

---

[132] Van Inwagen is not a fan of the introspection argument. In *An Essay on Free Will* (204-205), he argues that while we are in a privileged position to know our own mental states, we are not in a privileged position regarding free will. After all, he argues, an alien being, unbeknownst to us, may have implanted a device in our head that makes us think what we think, including, presumably, thinking that we have free will. Thus, we cannot actually know introspectively whether or not we have free will. With all due respect to Dr. Van Inwagen, I have no such device in my head and a quick MRI will confirm that fact. Introspectively, I am as aware of whether or not I

A third argument in favor of self-determination has to do with moral responsibility. If people are not self-determined, if they do not have free will, if they do not truly choose what they will or will not do, deciding who they will or will not be, how can anyone be held responsible for what they do or don't do? If we are causally determined and cannot act in any way other than in the way we do act, how can any act be deemed unacceptable? We are simply doing what we must do. When one person rapes another, molests another, takes from another, or intentionally injures another or kills another, in each case the person raping, molesting, taking, injuring, or killing is simply doing what he or she must do. The person has no choice in the matter. How, then, can that person be held accountable for his or her actions? If determinism is correct, no person ought to be held accountable for any action, for no one is free to choose what he or she will do. Yet as a society we (and all societies) do hold people accountable for their actions. We know, regardless of what determinists argue, that we are self-determined moral beings who are responsible for the choices we make.

Immanuel Kant explained it this way: "Will is a kind of causality belonging to living beings so far as they are rational. *Freedom* would then be the property this causality has of being able to work independently of *determinism* by alien causes."[133] Kant is saying that because we are rational beings we have a will that is exerted each time we make a decision or act in some way. Rational beings are *willing* beings in that we *will* to do this or that. This rational will is the essence of the person. It, more than any other aspect of us, is that which makes us who we are. Each time we decide, each time we say, *I will do this* or *I will not do that*, or *I think*

---

have free will as I am of whether or not I have a headache, or whether I am sad or happy.
[133] Kant, *Groundwork of the Metaphysics of Morals*, (pg 114 of the Patton edition).

this or *I think that*, we are exerting our will. Such events are experiences of our *self*, our inner self, our essence, mind, or will. Philosophers such as Hume, who searched for their inner self but could find it, evidently did not know what they were looking for and did not recognize it when they encountered it. Each expression of one's *will* is an expression of one's *self*.

Kant's point is that because we are rational, willing beings, we are free to choose. He is arguing that a rational, willing being cannot be a determined being. He is claiming that the ideas of free will and determinism are incompatible. And he is saying (in the pages following the above quotation) that we do have free will, and that is why we can be held morally accountable. Kant likes the word *autonomous*. We are autonomous—free, independent, rationally willing beings—who are then responsible for the choices we make. This being the case is the only reason we can hold anyone accountable for the things they do or do not do.

Determinism stands in opposition to all that we, as rational beings, know to be true about ourselves. It stands in opposition to how we treat each other based on what we know about ourselves as a species. One wonders why anyone would embrace an idea such as materialism that requires that one take such an incoherent position as determinism.

A fourth argument in favor of self-determination is what Van Inwagen refers to as the argument of deliberation. [134] I have already referred to the act of deliberation as part of the introspection argument. However, the act of deliberation can be used as a separate argument in favor of self-determination. The idea is this: when we deliberate between two or more alternative courses of action, we believe that each alternative is actually available to us and that we can, if we choose to, carry out whichever course of action we prefer. For example, on Tuesday afternoon I can

---

[134] Van Inwagen, *An Essay on Free Will*, 154-160

deliberate on three different activities to engage in on Tuesday evening. I can stay home and do some reading I need to do to be better prepared for the classes I teach on Wednesday, or I can go to the basketball game our men's team is playing that night, or I can take my wife out to dinner and then go see the movie we wanted to see but didn't get to over the weekend because of other family obligations. In deliberating about what to do Tuesday evening, I believe that all three of the alternatives I am considering are actually possible for me to do. I can stay home and read, go to the basketball game, or go out with my wife. Each of those possibilities is open to me. No one would deliberate on alternatives he or she did not believe were really possible. People might daydream or fantasize about the impossible, but no one deliberates on the impossible. We deliberate on those things that we believe are actually possible alternative courses of action.

How does acknowledging this feature of deliberation serve as an argument in favor of free will? It does so in this way: even those who advocate determinism, claiming that we do not have free will, engage in the activity or process of deliberation. They claim that they do not believe in free will, but their behavior demonstrates that they do. A determinist would probably reply to this argument by claiming that people think they have real alternatives when in reality they do not. They deliberate on what they think or assume are real alternatives but they are mistaken, because past physical events force each person into only one course of action— they make the only choice they can make based on past physical events. Of course, then, determinists are obligated to explain how past physical events can, in each and every case, determine the one and only "choice" a person can make. And that has not been done... nor can it be.

Determinists have an uphill battle because what they claim is true runs counter to the experience of every person. We know we are self-determined. We make real substantive

263

choices each day, the kind of choices that long past physical events cannot possibly determine.

Summary

Do we have free will, or are we somehow determined so that we have no choice but to do what we do? Philosophically, the question is discussed in the context of *free will* versus *determinism*. Are our actions freely chosen, or are they determined? Free will is the belief or position that the free will that we appear to have, we do, in fact, have. We are free to decide and act without outside forces determining our choices and actions. It is the position that, while there may be influences and predispositions that nudge us toward one choice or another, toward one behavior or another, ultimately humans remain free to choose. They actually do have the ability to choose between alternatives (doing this or that), and what they choose and what they do is freely chosen. Determinism is the belief or position that "all our mental states and acts, including choices and decisions, and all our actions are effects necessitated by preceding causes."[135] Determinism says that humans do not have free will, that the things we think and do, we must think and do and we have no choice in the matter. The cosmos is a cause and effect system and every effect (including what a person thinks and does) has been caused by something that preceded it. The causal chain that produces given effects in humans (as well as all other effects) began eons ago and continues to the present (and will continue into the future) causing the effects that occur in the cosmos. Those who work out of a deterministic paradigm usually embrace one of two positions in relation to free will: incompatibility and compatibility.

---

[135] Weatherford, "freedom and determinism, in *The Oxford Companion to Philosophy*, 313.

Determinism is deeply rooted in a materialistic view of the cosmos. However, one can be a determinist without believing that only physical things exist. It is also possible to embrace free will and still believe that the physical world is a law-abiding, cause and effect kind of a place.

There are four basic arguments in favor of humans being self-determined beings: first is the fact that the actual positive arguments that can be made regarding the nature of reality support a dualistic view of reality—which includes immaterial minds that are not determined by physical events.

A second argument in favor of free will is the *introspection* argument. It is the idea that I am aware of my own internal states and I know that I am deliberating on alternatives and making choices, and that no one or no thing other than me is determining what choice I make.

A third argument in favor of self-determination has to do with moral responsibility. If people are not self-determined, if they do not have free will, if they do not truly choose what they will or will not do, deciding who they will or will not be, how can anyone be held responsible for what they do or don't do? If we are causally determined and cannot act in any way other than in the way we do act, how can any act be deemed unacceptable?

A fourth argument in favor of self-determination is the deliberation argument. The idea is this: when we deliberate between two or more alternative courses of action, we believe that each alternative is actually available to us and that we can, if we choose to, carry out whichever course of action we prefer. This may be true, but how is it an argument in favor of determinism? Because even determinists, who deny free will engage in deliberation. Their actions demonstrate that regardless of what they say, they really do believe in free will.

Thought and Discussion Questions

1. Describe your basic response to the idea of determinism.
2. Explain incompatibilism and compatibilism as they relate to determinism.
3. Explain your views regarding free will.
4. Which argument in favor of free will do you feel is the strongest? Explain why.
5. Which argument in favor of free will do you feel is the weakest? Explain why.

Chapter 11
What Is The Purpose Of Life?

Where did I come from? Who am I? Why am I here? Why do I exist? Is there a point to any of this? Questions about the meaning or purpose of life are among the most important questions that can be asked. What is the purpose of life? How would one go about considering a question like that? Can that sort of question be answered in any definitive way? Isn't meaning or purpose in life a highly subjective concern? Perhaps. It seems, though, that one good way to begin thinking about the question is to consider what philosophers through the ages have said the purpose of life is or ought to be.

Flourishing

In Chapter 2 we briefly considered Aristotle and the role he played in the development of Greek philosophy. We will consider him again in Chapter 13 in considering the question, *how should human beings live*, when we look at his work in Virtue Ethics. In this section, however, I want to give you the opportunity to read what Aristotle had to say about the purpose of life, so I have included a section from *Nicomachean Ethics* Book 1, Chapters 4 through the first part of Chapter 7. In this material he discusses what the ancient Greeks would have identified as the purpose of life—happiness (flourishing or thriving), by which he meant *living well* and *doing well*. For Aristotle, to live well and do well was to be happy, and to be happy was the point of life. As you read, pay careful attention to how Aristotle defines words, explains concepts, and argues his case. The point here is not to have Aristotle *tell* us what the purpose of life is, but to let him explain to us what he thinks the purpose of life is, and then for us to evaluate his ideas.

> *Let us resume our inquiry and state, in view of the fact that all knowledge and every pursuit aims at some good, what it is that we say political science aims at and what is the highest of all goods achievable by action. Verbally there is very general agreement; for both the general run of men and people of superior refinement say that it is happiness, and identify living well and doing well with being happy; but with regard to what happiness is they differ, and the many do not give the same account as the wise. For the former think it is some plain and obvious thing, like pleasure, wealth, or honour; they differ, however, from one another- and often even the same man identifies it with different things, with health when he is ill, with wealth when he is poor; but, conscious of their ignorance, they admire those who proclaim some great ideal that is above their comprehension. Now some thought that apart from these many goods there is another which is self-subsistent and causes the goodness of all these as*

well. To examine all the opinions that have been held were perhaps somewhat fruitless; enough to examine those that are most prevalent or that seem to be arguable.

Let us not fail to notice, however, that there is a difference between arguments from and those to the first principles. For Plato, too, was right in raising this question and asking, as he used to do, 'are we on the way from or to the first principles?' There is a difference, as there is in a race-course between the course from the judges to the turning-point and the way back. For, while we must begin with what is known, things are objects of knowledge in two senses-some to us, some without qualification. Presumably, then, we must begin with things known to us. Hence any one who is to listen intelligently to lectures about what is noble and just, and generally, about the subjects of political science must have been brought up in good habits. For the fact is the starting-point, and if this is sufficiently plain to him, he will not at the start need the reason as well; and the man who has been well brought up has or can easily get startingpoints. And as for him who neither has nor can get them, let him hear the words of Hesiod:

> *Far best is he who knows all things himself; Good, he that hearkens when men counsel right; But he who neither knows, nor lays to heart Another's wisdom, is a useless wight.*

Let us, however, resume our discussion from the point at which we digressed. To judge from the lives that men lead, most men, and men of the most vulgar type, seem (not without some ground) to identify the good, or happiness, with pleasure; which is the reason why they love the life of enjoyment. For there are, we may say, three prominent types of life- that just mentioned, the political, and thirdly the contemplative life. Now the mass of mankind are evidently quite slavish in their tastes, preferring a life suitable to beasts, but they get some ground for their view from the fact that many of those in high places share the tastes of Sardanapallus. A consideration of the prominent types of life shows that people of superior refinement and of active disposition identify happiness with honour; for this is, roughly speaking, the end of the political life. But it seems too superficial to be what we are looking for, since it is thought to depend on those who bestow honour rather than on him who receives it, but the good we divine to be something proper to a man and not easily taken from him. Further, men seem to pursue honour in order that they may be assured of their goodness; at least it is by men of practical wisdom that they seek to be honoured, and among those who know them, and on the ground of their virtue; clearly, then, according to them, at any rate, virtue is better. And perhaps one might even suppose this to be, rather than honour, the end of the political life.

But even this appears somewhat incomplete; for possession of virtue seems actually compatible with being asleep, or with lifelong inactivity, and, further, with the greatest sufferings and misfortunes; but a man who was living so no one would call happy, unless he were maintaining a thesis at all costs. But enough of this; for the subject has been sufficiently treated even in the current discussions. Third comes the contemplative life, which we shall consider later.

The life of money-making is one undertaken under compulsion, and wealth is evidently not the good we are seeking; for it is merely useful and for the sake of something else. And so one might rather take the

270

aforenamed objects to be ends; for they are loved for themselves. But it is evident that not even these are ends; yet many arguments have been thrown away in support of them. Let us leave this subject, then.

We had perhaps better consider the universal good and discuss thoroughly what is meant by it, although such an inquiry is made an uphill one by the fact that the Forms have been introduced by friends of our own. Yet it would perhaps be thought to be better, indeed to be our duty, for the sake of maintaining the truth even to destroy what touches us closely, especially as we are philosophers or lovers of wisdom; for, while both are dear, piety requires us to honour truth above our friends.

The men who introduced this doctrine did not posit Ideas of classes within which they recognized priority and posteriority (which is the reason why they did not maintain the existence of an Idea embracing all numbers); but the term 'good' is used both in the category of substance and in that of quality and in that of relation, and that which is per se, i.e. substance, is prior in nature to the relative (for the latter is like an off shoot and accident of being); so that there could not be a common Idea set over all these goods. Further, since 'good' has as many senses as 'being' (for it is predicated both in the category of substance, as of God and of reason, and in quality, i.e. of the virtues, and in quantity, i.e. of that which is moderate, and in relation, i.e. of the useful, and in time, i.e. of the right opportunity, and in place, i.e. of the right locality and the like), clearly it cannot be something universally present in all cases and single; for then it could not have been predicated in all the categories but in one only. Further, since of the things answering to one Idea there is one science, there would have been one science of all the goods;

271

but as it is there are many sciences even of the things that fall under one category, e.g. of opportunity, for opportunity in war is studied by strategics and in disease by medicine, and the moderate in food is studied by medicine and in exercise by the science of gymnastics. And one might ask the question, what in the world they mean by 'a thing itself', is (as is the case) in 'man himself' and in a particular man the account of man is one and the same. For in so far as they are man, they will in no respect differ; and if this is so, neither will 'good itself' and particular goods, in so far as they are good. But again it will not be good any the more for being eternal, since that which lasts long is no whiter than that which perishes in a day. The Pythagoreans seem to give a more plausible account of the good, when they place the one in the column of goods; and it is they that Speusippus seems to have followed.

But let us discuss these matters elsewhere; an objection to what we have said, however, may be discerned in the fact that the Platonists have not been speaking about all goods, and that the goods that are pursued and loved for themselves are called good by reference to a single Form, while those which tend to produce or to preserve these somehow or to prevent their contraries are called so by reference to these, and in a secondary sense. Clearly, then, goods must be spoken of in two ways, and some must be good in themselves, the others by reason of these. Let us separate, then, things good in themselves from things useful, and consider whether the former are called good by reference to a single Idea. What sort of goods would one call good in themselves? Is it those that are pursued even when isolated from others, such as intelligence, sight, and certain pleasures and honours? Certainly, if we pursue these also for the

272

sake of something else, yet one would place them among things good in themselves. Or is nothing other than the Idea of good good in itself? In that case the Form will be empty. But if the things we have named are also things good in themselves, the account of the good will have to appear as something identical in them all, as that of whiteness is identical in snow and in white lead. But of honour, wisdom, and pleasure, just in respect of their goodness, the accounts are distinct and diverse. The good, therefore, is not some common element answering to one Idea.

But what then do we mean by the good? It is surely not like the things that only chance to have the same name. Are goods one, then, by being derived from one good or by all contributing to one good, or are they rather one by analogy? Certainly as sight is in the body, so is reason in the soul, and so on in other cases. But perhaps these subjects had better be dismissed for the present; for perfect precision about them would be more appropriate to another branch of philosophy. And similarly with regard to the Idea; even if there is some one good which is universally predicable of goods or is capable of separate and independent existence, clearly it could not be achieved or attained by man; but we are now seeking something attainable. Perhaps, however, some one might think it worth while to recognize this with a view to the goods that are attainable and achievable; for having this as a sort of pattern we shall know better the goods that are good for us, and if we know them shall attain them. This argument has some plausibility, but seems to clash with the procedure of the sciences; for all of these, though they aim at some good and seek to supply the deficiency of it, leave on one side the knowledge of the good. Yet that all the exponents of the arts should be ignorant of, and should not even seek, so great an aid is not probable. It is hard, too, to see how a weaver or a carpenter will be benefited in regard to his own craft by knowing this 'good itself', or how the man who has viewed the Idea itself will be a better doctor or general thereby. For a doctor seems not even to study health in this way, but the health of man, or perhaps rather the health of a particular man; it is individuals that he is healing. But enough of these topics.

Let us again return to the good we are seeking, and ask what it can be. It seems different in different actions and arts; it is different in medicine, in strategy, and in the other arts likewise. What then is the good of each? Surely that for whose sake everything else is done. In medicine this is health, in strategy victory, in architecture a house, in any other sphere something else, and in every action and pursuit the end; for it is for the sake of this that all men do whatever else they do. Therefore, if there is an end for all that we do, this will be the good achievable by action, and if there are more than one, these will be the goods achievable by action.

So the argument has by a different course reached the same point; but we must try to state this even more clearly. Since there are evidently more than one end, and we choose some of these (e.g. wealth, flutes, and in general instruments) for the sake of something else, clearly not all ends are final ends; but the chief good is evidently something final. Therefore, if there is only one final end, this will be what we are seeking, and if there are more than one, the most final of these will be what we are seeking. Now we call that which is in itself worthy of pursuit more final than that which is worthy of pursuit for the sake of something else, and that which is never desirable for the sake of something else more final than the things that are desirable both in themselves and for the sake of that other thing, and therefore we call final without qualification that which is always desirable in itself and never for the sake of something else. Now such a thing happiness, above all else, is held to be; for this we choose always for self and never for the sake of something else.

What is Aristotle trying to do here? Aristotle says he is looking for the "highest of all good achievable by action." In other words, he is asking, what is the very best thing we can do? He answers this question immediately by saying that most people, especially educated, thoughtful people, say that it is being happy, by which they mean living well and doing well. However, he adds, people have different opinions as to what it means to be happy, to live well and do well. Thus, the problem that Aristotle has set for himself in this section of his moral philosophy is to first determine whether or not it is appropriate to say that happiness is the highest of all good that can be achieved. If it turns out that it is, how is this living well and doing well to be understood? What constitutes living well and doing well?

In what, then, does happiness consist? Aristotle notes that for many people happiness is identified with pleasure. For others, happiness would be associated with the political, that is, with involvement and accomplishment in a sociopolitical context. For another smaller group, a life of contemplation would be a happy life. To Aristotle, identifying happiness with pleasure lowers it to the level of satisfying one's baser desires. Living well and doing well must involve more than satisfying one's appetites. The more refined person will link happiness to the honor that grows out of accomplishments associated with sociopolitical activity. This, too, Aristotle insists, is too superficial. Living well and doing well must require something more. Some suggest that virtue, rather than honor, is the end of a life of sociopolitical endeavors—virtues being character traits considered desirable and appropriate. Even, that, Aristotle observes, seems incomplete. There must be something else. Could it be financial success? No. Money is just a tool to be used. Making money does not constitute living well and doing well.

Aristotle then spends some time discussing what *the good* cannot be. At least part of his brief discussion is aimed at Plato's theory of the Forms and the Form of the good—a theory with which Aristotle disagrees. After his detour to address problems with the Platonic theory of the Form of the good (as he sees it), Aristotle refocuses on achieving the highest good. He discusses the idea that each kind of an endeavor (medical, strategic, architectural and so forth) has a good associated with it. The good of medical endeavors is healing and health. The good of strategy is victory. The good of architecture is a strong, beautiful building. But good things of these kinds, and others like them, are related to a specific endeavor and cannot be the highest good that can be achieved. What one good thing can be said to be the final end, the one good thing at which all endeavor is aimed? What is that one thing that is good and desirable in and of itself, a thing that is not a means to an end but is an end in itself? Aristotle says that happiness (as in living well and doing well) is that thing. Happiness is the goal people do and should aim for.

Is Aristotle right? Perhaps. Do we have enough information at this point to decide whether or not Aristotle is right? Probably not. Much of the rest of *Nicomachean Ethics* is given over to the task of explaining in more detail what happiness is and how it is attained. Basically, what he says is that working at incorporating positive (virtuous) character traits into one's life helps one live a life that can be described as flourishing or thriving (living well and doing well) which is the basis for being happy in life—which is the goal of life. So Aristotle's idea is that the goal of life is to be happy.

Pleasure

Another person who thought a great deal about the purpose of life was Epicurus. Epicurus was born in 341 BCE, six years after Plato died. He is the father of *Epicureanism*, a philosophy that says that the purpose of life is to minimize pain and maximize pleasure. Pleasure, according to Epicurus, is what people seek and what makes them happy. As we did with Aristotle, we need to allow Epicurus to explain his ideas to us so we can evaluate them.

Epicurus' letter to his friend Menoeceus (probably written in the late 4th century BCE) was an exhortation for his friend to embrace Epicureanism. As you read, note how Epicurus makes his case.

Greeting.
Let no one be slow to seek wisdom when he is young nor weary in the search thereof when he is grown old. For no age is too early or too late for the health of the soul. And to say that the season for studying philosophy has not yet come, or that it is past and gone, is like saying that the season for happiness is not yet or that it is now no more. Therefore, both old and young ought to seek wisdom, the former in order that, as age comes over him, he may be young in good things because of the grace of what has been, and the latter in order that, while he is young, he may at the same time be old, because he has no fear of the things which are to come. So we must exercise ourselves in the things which bring happiness, since, if that be present, we have everything, and, if that be absent, all our actions are directed toward attaining it.

Those things which without ceasing I have declared to you, those do, and exercise yourself in those, holding them to be the elements of right life. First believe that God is a living being immortal and happy, according to the notion of a god indicated by the common sense of humankind; and so of him anything that is at agrees not with about him whatever may uphold both his happyness and his immortality. For truly there are gods, and knowledge of them is evident; but they are not such as the multitude believe, seeing that people do not steadfastly maintain the notions they form respecting them. Not the person who denies the gods worshipped by the multitude, but he who affirms of the gods what the multitude believes about them is truly impious. For the utterances of the multitude about the gods are not true preconceptions but false assumptions; hence it is that the greatest evils happen to the wicked and the greatest blessings happen to the good from the hand of the gods, seeing that they are always favorable to their own good qualities and take pleasure in people like to themselves, but reject as alien whatever is not of their kind.

Accustom yourself to believe that death is nothing to us, for good and evil imply awareness, and death is the privation of all awareness; therefore a right understanding that death is nothing to us makes the mortality of life enjoyable, not by adding to life an unlimited time, but by taking away the yearning after immortality. For life has no terror; for those who thoroughly apprehend that there are no terrors for them in ceasing to live. Foolish, therefore, is the person who says that he fears death, not because it will pain when it comes, but because it pains in the prospect. Whatever causes no annoyance when it is present, causes only a groundless pain in the expectation. Death, therefore, the most awful of evils, is nothing to us, seeing that, when we are, death is not come, and, when death is come, we are not. It is nothing, then, either to the living or to the dead, for with the living it is not and the dead exist no longer. But in the world, at one time people shun death as the greatest of all evils, and at another time choose it as a respite from the evils in life. The wise person does not deprecate life nor does he fear the cessation of life. The thought of life is no offense to him, nor is the cessation of life regarded as an evil. And even as people choose of food not merely and simply the

278

larger portion, but the more pleasant, so the wise seek to enjoy the time which is most pleasant and not merely that which is longest. And he who admonishes the young to live well and the old to make a good end speaks foolishly, not merely because of the desirability of life, but because the same exercise at once teaches to live well and to die well. Much worse is he who says that it were good not to be born, but when once one is born to pass with all speed through the gates of Hades. For if he truly believes this, why does he not depart from life? It were easy for him to do so, if once he were firmly convinced. If he speaks only in mockery, his words are foolishness, for those who hear believe him not.

We must remember that the future is neither wholly ours nor wholly not ours, so that neither must we count upon it as quite certain to come nor despair of it as quite certain not to come.

We must also reflect that of desires some are natural, others are groundless; and that of the natural some are necessary as well as natural, and some natural only. And of the necessary desires some are necessary if we are to be happy, some if the body is to be rid of uneasiness, some if we are even to live. He who has a clear and certain understanding of these things will direct every preference and aversion toward securing health of body and tranquillity of mind, seeing that this is the sum and end of a happy life. For the end of all our actions is to be free from pain and fear, and, when once we have attained all this, the tempest of the soul is laid; seeing that the living creature has no need to go in search of something that is lacking, nor to look anything else by which the good of the soul and of the body will be fulfilled. When we are pained pleasure, then, and then only, do we feel the need of pleasure. For this reason we call pleasure the alpha and omega of a happy life. Pleasure is our first and kindred good. It is the starting-point of every choice and of every aversion, and to it we come back, inasmuch as we make feeling the rule by which to judge of every good thing. And since pleasure is our first and native good,

279

for that reason we do not choose every pleasure whatever, but often pass over many pleasures when a greater annoyance ensues from them. And often we consider pains superior to pleasures when submission to the pains for a long time brings us as a consequence a greater pleasure. While therefore all pleasure because it is naturally akin to us is good, not all pleasure is worthy of choice, just as all pain is an evil and yet not all pain is to be shunned. It is, however, by measuring one against another, and by looking at the conveniences and inconveniences, teat all these matters must be judged. Sometimes we treat the good as an evil, and the evil, on the contrary, as a good. Again, we regard. independence of outward things as a great good, not so as in all cases to use little, but so as to be contented with little if we have not much, being honestly persuaded that they have the sweetest enjoyment of luxury who stand least in need of it, and that whatever is natural is easily procured and only the vain and worthless hard to win. Plain fare gives as much pleasure as a costly diet, when one the pain of want has been removed, while bread an water confer the highest possible pleasure when they are brought to hungry lips. To habituate one's se therefore, to simple and inexpensive diet supplies al that is needful for health, and enables a person to meet the necessary requirements of life without shrinking and it places us in a better condition when we approach at intervals a costly fare and renders us fearless of fortune.

When we say, then, that pleasure is the end and aim, we do not mean the pleasures of the prodigal or the pleasures of sensuality, as we are understood to do by some through ignorance, prejudice, or willful misrepresentation. By pleasure we mean the absence of pain in the body and of trouble in the soul. It is not an unbroken succession of drinking-bouts and of merrymaking, not sexual love, not the enjoyment of the fish and other delicacies of a luxurious table, which produce a pleasant life; it is sober reasoning, searching out the grounds of every choice and avoidance, and banishing those beliefs through which the greatest disturbances take possession of the soul. Of all this is prudence. For this reason prudence is a more precious thing even than the other virtues, for ad a life of pleasure which is not also a life of prudence, honor, and justice; nor lead a life of prudence, honor, and justice, which is not also a life of pleasure. For the virtues have grown into one with a pleasant life, and a pleasant life is inseparable from them.

Who, then, is superior in your judgment to such a person? He holds a holy belief concerning the gods, and is altogether free from the fear of death. He has diligently considered the end fixed by nature, and understands how easily the limit of good things can be reached and attained, and how either the duration or the intensity of evils is but slight. Destiny which some introduce as sovereign over all things, he laughs to scorn, affirming rather that some things happen of necessity, others by chance, others through our own agency. For he sees that necessity destroys responsibility and that chance or fortune is inconstant; whereas our own actions are free, and it is to them that praise and blame naturally attach. It were better, indeed, to accept the legends of the gods than to bow beneath destiny which the natural philosophers have imposed. The one holds out some faint hope that we may escape if we honor the gods, while the necessity of the naturalists is deaf to all entreaties. Nor does he hold chance to be a god, as the world in general does, for in the acts of a god there is no disorder; nor to be a cause, though an uncertain one, for he believes that no good or evil is dispensed by chance to people so as to make life happy, though it supplies the starting-point of great good and great evil. He believes that the misfortune of the wise is better than the prosperity of the fool. It is better, in short, that what is well judged in action should not owe its successful issue to the aid of chance.

Exercise yourself in these and kindred precepts day and night, both by yourself and with him who is like to you; then never, either in waking or in dream,

will you be disturbed, but will live as a god among
people. For people lose all appearance of mortality
by living in the midst of immortal blessings.[136]

How, then, does Epicurus set out his philosophy of Epicureanism? Philosophers appear to agree that Epicurus is, to a degree, following Aristotle. There are, however, some basic differences. See if you can find the most obvious.

Epicurus begins by exhorting Menoeceus to study philosophy (seek wisdom) now, while he is young, and to remain steadfast in his study even in old age. Epicurus then, along with Aristotle, identifies happiness as that which people seek to attain. All activity, Epicurus asserts, is aimed at being happy. As part of this search for happiness, Epicurus urges his friend to believe in God and not fear death. Nor should Menoeceus worry too much about the future for, while it is not entirely beyond some measure of control, it is certainly not easily controlled. In other words, some things we can control and some we cannot. So don't get too worked up about all of it.

As Epicurus begins to focus more specifically on the idea of happiness, he asserts that the only way one can have a happy life is by securing the health of the body and the tranquility of the mind. We might say he is advocating that happiness grows out of physical health and mental and emotional peace of mind... not being all stressed out. To achieve this requires that we minimize pain and maximize pleasure, with a serious effort to maximize pleasure. He says, "...we call pleasure the alpha and the omega of a happy life." Alpha is the first letter of the Greek alphabet; Omega the last. So he is saying that pleasure is the beginning and the end of happiness.

Epicurus was aware that some pleasures can only be realized and enjoyed after enduring some pain. Thus, to have pleasure and be happy we have to endure some pain. Still,

---

[136] Translated into English by Robert Drew Hicks.

the goal is to minimize the pain and get to the pleasure part. Epicurus also stresses that when he speaks of pleasure, he is not necessarily referring to sensual pleasures. In fact, sensual pleasures are not the best form of pleasure and do not generate lasting happiness. What kind of pleasures, then, does Epicurus recommend? Basically, Epicurus is recommending sober reasoning—by which he means rational reflection on what to do or not do, and why. In other words, philosophical contemplation is about how to live life. Sounds a lot like what Aristotle said. To a degree it is. Yet it is different in one important way. Aristotle does not leave open a door for hedonistic pleasure to become the basis for happiness. Epicurus appears to have done just that. He has argued that the happy person is one who is in good shape physically and mentally, avoiding those things that cause distress. While he does advise against sensual overindulgence, he also focuses on the physical and mental pleasures as those that generate happiness. Thus, for Epicurus, the pleasures that result in a good physical and mental state become the basis for a happy life. Epicurus' happiness is clearly hedonistic in nature—a happy life is a life of pleasure. While in this letter to his friend Menoeceus, Epicurus suggests a focus on intellectual pleasures rather than sensual, the judgment of philosophers throughout history is that his is a hedonistic philosophy. The question to be asked, therefore, is, *can seeking pleasure be the purpose of life?* Most thoughtful people have said, no.

Aristotle and Epicurus each focus on happiness as the purpose of life, though each defines it differently. Throughout the centuries, the considered judgment of philosophers is that Epicurus' hedonistic approach leaves much to be desired. Aristotle, however, in the larger context of his moral philosophy, referred to as Virtue Ethics, may have identified something helpful.

283

Becoming

But there is yet another way of thinking about the purpose of life, one that is not rooted in the idea that life's purpose is to be happy. There is a passage in Plato's dialog, *Timaeus*, that will help set the stage for this part of the discussion.

> *Let me tell you then why the creator made this world of generation. He was good, and the good can never have any jealousy of anything. And being free from jealousy, he desired that all things should be as like himself as they could be. This is in the truest sense the origin of creation and of the world, as we shall do well in believing on the testimony of wise men: God desired that all things should be good and nothing bad, so far as this was attainable.*[137]

Here Plato suggests that God created the cosmos for a specific purpose, namely, that it (all parts of it, including humans) be perfected, that is, that it achieve its potential. He is talking about potential being actualized, about a process of *becoming*. We may have doubts about the material cosmos becoming anything more than it already is.[138] But the idea of human potential being actualized in a process of becoming is intriguing.

Considering the idea from a materialistic point of view, the idea seems rather severely limited. If we are born, live, and in a few years die and that's it, what are the chances of any significant becoming occurring? Not great. But from a dualistic perspective, the idea takes on dramatic potential. To make sense of the idea, we need to discuss human origin,

---

[137] Plato, *Timaeus*, translated by Benjamin Jowett.
[138] The idea is not entirely incoherent, however. Consider the acorn becoming an oak tree. Is it possible that the cosmos can become something other than what it is now, just as the acorn can? Certainly such a thing is possible.

human nature and then human potential.

Human Origins

Where did humans come from? There are only two possibilities. Humans can trace their origin either to non-living, non-conscious, non-rational matter, or to living, conscious, rational mind. Based on the arguments made in Chapter 6, I believe it can be demonstrated that that which has always existed and which is the source of all other things that exist is a living, conscious, rational mind. There is no coherent way to explain how non-living, non-conscious, non-rational matter generates that which is living, conscious, and rational. It has not and cannot be done. However, it is quite simple to explain how a living, conscious, rational mind produces other living, conscious, rational minds. A dualistic explanation of human origins is entirely coherent. A materialistic explanation, in my opinion, is not. Accepting this premise, we can say then that the eternally existing mind created other minds.

Human Nature

The eternally-existing mind (God) is a mind kind of a being, a rational substance. The other minds he created (us) are also rational substances, mind kind of beings. We are embodied while he is not, but our essential nature is that of a mind kind of a being, a mental substance. We are rational beings. That is what differentiates us from animals, animals that think but that are not rational—they do not engage in abstract conceptualization as do humans.

In Chapter 9 we discussed a number a features that, based upon rational reflection and observation, can be identified as basic features of human nature. We said that humans are: self-aware, self-determined, rational, capable of aesthetic appreciation and creation, rationally relational, culture builders and users, embodied minds, and enduring minds. We also noted a high degree of similarity between those *human* traits and a number of traits we are able to identify in God. Perhaps the similarity between the eternally-existing mind (God) and the other minds he created (humans) is no coincidence. Perhaps the other minds God created are essentially the same (stuff) as he is—mental substance. If that is the case, what are the implications?

Human Potential

What are the implications indeed! If our essence is the same as God's (if we are mental substances as he is), what kind of potential do we have? While it would be unwarranted to assume that humans could ever be equal to the eternally-existing mind that is responsible for the existence of the cosmos, it is logical to infer that other mental beings that God created have a potential similar to his own, a potential to become much more than we are in our present state of development. Why is this a logical inference? Because God creating other minds, minds that are the same kind of mental stuff God is, is analogous to humans producing offspring who are the same kinds of beings they are. I have three sons. None of them are me, but each of them is the same kind of a being I am, capable of the same kinds of activities and achievements of which I am capable. If this is an accurate analogy, and I believe it is, then because we are (metaphorically) God's offspring, it is logical to infer that we are the same kind of being God is and have, therefore, the potential to become like him—the acorn can become an oak.

The fact that we are embodied minds must be factored into the equation. But being embodied minds does not necessarily limit our potential to develop (evolve?) as mental beings. For instance, at our present level of development, to get thoughts from one mind into another, we must use a set of communication symbols, spoken, written, or gestured, in order to communicate. But is it possible that, given enough time, humans might develop telepathic abilities so that we can simply send thoughts from one mind to another without having to use written, spoken, or gestured symbols? I see no reason why, given sufficient time (perhaps hundreds of thousands of years), such evolutionary development is not possible.

What other kinds of skills might humans develop? At present we can create thoughts. The immaterial mind has the ability to create immaterial thoughts. It is an amazing creative process. We can think a thought we've never thought before. We can even think thoughts no one else has ever thought before. Albert Einstein had a few of those. The immaterial mind is capable of creating immaterial thoughts. Perhaps, given enough time, human minds will also learn how to move physical objects and to create physical matter, just as God did.

Obviously this is entirely speculative. But it is also entirely possible. An acorn can become an oak tree. What is a fetus capable of doing? Not much. But after it is born, given enough time, a human matures and develops skills that compared to a fetus are amazing. What if our existence in this world is something akin to a time of fetal development? What if our life right now is being lived out in the womb of the world and at some point in time we will be transitioned (born?) into the next phase of our existence where we will continue to mature along a developmental continuum? If this is the case, we have humankind on an evolutionary developmental continuum while each individual is on a personal developmental continuum that spans one's entire existence, not merely the physical phase of one's life. Humankind evolves, and each individual matures. So collectively and individually we are in the process of

287

becoming, we are in an ongoing developmental process of achieving our potential.

If this is the case, what are we to achieve during this physical part of our existence? If *becoming* is our purpose, what is it we are to become? What are we to achieve?[139] If we can humble ourselves (both as individuals and as a race of beings) enough to think of ourselves as very young children, clumsy, naive, unskilled, curious, rummaging about trying to figure things out, we might be able to draw a comparison that will be useful. What do young children need to learn? They need to learn all sorts of things. Children need to acquire a great deal of general knowledge about their world, about themselves and others, about how to meet their needs, how to get along, how to think analytically so they can solve problems and overcome challenges as part of their developmental process. Children need to learn lots of basic preparatory things just so they will be prepared to go to school where they will continue to learn the things they will need to know to be functional and productive in the world of adults. And even when they do become adults, there is still a lot to learn! Learning, growth, development and maturity never (or should never) stop occurring. Learning is life-long. Learning and growing is part of existing. *If the human mind is never finished existing, it is never finished learning, and developing.*

What, then, is the comparison between a human child who has much to learn and a human mind (a mental being) who has much to learn? We need to see ourselves, no matter how old or educated we are, as children who have a lot to learn. If we can manage to think of ourselves in that way, it may be easier to understand what it is we need to learn throughout this phase of our existence. I want to focus our thinking just briefly on four things that are foundational to

---

[139] The rest of the material in this section is borrowed from Rogers, *Becoming: A Philosophical Treatise on Human Potential.*

our development: identity, priorities, relational interaction, and discipline and self-control. These four things are basic but challenging. It may take us, depending on our family and life context, the whole of our physical lives to begin to make progress in these areas.

Identity

Because humans are self-aware, rational, and self-determined, we have a strong sense of personal identity. Sometimes it takes quite a while for us to figure out who we are, but for many people their personal identity has only to do with their immediate material context. That, however, is a limited (one dimensional) perspective, and there is, in reality, a great deal more than that to our identity. As I have argued, humans are dualistic beings. We are *mind-body beings* that live in two worlds, the physical world of the body and the mental world of the mind. Because the physical body decays and dies, the physical aspect of our existence is only one phase of our existence. It is a brief, temporary phase that helps prepare us for what comes next. To make the most of this preparatory phase, we need to understand it for what it is, which means understanding: 1) our own dualistic nature, and 2) the dualistic nature of reality—that there is a material and a non-material realm. We cannot grow as we might otherwise grow and mature as we might otherwise mature if we do not understand our own dualistic nature and the dualistic nature of reality.

Priorities

Another important lesson to be learned during this phase of our existence is how to prioritize life appropriately. This, of course, goes hand-in-hand with understanding our

289

identity, our own dualistic nature and the dualistic nature of reality. When we understand who we are and the kind of reality of which we are a part, prioritizing life appropriately is *theoretically* easier because we have a better idea of what is more and less important. I say *theoretically* easier because even when we know what is more important, what often happens is that the less important but urgent things of life cry out for attention, getting bumped up the list and treated as if they were more important than they really are.

What kinds of things are more important and what kinds of things are less important? Generally speaking, we normally attach more importance to things that are permanent and less importance to things that are temporary. For example, when we buy a home intending to live in it a long time, we understand the importance of keeping it properly maintained and attractively decorated. When we are traveling, however, and spending a night or two (or even more) in a hotel, we do not feel the need to maintain and decorate it. Since we are only there temporarily, such expenditures would be foolish.

If the physical phase of our existence is not permanent, if the body is destined to decay and die and it is the mind that is the enduring us, focusing too much attention on the physical aspect of our existence rather than the mental would appear to be unwise. Thus, activities that lead to development and insight related to the enduring us, to the growth and maturity of our essential mental selves, ought to be our primary priorities.

Relational Interaction

Part of prioritizing life appropriately involves understanding the importance of relationships with others. When we interact with another person, we are interacting with an embodied mind, with another dualistic being whose essential self transcends his or her physical body. Because minds are not temporary like physical bodies, but are enduring, the relational interactions that occur between enduring minds are highly significant.

I wonder how often we think of relational interacting as something that is multidimensional and transcendent? If the *essential us* is an enduring mind being, and the essential other with whom we are interacting is an enduring mind being, then those significant ongoing relational interactions are transcendent and enduring in nature. They are interactions along the enduring developmental continuum that are related to our levels of development and maturity on that continuum. Because they are transcendent in nature, they are more important than things that are not transcendent.

But even if we are not aware of the significance of the transcendental nature of many of our relational interactions, engaging other minds, interacting with them and relating to them at all levels is a fundamental part of the developmental process. Appropriate relational interaction, then, must surely be one of the things we need to learn during this phase of our existence.

How would one define appropriate relational interaction? Does God have something specific in mind? As children begin to interact with other children they must learn to be nice, not to hit or grab, but to be gentle, to share, and so forth. Just as each child must learn to interact in positive healthy ways with other children, adult humans must continue the process and learn to interact with other humans in positive healthy ways. We must learn to be kind, helpful, patient, tolerant, forgiving, considerate, compassionate, respectful, and so forth—all the things that enhance relational interactions between humans. We must learn to interact appropriately with people of our own culture (people who are like us) and with those of other cultures (people who are not like us) whose ways may seem strange to us.

Discipline and Self-control

Yet another lesson we need learn is to be disciplined and self-controlled. If we can come to think of ourselves as the offspring (children) of God, an idea that is thousands of years old, then we can readily understand his desire that we learn (sooner rather than later) to practice discipline and self-control.[140] We spend a great deal of time trying to teach our children self-control. Some learn easier and sooner than others. Even among siblings, some will learn easier and earlier to be disciplined and self-controlled. In this regard, God faces some of the same challenges parents face.

Why is it important to be disciplined and self-controlled? Because those who are undisciplined and who lack the ability to control their drives and impulses generally do not make the same kind of progress in life as those who are disciplined and self-controlled. If the goal is progress along a developmental continuum, then being disciplined and self-controlled sooner rather than later will enhance our progress.

Of course, all this becoming must surely be done in the context of the kind of living well and doing well that Aristotle focused on. If we are *becoming*, if we are in the process of achieving our full potential as a human being, we will incorporate into our lives the kinds of character traits (virtues) that are valued and appreciated and that help us live a happy, meaningful life. Becoming does not exclude happiness; it leads to the most satisfying kind of happiness the human can experience.

If the purpose of life is to become, to achieve our full potential, and if our becoming spans our entire existence,

---

[140] Though being disciplined and self-controlled are not the same thing, for the purpose of this discussion I am linking them together because they are complementary. A disciplined person is usually also self-controlled. However, a person can be self-controlled (in control of his or her drives and impulses) but not very disciplined in how he or she organizes and conducts daily affairs.

then we appear at this phase of our existence to be at the very beginning of a long and dynamic developmental trajectory that may in some way be analogous to an acorn becoming an oak tree.

Life's Purpose

So what is life's purpose? Is it to flourish, as Aristotle suggested, to live well and do well? Or is it to experience as much pleasure as we can, as Epicurus suggested? Or was Plato right, at least in part, when he suggested that becoming is the purpose of life? Did God create us for a specific purpose? If so, would it be simply for us to experience as much pleasure as possible? That idea appears to be rather shallow. Surely God can come up with a better purpose than that. Aristotle's idea, to live well and do well, comes closer to making good sense. It has much to commend it. But does it go far enough? Aristotle's purpose could be accomplished in an entirely materialistic context. It does not require a dualistic perspective. But Plato's idea, especially the modified, expanded version I have presented, is rooted in a dualistic perspective and requires not only that one live well and do well, as Aristotle suggested, but that one do so with a clear focus on the dualistic nature of reality.

So what is the purpose of life? Is it flourishing? Is it pleasure? Is it becoming? Or is there some other purpose?

Summary

Why am I here? Why are any of us here? What's the point? Is there a point? Why do we exist at all? What is the purpose of life? Aristotle had an opinion. He believed life's purpose is to flourish, to live well and to do well. For Aristotle, to live a life that can be described as flourishing is

293

to be happy. And happiness (the kind of happiness that grows out of living a flourishing kind of life) is the purpose of life. So live well and do well and be happy. Sounds pretty good from one point of view. But it can be understood and accomplished from a materialistic perspective. It is rooted in a *here and now* kind of happiness which involves a here and now kind of a purpose. This appears to be shortsighted.

Epicurus also had an opinion. He believed that experiencing as much pleasure as possible is the purpose of life. His is a hedonistic philosophy. It's all about pleasure. Surely the shortcomings of that approach are obvious.

Then there was Plato. Plato believed that life's purpose was to *become*. His idea of a cosmic becoming may seem odd to us, but if we adjust it a bit as I have done, the idea is an interesting one. It requires a dualistic perspective on reality and the nature of the human being. It requires understanding that the essential us is a mental being, a mental being who happens to be embodied, but a mental being nonetheless. It involves seeing one's total existence as unfolding in stages or phases, with this part of our existence being at the very beginning of a long and dynamic developmental process. Analogically, we might say that just as the acorn becomes the oak, so we can *become* like the eternally existing mind who created us as we travel along a developmental continuum.

Which view is correct? Is the purpose of life to flourish, to enjoy, or to become? Or is there some other purpose?

Thought and Discussion Questions

1. Describe and evaluate Aristotle's system of flourishing as you understand it.
2. Describe and evaluate Epicurus' system of pleasure as you understand it.

3. Describe and evaluate Plato's idea of becoming as Rogers narrows it (from cosmic to personal becoming) and explains the idea.

4. Explain how a materialistic perspective versus a dualistic perspective results in a different view regarding the purpose of life.

5. Explain and defend your own view about the purpose if life.

Chapter 12
Is There Life After Death?

"I'm not afraid of death; I just don't want to be there when it happens." Woody Allen.

"To the well-organized mind, death is but the next great adventure." J.K. Rowling.

"The fear of death follows from the fear of life. A man who lives fully is prepared to die at any time." Samuel Clemens.

Quotes about death could fill a book. On an individual basis, we don't talk about death a lot, but each of us thinks about it at some point, perhaps when a loved one dies. The old saying is that the only certainties in life are death and taxes. But if you know how, taxes can be avoided. Not so with death. It is inevitable. We know it's coming, and we don't like it. Why not? Because it is the end. Or is it? Is death the end or is there life after death? This question has haunted humans since there have been humans around to think about it.

Death As A Part Of Life

We are created through the process of procreation. The *I* that is *me* came into being when a sperm produced by my father fertilized an egg produced by my mother. Some of my father's DNA combined with some of my mother's DNA to create the unique strand of DNA that provided cells with the instructions they needed to build me. Following the instructions in the DNA, my cells constructed, me and nine months after I was conceived I was ready to be born. That's the way the process works. A body is constructed that is part of this physical world, a body that can eat, drink, breathe, sleep, walk, run, think, reproduce, do stuff, and make things. In other words, we are born to live in this world. It is actually a pretty nifty system. We are born to live.

But we are also born to die. The physical body is not meant to live forever. The body has a lifespan. Cellular replication can only be carried on for a finite period of time. The body gets old, wears out and ceases to function. We are born; we live; we die. While we live, we produce the next generation. We die but they carry on, also reproducing the next generation. Then they die. Each generation produces the next and then dies. It is the cycle of life. Birth, life, death. Thus, death is part of the cycle of life. Just as we are born to live, we are born to die. Death is coming. There's no denying it. Sometimes we can delay it a few more years, but eventually our time arrives. Eventually we die. And under normal circumstances we are not looking forward to it. Why not? Because, for most people, it involves elements of uncertainty and finality with which we are not comfortable. Why are we not comfortable? Because many of us are not sure about whether or not there is life after death or, if there is, under what conditions we will live it. For many people there are just too many uncertainties for us to be entirely comfortable with the event.

Ancient Theories Of Death

We are certainly not the first people to be concerned about death. As noted already, questions about death are as old of humankind. In this section we will look at some ancient theories about death, the main question being, is there life after death? The ancients considered this question under the heading: the immortality of the soul. The question is: is there a part of us (a conscious individuated self) that lives on after the body dies? Or, asked another way, after my body dies, do I still exist?

The Ancient Greeks

It is likely the case that the average ancient Greek embraced the Homeric conception of the Hadean underworld afterlife. Zeus' brother, Hades, was the ruler of the underworld, also referred to as Hades. The souls of the dead went to Hades where they lived a shadowy existence in the underworld as shades, the spirits or ghosts of the dead. Obviously this is a belief in the immortality of the soul. The body dies but something of the person, the soul or spirit of that person, continues to exist in another realm. In Homer's *Odyssey*, Odysseus has a vision of the underworld.

It should not be assumed, however, that the serious thinkers in post-Homeric Greece also embraced the idea. Some of them may have; others may have been agnostic in their views, claiming that there was not sufficient evidence to have knowledge regarding immortality.

Pythagoras and the Pythagoreans

Pythagoras (570 to ca. 490 BCE) was one of the more influential thinkers in ancient Greece. Born on Samos (an

Island off the coast of Turkey), he moved to Croton (in Southern Italy) when he was around forty years old. He founded a religious society that was ascetic in nature, requiring strict self-discipline including silence and not eating meat or beans. Pythagoras likely believed in the immortality of the soul and taught the idea of *metempsychosis* (sometimes referred to as *transmigration* of souls) that is, that the soul is reincarnated. Specifically, he believed that the human soul could be reincarnated in plants and animals as well as in human form.

Pythagoras was considered to be an expert on the soul and religious teaching and practices related to death. Huffman notes that, "Herodotus describes Pythagorean practices as "rituals" and gives as an example that the Pythagoreans agree with the Egyptians in not allowing the dead to be buried in wool."[141]

Plato

The reason Pythagoreanism is important is that Plato, one of the most influential philosophers in history, was significantly influenced by Pythagorean beliefs. Brickhouse provides a concise summary of Pythagoras' influence on Plato.

Diogenes Laertius (3.6) claims that Plato visited several Pythagoreans in Southern Italy (one of whom, Theodorus, is also mentioned as a friend to Socrates in Plato's Theaetetus). In the Seventh Letter, we learn that Plato was a friend of Archytas of Tarentum, a well-known Pythagorean statesman and thinker (see 339d-e), and in the Phaedo, Plato has Echecrates, another Pythagorean, in the group around Socrates

---

141 Huffman, "Pythagoras," *Stanford Encyclopedia of Philosophy.*

on his final day in prison. Plato's Pythagorean influences seem especially evident in his fascination with mathematics, and in some of his political ideals (see Plato's political philosophy), expressed in various ways in several dialogues.[142]

Perhaps the best way to understand how Pythagoreanism impacted Plato is to read his dialog, *Phaedo*. In this dialog, Socrates has been convicted and sentenced to death. He has been in prison for a month waiting for the day of execution to arrive. On the day of his execution his friends have gathered to be with him. Surprisingly, Socrates is upbeat and wants to do what he loves—have a philosophical discussion. The dialog is about Socrates' last philosophical conversation, which happens to be on the subject of the immortality of the soul.

PHAEDO
By Plato
translated by Benjamin Jowett

PERSONS OF THE DIALOGUE
PHAEDO, who is the narrator of the dialogue to
ECHECRATES of Phlius
SOCRA TES
APOLLODORUS
SIMMIAS
CEBES
CRITO
ATTENDANT OF THE PRISON PHAEDO

SCENE: The prison cell of Socrates

---

142 Brickhouse and Smith, "Plato," *Internet Encyclopedia of Philosophy*.

Echecrates *Were you yourself, Phaedo, in the prison with Socrates on the day when he drank the poison?*
Phaedo *Yes, Echecrates, I was.*
Ech *I wish that you would tell me about his death. What did he say in his last hours? We were informed that he died by taking poison, but no one knew anything more; for no Phliasian ever goes to Athens now, and a long time has elapsed since any Athenian found his way to Phlius, and therefore we had no clear account.*
Phaed *Did you not hear of the proceedings at the trial?*
Ech *Yes; someone told us about the trial, and we could not understand why, having been condemned, he was put to death, as appeared, not at the time, but long afterwards. What was the reason of this?*
Phaed *An accident, Echecrates. The reason was that the stern of the ship which the Athenians send to Delos happened to have been crowned on the day before he was tried.*
Ech *What is this ship?*
Phaed *This is the ship in which, as the Athenians say, Theseus went to Crete when he took with him the fourteen youths, and was the saviour of them and of himself. And*
they were said to have vowed to Apollo at the time, that if they were saved they would make an annual pilgrimage to Delos. Now this custom still continues, and the whole period of the voyage to and from Delos, beginning when the priest of Apollo crowns the stern of the ship, is a holy season, during which the city is not allowed to be polluted by public executions; and often, when the vessel is detained by adverse winds, there may be a very considerable delay. As I was saying, the ship was crowned on the day before the trial, and this was the reason why Socrates lay in

*prison and was not put to death until long after he
was condemned.*

Ech *What was the manner of his death, Phaedo?
What was said or done? And which of his friends had
he with him? Or were they not allowed by the
authorities to be present? And did he die alone?*

Phaed *No; there were several of his friends with him.*

Ech *If you have nothing to do, I wish that you would
tell me what passed, as exactly as you can.*

Phaed *I have nothing to do, and will try to gratify
your wish. For to me, too, there is no greater
pleasure than to have Socrates brought to my
recollection, whether I speak myself or hear another
speak of him.*

Ech *You will have listeners who are of the same mind
with you, and I hope that you will be as exact as you
can.*

Phaed *I remember the strange feeling which came
over me at being with him. For I could hardly believe
that I was present at the death of a friend, and
therefore I did not pity him, Echecrates; his mien and
his language were so noble and fearless in the hour
of death that to me he appeared blessed. I thought
that in going to the other world he could not be
without a divine call, and that he would be happy, if
any man ever was, when he arrived there, and
therefore I did not pity him as might seem natural at
such a time. But neither could I feel the pleasure
which I usually felt in philosophical discourse (for
philosophy was the theme of which we spoke). I was
pleased, and I was also pained, because I knew that
he was soon to die, and this strange mixture of feeling
was shared by us all; we were laughing and weeping
by turns, especially the excitable Apollodorus you
know the sort of man?*

Ech *Yes.*

Phaed *He was quite overcome; and I myself and all of us were greatly moved.*

Ech *Who were present?*

Phaed *Of native Athenians there were, besides Apollodorus, Critobulus and his father Crito, Hermogenes, Epigenes, Aeschines, and Antisthenes; likewise Ctesippus of the deme of Paeania, Menexenus, and some others; but Plato, if I am not mistaken, was ill.*

Ech *Were there any strangers?*

Phaed *Yes, there were; Simmias the Theban, and Cebes, and Phaedondes; Euclid and Terpison, who came from Megara.*

Ech *And was Aristippus there, and Cleombrotus?*

Phaed *No, they were said to be in Aegina.*

Ech *Anyone else?*

Phaed *I think that these were about all.*

Ech *And what was the discourse of which you spoke?*

Phaed *I will begin at the beginning, and endeavor to repeat the entire conversation. You must understand that we had been previously in the habit of assembling early in the morning at the court in which the trial was held, and which is not far from the prison. There we remained talking with one another until the opening of the prison doors (for they were not opened very early), and then went in and generally passed the day with Socrates. On the last morning the meeting was earlier than usual; this was owing to our having heard on the previous evening that the sacred ship had arrived from Delos, and therefore we agreed to meet very early at the accustomed place. On our going to the prison, the jailer who answered the door, instead of admitting us, came out and bade us wait and he would call us. "For the Eleven," he said, "are now with Socrates; they are taking off his chains, and giving orders that*

*he is to die today." He soon returned and said that
we might come in. On entering we found Socrates just
released from chains, and Xanthippe, whom you
know, sitting by him, and holding his child in her
arms.*

*When she saw us she uttered a cry and said, as
women will: "O Socrates, this is the last time that
either you will converse with your friends, or they
with you." Socrates turned to Crito and said:
"Crito, let someone take her home." Some of Crito's
people accordingly led her away, crying out and
beating herself. And when she was gone, Socrates,
sitting up on the couch, began to bend and rub his leg,
saying, as he rubbed: "How singular is the thing
called pleasure, and how curiously related to pain,
which might be thought to be the opposite of it; for
they never come to a man together, and yet he who
pursues either of them is generally compelled to take
the other. They are two, and yet they grow together
out of one head or stem; and I cannot help thinking
that if Aesop had noticed them, he would have made a
fable about God trying to reconcile their strife, and
when he could not, he fastened their heads together;
and this is the reason why when one comes the other
follows, as I find in my own case pleasure comes
following after the pain in my leg, which was caused
by the chain."*

*Upon this Cebes said: I am very glad indeed,
Socrates, that you mentioned the name of Aesop. For
that reminds me of a question which has been asked
by others, and was asked of me only the day before
yesterday by Evenus the poet, and as he will be sure
to as again, you may as well tell me what I should say
to him, if you would like him to have an answer. He
wanted to know why you who never before wrote a
line of poetry, now that you are in prison are putting*

Aesop into verse, and also composing that hymn in honor of Apollo.

Tell him, Cebes, he replied, that I had no idea of rivalling him or his poems; which is the truth, for I knew that I could not do that. But I wanted to see whether I could purge away a scruple which I felt about certain dreams. In the course of my life I have often had intimations in dreams "that I should make music." The same dream came to me sometimes in one form, and sometimes in another, but always saying the same or nearly the same words: Make and cultivate music, said the dream. And hitherto I had imagined that this was only intended to exhort and encourage me in the study of philosophy, which has always been the pursuit of my life, and is the noblest and best of music. The dream was bidding me to do what I was already doing, in the same way that the competitor in a race is bidden by the spectators to run when he is already running. But I was not certain of this, as the dream might have meant music in the popular sense of the word, and being under sentence of death, and the festival giving me a respite, I thought that I should be safer if I satisfied the scruple, and, in obedience to the dream, composed a few verses before I departed. And first I made a hymn in honor of the god of the festival, and then considering that a poet, if he is really to be a poet or maker, should not only put words together but make stories, and as I have no invention, I took some fables of esop, which I had ready at hand and knew, and turned them into verse. Tell Evenus this, and bid him be of good cheer; that I would have him come after me if he be a wise man, and not tarry; and that to-day I am likely to be going, for the Athenians say that I must.

Simmias said: What a message for such a man! having been a frequent companion of his, I should say that, as far as I know him, he will never take your advice unless he is obliged.

Why, said Socrates,-is not Evenus a philosopher?

I think that he is, said Simmias.

Then he, or any man who has the spirit of philosophy, will be willing to die, though he will not take his own life, for that is held not to be right.

Here he changed his position, and put his legs off the couch on to the ground, and during the rest of the conversation he remained sitting.

Why do you say, inquired Cebes, that a man ought not to take his own life, but that the philosopher will be ready to follow the dying? Socrates replied: And have you, Cebes and Simmias, who are acquainted with Philolaus, never heard him speak of this?

I never understood him, Socrates.

My words, too, are only an echo; but I am very willing to say what I have heard: and indeed, as I am going to another place, I ought to be thinking and talking of the nature of the pilgrimage which I am about to make. What can I do better in the interval between this and the setting of the sun?

Then tell me, Socrates, why is suicide held not to be right? as I have certainly heard Philolaus affirm when he was staying with us at Thebes: and there are others who say the same, although none of them has ever made me understand him.

But do your best, replied Socrates, and the day may come when you will understand. I suppose that you wonder why, as most things which are evil may be accidentally good, this is to be the only exception (for may not death, too, be better than life in some cases?), and why, when a man is better dead, he is not permitted to be his own benefactor, but must wait for the hand of another.

By Jupiter! yes, indeed, said Cebes, laughing, and speaking in his native Doric.

I admit the appearance of inconsistency, replied Socrates, but there may not be any real inconsistency after all in this. There is a doctrine uttered in secret that man is a prisoner who has no right to open the door of his prison and run away; this is a great mystery which I do not quite understand. Yet I, too, believe that the gods are our guardians, and that we are a possession of theirs. Do you not agree?

Yes, I agree to that, said Cebes.

And if one of your own possessions, an ox or an ass, for example took the liberty of putting himself out of the way when you had given no intimation of your wish that he should die, would you not be angry with him, and would you not punish him if you could?

Certainly, replied Cebes.

Then there may be reason in saying that a man should wait, and not take his own life until God summons him, as he is now summoning me.

Yes, Socrates, said Cebes, there is surely reason in that. And yet how can you reconcile this seemingly true belief that God is our guardian and we his possessions, with that willingness to die which we were attributing to the philosopher? That the wisest of men should be willing to leave this service in which they are ruled by the gods who are the best of rulers is not reasonable, for surely no wise man thinks that when set at liberty he can take better care of himself than the gods take of him. A fool may perhaps think this-he may argue that he had better run away from his master, not considering that his duty is to remain to the end, and not to run away from the good, and that there is no sense in his running away. But the wise man will want to be ever with him who is better than himself. Now this, Socrates, is the reverse of

*what was just now said; for upon this view the wise
man should sorrow and the fool rejoice at passing out
of life.*

*The earnestness of Cebes seemed to please Socrates.
Here, said he, turning to us, is a man who is always
inquiring, and is not to be convinced all in a moment,
nor by every argument.*

*And in this case, added Simmias, his objection does
appear to me to have some force. For what can be the
meaning of a truly wise man wanting to fly away and
lightly leave a master who is better than himself? And
I rather imagine that Cebes is referring to you; he
thinks that you are too ready to leave us, and too
ready to leave the gods who, as you acknowledge, are
our good rulers.*

*Yes, replied Socrates; there is reason in that. And this
indictment you think that I ought to answer as if I
were in court?*

That is what we should like, said Simmias.

*Then I must try to make a better impression upon you
than I did when defending myself before the judges.
For I am quite ready to acknowledge, Simmias and
Cebes, that I ought to be grieved at death, if I were
not persuaded that I am going to other gods who are
wise and good (of this I am as certain as I can be of
anything of the sort) and to men departed (though I
am not so certain of this), who are better than those
whom I leave behind; and therefore I do not grieve as
I might have done, for I have good hope that there is
yet something remaining for the dead, and, as has
been said of old, some far better thing for the good
than for the evil.*

*But do you mean to take away your thoughts with you,
Socrates? said Simmias. Will you not communicate
them to us?-the benefit is one in which we too may
hope to share. Moreover, if you succeed in*

convincing us, that will be an answer to the charge
against yourself.
I will do my best, replied Socrates. But you must first
let me hear what Crito wants; he was going to say
something to me.
Only this, Socrates, replied Crito: the attendant who
is to give you the poison has been telling me that you
are not to talk much, and he wants me to let you know
this; for that by talking heat is increased, and this
interferes with the action of the poison; those who
excite themselves are sometimes obliged to drink the
poison two or three times.
Then, said Socrates, let him mind his business and be
prepared to give the poison two or three times, if
necessary; that is all.
I was almost certain that you would say that, replied
Crito; but I was obliged to satisfy him.
Never mind him, he said.
And now I will make answer to you, O my judges, and
show that he who has lived as a true philosopher has
reason to be of good cheer when he is about to die,
and that after death he may hope to receive the
greatest good in the other world. And how this may
be, Simmias and Cebes, I will endeavor to explain.
For I deem that the true disciple of philosophy is
likely to be misunderstood by other men; they do not
perceive that he is ever pursuing death and dying;
and if this is true, why, having had the desire of death
all his life long, should he repine at the arrival of that
which he has been always pursuing and desiring?
Simmias laughed and said: Though not in a laughing
humor, I swear that I cannot help laughing when I
think what the wicked world will say when they hear
this. They will say that this is very true, and our
people at home will agree with them in saying that
the life which philosophers desire is truly death, and

that they have found them out to be deserving of the death which they desire.

And they are right, Simmias, in saying this, with the exception of the words "They have found them out"; for they have not found out what is the nature of this death which the true philosopher desires, or how he deserves or desires death. But let us leave them and have a word with ourselves: Do we believe that there is such a thing as death?

To be sure, replied Simmias.

And is this anything but the separation of soul and body? And being dead is the attainment of this separation; when the soul exists in herself, and is parted from the body and the body is parted from the soul-that is death?

Exactly: that and nothing else, he replied.

And what do you say of another question, my friend, about which I should like to have your opinion, and the answer to which will probably throw light on our present inquiry: Do you think that the philosopher ought to care about the pleasures-if they are to be called pleasures-of eating and drinking?

Certainly not, answered Simmias.

And what do you say of the pleasures of love-should he care about them?

By no means.

And will he think much of the other ways of indulging the bodyfor example, the acquisition of costly raiment, or sandals, or other adornments of the body? Instead of caring about them, does he not rather despise anything more than nature needs? What do you say? I should say the true philosopher would despise them. Would you not say that he is entirely concerned with the soul and not with the body? He would like, as far as he can, to be quit of the body and turn to the soul. That is true.

In matters of this sort philosophers, above all other men, may be observed in every sort of way to dissever the soul from the body.

That is true.

Whereas, Simmias, the rest of the world are of opinion that a life which has no bodily pleasures and no part in them is not worth having; but that he who thinks nothing of bodily pleasures is almost as though he were dead.

That is quite true.

What again shall we say of the actual acquirement of knowledge? Is the body, if invited to share in the inquiry, a hinderer or a helper? I mean to say, have sight and hearing any truth in them? Are they not, as the poets are always telling us, inaccurate witnesses? and yet, if even they are inaccurate and indistinct, what is to be said of the other senses?-for you will allow that they are the best of them?

Certainly, he replied.

Then when does the soul attain truth?-for in attempting to consider anything in company with the body she is obviously deceived.

Yes, that is true.

Then must not existence be revealed to her in thought, if at all?

Yes.

And thought is best when the mind is gathered into herself and none of these things trouble her-neither sounds nor sights nor pain
nor any pleasure-when she has as little as possible to do with the
body, and has no bodily sense or feeling, but is aspiring after being?

That is true.

*And in this the philosopher dishonors the body; his
soul runs away from the body and desires to be alone
and by herself?*

That is true.

*Well, but there is another thing, Simmias: Is there or
is there not an absolute justice?*

Assuredly there is.

And an absolute beauty and absolute good?

Of course.

But did you ever behold any of them with your eyes?

Certainly not.

*Or did you ever reach them with any other bodily
sense? (and I speak not of these alone, but of absolute
greatness, and health, and strength, and of the
essence or true nature of everything). Has the reality
of them ever been perceived by you through the
bodily organs? or rather, is not the nearest approach
to the knowledge of their several natures made by
him who so orders his intellectual vision as to have
the most exact conception of the essence of that which
he considers?*

Certainly .

*And he attains to the knowledge of them in their
highest purity who goes to each of them with the mind
alone, not allowing when in the act of thought the
intrusion or introduction of sight or any other sense
in the company of reason, but with the very light of
the mind in her clearness penetrates into the very
fight of truth in each; he has got rid, as far as he can,
of eyes and ears and of the whole body, which he
conceives of only as a disturbing element, hindering
the soul from the acquisition of knowledge when in
company with her-is not this the sort of man who, if
ever man did, is likely to attain the knowledge of
existence?*

There is admirable truth in that, Socrates, replied Simmias.

And when they consider all this, must not true philosophers make a reflection, of which they will speak to one another in such words as these: We have found, they will say, a path of speculation which seems to bring us and the argument to the conclusion that while we are in the body, and while the soul is mingled with this mass of evil, our desire will not be satisfied, and our desire is of the truth. For the body is a source of endless trouble to us by reason of the mere requirement of food; and also is liable to diseases which overtake and impede us in the search after truth: and by filling us so full of loves, and lusts, and fears, and fancies, and idols, and every sort of folly, prevents our ever having, as people say, so much as a thought. For whence come wars, and fightings, and factions? whence but from the body and the lusts of the body? For wars are occasioned by the love of money, and money has to be acquired for the sake and in the service of the body; and in consequence of all these things the time which ought to be given to philosophy is lost. Moreover, if there is time and an inclination toward philosophy, yet the body introduces a turmoil and confusion and fear into the course of speculation, and hinders us from seeing the truth: and all experience shows that if we would have pure knowledge of anything we must be quit of the body, and the soul in herself must behold all things in themselves: then I suppose that we shall attain that which we desire, and of which we say that we are lovers, and that is wisdom, not while we live, but after death, as the argument shows; for if while in company with the body the soul cannot have pure knowledge, one of two things seems to follow-either knowledge is not to be attained at all, or, if at all,

313

after death. For then, and not till then, the soul will
be in herself alone and without the body. In this
present life, I reckon that we make the nearest
approach to knowledge when we have the least
possible concern or interest in the body, and are not
saturated with the bodily nature, but remain pure
until the hour when God himself is pleased to release
us. And then the foolishness of the body will be
cleared away and we shall be pure and hold converse
with other pure souls, and know of ourselves the clear
light everywhere; and this is surely the light of truth.
For no impure thing is allowed to approach the pure.
These are the sort of words, Simmias, which the true
lovers of wisdom cannot help saying to one another,
and thinking. You will agree with me in that?
Certainly, Socrates.
But if this is true, O my friend, then there is great
hope that, going whither I go, I shall there be
satisfied with that which has been the chief concern
of you and me in our past lives. And now that the
hour of departure is appointed to me, this is the hope
with which I depart, and not I only, but every man
who believes that he has his mind purified.
Certainly, replied Simmias.
And what is purification but the separation of the soul
from the body, as I was saying before; the habit of the
soul gathering and collecting herself into herself, out
of all the courses of the body; the dwelling in her own
place alone, as in another life, so also in this, as far
as she can; the release of the soul from the chains of
the body?
Very true, he said.
And what is that which is termed death, but this very
separation and release of the soul from the body?
To be sure, he said.

*And the true philosophers, and they only, study and
are eager to release the soul. Is not the separation
and release of the soul from the body their especial
study?*

That is true.

*And as I was saying at first, there would be a
ridiculous contradiction in men studying to live as
nearly as they can in a state of death, and yet
repining when death comes.*

Certainly .

*Then, Simmias, as the true philosophers are ever
studying death, to them, of all men, death is the least
terrible. Look at the matter in this way: how
inconsistent of them to have been always enemies of
the body, and wanting to have the soul alone, and
when this is granted to them, to be trembling and
repining; instead of rejoicing at their departing to
that place where, when they arrive, they hope to gain
that which in life they loved (and this was wisdom),
and at the same time to be rid of the company of their
enemy. Many a man has been willing to go to the
world below in the hope of seeing there an earthly
love, or wife, or son, and conversing with them. And
will he who is a true lover of wisdom, and is
persuaded in like manner that only in the world
below he can worthily enjoy her, still repine at death?
Will he not depart with joy? Surely he will, my friend,
if he be a true philosopher. For he will have a firm
conviction that there only, and nowhere else, he can
find wisdom in her purity. And if this be true, he
would be very absurd, as I was saying, if he were to
fear death.*

He would, indeed, replied Simmias.

*And when you see a man who is repining at the
approach of death, is not his reluctance a sufficient
proof that he is not a lover of wisdom, but a lover of*

315

the body, and probably at the same time a lover of
either money or power, or both?
That is very true, he replied.
There is a virtue, Simmias, which is named courage.
Is not that a special attribute of the philosopher?
Certainly .
Again, there is temperance. Is not the calm, and
control, and disdain of the passions which even the
many call temperance, a quality belonging only to
those who despise the body and live in philosophy?
That is not to be denied.
For the courage and temperance of other men, if you
will consider them, are really a contradiction.
Well, he said, you are aware that death is regarded
by men in general as a great evil.
That is true, he said.
And do not courageous men endure death because
they are afraid of yet greater evils?
That is true.
Then all but the philosophers are courageous only
from fear, and because they are afraid; and yet that a
man should be courageous from fear, and because he
is a coward, is surely a strange thing.
Very true.
And are not the temperate exactly in the same case?
They are temperate because they are intemperate-
which may seem to be a contradiction, but is
nevertheless the sort of thing which happens with this
foolish temperance. For there are pleasures which
they must have, and are afraid of losing; and
therefore they abstain from one class of pleasures
because they are overcome by another: and whereas
intemperance is defined as "being under the
dominion of pleasure," they overcome only because
they are overcome by pleasure. And that is what I

*mean by saying that they are temperate through
intemperance.*

That appears to be true.

*Yet the exchange of one fear or pleasure or pain for
another fear or pleasure or pain, which are measured
like coins, the greater with the less, is not the
exchange of virtue. O my dear Simmias, is there not
one true coin for which all things ought to
exchange?-and that is wisdom; and only in exchange
for this, and in company with this, is anything truly
bought or sold, whether courage or temperance or
justice. And is not all true virtue the companion of
wisdom, no matter what fears or pleasures or other
similar goods or evils may or may not attend her? But
the virtue which is made up of these goods, when they
are severed from wisdom and exchanged with one
another, is a shadow of virtue only, nor is there any
freedom or health or truth in her; but in the true
exchange there is a purging away of all these things,
and temperance, and justice, and courage, and
wisdom herself are a purgation of them.*

*And I conceive that the founders of the mysteries had
a real*

*meaning and were not mere triflers when they
intimated in a figure long ago that he who passes
unsanctified and uninitiated into the world below will
live in a slough, but that he who arrives there after
initiation and purification will dwell with the gods.
For*

*"many," as they say in the mysteries, "are the
thyrsus bearers, but few are the mystics,"-meaning,
as I interpret the words, the true philosophers. In the
number of whom I have been seeking, according to
my ability, to find a place during my whole life;
whether I have sought in a right way or not, and
whether I have succeeded or not, I shall truly know in*

317

a little while, if God will, when I myself arrive in the other world: that is my belief. And now, Simmias and Cebes, I have answered those who charge me with not grieving or repining at parting from you and my masters in this world; and I am right in not repining, for I believe that I shall find other masters and friends who are as good in the world below. But all men cannot believe this, and I shall be glad if my words have any more success with you than with the judges of the Athenians.

Cebes answered: I agree, Socrates, in the greater part of what you say. But in what relates to the soul, men are apt to be incredulous; they fear that when she leaves the body her place may be nowhere, and that on the very day of death she may be destroyed and perish immediately on her release from the body, issuing forth like smoke or air and vanishing away into nothingness. For if she could only hold together and be herself after she was released from the evils of the body, there would be good reason to hope, Socrates, that what you say is true. But much persuasion and many arguments are required in order to prove that when the man is dead the soul yet exists, and has any force of intelligence.

True, Cebes, said Socrates; and shall I suggest that we talk a little of the probabilities of these things? I am sure, said Cebes, that I should greatly like to know your opinion about them.

I reckon, said Socrates, that no one who heard me now, not even if he were one of my old enemies, the comic poets, could accuse me of idle talking about matters in which I have no concern. Let us, then, if you please, proceed with the inquiry. Whether the souls of men after death are or are not in the world below, is a question which may be argued in this manner: The ancient doctrine of which I have been

318

speaking affirms that they go from this into the other world, and return hither, and are born from the dead. Now if this be true, and the living come from the dead, then our souls must be in the other world, for if not, how could they be born again? And this would be conclusive, if there were any real evidence that the living are only born from the dead; but if there is no evidence of this, then other arguments will have to be adduced.

That is very true, replied Cebes.

Then let us consider this question, not in relation to man only, but in relation to animals generally, and to plants, and to everything of which there is generation, and the proof will be easier. Are not all things which have opposites generated out of their opposites? I mean such things as good and evil, just and unjust- and there are innumerable other opposites which are generated out of opposites. And I want to show that this holds universally of all opposites; I mean to say, for example, that anything which becomes greater must become greater after being less.

True.

And that which becomes less must have been once greater and then be come less.

Yes.

And the weaker is generated from the stronger, and the swifter from the slower.

Very true.

And the worse is from the better, and the more just is from the more unjust.

Of course.

And is this true of all opposites? and are we convinced that all of them are generated out of opposites?

Yes.

And in this universal opposition of all things, are there not also two intermediate processes which are ever going on, from one to the other, and back again; where there is a greater and a less there is also an intermediate process of increase and diminution, and that which grows is said to wax, and that which decays to wane?

Yes, he said.

And there are many other processes, such as division and composition, cooling and heating, which equally involve a passage into and out of one another. And this holds of all opposites, even though not always expressed in words-they are generated out of one another, and there is a passing or process from one to the other of them?

Very true, he replied.

Well, and is there not an opposite of life, as sleep is the opposite of waking?

True, he said.

And what is that?

Death, he answered.

And these, then, are generated, if they are opposites, the one from the other, and have there their two intermediate processes also?

Of course.

Now, said Socrates, I will analyze one of the two pairs of opposites which I have mentioned to you, and also its intermediate processes, and you shall analyze the other to me. The state of sleep is opposed to the state of waking, and out of sleeping waking is generated, and out of waking, sleeping, and the process of generation is in the one case falling asleep, and in the other waking up. Are you agreed about that?

Quite agreed.
Then suppose that you analyze life and death to me in
the same manner. Is not death opposed to life?
Yes.
And they are generated one from the other?
Yes.
What is generated from life?
Death.
And what from death?
I can only say in answer-life.
Then the living, whether things or persons, Cebes,
are generated from the dead?
That is clear, he replied.
Then the inference is, that our souls are in the world
below?
That is true.
And one of the two processes or generations is
visible-for surely the act of dying is visible?
Surely, he said.
And may not the other be inferred as the complement
of nature, who is not to be supposed to go on one leg
only? And if not, a corresponding process of
generation in death must also be assigned to her?
Certainly, he replied.
And what is that process?
Revival.
And revival, if there be such a thing, is the birth of the
dead into the world of the living?
Quite true.
Then there is a new way in which we arrive at the
inference that the living come from the dead, just as
the dead come from the living; and if this is true, then
the souls of the dead must be in some place out of
which they come again. And this, as I think, has been
satisfactorily proved.

321

*Yes, Socrates, he said; all this seems to flow
necessarily out of our previous admissions.
And that these admissions are not unfair, Cebes, he
said, may be shown, as I think, in this way: If
generation were in a straight line only, and there
were no compensation or circle in nature, no turn or
return into one another, then you know that all things
would at last have the same form and pass into the
same state, and there would be no more generation of
them.
What do you mean? he said.
A simple thing enough, which I will illustrate by the
case of sleep, he replied. You know that if there were
no compensation of sleeping and waking, the story of
the sleeping Endymion would in the end have no
meaning, because all other things would be asleep,
too, and he would not be thought of. Or if there were
composition only, and no division of substances, then
the chaos of Anaxagoras would come again. And in
like manner, my dear Cebes, if all things which
partook of life were to die, and after they were dead
remained in the form of death, and did not come to
life again, all would at last die, and nothing would be
alive-how could this be otherwise? For if the living
spring from any others who are not the dead, and
they die, must not all things at last be swallowed up
in death?
There is no escape from that, Socrates, said Cebes;
and I think that what you say is entirely true.
Yes, he said, Cebes, I entirely think so, too; and we
are not walking
in a vain imagination; but I am confident in the belief
that there truly is such a thing as living again, and
that the living spring from the dead, and that the
souls of the dead are in existence, and that the good
souls have a better portion than the evil.*

322

Cebes added: Your favorite doctrine, Socrates, that knowledge is simply recollection, if true, also necessarily implies a previous time in which we learned that which we now recollect. But this would be impossible unless our soul was in some place before existing in the human form; here, then, is another argument of the soul's immortality.

But tell me, Cebes, said Simmias, interposing, what proofs are given of this doctrine of recollection? I am not very sure at this moment that I remember them.

One excellent proof, said Cebes, is afforded by questions. If you put a question to a person in a right way, he will give a true answer of himself; but how could he do this unless there were knowledge and right reason already in him? And this is most clearly shown when he is taken to a diagram or to anything of that sort.

But if, said Socrates, you are still incredulous, Simmias, I would ask you whether you may not agree with me when you look at the matter in another way; I mean, if you are still incredulous as to whether knowledge is recollection.

Incredulous, I am not, said Simmias; but I want to have this doctrine of recollection brought to my own recollection, and, from what Cebes has said, I am beginning to recollect and be convinced; but I should still like to hear what more you have to say.

This is what I would say, he replied: We should agree, if I am not mistaken, that what a man recollects he must have known at some previous time.

Very true.

And what is the nature of this recollection? And, in asking this, I mean to ask whether, when a person has already seen or heard or in any way perceived anything, and he knows not only that, but something else of which he has not the same, but another

knowledge, we may not fairly say that he recollects
that which comes into his mind. Are we agreed about
that?

What do you mean?

I mean what I may illustrate by the following
instance: The knowledge of a lyre is not the same as
the knowledge of a man?

True.

And yet what is the feeling of lovers when they
recognize a lyre, or a garment, or anything else
which the beloved has been in the habit of using? Do
not they, from knowing the lyre, form in the mind's
eye an image of the youth to whom the lyre belongs?
And this is recollection: and in the same way anyone
who sees Simmias may remember Cebes; and there
are endless other things of the same nature.

Yes, indeed, there are-endless, replied Simmias.

And this sort of thing, he said, is recollection, and is
most commonly a process of recovering that which
has been forgotten through time and inattention.

Very true, he said.

Well; and may you not also from seeing the picture of
a horse or a lyre remember a man? and from the
picture of Simmias, you may be led to remember
Cebes?

True.

Or you may also be led to the recollection of Simmias
himself? True, he said.

And in all these cases, the recollection may be
derived from things either like or unlike?

That is true.

And when the recollection is derived from like things,
then there is sure to be another question, which is,
whether the likeness of that which is recollected is in
any way defective or not.

Very true, he said.

*And shall we proceed a step further, and affirm that
there is such a thing as equality, not of wood with
wood, or of stone with stone, but that, over and above
this, there is equality in the abstract? Shall we affirm
this?*

*Affirm, yes, and swear to it, replied Simmias, with all
the confidence in life.*

And do we know the nature of this abstract essence?

To be sure, he said.

*And whence did we obtain this knowledge? Did we
not see equalities of material things, such as pieces of
wood and stones, and gather from them the idea of an
equality which is different from them?-you will admit
that? Or look at the matter again in this way: Do not
the same pieces of wood or stone appear at one time
equal, and at another time unequal?*

That is certain.

*But are real equals ever unequal? or is the idea of
equality ever inequality?*

That surely was never yet known, Socrates.

*Then these (so-called) equals are not the same with
the idea of equality?*

I should say, clearly not, Socrates.

*And yet from these equals, although differing from
the idea of equality, you conceived and attained that
idea?*

Very true, he said.

Which might be like, or might be unlike them?

Yes.

*But that makes no difference; whenever from seeing
one thing you conceived another, whether like or
unlike, there must surely have been an act of
recollection?*

Very true.

*But what would you say of equal portions of wood
and stone, or other material equals? and what is the*

impression produced by them? Are they equals in the same sense as absolute equality? or do they fall short of this in a measure?

Yes, he said, in a very great measure, too.

And must we not allow that when I or anyone look at any object, and perceive that the object aims at being some other thing, but falls short of, and cannot attain to it-he who makes this observation must have had previous knowledge of that to which, as he says, the other, although similar, was inferior?

Certainly.

And has not this been our case in the matter of equals and of absolute equality?

Precisely.

Then we must have known absolute equality previously to the time when we first saw the material equals, and reflected that all these apparent equals aim at this absolute equality, but fall short of it?

That is true.

And we recognize also that this absolute equality has only been known, and can only be known, through the medium of sight or touch, or of some other sense. And this I would affirm of all such conceptions.

Yes, Socrates, as far as the argument is concerned, one of them is the same as the other.

And from the senses, then, is derived the knowledge that all sensible things aim at an idea of equality of which they fall short-is not that true?

Yes.

Then before we began to see or hear or perceive in any way, we must have had a knowledge of absolute equality, or we could not have referred to that the equals which are derived from the senses for to that they all aspire, and of that they fall short? That, Socrates, is certainly to be inferred from the previous statements.

326

And did we not see and hear and acquire our other senses as soon as we were born?

Certainly.

Then we must have acquired the knowledge of the ideal equal at some time previous to this?

Yes.

That is to say, before we were born, I suppose?

True.

And if we acquired this knowledge before we were born, and were born having it, then we also knew before we were born and at the instant of birth not only equal or the greater or the less, but all other ideas; for we are not speaking only of equality absolute, but of beauty, goodness, justice, holiness, and all which we stamp with the name of essence in the dialectical process, when we ask and answer questions. Of all this we may certainly affirm that we acquired the knowledge before birth?

That is true.

But if, after having acquired, we have not forgotten that which we acquired, then we must always have been born with knowledge, and shall always continue to know as long as life lasts-for knowing is the acquiring and retaining knowledge and not forgetting. Is not forgetting, Simmias, just the losing of knowledge?

Quite true, Socrates.

But if the knowledge which we acquired before birth was lost by us at birth, and afterwards by the use of the senses we recovered that which we previously knew, will not that which we call learning be a process of recovering our knowledge, and may not this be rightly termed recollection by us? Very true. For this is clear, that when we perceived something, either by the help of sight or hearing, or some other sense, there was no difficulty in receiving from this a conception of some other thing like or unlike which had been forgotten and which was associated with this; and therefore, as I was saying, one of two alternatives follows: either we had this knowledge at birth, and continued to know through life; or, after birth, those who are said to learn only remember, and learning is recollection only.

Yes, that is quite true, Socrates.

And which alternative, Simmias, do you prefer? Had we the knowledge at our birth, or did we remember afterwards the things which we knew previously to our birth? I cannot decide at the moment. At any rate you can decide whether he who has knowledge ought or ought not to be able to give a reason for what he knows.

Certainly, he ought.

But do you think that every man is able to give a reason about these very matters of which we are speaking? I wish that they could, Socrates, but I greatly fear that to-morrow at this time there will be no one able to give a reason worth having.

Then you are not of opinion, Simmias, that all men know these things? Certainly not.

Then they are in process of recollecting that which they learned before.

Certainly.

But when did our souls acquire this knowledge?-not since we were born as men? Certainly not.

And therefore previously? Yes.

Then, Simmias, our souls must have existed before they were in the form of man-without bodies, and must have had intelligence.

Unless indeed you suppose, Socrates, that these notions were given us at the moment of birth; for this is the only time that remains.

Yes, my friend, but when did we lose them? for they are not in us when we are born-that is admitted. Did we lose them at the moment of receiving them, or at some other time? No, Socrates, I perceive that I was unconsciously talking nonsense.

Then may we not say, Simmias, that if, as we are always repeating, there is an absolute beauty, and goodness, and essence in general, and to this, which is now discovered to be a previous condition of our being, we refer all our sensations, and with this compare

them assuming this to have a prior existence, then our souls must have had a prior existence, but if not, there would be no force in the argument? There can be no doubt that if these absolute ideas existed before we were born, then our souls must have existed before we were born, and if not the ideas, then not the souls.

Yes, Socrates; I am convinced that there is precisely the same necessity for the existence of the soul before birth, and of the essence of which you are speaking: and the argument arrives at a result which happily agrees with my own notion. For there is nothing which to my mind is so evident as that beauty, goodness, and other notions of which you were just now speaking have a most real and absolute existence; and I am satisfied with the proof.

Well, but is Cebes equally satisfied? for I must convince him too.

I think, said Simmias, that Cebes is satisfied: although he is the most incredulous of mortals, yet I believe that he is convinced of the existence of the soul before birth. But that after death the soul will continue to exist is not yet proven even to my own satisfaction. I cannot get rid of the feeling of the many to which Cebes was referring-the feeling that when the man dies the soul may be scattered, and that this may be the end of her. For admitting that she may be generated and created in some other place, and may have existed before entering the human body, why after having entered in and gone out again may she not herself be destroyed and come to an end? Very true, Simmias, said Cebes; that our soul existed before we were born was the first half of the argument, and this appears to have been proven; that the soul will exist after death as well as before birth is the other half of which the proof is still wanting, and has to be supplied.

But that proof, Simmias and Cebes, has been already given, said Socrates, if you put the two arguments together-I mean this and the former one, in which we admitted that everything living is born of the dead. For if the soul existed before birth, and in coming to life and being born can be born only from death and dying, must she not after death continue to exist, since she has to be born again? surely the proof which you desire has been already furnished. Still I suspect that you and Simmias would be glad to probe the argument further; like children, you are haunted with a fear that when the soul leaves the body, the wind may really blow her away and scatter her; especially if a man should happen to die in stormy weather and not when the sky is calm.

Cebes answered with a smile: Then, Socrates, you must argue us out of our fears-and yet, strictly speaking, they are not our fears, but there is a child within us to whom death is a sort of hobgoblin; him too we must persuade not to be afraid when he is alone with him in the dark.

Socrates said: Let the voice of the charmer be applied daily until you have charmed him away.

And where shall we find a good charmer of our fears,
Socrates, when you are gone?
Hellas, he replied, is a large place, Cebes, and has
many good men,
and there are barbarous races not a few: seek for him
among them all, far and wide, sparing neither pains
nor money; for there is no better way of using your
money. And you must not forget to seek for him
among yourselves too; for he is nowhere more likely
to be found.
The search, replied Cebes, shall certainly be made.
And now, if you please, let us return to the point of
the argument at which we digressed.
By all means, replied Socrates; what else should I
please?
Very good, he said.
Must we not, said Socrates, ask ourselves some
question of this sort?-What is that which, as we
imagine, is liable to be scattered away, and about
which we fear? and what again is that about which
we have no fear? And then we may proceed to inquire
whether that which suffers dispersion is or is not of
the nature of soul-our hopes and fears as to our own
souls will turn upon that.
That is true, he said.
Now the compound or composite may be supposed to
be naturally capable of being dissolved in like
manner as of being compounded; but that which is
uncompounded, and that only, must be, if anything is,
indissoluble.
Yes; that is what I should imagine, said Cebes.
And the uncompounded may be assumed to be the
same and unchanging, where the compound is always
changing and never the same?
That I also think, he said.

331

Then now let us return to the previous discussion. Is that idea or essence, which in the dialectical process we define as essence of true existence-whether essence of equality, beauty, or anything else: are these essences, I say, liable at times to some degree of change? or are they each of them always what they are, having the same simple, self-existent and unchanging forms, and not admitting of variation at all, or in any way, or at any time?

They must be always the same, Socrates, replied Cebes.

And what would you say of the many beautiful- whether men or horses or garments or any other things which may be called equal or beautiful-are they all unchanging and the same always, or quite the reverse? May they not rather be described as almost always changing and hardly ever the same either with themselves or with one another? The latter, replied Cebes; they are always in a state of change.

And these you can touch and see and perceive with the senses, but the unchanging things you can only perceive with the mind-they are invisible and are not seen?

That is very true, he said.

Well, then, he added, let us suppose that there are two sorts of existences, one seen, the other unseen. Let us suppose them.

The seen is the changing, and the unseen is the unchanging. That may be also supposed.

And, further, is not one part of us body, and the rest of us soul? To be sure.

Clearly to the seen: no one can doubt that.

And is the soul seen or not seen?

Not by man, Socrates.

And by "seen" and "not seen" is meant by us that which is or is not visible to the eye of man?

Yes, to the eye of man.

And what do we say of the soul? is that seen or not seen?

Not seen.

Unseen then?

Yes.

Then the soul is more like to the unseen, and the body to the seen? That is most certain, Socrates.

And were we not saying long ago that the soul when using the body as an instrument of perception, that is to say, when using the sense of sight or hearing or some other sense (for the meaning of perceiving through the body is perceiving through the senses)were we not saying that the soul too is then dragged by the body into the region of the changeable, and wanders and is confused; the world spins round her, and she is like a drunkard when under their influence?

Very true.

But when returning into herself she reflects; then she passes into the realm of purity, and eternity, and immortality, and unchangeableness, which are her kindred, and with them she ever lives, when she is by herself and is not let or hindered; then she ceases from her erring ways, and being in communion with the unchanging is unchanging. And this state of the soul is called wisdom?

That is well and truly said, Socrates, he replied.

And to which class is the soul more nearly alike and akin, as far as may be inferred from this argument, as well as from the preceding one?

I think, Socrates, that, in the opinion of everyone who follows the

argument, the soul will be infinitely more like the unchangeable even the most stupid person will not deny that.

And the body is more like the changing?

Yes.

Yet once more consider the matter in this light: When the soul and the body are united, then nature orders the soul to rule and govern, and the body to obey and serve.

Now which of these two functions is akin to the divine? and which to the mortal? Does not the divine appear to you to be that which naturally orders and rules, and the mortal that which is subject and servant?

True.

And which does the soul resemble? The soul resembles the divine and the body the mortal-there can be no doubt of that, Socrates.

Then reflect, Cebes: is not the conclusion of the whole matter this?--that the soul is in the very likeness of the divine, and immortal, and intelligible, and uniform, and indissoluble, and unchangeable; and the body is in the very likeness of the human, and mortal, and unintelligible, and multiform, and dissoluble, and changeable. Can this, my dear Cebes, be denied?

No, indeed.

But if this is true, then is not the body liable to speedy dissolution? and is not the soul almost or altogether indissoluble?

Certainly .

And do you further observe, that after a man is dead, the body, which is the visible part of man, and has a visible framework, which is called a corpse, and which would naturally be dissolved and decomposed and dissipated, is not dissolved or decomposed at once, but may remain for a good while, if the constitution be sound at the time of death, and the season of the year favorable? For the body when

shrunk and embalmed, as is the custom in Egypt, may
remain almost entire through infinite ages; and even
in decay, still there are some portions, such as the
bones and ligaments, which are practically
indestructible. You allow that?
Yes.
And are we to suppose that the soul, which is
invisible, in passing to the true Hades, which like her
is invisible, and pure, and noble, and on her way to
the good and wise God, whither, if God will, my soul
is also soon to go-that the soul, I repeat, if this be her
nature and origin, is blown away and perishes
immediately on quitting the body as the many say?
That can never be, dear Simmias and Cebes The truth
rather is that the soul which is pure at departing
draws after her no bodily taint, having never
voluntarily had connection with the body, which she
is ever avoiding, herself gathered into herself (for
such abstraction has been the study of her life). And
what does this mean but that she has been a true
disciple of philosophy and has practised how to die
easily? And is not philosophy the practice of death?
Certainly.
That soul, I say, herself invisible, departs to the
invisible world to the divine and immortal and
rational: thither arriving, she lives in bliss and is
released from the error and folly of men, their fears
and wild passions and all other human ills, and
forever dwells, as they say of the initiated, in
company with the gods. Is not this true, Cebes?
Yes, said Cebes, beyond a doubt.
But the soul which has been polluted, and is impure
at the time of her departure, and is the companion
and servant of the body always, and is in love with
and fascinated by the body and by the desires and
pleasures of the body, until she is led to believe that

335

*the truth only exists in a bodily form, which a man
may touch and see and taste and use for the purposes
of his lusts-the soul, I mean, accustomed to hate and
fear and avoid the intellectual principle, which to the
bodily eye is dark and invisible, and can be attained
only by philosophy-do you suppose that such a soul
as this will depart pure and unalloyed?
That is impossible, he replied.
She is engrossed by the corporeal, which the
continual association and constant care of the body
have made natural to her.
Very true.
And this, my friend, may be conceived to be that
heavy, weighty, earthy element of sight by which such
a soul is depressed and dragged down again into the
visible world, because she is afraid of the invisible
and of the world below-prowling about tombs and
sepulchres, in the neighborhood of which, as they tell
us, are seen certain ghostly apparitions of souls
which have not departed pure, but are cloyed with
sight and therefore visible.
That is very likely, Socrates.
Yes, that is very likely, Cebes; and these must be the
souls, not of the good, but of the evil, who are
compelled to wander about such places in payment of
the penalty of their former evil way of life; and they
continue to wander until the desire which haunts
them is satisfied and they are imprisoned in another
body. And they may be supposed to be fixed in the
same natures which they had in their former life.
What natures do you mean, Socrates?
I mean to say that men who have followed after
gluttony, and wantonness, and drunkenness, and have
had no thought of avoiding them, would pass into
asses and animals of that sort. What do you think? I
think that exceedingly probable.*

336

*And those who have chosen the portion of injustice,
and tyranny, and violence, will pass into wolves, or
into hawks and kites; whither else can we suppose
them to go?*

*Yes, said Cebes; that is doubtless the place of natures
such as theirs.*

*And there is no difficulty, he said, in assigning to all
of them places answering to their several natures and
propensities?*

There is not, he said.

*Even among them some are happier than others; and
the happiest both in themselves and their place of
abode are those who have practised the civil and
social virtues which are called temperance and
justice, and are acquired by habit and attention
without philosophy and mind.*

Why are they the happiest?

*Because they may be expected to pass into some
gentle, social nature which is like their own, such as
that of bees or ants, or even back again into the form
of man, and just and moderate men spring from them.
That is not impossible.*

*But he who is a philosopher or lover of learning, and
is entirely pure at departing, is alone permitted to
reach the gods. And this is the reason, Simmias and
Cebes, why the true votaries of philosophy abstain
from all fleshly lusts, and endure and refuse to
give themselves up to them-not because they fear
poverty or the ruin of their families, like the lovers of
money, and the world in general; nor like the lovers
of power and honor, because they dread the dishonor
or disgrace of evil deeds.*

*No, Socrates, that would not become them, said
Cebes.*

*No, indeed, he replied; and therefore they who have a
care of their souls, and do not merely live in the*

337

*fashions of the body, say farewell to all this; they will
not walk in the ways of the blind: and when
philosophy offers them purification and release from
evil, they feel that they ought not to resist her
influence, and to her they incline, and whither she
leads they follow her.*

What do you mean, Socrates?

*I will tell you, he said. The lovers of knowledge are
conscious that their souls, when philosophy receives
them, are simply fastened and glued to their bodies:
the soul is only able to view existence through the
bars of a prison, and not in her own nature; she is
wallowing in the mire of all ignorance; and
philosophy, seeing the terrible nature of her
confinement, and that the captive through desire is
led to conspire in her own captivity (for the lovers of
knowledge are aware that this was the original state
of the soul, and that when she was in this state
philosophy received and gently counseled her, and
wanted to release her, pointing out to her that the eye
is full of deceit, and also the ear and other senses,
and persuading her to retire from them in all but the
necessary use of them and to be gathered up and
collected into herself, and to trust only to herself and
her own intuitions of absolute existence, and mistrust
that which comes to her through others and is subject
to vicissitude)-philosophy shows her that this is
visible and tangible, but that what she sees in her
own nature is intellectual and invisible. And the soul
of the true philosopher thinks that she ought not to
resist this deliverance, and therefore abstains from
pleasures and desires and pains and fears, as far as
she is able; reflecting that when a man has great joys
or sorrows or fears or desires he suffers from them,
not the sort of evil which might be anticipated-as, for
example, the loss of his health or property, which he*

338

has sacrificed to his lusts-but he has suffered an evil greater far, which is the greatest and worst of all evils, and one of which he never thinks.

And what is that, Socrates? said Cebes.

Why, this: When the feeling of pleasure or pain in the soul is most intense, all of us naturally suppose that the object of this intense feeling is then plainest and truest: but this is not the case.

Very true.

And this is the state in which the soul is most enthralled by the body.

How is that?

Why, because each pleasure and pain is a sort of nail which nails and rivets the soul to the body, and engrosses her and makes her believe that to be true which the body affirms to be true; and from agreeing with the body and having the same delights she is obliged to have the same habits and ways, and is not likely ever to be pure at her departure to the world below, but is always saturated with the body; so that she soon sinks into another body and there germinates and grows, and has therefore no part in the communion of the divine and pure and simple.

That is most true, Socrates, answered Cebes.

And this, Cebes, is the reason why the true lovers of knowledge are temperate and brave; and not for the reason which the world gives.

Certainly not.

Certainly not! For not in that way does the soul of a philosopher reason; she will not ask philosophy to release her in order that when released she may deliver herself up again to the thraldom of pleasures and pains, doing a work only to be undone again, weaving instead of unweaving her Penelope's web. But she will make herself a calm of passion and follow Reason, and dwell in her, beholding the true

*and divine (which is not matter of opinion), and
thence derive nourishment. Thus she seeks to live
while she lives, and after death she hopes to go to her
own kindred and to be freed from human ills. Never
fear, Simmias and Cebes, that a soul which has been
thus nurtured and has had these pursuits, will at her
departure from the body be scattered and blown away
by the winds and be nowhere and nothing.*

*When Socrates had done speaking, for a considerable
time there was silence; he himself and most of us
appeared to be meditating on what had been said;
only Cebes and Simmias spoke a few words to one
another. And Socrates observing this asked them
what they thought of the argument, and whether there
was anything wanting? For, said he, much is still
open to suspicion and attack, if anyone were disposed
to sift the matter thoroughly. If you are talking of
something else I would rather not interrupt you, but if
you are still doubtful about the argument do not
hesitate to say exactly what you think, and let us have
anything better which you can suggest; and if I am
likely to be of any use, allow me to help you.*

*Simmias said: I must confess, Socrates, that doubts
did arise in our minds, and each of us was urging and
inciting the other to put the question which he wanted
to have answered and which neither of us liked to ask,
fearing that our importunity might be troublesome
under present circumstances.*

*Socrates smiled and said: O Simmias, how strange
that is; I am not very likely to persuade other men
that I do not regard my present situation as a
misfortune, if I am unable to persuade you, and you
will keep fancying that I am at all more troubled now
than at any other time. Will you not allow that I have
as much of the spirit of prophecy in me as the swans?
For they, when they perceive that they must die,*

340

*having sung all their life long, do then sing more than
ever, rejoicing in the thought that they are about to
go away to the god whose ministers they are. But men,
because they are themselves afraid of death,
slanderously affirm of the swans that they sing a
lament at the last, not considering that no bird sings
when cold, or hungry, or in pain, not even the
nightingale, nor the swallow, nor yet the hoopoe;
which are said indeed to tune a lay of sorrow,
although I do not believe this to be true of them any
more than of the swans. But because they are sacred
to Apollo and have the gift of prophecy and anticipate
the good things of another world, therefore they sing
and rejoice in that day more than they ever did before.
And I, too, believing myself to be the consecrated
servant of the same God, and the fellow servant of the
swans, and thinking that I have received from my
master gifts of prophecy which are not inferior to
theirs, would not go out of life less merrily than the
swans. Cease to mind then about this, but speak and
ask anything which you like, while the eleven
magistrates of Athens allow.*

*Well, Socrates, said Simmias, then I will tell you my
difficulty, and Cebes will tell you his. For I dare say
that you, Socrates, feel, as I do, how very hard or
almost impossible is the attainment of any certainty
about questions such as these in the present life. And
yet I should deem him a coward who did not prove
what is said about them to the uttermost, or whose
heart failed him before he had examined them on
every side. For he should persevere until he has
attained one of two things: either he should discover
or learn the truth about them; or, if this is impossible,
I would have him take the best and most irrefragable
of human notions, and let this be the raft upon which
he sails through life-not without risk, as I admit, if he*

341

*cannot find some word of God which will more surely
and safely carry him. And now, as you bid me, I will
venture to question you, as I should not like to
reproach myself hereafter with not having said at the
time what I think. For when I consider the matter
either alone or with Cebes, the argument does
certainly appear to me, Socrates, to be not sufficient.
Socrates answered: I dare say, my friend, that you
may be right, but I should like to know in what
respect the argument is not sufficient.*

*In this respect, replied Simmias: Might not a person
use the same argument about harmony and the lyre-
might he not say that harmony is a thing invisible,
incorporeal, fair, divine, abiding in the lyre which is
harmonized, but that the lyre and the strings are
matter and material, composite, earthy, and akin to
mortality? And when someone breaks the lyre, or cuts
and rends the strings, then he who takes this view
would argue as you do, and on the same analogy, that
the harmony survives and has not perished; for you
cannot imagine, as we would say, that the lyre
without the strings, and the broken strings themselves,
remain, and yet that the harmony, which is of
heavenly and immortal nature and kindred, has
perished-and perished too before the mortal. The
harmony, he would say, certainly exists somewhere,
and the wood and strings will decay before that
decays. For I suspect, Socrates, that the notion of the
soul which we are all of us inclined to entertain,
would also be yours, and that you too would conceive
the body to be strung up, and held together, by the
elements of hot and cold, wet and dry, and the like,
and that the soul is the harmony or due proportionate
admixture of them. And, if this is true, the inference
clearly is that when the strings of the body are unduly
loosened or overstrained through disorder or other*

*injury, then the soul, though most divine, like other
harmonies of music or of the works of art, of course
perishes at once, although the material remains of the
body may last for a considerable time, until they are
either decayed or burnt. Now if anyone maintained
that the soul, being the harmony of the elements of
the body, first perishes in that which is called death,
how shall we answer him?
Socrates looked round at us as his manner was, and
said, with a smile: Simmias has reason on his side;
and why does not some one of you who is abler than
myself answer him? for there is force in his attack
upon me. But perhaps, before we answer him, we had
better also hear what Cebes has to say against the
argument-this will give us time for reflection, and
when both of them have spoken, we may either assent
to them if their words appear to be in consonance
with the truth, or if not, we may take up the other side,
and argue with them. Please to tell me then, Cebes,
he said, what was the difficulty which troubled you?
Cebes said: I will tell you. My feeling is that the
argument is still in the same position, and open to the
same objections which were urged before; for I am
ready to admit that the existence of the soul before
entering into the bodily form has been very
ingeniously, and, as I may be allowed to say, quite
sufficiently proven; but the existence of the soul after
death is still, in my judgment, unproven.
Now my objection is not the same as that of Simmias;
for I am not disposed to deny that the soul is stronger
and more lasting than the body, being of opinion that
in all such respects the soul very far excels the body.
Well, then, says the argument to me, why do you
remain unconvinced? When you see that the weaker
is still in existence after the man is dead, will you not
admit that the more lasting must also survive during*

*the same period of time? Now I, like Simmias, must
employ a figure; and I shall ask you to consider
whether the figure is to the point.*

*The parallel which I will suppose is that of an old
weaver, who dies, and after his death somebody says:
He is not dead, he must be alive; and he appeals to
the coat which he himself wove and wore, and which
is still whole and undecayed. And then he proceeds to
ask of someone who is incredulous, whether a man
lasts longer, or the coat which is in use and wear;
and when he is answered that a man lasts far longer,
thinks that he has thus certainly demonstrated the
survival of the man, who is the more lasting, because
the less lasting remains. But that, Simmias, as I would
beg you to observe, is not the truth; everyone sees
that he who talks thus is talking nonsense. For the
truth is that this weaver, having worn and woven
many such coats, though he outlived several of them,
was himself outlived by the last; but this is surely very
far from proving that a man is slighter and weaker
than a coat. Now the relation of the body to the soul
may be expressed in a similar figure; for you may say
with reason that the soul is lasting, and the body
weak and short-lived in comparison. And every soul
may be said to wear out many bodies, especially in
the course of a long life. For if while the man is alive
the body deliquesces and decays, and yet the soul
always weaves her garment anew and repairs the
waste, then of course, when the soul perishes, she
must have on her last garment, and this only will
survive her; but then again when the soul is dead the
body will at last show its native weakness, and soon
pass into decay. And therefore this is an argument on
which I would rather not rely as proving that the soul
exists after death.*

For suppose that we grant even more than you affirm
as within the range of possibility, and besides
acknowledging that the soul existed before birth
admit also that after death the souls of some are
existing still, and will exist, and will be born and die
again and again, and that there is a natural strength
in the soul which will hold out and be born many
times-for all this, we may be still inclined to think that
she will weary in the labors of successive births, and
may at last succumb in one of her deaths and utterly
perish; and this death and dissolution of the body
which brings destruction to the soul may be unknown
to any of us, for no one of us can have had any
experience of it: and if this be true, then I say that he
who is confident in death has but a foolish confidence,
unless he is able to prove that the soul is altogether
immortal and imperishable. But if he is not able to
prove this, he who is about to die will always have
reason to fear that when the body is disunited, the
soul also may utterly perish.
All of us, as we afterwards remarked to one another,
had an unpleasant feeling at hearing them say this.
When we had been so firmly convinced before, now to
have our faith shaken seemed to introduce a
confusion and uncertainty, not only into the previous
argument, but into any future one; either we were not
good judges, or there were no real grounds of belief.
Ech *There I feel with you-indeed I do, Phaedo, and*
when you were speaking, I was beginning to ask
myself the same question: What argument can I ever
trust again? For what could be more convincing than
the argument of Socrates, which has now fallen into
discredit? That the soul is a harmony is a doctrine
which has always had a wonderful attraction for me,
and, when mentioned, came back to me at once, as
my own original conviction. And now I must begin

345

*again and find another argument which will assure
me that when the man is dead the soul dies not with
him. Tell me, I beg, how did Socrates proceed? Did
he appear to share the unpleasant feeling which you
mention? or did he receive the interruption calmly
and give a sufficient answer? Tell us, as exactly as
you can, what passed.*

Phaed *Often, Echecrates, as I have admired Socrates,
I never admired him more than at that moment. That
he should be able to answer was nothing, but what
astonished me was, first, the gentle and pleasant and
approving manner in which he regarded the words of
the young men, and then his quick sense of the wound
which had been inflicted by the argument, and his
ready application of the healing art. He might be
compared to a general rallying his defeated and
broken army, urging them to follow him and return to
the field of argument.*

Ech *How was that?*

Phaed *You shall hear, for I was close to him on his
right hand, seated on a sort of stool, and he on a
couch which was a good deal higher. Now he had a
way of playing with my hair, and then he smoothed
my head, and pressed the hair upon my neck, and
said: Tomorrow, Phaedo, I suppose that these fair
locks of yours will be severed.*

Yes, Socrates, I suppose that they will, I replied.

Not so if you will take my advice.

What shall I do with them? I said.

*Today, he replied, and not tomorrow, if this argument
dies and cannot be brought to life again by us, you
and I will both shave our locks; and if I were you,
and could not maintain my ground against Simmias
and Cebes, I would myself take an oath, like the
Argives, not to wear hair any more until I had
renewed the conflict and defeated them.*

346

*Yes, I said, but Heracles himself is said not to be a
match for two.*

*Summon me then, he said, and I will be your Iolaus
until the sun goes down.*

*I summon you rather, I said, not as Heracles
summoning Iolaus, but as Iolaus might summon
Heracles.*

*That will be all the same, he said. But first let us take
care that we avoid a danger.*

And what is that? I said.

*The danger of becoming misologists, he replied,
which is one of the very worst things that can happen
to us. For as there are misanthropists or haters of
men, there are also misologists or haters of ideas,
and both spring from the same cause, which is
ignorance of the world. Misanthropy arises from the
too great confidence of inexperience; you trust a man
and think him altogether true and good and faithful,
and then in a little while he turns out to be false and
knavish; and then another and another, and when this
has happened several times to a man, especially
within the circle of his most trusted friends, as he
deems them, and he has often quarreled with them, he
at last hates all men, and believes that no one has any
good in him at all. I dare say that you must have
observed this.*

Yes, I said.

*And is not this discreditable? The reason is that a
man, having to deal with other men, has no
knowledge of them; for if he had knowledge he would
have known the true state of the case, that few are the
good and few the evil, and that the great majority are
in the interval between them.*

How do you mean? I said.

*I mean, he replied, as you might say of the very large
and very small, that nothing is more uncommon than*

347

*a very large or a very small man; and this applies
generally to all extremes, whether of great and small,
or swift and slow, or fair and foul, or black and
white: and whether the instances you select be men or
dogs or anything else, few are the extremes, but many
are in the mean between them. Did you never observe
this?*

Yes, I said, I have.

*And do you not imagine, he said, that if there were a
competition of evil, the first in evil would be found to
be very few?*

Yes, that is very likely, I said.

*Yes, that is very likely, he replied; not that in this
respect arguments are like men-there I was led on by
you to say more than I had intended; but the point of
comparison was that when a simple man who has no
skill in dialectics believes an argument to be true
which he afterwards imagines to be false, whether
really false or not, and then another and another, he
has no longer any faith left, and great disputers, as
you know, come to think, at last that they have grown
to be the wisest of mankind; for they alone perceive
the utter unsoundness and instability of all arguments,
or, indeed, of all things, which, like the currents in
the Euripus, are going up and down in never-ceasing
ebb and flow.*

That is quite true, I said.

*Yes, Phaedo, he replied, and very melancholy too, if
there be such a thing as truth or certainty or power of
knowing at all, that a man should have lighted upon
some argument or other which at first seemed true
and then turned out to be false, and instead of
blaming himself and his own want of wit, because he
is annoyed, should at last be too glad to transfer the
blame from himself to arguments in general; and*

forever afterwards should hate and revile them, and
lose the truth and knowledge of existence.
Yes, indeed, I said; that is very melancholy.
Let us, then, in the first place, he said, be careful of
admitting into our souls the notion that there is no
truth or health or soundness in any arguments at all;
but let us rather say that there is as yet no health in
us, and that we must quit ourselves like men and do
our best to gain health-you and all other men with a
view to the whole of your future life, and I myself with
a view to death. For at this moment I am sensible that
I have not the temper of a philosopher; like the vulgar,
I am only a partisan. For the partisan, when he is
engaged in a dispute, cares nothing about the rights
of the question, but is anxious only to convince his
hearers of his own assertions. And the difference
between him and me at the present moment is only
this-that whereas he seeks to convince his hearers
that what he says is true, I am rather seeking to
convince myself; to convince my hearers is a
secondary matter with me. And do but see how much
I gain by this. For if what I say is true, then I do well
to be persuaded of the truth, but if there be nothing
after death, still, during the short time that remains, I
shall save my friends from lamentations, and my
ignorance will not last, and therefore no harm will be
done. This is the state of mind, Simmias and Cebes, in
which I approach the argument. And I would ask you
to be thinking of the truth and not of Socrates: agree
with me, if I seem to you to be speaking the truth; or
if not, withstand me might and main, that I may not
deceive you as well as myself in my enthusiasm, and,
like the bee, leave my sting in you before I die.
And now let us proceed, he said. And first of all let
me be sure that I have in my mind what you were
saying. Simmias, if I remember rightly, has fears and

misgivings whether the soul, being in the form of harmony, although a fairer and diviner thing than the body, may not perish first. On the other hand, Cebes appeared to grant that the soul was more lasting than the body, but he said that no one could know whether the soul, after having worn out many bodies, might not perish herself and leave her last body behind her; and that this is death, which is the destruction not of the body but of the soul, for in the body the work of destruction is ever going on. Are not these, Simmias and Cebes, the points which we have to consider? They both agreed to this statement of them.

He proceeded: And did you deny the force of the whole preceding argument, or of a part only?

Of a part only, they replied.

And what did you think, he said, of that part of the argument in which we said that knowledge was recollection only, and inferred from this that the soul must have previously existed somewhere else before she was enclosed in the body? Cebes said that he had been wonderfully impressed by that part of the argument, and that his conviction remained unshaken. Simmias agreed, and added that he himself could hardly imagine the possibility of his ever thinking differently about that.

But, rejoined Socrates, you will have to think differently, my Theban friend, if you still maintain that harmony is a compound, and that the soul is a harmony which is made out of strings set in the frame of the body; for you will surely never allow yourself to say that a harmony is prior to the elements which compose the harmony.

No, Socrates, that is impossible.

But do you not see that you are saying this when you say that the soul existed before she took the form and body of man, and was made up of elements which as yet had no existence? For harmony is not a sort of thing like the soul, as you suppose; but first the lyre, and the strings, and the sounds exist in a state of discord, and then harmony is made last of all, and perishes first. And how can such a notion of the soul as this agree with the other?

Not at all, replied Simmias.

And yet, he said, there surely ought to be harmony when harmony is the theme of discourse.

There ought, replied Simmias.

But there is no harmony, he said, in the two propositions that knowledge is recollection, and that the soul is a harmony. Which of them, then, will you retain?

I think, he replied, that I have a much stronger faith, Socrates, in the first of the two, which has been fully demonstrated to me, than in the latter, which has not been demonstrated at all, but rests only on probable and plausible grounds; and I know too well that these arguments from probabilities are impostors, and unless great caution is observed in the use of them they are apt to be deceptive- in geometry, and in other things too. But the doctrine of knowledge and recollection has been proven to me on trustworthy grounds; and the proof was that the soul must have existed before she came into the body, because to her belongs the essence of which the very name implies existence. Having, as I am convinced, rightly accepted this conclusion, and on sufficient grounds, I must, as I suppose, cease to argue or allow others to argue that the soul is a harmony .

Let me put the matter, Simmias, he said, in another point of view: Do you imagine that a harmony or any other composition can be in a state other than that of the elements out of which it is compounded?

Certainly not.

Or do or suffer anything other than they do or suffer?
He agreed.
Then a harmony does not lead the parts or elements
which make up the harmony, but only follows them.
He assented.
For harmony cannot possibly have any motion, or
sound, or other quality which is opposed to the parts.
That would be impossible, he replied.
And does not every harmony depend upon the manner
in which the elements are harmonized?
I do not understand you, he said.
I mean to say that a harmony admits of degrees, and
is more of a harmony, and more completely a
harmony, when more completely harmonized, if that
be possible; and less of a harmony, and less
completely a harmony, when less harmonized.
True.
But does the soul admit of degrees? or is one soul in
the very least degree more or less, or more or less
completely, a soul than another?
Not in the least.
Yet surely one soul is said to have intelligence and
virtue, and to be good, and another soul is said to
have folly and vice, and to be an evil soul: and this is
said truly? Yes, truly.
But what will those who maintain the soul to be a
harmony say of this presence of virtue and vice in the
soul? Will they say that there is another harmony,
and another discord, and that the virtuous soul is
harmonized, and herself being a harmony has
another harmony within her, and that the vicious soul
is inharmonical and has no harmony within her?
I cannot say, replied Simmias; but I suppose that
something of that kind would be asserted by those
who take this view. And the admission is already
made that no soul is more a soul than another; and

*this is equivalent to admitting that harmony is not
more or less harmony, or more or less completely a
harmony?*

Quite true.

*And that which is not more or less a harmony is not
more or less harmonized?*

True.

*And that which is not more or less harmonized cannot
have more or less of harmony, but only an equal
harmony?*

Yes, an equal harmony.

*Then one soul not being more or less absolutely a
soul than another, is not more or less harmonized?*

Exactly .

*And therefore has neither more nor less of harmony
or of discord? She has not.*

*And having neither more nor less of harmony or of
discord, one soul has no more vice or virtue than
another, if vice be discord and virtue harmony?*

Not at all more.

*Or speaking more correctly, Simmias, the soul, if she
is a harmony, will never have any vice; because a
harmony, being absolutely a harmony, has no part in
the inharmonical?*

No.

*And therefore a soul which is absolutely a soul has no
vice?*

*How can she have, consistently with the preceding
argument? Then, according to this, if the souls of all
animals are equally and absolutely souls, they will be
equally good?*

I agree with you, Socrates, he said.

*And can all this be true, think you? he said; and are
all these consequences admissible-which nevertheless
seem to follow from the assumption that the soul is a
harmony?*

Certainly not, he said.

Once more, he said, what ruling principle is there of human things

other than the soul, and especially the wise soul? Do you know of any? Indeed, I do not.

And is the soul in agreement with the affections of the body? or is she at variance with them? For example, when the body is hot and thirsty, does not the soul incline us against drinking? and when the body is hungry, against eating? And this is only one instance out of ten thousand of the opposition of the soul to the things of the body.

Very true.

But we have already acknowledged that the soul, being a harmony, can never utter a note at variance with the tensions and relaxations and vibrations and other affections of the strings out of which she is composed; she can only follow, she cannot lead them?

Yes, he said, we acknowledged that, certainly.

And yet do we not now discover the soul to be doing the exact

opposite-leading the elements of which she is believed to be composed; almost always opposing and coercing them in all sorts of ways throughout life, sometimes more violently with the pains of medicine and gymnastic; then again more gently; threatening and also reprimanding the desires, passions, fears, as if talking to a thing which is not herself, as Homer in the "Odyssey" represents Odysseus doing in the words, "He beat his breast, and thus reproached his heart: Endure, my heart; far worse hast thou endured!" - Do you think that Homer could have written this under the idea that the soul is a harmony capable of being led by the affections of the body, and

*not rather of a nature which leads and masters them;
and herself a far diviner thing than any harmony?
Yes, Socrates, I quite agree to that.
Then, my friend, we can never be right in saying that
the soul is a harmony, for that would clearly
contradict the divine Homer as well as ourselves.
True, he said.
Thus much, said Socrates, of Harmonia, your Theban
goddess,
Cebes, who has not been ungracious to us, I think;
but what shall I say to the Theban Cadmus, and how
shall I propitiate him?
I think that you will discover a way of propitiating
him, said Cebes; I am sure that you have answered
the argument about harmony in a manner that I could
never have expected. For when Simmias mentioned
his objection, I quite imagined that no answer could
be given to him, and therefore I was surprised at
finding that his argument could not sustain the first
onset of yours; and not impossibly the other, whom
you call Cadmus, may share a similar fate.
Nay, my good friend, said Socrates, let us not boast,
lest some evil eye should put to flight the word which
I am about to speak. That, however, may be left in the
hands of those above, while I draw near in Homeric
fashion, and try the mettle of your words. Briefly, the
sum of your objection is as follows: You want to have
proven to you that the soul is imperishable and
immortal, and you think that the philosopher who is
confident in death has but a vain and foolish
confidence, if he thinks that he will fare better than
one who has led another sort of life, in the world
below, unless he can prove this; and you say that the
demonstration of the strength and divinity of the soul,
and of her existence prior to our becoming men, does
not necessarily imply her immortality. Granting that*

the soul is longlived, and has known and done much in a former state, still she is not on that account immortal; and her entrance into the human form may be a sort of disease which is the beginning of dissolution, and may at last, after the toils of life are over, end in that which is called death. And whether the soul enters into the body once only or many times, that, as you would say, makes no difference in the fears of individuals. For any man, who is not devoid of natural feeling, has reason to fear, if he has no knowledge or proof of the soul's immortality. That is what I suppose you to say, Cebes, which I designedly repeat, in order that nothing may escape us, and that you may, if you wish, add or subtract anything.

But, said Cebes, as far as I can see at present, I have nothing to add or subtract; you have expressed my meaning.

Socrates paused awhile, and seemed to be absorbed in reflection.

At length he said: This is a very serious inquiry which you are raising, Cebes, involving the whole question of generation and corruption, about which I will, if you like, give you my own experience; and you can apply this, if you think that anything which I say will avail towards the solution of your difficulty.

I should very much like, said Cebes, to hear what you have to say.

Then I will tell you, said Socrates. When I was young, Cebes, I had a prodigious desire to know that department of philosophy which is called Natural Science; this appeared to me to have lofty aims, as being the science which has to do with the causes of things, and which teaches why a thing is, and is created and destroyed; and I was always agitating myself with the consideration of such questions as these: Is the growth of animals the result of some decay which the hot and cold principle contracts, as some have said? Is the blood the element with which we think, or the air, or the fire? or perhaps nothing of this sort-but the brain may be the originating power of the perceptions of hearing and sight and smell, and memory and opinion may come from them, and science may be based on memory and opinion when no longer in motion, but at rest. And then I went on to examine the decay of them, and then to the things of heaven and earth, and at last I concluded that I was wholly incapable of these inquiries, as I will satisfactorily prove to you. For I was fascinated by them to such a degree that my eyes grew blind to things that I had seemed to myself, and also to others, to know quite well; and I forgot what I had before thought to be self-evident, that the growth of man is the result of eating and drinking; for when by the digestion of food flesh is added to flesh and bone to bone, and whenever there is an aggregation of congenial elements, the lesser bulk becomes larger and the small man greater. Was not that a reasonable notion?

Yes, said Cebes, I think so.

Well; but let me tell you something more. There was a time when I thought that I understood the meaning of greater and less pretty well; and when I saw a great man standing by a little one I fancied that one was taller than the other by a head; or one horse would appear to be greater than another horse: and still more clearly did I seem to perceive that ten is two more than eight, and that two cubits are more than one, because two is twice one.

And what is now your notion of such matters? said Cebes.

I should be far enough from imagining, he replied, that I knew the cause of any of them, indeed I should,

357

*for I cannot satisfy myself that when one is added to
one, the one to which the addition is made becomes
two, or that the two units added together make two by
reason of the addition. For I cannot understand how,
when separated from the other, each of them was one
and not two, and now, when they are brought
together, the mere juxtaposition of them can be the
cause of their becoming two: nor can I understand
how the division of one is the way to make two; for
then a different cause would produce the same effect-
as in the former instance the addition and
juxtaposition of one to one was the cause of two, in
this the separation and subtraction of one from the
other would be the cause. Nor am I any longer
satisfied that I understand the reason why one or
anything else either is generated or destroyed or is at
all, but I have in my mind some confused notion of
another method, and can never admit this.*

*Then I heard someone who had a book of Anaxagoras,
as he said, out of which he read that mind was the
disposer and cause of all, and I was quite delighted at
the notion of this, which appeared admirable, and I
said to myself: If mind is the disposer, mind will
dispose all for the best, and put each particular in the
best place; and I argued that if anyone desired to find
out the cause of the generation or destruction or
existence of anything, he must find out what state of
being or suffering or doing was best for that thing,
and therefore a man had only to consider the best for
himself and others, and then he would also know the
worse, for that the same science comprised both. And
I rejoiced to think that I had found in Anaxagoras a
teacher of the causes of existence such as I desired,
and I imagined that he would tell me first whether the
earth is flat or round; and then he would further
explain the cause and the necessity of this, and would*

teach me the nature of the best and show that this was best; and if he said that the earth was in the centre, he would explain that this position was the best, and I should be satisfied if this were shown to me, and not want any other sort of cause. And I thought that I would then go and ask him about the sun and moon and stars, and that he would explain to me their comparative swiftness, and their returnings and various states, and how their several affections, active and passive, were all for the best. For I could not imagine that when he spoke of mind as the disposer of them, he would give any other account of their being as they are, except that this was best; and I thought when he had explained to me in detail the cause of each and the cause of all, he would go on to explain to me what was best for each and what was best for all. I had hopes which I would not have sold for much, and I seized the books and read them as fast as I could in my eagerness to know the better and the worse.

What hopes I had formed, and how grievously was I disappointed!

As I proceeded, I found my philosopher altogether forsaking mind or any other principle of order, but having recourse to air, and ether, and water, and other eccentricities. I might compare him to a person who began by maintaining generally that mind is the cause of the actions of Socrates, but who, when he endeavored to explain the causes of my several actions in detail, went on to show that I sit here because my body is made up of bones and muscles; and the bones, as he would say, are hard and have ligaments which divide them, and the muscles are elastic, and they cover the bones, which have also a covering or environment of flesh and skin which contains them; and as the bones are lifted at their

359

joints by the contraction or relaxation of the muscles,
I am able to bend my limbs, and this is why I am
sitting here in a curved posture: that is what he would
say, and he would have a similar explanation of my
talking to you, which he would attribute to sound, and
air, and hearing, and he would assign ten thousand
other causes of the same sort, forgetting to mention
the true cause, which is that the Athenians have
thought fit to condemn me, and accordingly I have
thought it better and more right to remain here and
undergo my sentence; for I am inclined to think that
these muscles and bones of mine would have gone off
to Megara or Boeotia-by the dog of Egypt they would,
if they had been guided only by their own idea of
what was best, and if I had not chosen as the better
and nobler part, instead of playing truant and
running away, to undergo any punishment which the
State inflicts. There is surely a strange confusion of
causes and conditions in all this. It may be said,
indeed, that without bones and muscles and the other
parts of the body I cannot execute my purposes. But
to say that I do as I do because of them, and that this
is the way in which mind acts, and not from the
choice of the best, is a very careless and idle mode of
speaking. I wonder that they cannot distinguish the
cause from the condition, which the many, feeling
about in the dark, are always mistaking and
misnaming. And thus one man makes a vortex all
round and steadies the earth by the heaven; another
gives the air as a support to the earth, which is a sort
of broad trough. Any power which in disposing them
as they are disposes them for the best never enters
into their minds, nor do they imagine that there is any
superhuman strength in that; they rather expect to
find another Atlas of the world who is stronger and
more everlasting and more containing than the good

is, and are clearly of opinion that the obligatory and containing power of the good is as nothing; and yet this is the principle which I would fain learn if anyone would teach me. But as I have failed either to discover myself or to learn of anyone else, the nature of the best, I will exhibit to you, if you like, what I have found to be the second best mode of inquiring into the cause.

I should very much like to hear that, he replied. Socrates proceeded: I thought that as I had failed in the contemplation of true existence, I ought to be careful that I did not lose the eye of my soul; as people may injure their bodily eye by observing and gazing on the sun during an eclipse, unless they take the precaution of only looking at the image reflected in the water, or in some similar medium. That occurred to me, and I was afraid that my soul might be blinded altogether if I looked at things with my eyes or tried by the help of the senses to apprehend them. And I thought that I had better have recourse to ideas, and seek in them the truth of existence. I dare say that the simile is not perfect-for I am very far from admitting that he who contemplates existence through the medium of ideas, sees them only "through a glass darkly," any more than he who sees them in their working and effects. However, this was the method which I adopted: I first assumed some principle which I judged to be the strongest, and then I affirmed as true whatever seemed to agree with this, whether relating to the cause or to anything else; and that which disagreed I regarded as untrue. But I should like to explain my meaning clearly, as I do not think that you understand me.

No, indeed, replied Cebes, not very well.

There is nothing new, he said, in what I am about to tell you; but only what I have been always and

*everywhere repeating in the previous discussion and
on other occasions: I want to show you the nature of
that cause which has occupied my thoughts, and I
shall have to go back to those familiar words which
are in the mouth of everyone, and first of all assume
that there is an absolute beauty and goodness and
greatness, and the like; grant me this, and I hope to
be able to show you the nature of the cause, and to
prove the immortality of the soul.*

*Cebes said: You may proceed at once with the proof,
as I readily grant you this.*

*Well, he said, then I should like to know whether you
agree with me in the next step; for I cannot help
thinking that if there be anything beautiful other than
absolute beauty, that can only be beautiful in as far
as it partakes of absolute beauty-and this I should say
of everything. Do you agree in this notion of the
cause?*

Yes, he said, I agree.

*He proceeded: I know nothing and can understand
nothing of any other of those wise causes which are
alleged; and if a person says to me that the bloom of
color, or form, or anything else of that sort is a
source of beauty, I leave all that, which is only
confusing to me, and simply and singly, and perhaps
foolishly, hold and am assured in my own mind that
nothing makes a thing beautiful but the presence and
participation of beauty in whatever way or manner
obtained; for as to the manner I am uncertain, but I
stoutly contend that by beauty all beautiful things
become beautiful. That appears to me to be the only
safe answer that I can give, either to myself or to any
other, and to that I cling, in the persuasion that I
shall never be overthrown, and that I may safely
answer to myself or any other that by beauty beautiful*

362

things become beautiful. Do you not agree to that?
Yes, I agree.
And that by greatness only great things become great
and greater greater, and by smallness the less
becomes less.
True.
Then if a person remarks that A is taller by a head
than B, and B less by a head than A, you would refuse
to admit this, and would stoutly contend that what
you mean is only that the greater is greater by, and
by reason of, greatness, and the less is less only by,
or by reason of, smallness; and thus you would avoid
the danger of saying that the greater is greater and
the less by the measure of the head, which is the same
in both, and would also avoid the monstrous
absurdity of supposing that the greater man is greater
by reason of the head, which is small. Would you not
be afraid of that?
Indeed, I should, said Cebes, laughing. In like
manner you would be afraid to say that ten exceeded
eight by, and by reason of, two; but would say by, and
by reason of, number; or that two cubits exceed one
cubit not by a half, but by magnitude?-that is what
you would say, for there is the same danger in both
cases.
Very true, he said.
Again, would you not be cautious of affirming that the
addition of one to one, or the division of one, is the
cause of two? And you would loudly asseverate that
you know of no way in which anything comes into
existence except by participation in its own
proper essence, and consequently, as far as you know,
the only cause of two is the participation in duality;
that is the way to make two, and the participation in
one is the way to make one. You would say: I will let
alone puzzles of division and addition-wiser

363

*heads than mine may answer them; inexperienced as
I am, and ready to start, as the proverb says, at my
own shadow, I cannot afford to give up the sure
ground of a principle. And if anyone assails you there,
you would not mind him, or answer him until
you had seen whether the consequences which follow
agree with one another or not, and when you are
further required to give an explanation of this
principle, you would go on to assume a higher
principle, and the best of the higher ones, until you
found a resting-place; but you would not refuse the
principle and the consequences in your reasoning like
the Eristics-at least if you wanted to discover real
existence. Not that this confusion signifies to them
who never care or think about the matter at all, for
they have the wit to be well pleased with themselves,
however great may be the turmoil of their ideas. But
you, if you are a philosopher, will, I believe, do as I
say.*

*What you say is most true, said Simmias and Cebes,
both speaking at once.*

Ech *Yes, Phaedo; and I don't wonder at their
assenting. Anyone who has the least sense will
acknowledge the wonderful clear. of Socrates'
reasoning.*

Phaed *Certainly, Echecrates; and that was the
feeling of the whole company at the time.*

Ech *Yes, and equally of ourselves, who were not of
the company, and are now listening to your recital.
But what followed?*

Phaedo *After all this was admitted, and they had
agreed about the existence of ideas and the
participation in them of the other things which derive
their names from them, Socrates, if I remember
rightly, said: This is your way of speaking; and yet
when you say that Simmias is greater than Socrates*

364

*and less than Phaedo, do you not predicate of
Simmias both greatness and smallness?*

Yes, I do.

*But still you allow that Simmias does not really
exceed Socrates, as the words may seem to imply,
because he is Simmias, but by reason of the size
which he has; just as Simmias does not exceed
Socrates because he is Simmias, any more than
because Socrates is Socrates, but because he has
smallness when compared with the greatness of
Simmias?*

True.

*And if Phaedo exceeds him in size, that is not because
Phaedo is Phaedo, but because Phaedo has greatness
relatively to Simmias, who is comparatively smaller?*

That is true.

*And therefore Simmias is said to be great, and is also
said to be small, because he is in a mean between
them, exceeding the smallness of the one by his
greatness, and allowing the greatness of the other to
exceed his smallness. He added, laughing, I am
speaking like a book, but I believe that what I am now
saying is true.*

Simmias assented to this.

*The reason why I say this is that I want you to agree
with me in thinking, not only that absolute greatness
will never be great and also small, but that greatness
in us or in the concrete will never admit the small or
admit of being exceeded: instead of this, one of two
things will happen-either the greater will fly or retire
before the opposite, which is the less, or at the
advance of the less will cease to exist; but will not, if
allowing or admitting smallness, be changed by that;
even as I, having received and admitted smallness
when compared with Simmias, remain just as I was,
and am the same small person. And as the idea of*

365

greatness cannot condescend ever to be or become
small, in like manner the smallness in us cannot be or
become great; nor can any other opposite which
remains the same ever be or become its own opposite,
but either passes away or perishes in the change.
That, replied Cebes, is quite my notion.
One of the company, though I do not exactly
remember which of them, on hearing this, said: By
Heaven, is not this the direct contrary of what was
admitted before-that out of the greater came the less
and out of the less the greater, and that opposites are
simply generated from opposites; whereas now this
seems to be utterly denied.
Socrates inclined his head to the speaker and listened.
I like your courage, he said, in reminding us of this.
But you do not observe that there is a difference in
the two cases. For then we were speaking of
opposites in the concrete, and now of the essential
opposite which, as is affirmed, neither in us nor in
nature can ever be at variance with itself: then, my
friend, we were speaking of things in which opposites
are inherent and which are called after them, but now
about the opposites which are inherent in them and
which give their name to them; these essential
opposites will never, as we maintain, admit of
generation into or out of one another. At the same
time, turning to Cebes, he said: Were you at all
disconcerted, Cebes, at our friend's objection?
That was not my feeling, said Cebes; and yet I cannot
deny that I am apt to be disconcerted.
Then we are agreed after all, said Socrates, that the
opposite will never in any case be opposed to itself?
To that we are quite agreed, he replied.
Yet once more let me ask you to consider the question
from another

*point of view, and see whether you agree with me:
There is a thing which you term heat, and another
thing which you term cold?
Certainly.
But are they the same as fire and snow?
Most assuredly not.
Heat is not the same as fire, nor is cold the same as
snow?
No.
And yet you will surely admit that when snow, as
before said, is under the influence of heat, they will
not remain snow and heat; but at the advance of the
heat the snow will either retire or perish?
Very true, he replied.
And the fire too at the advance of the cold will either
retire or perish; and when the fire is under the
influence of the cold, they will not remain, as before,
fire and cold.
That is true, he said.
And in some cases the name of the idea is not
confined to the idea; but anything else which, not
being the idea, exists only in the form of the idea, may
also lay claim to it. I will try to make this clearer by
an example: The odd number is always called by the
name of odd?
Very true.
But is this the only thing which is called odd? Are
there not other things which have their own name,
and yet are called odd, because, although not the
same as oddness, they are never without oddness?-
that is what I mean to ask-whether numbers such as
the
number three are not of the class of odd. And there
are many other examples: would you not say, for
example, that three may be called by its proper name,
and also be called odd, which is not the same with*

367

three? and this may be said not only of three but also of five,

and every alternate number-each of them without being oddness is odd, and in the same way two and four, and the whole series of alternate numbers, has every number even, without being evenness. Do you admit that?

Yes, he said, how can I deny that?

Then now mark the point at which I am aiming: not only do essential opposites exclude one another, but also concrete things, which, although not in themselves opposed, contain opposites; these, I say, also reject the idea which is opposed to that which is contained in them, and at the advance of that they either perish or withdraw. There is the number three for example; will not that endure annihilation or anything sooner than be converted into an even number, remaining three? Very true, said Cebes. And yet, he said, the number two is certainly not opposed to the number three?

It is not.

Then not only do opposite ideas repel the advance of one another, but also there are other things which repel the approach of opposites.

That is quite true, he said.

Suppose, he said, that we endeavor, if possible, to determine what these are.

By all means.

Are they not, Cebes, such as compel the things of which they have

possession, not only to take their own form, but also the form of some opposite?

What do you mean?

I mean, as I was just now saying, and have no need to repeat to you, that those things which are possessed

by the number three must not only be three in number,
but must also be odd.
Quite true.
And on this oddness, of which the number three has
the impress,
the opposite idea will never intrude? No.
And this impress was given by the odd principle? Yes.
And to the odd is opposed the even?
True.
Then the idea of the even number will never arrive at
three?
No.
Then three has no part in the even?
None.
Then the triad or number three is uneven?
Very true.
To return then to my distinction of natures which are
not opposites, and yet do not admit opposites: as, in
this instance, three, although not opposed to the even,
does not any the more admit of the even, but always
brings the opposite into play on the other side; or as
two does not receive the odd, or fire the cold-from
these examples (and there are many more of them)
perhaps you may be able to arrive at the general
conclusion that not only opposites will not receive
opposites, but also that nothing which brings the
opposite
will admit the opposite of that which it brings in that
to which it is brought. And here let me recapitulate-
for there is no harm in repetition. The number five
will not admit the nature of the even, any more than
ten, which is the double of five, will admit the
nature of the odd-the double, though not strictly
opposed to the odd, rejects the odd altogether. Nor
again will parts in the ratio of 3:2, nor any fraction in
which there is a half, nor again in which there is a

369

*third, admit the notion of the whole, although they
are not opposed to the whole. You will agree to that?
Yes, he said, I entirely agree and go along with you in
that.*

*And now, he said, I think that I may begin again; and
to the question which I am about to ask I will beg you
to give not the old safe answer, but another, of which
I will offer you an example; and I hope that you will
find in what has been just said another foundation
which is as safe. I mean that if anyone asks you
"what that is, the inherence of which makes the body
hot," you will reply not heat (this is what I call the
safe and stupid answer), but fire, a far better answer,
which we are now in a condition to give. Or if anyone
asks you "why a body is diseased," you will not say
from disease, but from fever; and instead of saying
that oddness is the cause of odd numbers, you will
say that the monad is the cause of them: and so of
things in general, as I dare say that you will
understand sufficiently without my adducing any
further examples.*

Yes, he said, I quite understand you.

*Tell me, then, what is that the inherence of which will
render the body alive?*

The soul, he replied.

And is this always the case?

Yes, he said, of course.

*Then whatever the soul possesses, to that she comes
bearing life? Yes, certainly.*

And is there any opposite to life?

There is, he said.

And what is that?

Death.

*Then the soul, as has been acknowledged, will never
receive the opposite of what she brings. And now, he*

said, what did we call that principle which repels the even?

The odd.

And that principle which repels the musical, or the just?

The unmusical, he said, and the unjust.

And what do we call the principle which does not admit of death? The immortal, he said.

And does the soul admit of death?

No.

Then the soul is immortal?

Yes, he said.

And may we say that this is proven?

Yes, abundantly proven, Socrates, he replied.

And supposing that the odd were imperishable, must not three be

imperishable?

Of course.

And if that which is cold were imperishable, when the warm principle came attacking the snow, must not the snow have retired whole and unmelted-for it could never have perished, nor could it have remained and admitted the heat?

True, he said.

Again, if the uncooling or warm principle were imperishable, the

fire when assailed by cold would not have perished or have been extinguished, but would have gone away unaffected?

Certainly, he said.

And the same may be said of the immortal: if the immortal is also imperishable, the soul when attacked by death cannot perish; for the preceding argument shows that the soul will not admit of death, or ever be dead, any more than three or the odd number

will admit of the even, or fire or the heat in the fire, of
the cold. Yet a person may say: "But although the
odd will not become even at the approach of the even,
why may not the odd perish and the even take the
place of the odd?" Now to him who makes this
objection, we cannot answer that the odd principle is
imperishable; for this has not been acknowledged,
but if this had been acknowledged, there would have
been no difficulty in contending that at the approach
of the even the odd principle and the number
three took up their departure; and the same argument
would have held good of fire and heat and any other
thing.
Very true.
And the same may be said of the immortal: if the
immortal is also imperishable, then the soul will be
imperishable as well as immortal; but if not, some
other proof of her imperishableness will have to be
given.
No other proof is needed, he said; for if the immortal,
being eternal, is liable to perish, then nothing is
imperishable.
Yes, replied Socrates, all men will agree that God,
and the essential form of life, and the immortal in
general, will never perish.
Yes, all men, he said-that is true; and what is more,
gods, if I am not mistaken, as well as men.
Seeing then that the immortal is indestructible, must
not the soul, if she is immortal, be also imperishable?
Most certainly.
Then when death attacks a man, the mortal portion of
him may be supposed to die, but the immortal goes
out of the way of death and is preserved safe and
sound?
True.

Then, Cebes, beyond question the soul is immortal and imperishable, and our souls will truly exist in another world!

I am convinced, Socrates, said Cebes, and have nothing more to

object; but if my friend Simmias, or anyone else, has any further objection, he had better speak out, and not keep silence, since I do not know how there can ever be a more fitting time to which he can defer the discussion, if there is anything which he wants to say or have said.

But I have nothing more to say, replied Simmias; nor do I see any room for uncertainty, except that which arises necessarily out of the greatness of the subject and the feebleness of man, and which I cannot help feeling.

Yes, Simmias, replied Socrates, that is well said: and more than

that, first principles, even if they appear certain, should be carefully considered; and when they are satisfactorily ascertained, then, with a sort of hesitating confidence in human reason, you may, I think, follow the course of the argument; and if this is clear, there will be no need for any further inquiry.

That, he said, is true.

But then, O my friends, he said, if the soul is really immortal, what care should be taken of her, not only in respect of the portion of time which is called life, but of eternity! And the danger of neglecting her from this point of view does indeed appear to be awful. If death had only been the end of all, the wicked would have had a good bargain in dying, for they would have been happily quit not only of their body, but of their own evil together with their souls.

But now, as the soul plainly appears to be immortal, there is no release or salvation from evil except the

attainment of the highest virtue and wisdom. For the
soul when on her progress to the world below takes
nothing with her but nurture and education; which
are indeed said greatly to benefit or greatly to injure
the departed, at the very beginning of its pilgrimage
in the other world.

For after death, as they say, the genius of each
individual, to whom he belonged in life, leads him to
a certain place in which the dead are gathered
together for judgment, whence they go into the world
below, following the guide who is appointed to
conduct them from this world to the other: and when
they have there received their due and remained their
time, another guide brings them back again after
many revolutions of ages. Now this journey to the
other world is not, as Aeschylus says in the
"Telephus," a single and straight path-no guide
would be wanted for that, and no one could miss a
single path; but there are many partings of the road,
and windings, as I must infer from the rites and
sacrifices which are offered to the gods below in
places where three ways meet on earth.

The wise and orderly soul is conscious of her
situation and follows in the path; but the soul which
desires the body, and which, as I was relating before,
has long been fluttering about the lifeless frame and
the world of sight, is after many struggles and many
sufferings hardly and with violence carried away by
her attendant genius, and when she arrives at the
place where the other souls are gathered, if she be
impure and have done impure deeds, or been
concerned in foul murders or other crimes which are
the brothers of these, and the works of brothers in
crime-from that soul everyone flees and turns away;
no one will be her companion, no one her guide, but
alone she wanders in extremity of evil until certain

times are fulfilled, and when they are fulfilled, she is borne irresistibly to her own fitting habitation; as every pure and just soul which has passed through life in the company and under the guidance of the gods has also her own proper home.

Now the earth has divers wonderful regions, and is indeed in

nature and extent very unlike the notions of geographers, as I believe on the authority of one who shall be nameless.

What do you mean, Socrates? said Simmias. I have myself heard many descriptions of the earth, but I do not know in what you are putting your faith, and I should like to know.

Well, Simmias, replied Socrates, the recital of a tale does not, I think, require the art of Glaucus; and I know not that the art of Glaucus could prove the truth of my tale, which I myself should never be able to prove, and even if I could, I fear, Simmias, that my life would come to an end before the argument was completed.

I may describe to you, however, the form and regions of the earth according to my conception of them.

That, said Simmias, will be enough.

Well, then, he said, my conviction is that the earth is a round body

in the center of the heavens, and therefore has no need of air or any similar force as a support, but is kept there and hindered from falling or inclining any way by the equability of the surrounding heaven and by her own equipoise. For that which, being in equipoise, is in the center of that which is equably diffused, will not incline any way in any degree, but will always remain in the same state and not deviate. And this is my first notion.

Which is surely a correct one, said Simmias.

Also I believe that the earth is very vast, and that we who dwell in the region extending from the river Phasis to the Pillars of Heracles, along the borders of the sea, are just like ants or frogs about a marsh, and inhabit a small portion only, and that many others dwell in many like places. For I should say that in all parts of the earth there are hollows of various forms and sizes, into which the water and the mist and the air collect; and that the true earth is pure and in the pure heaven, in which also are the stars- that is the heaven which is commonly spoken of as the ether, of which this is but the sediment collecting in the hollows of the earth. But we who live in these hollows are deceived into the notion that we are dwelling above on the surface of the earth; which is just as if a creature who was at the bottom of the sea were to fancy that he was on the surface of the water, and that the sea was the heaven through which he saw the sun and the other stars-he having never come to the surface by reason of his feebleness and sluggishness, and having never lifted up his head and seen, nor ever heard from one who had seen, this region which is so much purer and fairer than his own. Now this is exactly our case: for we are dwelling in a hollow of the earth, and fancy that we are on the surface; and the air we call the heaven, and in this we imagine that the stars move. But this is also owing to our feebleness and sluggishness, which prevent our reaching the surface of the air: for if any man could arrive at the exterior limit, or take the wings of a bird and fly upward, like a fish who puts his head out and sees this world, he would see a world beyond; and, if the nature of man could sustain the sight, he would acknowledge that this was the place of the true heaven and the true light and the true stars. For this earth, and the stones, and the entire region which surrounds us, are spoilt and corroded, like the things in the sea which are corroded by the brine; for in the sea too there is hardly any noble or perfect growth, but clefts only, and sand, and an endless slough of mud: and even the shore is not to be compared to the fairer sights of this world. And greater far is the superiority of the other. Now of that upper earth which is under the heaven, I can tell you a charming tale, Simmias, which is well worth hearing. And we, Socrates, replied Simmias, shall be charmed to listen.

The tale, my friend, he said, is as follows: In the first place, the earth, when looked at from above, is like one of those balls which have leather coverings in twelve pieces, and is of divers colors, of which the colors which painters use on earth are only a sample. But there the whole earth is made up of them, and they are brighter far and clearer than ours; there is a purple of wonderful luster, also the radiance of gold, and the white which is in the earth is whiter than any chalk or snow. Of these and other colors the earth is made up, and they are more in number and fairer than the eye of man has ever seen; and the very hollows (of which I was speaking) filled with air and water are seen like light flashing amid the other colors, and have a color of their own, which gives a sort of unity to the variety of earth. And in this fair region everything that growstrees, and flowers, and fruits-is in a like degree fairer than any here; and there are hills, and stones in them in a like degree smoother, and more transparent, and fairer in color than our highly valued emeralds and sardonyxes and jaspers, and other gems, which are but minute fragments of them: for there all the stones are like our precious stones, and fairer still. The reason of this is that they are pure, and not, like our precious

stones, infected or corroded by the corrupt briny
elements which coagulate among us, and which breed
foulness and disease both in earth and stones, as well
as in animals and plants. They are the jewels of the
upper earth, which also shines with gold and silver
and the like, and they are visible to sight and large
and abundant and found in every region of the earth,
and blessed is he who sees them. And upon the earth
are animals and men, some in a middle region, others
dwelling about the air as we dwell about the sea;
others in islands which the air flows round, near the
continent: and in a word, the air is used by them as
the water and the sea are by us, and the ether is to
them what the air is to us. Moreover, the
temperament of their seasons is such that they have
no disease, and live much longer than we do, and
have sight and hearing and smell, and all the other
senses, in far greater perfection, in the same degree
that air is purer than water or the ether than air. Also
they have temples and sacred places in which the
gods really dwell, and they hear their voices and
receive their answers, and are conscious of them and
hold converse with them, and they see the sun, moon,
and stars as they really are, and their other
blessedness is of a piece with this.
Such is the nature of the whole earth, and of the
things which are around the earth; and there are
divers regions in the hollows on the face of the globe
everywhere, some of them deeper and also wider than
that which we inhabit, others deeper and with a
narrower opening than ours, and some are shallower
and wider; all have numerous perforations, and
passages broad and narrow in the interior of the
earth, connecting them with one another; and there
flows into and out of them, as into basins, a vast tide
of water, and huge subterranean streams of perennial

378

rivers, and springs hot and cold, and a great fire, and great rivers of fire, and streams of liquid mud, thin or thick (like the rivers of mud in Sicily, and the lava-streams which follow them), and the regions about which they happen to flow are filled up with them. And there is a sort of swing in the interior of the earth which moves all this up and down. Now the swing is in this wise: There is a chasm which is the vastest of them all, and pierces right through the whole earth; this is that which Homer describes in the words, "Far off, where is the inmost depth beneath the earth"; and which he in other places, and many other poets, have called Tartarus. And the swing is caused by the streams flowing into and out of this chasm, and they each have the nature of the soil through which they flow. And the reason why the streams are always flowing in and out is that the watery element has no bed or bottom, and is surging and swinging up and down, and the surrounding wind and air do the same; they follow the water up and down, hither and thither, over the earth- just as in respiring the air is always in process of inhalation and exhalation; and the wind swinging with the water in and out produces fearful and irresistible blasts: when the waters retire with a rush into the lower parts of the earth, as they are called, they flow through the earth into those regions, and fill them up as with the alternate motion of a pump, and then when they leave those regions and rush back hither, they again fill the hollows here, and when these are filled, flow through subterranean channels and find their way to their several places, forming seas, and lakes, and rivers, and springs. Thence they again enter the earth, some of them making a long circuit into many lands, others going to few places and those not distant, and again fall into Tartarus, some at a point a good deal lower than that at which they rose, and others not much lower, but all in some degree lower than the point of issue. And some burst forth again on the opposite side, and some on the same side, and some wind round the earth with one or many folds, like the coils of a serpent, and descend as far as they can, but always return and fall into the lake. The rivers on either side can descend only to the center and no further, for to the rivers on both sides the opposite side is a precipice.

Now these rivers are many, and mighty, and diverse, and there are four principal ones, of which the greatest and outermost is that called Oceanus, which flows round the earth in a circle; and in the opposite direction flows Acheron, which passes under the earth through desert places, into the Acherusian Lake: this is the lake to the shores of which the souls of the many go when they are dead, and after waiting an appointed time, which is to some a longer and to some a shorter time, they are sent back again to be born as animals. The third river rises between the two, and near the place of rising pours into a vast region of fire, and forms a lake larger than the Mediterranean Sea, boiling with water and mud; and proceeding muddy and turbid, and winding about the earth, comes, among other places, to the extremities of the Acherusian Lake, but mingles not with the waters of the lake, and after making many coils about the earth plunges into Tartarus at a deeper level. This is that Pyriphlegethon, as the stream is called, which throws up jets of fire in all sorts of places. The fourth river goes out on the opposite side, and falls first of all into a wild and savage region, which is all of a dark-blue color, like lapis lazuli; and this is that river which is called the Stygian River, and falls into and forms the Lake Styx, and after falling into the lake and receiving strange powers in the waters, passes under the earth, winding round in the opposite direction to Pyriphlegethon, and meeting in the Acherusian Lake from the opposite side. And the water of this river too mingles with no other, but flows round in a circle and falls into Tartarus over against Pyriphlegethon, and the name of this river, as the poet says, is Cocytus.

Such is the name of the other world; and when the dead arrive at the place to which the genius of each severally conveys them, first of all they have sentence passed upon them, as they have lived well and piously or not. And those who appear to have lived neither well nor ill, go to the river Acheron, and mount such conveyances as they can get, and are carried in them to the lake, and there they dwell and are purified of their evil deeds, and suffer the penalty of the wrongs which they have done to others, and are absolved, and receive the rewards of their good deeds according to their deserts. But those who appear to be incurable by reason of the greatness of their crimes-who have committed many and terrible deeds of sacrilege, murders foul and violent, or the like-such are hurled into Tartarus, which is their suitable destiny, and they never come out. Those again who have committed crimes, which, although great, are not unpardonable-who in a moment of anger, for example, have done violence to a father or mother, and have repented for the remainder of their lives, or who have taken the life of another under like extenuating circumstances-these are plunged into Tartarus, the pains of which they are compelled to undergo for a year, but at the end of the year the wave casts them forth-mere homicides by way of Cocytus, parricides and matricides by Pyriphlegethon-and they are borne to the Acherusian

Lake, and there they lift up their voices and call upon the victims whom they have slain or wronged, to have pity on them, and to receive them, and to let them come out of the river into the lake. And if they prevail, then they come forth and cease from their troubles; but if not, they are carried back again into Tartarus and from thence into the rivers unceasingly, until they obtain mercy from those whom they have wronged: for that is the sentence inflicted upon them by their judges. Those also who are remarkable for having led holy lives are released from this earthly prison, and go to their pure home which is above, and dwell in the purer earth; and those who have duly purified themselves with philosophy live henceforth altogether without the body, in mansions fairer far than these, which may not be described, and of which the time would fail me to tell.

Wherefore, Simmias, seeing all these things, what ought not we to do in order to obtain virtue and wisdom in this life? Fair is the prize, and the hope great.

I do not mean to affirm that the description which I have given of the soul and her mansions is exactly true—a man of sense ought hardly to say that. But I do say that, inasmuch as the soul is shown to be immortal, he may venture to think, not improperly or unworthily, that something of the kind is true. The venture is a glorious one, and he ought to comfort himself with words like these, which is the reason why lengthen out the tale. Wherefore, I say, let a man be of good cheer about his soul, who has cast away the pleasures and ornaments of the body as alien to him, and rather hurtful in their effects, and has followed after the pleasures of knowledge in this life; who has adorned the soul in her own proper jewels, which are temperance, and justice, and courage, and nobility, *and truth-in these arrayed she is ready to go on her journey to the world below, when her time comes. You, Simmias and Cebes, and all other men, will depart at some time or other. Me already, as the tragic poet would say, the voice of fate calls. Soon I must drink the poison; and I think that I had better repair to the bath first, in order that the women may not have the trouble of washing my body after I am dead.*

When he had done speaking, Crito said: And have you any commands for us, Socrates-anything to say about your children, or any other matter in which we can serve you?

Nothing particular, he said: only, as I have always told you, I would have you look to yourselves; that is a service which you may always be doing to me and mine as well as to yourselves. And you need not make professions; for if you take no thought for yourselves, and walk not according to the precepts which I have given you, not now for the first time, the warmth of your professions will be of no avail.

We will do our best, said Crito. But in what way would you have us bury you?

In any way that you like; only you must get hold of me, and take care that I do not walk away from you. Then he turned to us, and added with a smile: I cannot make Crito believe that I am the same Socrates who have been talking and conducting the argument; he fancies that I am the other Socrates whom he will soon see, a dead body and he asks, How shall he bury me? And though I have spoken many words in the endeavor to show that when I have drunk the poison I shall leave you and go to the joys of the blessed- these words of mine, with which I comforted you and myself, have had, I perceive, no effect upon Crito and

therefore I want you to be surety for me now, as he was surety
for me at the trial: but let the promise be of another sort; for he was my surety to the judges that I would remain, but you must be my surety to him that I shall not remain, but go away and depart; and then he will suffer less at my death, and not be grieved when he sees my body being burned or buried. I would not have him sorrow at my hard lot, or say at the burial, Thus we lay out Socrates, or, Thus we follow him to the grave or bury him; for false words are not only evil in themselves, but they infect the soul with evil. Be of good cheer, then, my dear Crito, and say that you are burying my body only, and do with that as is usual, and as you think best.

When he had spoken these words, he arose and went into the bath chamber with Crito, who bade us wait; and we waited, talking and thinking of the subject of discourse, and also of the greatness of our sorrow; he was like a father of whom we were being bereaved, and we were about to pass the rest of our lives as orphans. When he had taken the bath his children were brought to him-(he had two young sons and an elder one); and the women of his family also came, and he talked to them and gave them a few directions in the presence of Crito; and he then dismissed them and returned to us.

Now the hour of sunset was near, for a good deal of time had passed while he was within. When he came out, he sat down with us again after his bath, but not much was said. Soon the jailer, who was the servant of the Eleven, entered and stood by him, saying: To you, Socrates, whom I know to be the noblest and gentlest and best of all who ever came to this place, I will not impute the angry feelings of other men, who rage and swear at me when, in obedience to the

*authorities, I bid them drink the poison-indeed, I am
sure that you will not be angry with me; for others, as
you are aware, and not I, are the guilty cause. And so
fare you well, and try to bear lightly what must needs
be; you know my errand. Then bursting into tears he
turned away and went out.*

*Socrates looked at him and said: I return your good
wishes, and will do as you bid. Then, turning to us, he
said, How charming the man is: since I have been in
prison he has always been coming to see me, and at
times he would talk to me, and was as good as could
be to me, and now see how generously he sorrows for
me.*

*But we must do as he says, Crito; let the cup be
brought, if the poison is prepared: if not, let the
attendant prepare some.*

*Yet, said Crito, the sun is still upon the hilltops, and
many a one has taken the draught late, and after the
announcement has been made to him, he has eaten
and drunk, and indulged in sensual delights; do not
hasten then, there is still time.*

*Socrates said: Yes, Crito, and they of whom you
speak are right in doing thus, for they think that they
will gain by the delay; but I am right in not doing
thus, for I do not think that I should gain anything by
drinking the poison a little later; I should be sparing
and saving a life which is already gone: I could only
laugh at myself for this. Please then to do as I say,
and not to refuse me.*

*Crito, when he heard this, made a sign to the servant,
and the servant went in, and remained for some time,
and then returned with the jailer carrying a cup of
poison. Socrates said: You, my good friend, who are
experienced in these matters, shall give me directions
how I am to proceed. The man answered: You have
only to walk about until your legs are heavy, and then*

to lie down, and thè poison will act. At the same time
he handed the cup to Socrates, who in the easiest and
gentlest manner, without the least fear or change of
color or feature, looking at the man with all his eyes,
Echecrates, as his manner was, took the cup and
said: What do you say about making a libation out of
this cup to any god? May I, or not? The man
answered: We only prepare, Socrates, just so much as
we deem enough. I understand, he said: yet I may and
must pray to the gods to prosper my journey from this
to that other world may this, then, which is my prayer,
be granted to me. Then holding the cup to his lips,
quite readily and cheerfully he drank off the poison.
And hitherto most of us had been able to control our
sorrow; but now when we saw him drinking, and saw
too that he had finished the draught, we could no
longer forbear, and in spite of myself my own tears
were flowing fast; so that I covered my face and wept
over myself, for certainly I was not weeping over him,
but at the thought of my own calamity in having lost
such a companion.
Nor was I the first, for Crito, when he found himself
unable to restrain his tears, had got up and moved
away, and I followed; and at that moment.
Apollodorus, who had been weeping all the time,
broke out in a loud cry which made cowards of us all.
Socrates alone retained his calmness: What is this
strange outcry? he said. I sent away the women
mainly in order that they might not offend in this way,
for I have heard that a man should die in peace. Be
quiet, then, and have patience.
When we heard that, we were ashamed, and refrained
our tears; and he walked about until, as he said, his
legs began to fail, and then he lay on his back,
according to the directions, and the man who gave
him the poison now and then looked at his feet and

legs; and after a while he pressed his foot hard and asked him if he could feel; and he said, no; and then his leg, and so upwards and upwards, and showed us that he was cold and stiff. And he felt them himself, and said: When the poison reaches the heart, that will be the end. He was beginning to grow cold about the groin, when he uncovered his face, for he had covered himself up, and said (they were his last words)-he said: Crito, I owe a cock to Asclepius; will you remember to pay the debt? The debt shall be paid, said Crito; is there anything else? There was no answer to this question; but in a minute or two a movement was heard, and the attendants uncovered him; his eyes were set, and Crito closed his eyes and mouth.
Such was the end, Echecrates, of our friend, whom I may truly call the wisest, and justest, and best of all the men whom I have ever known.

In one of Plato's earlier dialogs, *Apology*, Socrates is unsure about immortality. But by the time Plato wrote this later dialog, he had become convinced and made it clear that he had embraced the idea of immortality. In answer to Crito's question: *But in what way would you have us bury you?* Socrates replied:

In any way that you like; only you must get hold of me, and take care that I do not walk away from you. Then he turned to us, and added with a smile: I cannot make Crito believe that I am the same Socrates who have been talking and conducting the argument; he fancies that I am the other Socrates whom he will soon see, a dead body and he asks, How shall he bury me? And though I have spoken many words in the endeavor to show that when I have drunk the poison I

387

shall leave you and go to the joys of the blessed-
these words of mine, with which I comforted you and
myself, have had, I perceive, no effect upon Crito and
therefore I want you to be surety for me now, as he
was surety for me at the trial: but let the promise be
of another sort; for he was my surety to the judges
that I would remain, but you must be my surety to him
that I shall not remain, but go away and depart; and
then he will suffer less at my death, and not be
grieved when he sees my body being burned or buried.
I would not have him sorrow at my hard lot, or say at
the burial, Thus we lay out Socrates, or, Thus we
follow him to the grave or bury him; for false words
are not only evil in themselves, but they infect the
soul with evil. Be of good cheer, then, my dear Crito,
and say that you are burying my body only, and do
with that as is usual, and as you think best.

Bury me any way you want, Socrates said, (and here I'm paraphrasing) because I won't be there. I will be somewhere else enjoying other blessings and experiences. The *I* Socrates referred to, the part of him that was separate from his body, was his true self, his will, his mental essence. The body would die, but *he* would continue to live. It is an interesting concept, isn't it?

What arguments does Plato make in this dialog to support his belief in the immortality of the soul? He makes three: *the cyclical argument, the argument from recollection,* and *the affinity argument*. The *cyclical argument* can be summarized as follows:

1. Things come to be what they are based on their having been an opposite—large things were at one time small, dead things were at one time living things.
2. Between opposites there are two opposite processes: for example, between smaller and larger, there are the processes

of decrease and increase, as in smaller can increase, becoming larger.

3. If the two opposite processes did not balance each other out, everything would eventually end up in the same state: for instance, if increase did not balance out decrease, everything would continue to get smaller and smaller.

4. Being dead and being alive are opposite states, and dying and coming to life are opposites processes. Coming to life, then, must balance out dying.

5. Therefore, everything that dies must come to life again.

Is this a good argument? If not, can you identify what you consider its weak point to be?

The *argument from recollection* appears to be an original Platonic argument and is utilized in two other of Plato's dialogs: *Meno* and *Phaedrus*. The idea is that much of the knowledge we have is innate and must be remembered rather than learned. The argument can be summarized as follows:

1. Things in the world may appear to be equal to each other. In fact they are not truly equal.

2. Therefore, a true equality (equality being understood as concept or form that exists) does not exist between them.

3. Noting the inequality that exists in the world, we are reminded of the concept of equality, that is, we know that equality as a concept exists, but we do not see it in the world.

4. The only way this is possible is for us to have had prior knowledge of the idea or concept of equality.

5. Knowledge of true equality cannot come from sensory perception (because true equality does not exist in the world), so it is necessary that we acquired our knowledge of equality before we were born.

6. Therefore, our soul (or mind) must have existed before we were born so we could acquire this knowledge.

Is this a good argument? If not, what is wrong with

389

it?

Plato's third argument in support of immortality is the *affinity argument*. It is based on the idea of an affinity or likeness between two different kinds of realities. It may be summarized as follows:

1. There are two different aspects to the one true reality: (1) a material aspect—the physical world of material objects, including physical human bodies, and (2) an immaterial aspect—the world of mental realities, including minds, thoughts, concepts, and so on. Things that are part of the material aspect are constantly changing. There is death and decay. Things that are part of the immaterial aspect are enduring, endless.
2. The soul is more like or has an affinity with or to the immaterial aspect of reality.
3. Therefore, if it has been properly educated and trained, that is, if it is appropriately philosophically (and spiritually) oriented, the soul of a dead person will make its way into the immaterial world.

It must be understood that Plato's argument here is designed to argue a possibility. The properly enlightened soul can (is more likely to be able to) find its way to the immaterial realm. The unenlightened soul cannot. So the enlightened soul can be immortal. [143]

Once again, the question is, is this a convincing argument? Over the centuries, most people have felt like Plato failed to present convincing arguments regarding the immortality of the soul. What we must understand is whether or not the human soul is immortal, whether or not there is life after death, does not depend on whether or not Plato presented convincing arguments. Personally, I do not believe Plato made his case. That does not mean, however, that there

---

[143] Connolly, "Plato's Phaedo," *Internet Encyclopedia of Philosophy.*

is no life after death. It just means that Plato did not provide us with convincing arguments.

Epicurus

We have little of Epicurus' original material to study. Some has survived and material from his followers also provide insight into his beliefs and philosophy. From what we can gather, Epicurus' views regarding death and immortality were very different from Plato's. One of his followers, Lucretius (1st century BCE), wrote a poem that reflects Epicurus' views on death. The poem is entitled, *Against the Fear of Death* (translation by John Dryden).

> *What has this bugbear Death to frighten man,*
> *If souls can die, as well as bodies can?*
> *For, as before our birth we feel no pain,*
> *When Punic arms infested land and main,*
> *When heaven and earth were in confusion hurl'd*
> *For the debated empire of the world,*
> *Which awed with dreadful expectation lay,*
> *Soon to be slaves, uncertain who should sway:*
> *So, when our mortal frame shall be disjoin'd,*
> *The lifeless lump uncoupled from the mind,*
> *From sense of grief and pain we shall be free;*
> *We shall not feel, because we shall not be.*
> *Though earth in seas, and seas in heaven were lost,*
> *We should not move, we only should be toss'd.*
> *Nay, e'en suppose when we have suffered fate*
> *The soul should feel in her divided state,*
> *What's that to us? for we are only we,*
> *While souls and bodies in our frame agree.*
> *Nay, though our atoms should revolve by chance,*
> *And matter leap into the former dance;*
> *Though time our life and motion could restore,*

And make our bodies what they were before,
What gain to us would all this bustle bring?
The new-made man would be another thing.
When once an interrupting pause is made,
That individual being is decay'd.
We, who are dead and gone, shall bear no part
In all the pleasures, nor shall feel the smart,
Which to that other mortal shall accrue,
Whom to our matter time shall mold anew.
For backward if you look on that long space
Of ages past, and view the changing face
Of matter, toss'd and variously combin'd
In sundry shapes, 'tis easy for the mind
From thence to infer, that seeds of things have been
In the same order as they now are seen:
Which yet our dark remembrance cannot trace,
Because a pause of life, a gaping space,
Has come betwixt, where memory lies dead,
And all the wandering motions from the sense are fled.
For whosoe'er shall in misfortune live,
Must be, when those misfortunes shall arrive;
And since the man who is not, feels not woe,
(For death exempts him, and wards off the blow,
Which we, the living, only feel and bear,)
What is there left for us in death to fear?
When once that pause of life has come between
'Tis just the same as we had never been.

What is the point of the poem? It is that death is nothing to fear because we just cease to be. What will be will be, the same as it was before we came to be. Since before we existed we were not afraid of not existing, why be afraid of not existing again? Personally, I do not agree with Lucretius, but I see his logic.

The material we have from Epicurus that addresses this idea of the fear of death is a letter to his friend

Menoeceus. It is a more straightforward comment on the subject. Since we looked at the entire letter in an earlier chapter, I will include here only those sections that have to do with his views on death.

Accustom yourself to believing that death is nothing to us, for good and evil imply the capacity for sensation, and death is the privation of all sentience; therefore a correct understanding that death is nothing to us makes the mortality of life enjoyable, not by adding to life a limitless time, but by taking away the yearning after immortality. For life has no terrors for him who has thoroughly understood that there are no terrors for him in ceasing to live. Foolish, therefore, is the man who says that he fears death, not because it will pain when it comes, but because it pains in the prospect. Whatever causes no annoyance when it is present, causes only a groundless pain in the expectation. Death, therefore, the most awful of evils, is nothing to us, seeing that, when we are, death is not come, and, when death is come, we are not. It is nothing, then, either to the living or to the dead, for with the living it is not and the dead exist no longer.

Epicurus thoughts can be summarized as follows:

1. Either I am alive and exist, or dead and no longer exist.
2. When I am alive, I exist.
3. When I am alive, non-existence is of no concern to me.
4. Therefore, when I am alive, death is of no concern to me.
5. When I am dead, I do not exist.
6. When I do not exist, death is of no concern to me.
7. Therefore, when I am dead, death is of no concern to me.
8. Therefore, whether I am dead or alive, death is of no concern to me.

393

Kenny explains that Epicurus had accepted (with some modifications) the atomism of Democritus, and believed that the soul consisted of atoms (that is, that it was a physical thing). "At death the atoms of the soul are dispersed, and cease to be capable of sensation because they no longer occupy their appropriate place in a body."[144]

Epicurus, of course, is not offering an argument but simply an assertion, explaining to his friend what he (Epicurus) believes and hopes his friend will embrace. Many people today embrace the same idea—that the human being is entirely physical in nature and that when the physical body dies, the "person" ceases to exist.

Jesus

Jesus did not share Epicurus' belief that the human being was only a physical creature that ceased to exist upon the death of the body. Jesus' philosophy and theology was part of a long tradition of Hebrew thought that, by the 1st century CE, included some selected Greek ideas concerning death and immortality. Jesus taught that there would be a day of reckoning at the end of time when all people will be resurrected from the dead and experience the consequences of the choices they had made during their lives. "*Do not be amazed at this, for a time is coming when all who are in their graves will hear his voice and come out—those who have done what is good will rise to live, and those who have done what is evil will rise to be condemned*," (John 5:28-29).

Jesus' followers embraced that idea, teaching the resurrection of the dead and the immortality of the soul. The Apostle Paul gives what is perhaps the most concise statement of the idea.

---

[144] Kenny, *An Illustrated Brief History of Western Philosophy*, 94.

So will it be with the resurrection of the dead. The body that is sown is perishable, it is raised imperishable; it is sown in dishonor, it is raised in glory; it is sown in weakness, it is raised in power; it is sown a natural body, it is raised a spiritual body.

If there is a natural body, there is also a spiritual body. So it is written: "The first man Adam became a living being;" the last Adam, a life-giving spirit. The spiritual did not come first, but the natural, and after that the spiritual. The first man was of the dust of the earth; the second man is of heaven. As was the earthly man, so are those who are of the earth; and as is the heavenly man, so also are those who are of heaven. And just as we have borne the image of the earthly man, so shall we bear the image of the heavenly man.

I declare to you, brothers and sisters, that flesh and blood cannot inherit the kingdom of God, nor does the perishable inherit the imperishable. Listen, I tell you a mystery: We will not all sleep, but we will all be changed—in a flash, in the twinkling of an eye, at the last trumpet. For the trumpet will sound, the dead will be raised imperishable, and we will be changed. For the perishable must clothe itself with the imperishable, and the mortal with immortality. When the perishable has been clothed with the imperishable, and the mortal with immortality, then the saying that is written will come true: "Death has been swallowed up in victory."

"Where, O death, is your victory? Where, O death, is your sting?" The sting of death is sin, and the power of sin is the law. But thanks be to God! He gives us the victory through our Lord Jesus Christ, (1 Corinthians 15:42-57).

The immortality of the soul and the resurrection of the dead are foundational beliefs of the Christian faith. The ideas, however, are usually asserted and accepted rather than argued. By itself that does not mean that the beliefs are without foundation. It just means that neither Jesus nor his followers felt the need to present rational arguments in support of the ideas.

Death

So what are we left with, then, to guide us in our thinking regarding death? Is death the end of each person's existence? Or is there life after death? One way to approach the subject is to consider it in light of two alternative perspectives: materialism and dualism.

If Materialism Is True

Materialism is the idea that only physical things exist. If materialism is true and only physical things exist, then humans are only physical organisms—a physical body enabled and controlled by a physical brain. If this is the case, when the body dies and the brain ceases to function, the person you are ceases to exist. There is no life after death. While many people do embrace this idea, many others do not. In Chapter 9, I offered specific arguments demonstrating that materialism is at best a questionable theory. There is no point in duplicating that material here. Instead it might be appropriate to ask if the prospect of extinction is coherent. I do not believe it is. If materialism is true and only physical things exist and those exist as they do (in this present state of existence) only because of random chance, then not only is there no life after death, but life has no purpose beyond one's simple biological presence and process. I'm born, I live, I reproduce, I die. That's it. And if that is it, life is as pointless as it can possibly be. If materialism is true, Epicurus was right and pleasure is the point and purpose of life. There can be no other possible conclusion. You are born and you die. In between birth and death, stuff happens. You should do all you can to be sure that it is as pleasurable as possible. Nothing else matters, because when you die you cease to exist. You *are* and then you *aren't*. Can that really be the way things are? I do not think so. That particular position ignores the reality of a mental life that suggests a dualistic reality. To ignore such evidence is illogical and results, therefore, in an incoherent position.

If Dualism Is True

Materialism is a very bleak perspective from which to think about and live life. Dualism, however, has much more to offer. If dualism is true, the soul or mind is an essence that is not physical in nature and, therefore, not subject to the physical decay that characterizes objects composed of physical matter. The body dies; the mind endures. If that which has always existed is mind rather than matter (see the cosmological argument in Chapter 6), then mind is clearly enduring in nature. It does not get old and wear out. Thus, when the body dies, the mind or soul survives and the *person* (the part of us with which we think and decide) remains an individuated self, an entity or being with the same identity it had while embodied. There is no extinction; there is no ceasing to exist.

Death As A Birth

If one embraces a dualistic perspective, death can be thought of as a birth or a transition into another phase of life. Just as a baby's time of development in the womb will come to an end in the process of birth where it will be transitioned into a new phase of its existence, so, too, our time in this physical world can be thought of as a time of development that will end in death. But death can also be thought of as a birth, a transition into the new phase of existence. In this new phase of existence we will continue to experience, encounter, learn, and mature as we move along a developmental trajectory toward our fully realized potential.

Some of this terminology may be new but the idea itself is not new. It is the idea of becoming. A dualistic reality allows for the idea of becoming. A materialistic perspective does not.

Summary

Death is a part of life. From one point of view, we are born to die. That reality can be startling. What is this thing called death that we all must experience? It is the end of physical life, but is it the end of existence? The answer to that question, of course, is determined by whether reality is materialistic in nature or dualistic. If only material things exist, then when the body dies, the individual ceases to exist. If, however, reality is dualistic in nature and non-material things exist, then while physical life may end, existence does not end. Minds or souls are mental essences that are enduring. They are not subject to the decay of physical things. If a person is a mental being, a soul, then when the body dies, the soul lives on.

Is there life after death? During this stage of our lives we raise the question. At some point in the not too distance future, we will have a definitive answer.

Thought and Discussion Questions
1. Discuss your reaction to Crito's question to Socrates, "How shall we bury you?" and Socrates' answer, "Any way

you like. I won't be there." What are the implications of Socrates' answer?

2. Discuss your reaction to Epicurus' perspective that death is nothing to fear because death is simply the end of existence.

3. Discuss your thinking about Jesus' concept of life after death being linked to a resurrection.

4. Discuss the idea of death being compared to a birth, or a transition into another phase of existence.

5. Discuss your own views about death and life after death.

Chapter 13
How Should Human Beings Live?

In the last chapter we considered whether or not there is life after death, an important question indeed. An equally important question is how we ought to live the life we have before death comes our way. Philosophical questions about how life ought to be lived come under the heading of moral philosophy. How life ought to be lived was a topic of concern for the ancient Hebrews as well as for the Greeks. The Hebrews had an entire genre of literature, called *wisdom literature*, which focused on advice for living a life of wisdom. The Greeks, of course, set the standards for rational reflection on how life ought to be lived, or on what constituted living a good life. Socrates is known as the Father of Moral Philosophy. His student, Plato, believed that absolute knowledge about morality was available, and his student, Aristotle, produced the most detailed analysis of moral philosophy in the ancient world—*Nicomachean Ethics*.

So how should life be lived? To even attempt an answer to that question, we must first ask and answer two other basic questions: 1) *what makes humans moral beings,* and 2) *what makes an act moral or immoral?*

What Makes Humans Moral Beings

The same things that make us *human* beings make us *moral* beings. To be a human being is to be a moral being. So what makes human beings moral beings? In a nutshell, it is this: humans are rational and enjoy second level awareness (not just being aware but being aware of being aware), which allows us to make choices, or to be self-determined. Being rational, having second-level awareness, and being self-determined beings make us moral beings. Let us consider each of these separately.

Humans are rational. We engage in high-level abstract conceptualization. We can think about the idea of existence and what it means that we exist. We can think about existing in time and space and ask, what if I existed in a different time and space? We can project ourselves into different times and spaces, into different circumstances and situations. We can think about concepts such as beauty, and create art that represents conceptions of what is beautiful. We think mathematically and symbolically. We are rational beings.

Humans are self-aware, that is, aware of our own individuated existence. I exist separate from other people and objects. I am me. But humans are not the only self-aware species. Lots of mammals are self-aware. Elephants, chimps, and dogs can recognize themselves in a mirror. But we have what I refer to as second-level awareness. We are not only self-aware, we are aware that we are aware and can contemplate what that awareness means. It is, from one point of view, a very personal introspective application of our high level of rationality. I exist and I know it. I am rational, and I can contemplate my existence, my reality, my meaning. I

401

have a life to live. Should I live it this way or that way? Should I live as if I am the only one who matters, or should I consider other people's needs and feelings? Should I live as if my view of right and wrong, of good and evil, is all that matters, or should I consider that morality may depend on something other than my own personal or cultural perspective? In other words, I have choices to make. Because I am rational and have second-level awareness, I have choices to make. I am self-determined. I can decide to do this or to do that, and I am then responsible for the choice I make.

Humans are rational, have second-level awareness, and are self-determined. That makes us moral beings. Humans are not *amoral*. Humans (at least fully functional humans) are moral beings who can act either morally or immorally. There are no amoral humans. Animals are amoral. They cannot contemplate goodness and justice; they cannot ask, what is the right thing to do? Their behaviors are instinctive or trained. Animal behavior does not grow out of moral contemplation. Human behavior does. Mature humans ask themselves, what is the right thing to do?[145] That is the behavior of a moral being.

That which differentiates us from animals is our rationality, our second-level awareness, and our self-determination. Those three things make us human beings, and they also make us moral beings—beings with *intrinsic value*. Since we are moral beings, we ought to live moral lives. But what is entailed in living a moral life? To answer that we need to discover what it is that makes an act moral or immoral.

---

[145] Most of us have known people or known of people who did not seem to care about the right thing to do. Within the species, there are extremely selfish people. But generally speaking, humankind has always been concerned about living well and living right, and asking, what is the right thing to do? That's why there is such a thing as moral philosophy.

What Makes An Act Moral Or Immoral

Because human beings are moral beings, morality cannot be separated from our humanness. Humanness carries with it an intrinsic value. Humans have worth simply by virtue of their humanness. Since humanness entails rationality, second-level awareness, and self-determination, humans are moral beings with intrinsic value. Morality—that which makes an act moral or immoral—must be linked to the intrinsic value of humanness.

It is when we understand the intrinsic value of humanness that we are in a position to determine what makes an act moral or immoral. I propose that morality involves recognizing the intrinsic value of humanness (one's own and that of others), along with actions, reactions, and interactions that reflect an appreciation of human value. Immorality involves a failure to recognize the intrinsic value of humanness (one's own and that of others), along with a subsequent failure to act, react and interact in ways that reflect an appreciation of human value. Thus, an act is moral if it recognizes and or enhances human value, and is immoral if it fails to recognize or in some way diminishes the value of humanness.

This way of thinking about what is moral and immoral can be referred to as metamorality, *that is, it is the underlying or foundational concept of morality that allows us to begin thinking about moral character and moral behavior. The* metamorality *must be in place as an underlying concept before we can begin to think about how it will express or manifest itself in one's character (one's habitual way of being) and in specific behaviors in response to specific moral dilemmas. While* metamorality *is an appreciation of humanness,* morality *is that*

403

appreciation expressed, generally, in one's character, and specifically, in actions related to given situations.

For instance, if I have an underlying appreciation for humanness that expresses itself in my character, my habitual behaviors will be those that reflect that appreciation. I will interact with people in ways that are consistent with my appreciation of their humanness. I will be respectful, courteous, honest, kind, charitable, and so forth, because I value what they are—a human being. My character will also reflect the value I have for myself as a human being. In valuing the humanness of others, I value my own. In devaluing the humanness of others, I devalue my own. If I am a moral person, my characteristic behavior will reflect an appreciation of or for humanness. Likewise, in specific situations, concerns, or crisis where specific needs arise, if I am a moral person, my behavior toward my fellow human beings in those specific instances (my sympathy, my willingness to help, and the way I go about helping) will reflect my appreciation of their humanness. If I value humanness, my character in general and my actions in given situations will reflect that value.[146]

This is my definition and explanation of what makes an act moral or immoral. Different ethicists will define and explain morality differently. But I'm going to proceed on the basis of this definition and explanation and look at a few of the major ethical systems that have been proposed over the centuries, systems that have had significant impact on the development of moral philosophy in the west.

---

[146] Rogers, *21st Century Ethics*, 184-186.

Systems For Moral Thinking And Acting

As we think about the ethical theories or moral systems that have been proposed throughout the centuries, we need to ask: *What would a fully functional moral paradigm look like? What features would it need to be viable, to provide one with an effective framework for moral thinking and acting in contemporary society?* It would need five features. A functional moral theory would need:

1. *A thorough and effective definition/explanation of morality.* It is impossible to think about morality, to discuss morality, and to determine what the moral thing to do in any given situation is if we do not know what morality is. So a functional moral theory must begin by explaining what morality is, by defining morality.

2. *A proper focus on the development of moral character.* From the very beginning of moral philosophy, the focus was on the kind of person one ought to be. Only recently (the past few hundred years) has the focus shifted to behaviors in specific circumstances. While the question, *What is the right thing to do?* is a good and valid question, so is the question, *What kind of a person ought one to be?* Both questions deserve to be asked and answered. However, when considering what the proper behavior in a given situation might be, it is apparent that one who is of high moral character, one who habitually does the right kinds of things in general, will be likely (perhaps more likely) to do the right thing in a specific situation. Thus, a functional moral theory will be one that focuses on the development of moral character.

3. *A mechanism for discovering the moral thing to do in a given situation.* While a proper focus on

moral character is an essential feature of a functional moral theory, so is the inclusion of a mechanism for determining the moral thing to do in a given situation. A person may be of the highest moral character and find himself completely confounded when confronted by a moral dilemma to which he has not given much thought. A moral theory that stresses only moral character and provides no mechanism for determining right action in a given situation is incomplete. Therefore, a functional moral theory will include a mechanism for discovering the moral thing to do in a specific situation.

4. *A proper focus on motive and intention.* Why one does what one does is of crucial importance. Two people can perform the same act, say, giving money to a poor person. One can do it out of compassion for the poor person, wanting to help, the other can do it for appearances sake, to impress and generate positive regard from others. The end result for the poor person is the same in either case, but the givers gave for very different reasons. One motive was altruistic, the other egoistic, one others-centered, the other self-centered. But if the outcome for the poor person is the same, why does motive matter? Because motive and intention provide the foundation for human behavior. What we do (action) and why we do it (motive) are connected because we are rational self-determined people. We decide who and what we are and we do so for reasons. Reasons (motive and intentions) matter. So a functional moral theory will provide a proper focus on motive and intentions.

5. *A proper focus on consequences.* As important as motives and intentions are, consequences are equally important. What happens is as important as why it happens. A moral theory that focuses only on motive and intention is lopsided. There must be a

focus on consequences as well. Humans act for reasons. And actions have consequences that matter. What happens to me matters; and what happens to you matters. Why? Because as human beings, we matter. So consequences also matter.

These five features must be present in a moral theory if it is to be [fully] viable in contemporary society as a means for moral thinking and acting.[147]

In the next four sections we will look at four ethical theories. We should look at each in relation to the standards outlined above and see how well they might work as a framework for moral thinking and acting in our contemporary context.

Virtue Ethics[148]

One of the most popular ethical theories embraced today is Virtue Ethics, a system originally outlined by Aristotle. Aristotle had proposed that life had a purpose, a goal toward which it moved. That goal was the realization of a person's potential, which would lead to that person being happy. The ancient Greek concept of happiness was different from ours. For Aristotle, the idea of happiness (*eudaimonia*) meant flourishing or thriving. To achieve that goal, one had to be an *arête* kind of a person, an excellent person, one who over the course of his life developed traits that resulted in him being an excellent person. For Aristotle, the character of an excellent person involved a group of traits that represented a mean between two extremes. The list of traits

---

[147] Rogers, *21st Century Ethics*, 203-205.
[148] Borrowed (with some minor editing) from Rogers, *21st Century Ethics*, 166-169.

that Aristotle believed to result in *arête* included the traits listed below:

The Deficiency	The Virtuous Mean	The Excess
Cowardice	Courage	Foolhardiness
Lack of restraint	Temperate	Ascetic self-denial
Stinginess	Liberality	Wastefulness
Pettiness	Magnanimous	Ostentatious
Overly humble	Proud	Arrogance
Indolent	Ambitious	Overreaching
Disagreeable	Good Tempered	Overly affable
Unfriendly surliness	Friendliness	Overly friendly
Deceitfulness	Truthfulness	Exaggeration
Humorless	Wittiness	Buffoonery
Shamelessness	Modesty	Bashfulness
Callousness	Just	Vengeful

Look at and think carefully about the traits in the middle column—The Virtuous Mean. Think about the kind of person a man would be if those traits characterized him. Most of us would like to be friends with that kind of a person. Most of us would like to be that kind of a person. Clearly, Aristotle believed that to be a person who would flourish in life (who had a good life and was happy), one had to be a certain kind of a person—a good person, a person who got along well with others and was respected and liked.

But what about moral behavior? What about knowing how to live a moral life? If the middle column represents the kind of person a virtuous person is, then the other two columns represent the kind of person the virtuous person will not be. The virtuous person, for example, who is just will not be calloused (or the things associated with it—cold, unfeeling, uncaring, unsympathetic, and so forth) or vengeful (or the things associated with it—intolerant, mean-spirited, violent, and so forth). If the virtuous man is truthful, he will not be a liar. The list of what a virtuous man is also serves as a list of things he is not. Aristotle's list becomes a moral code of how to live in order to be an excellent person.

Also, we must remember that for Aristotle, the virtues could not be attained and lived apart from reason. Humans are rational animals, according to Aristotle. To live a fully human life, one must live a life of reason. Reason (*phronesis*, practical wisdom) is the foundation and driving force behind the development of each virtue. A virtuous person is also a rational person, and for Aristotle the highest form of rational endeavor was contemplation—the kind of philosophical contemplation that characterized his life.

Aristotle's moral philosophy was developed in the 4th century BCE. Some have asked, can a moral theory developed 2,500 years ago provide a meaningful framework for moral thinking and acting in the modern world? Perhaps. Perhaps not. Maybe it would need to be tweaked just a bit. Contemporary ethicists have offered adjusted versions of Virtue Ethics. Are contemporary expressions of Virtue Ethics substantially different from Aristotelian Virtue Ethics? In some ways, yes; in others no.[149] One of the differences between the ancient and the modern will be in what we include in our list of virtues that would lead to or result in an excellent life in contemporary society. Rachels has developed a list of virtues that most contemporary people would agree are essential traits for achieving excellence in life.

---

[149] The substantial difference is that some of Aristotle's conclusions regarding manual labor, slavery and women have been rejected. See Simpson, "Contemporary Virtue Ethics and Aristotle."

Virtues Valued in Contemporary [Western] Society

Benevolence	Fairness	Reasonableness
Civility	Friendliness	Self-confidence
Compassion	Generosity	Self-control
Conscientiousness	Honesty	Self-discipline
Cooperativeness	Industriousness	Self-reliance
Courage	Justice	Tactfulness
Courteousness	Loyalty	Thoughtfulness
Dependability	Moderation	Tolerance[150]

Rachels' list has twice as many items in it as Aristotle's. Why? Perhaps because contemporary life is more complex and it takes more virtues to be an excellent person today than it did 2,500 years ago. But perhaps the difference is simply two different moral philosophers, each developing his own list, one being more specific than the other. I doubt that Aristotle would be unhappy with Rachels' list. Other than some of Aristotle's culturally shaped views that can no longer be embraced, the basic differences between ancient and modern Virtue Ethics appear to be insignificant.

Many ethicists today believe that Aristotle's ancient focus on the kind of person one ought to be is precisely what contemporary society needs if we are to be a moral society. Others feel that Virtue Ethics provides a good foundation for thinking about morality, but that it lacks a mechanism for solving the complex moral dilemmas that exist in our society. Review the features of a functional moral system discussed earlier in this chapter and evaluate Virtue Ethics in light of that list. Does Virtue Ethics measure up, or should we look for a different kind of a moral theory to use in our contemporary society?

---

[150] Rachels, "The Ethics of Virtue," in *Ethics: History, Theory, and Contemporary Issues*, 697.

Kantian Ethics[151]

Immanuel Kant (born 1724) was not only one of the most influential philosophers of the Enlightenment but of all time. His books, especially *Critique of Pure Reason*, changed the course of Western Philosophy. Kant was also a devout Christian with a deep interest in moral philosophy. His ethical theory remains one of the most influential in history. His book, *The Groundwork of the Metaphysics of Morals*, is an introductory volume on his moral theory.

Kant's opening sentence of Chapter 1 of *Groundwork* is: "It is impossible to conceive anything at all in the world, or even out of it, which can be taken as good without qualification, except a *good will*."[152] What did he mean? What is a good will? For Kant, a good will is one's desire to do the right thing. The human will is that aspect of our nature with which we determine our actions. To *will* a thing is to decide it, to want to bring it about. I can *will* that I should respond with respect and courtesy each time I encounter another person. I can *will* that I keep each promise that I make. Kant is making the bold claim that the only thing that is intrinsically good, good in and of itself, is a good will—a *will* that *wills* to do the right thing. A person with a good will is a person who wants, in each case, to do the right thing, the moral thing.

Kant is not saying that the only thing that is good is a good will. He knows that are many things that are good. He goes on in his opening paragraph of *Groundwork* to say, "Intelligence, wit, judgment and any other talents of the mind we may care to name, or courage, resolution, and constancy of purpose, as qualities of temperament, are without doubt good and desirable in many respects." He goes on to explain,

---

[151] Borrowed (with slight editing) from Rogers, *21st Century Ethics*, 106-117.
[152] Kant, *Groundwork*, 1: 393, 1.

however, that they can also be bad and hurtful. Any of those kinds of things can also be used badly. Thieves might be intelligent and courageous. But their intelligence and courage, if used for immoral purposes become bad things. Thus those "contingently" good things (things that can be good or bad depending on how they are used) cannot be intrinsically good. For Kant, only a good will is intrinsically good.

Kant also points out that the good of a good will is not dependent upon consequences in any way. If one wills (intends) to do good, it is good (because it is the product of a good will) even if the results are less than desirable. In Kant's view, one may will to always tell the truth. In the process of being a truth-teller, however, one may tell a truth that results in something very bad happening to someone else. For Kant, that bad outcome is irrelevant. The will to be a truth-teller and the subsequent actual truth-telling cannot be diminished by negative consequences. For Kant, a good will is good all the time and is good in and of itself. It is intrinsically good.

Another of Kant's foundational ideas in his quest for *the supreme principle of morality* (in addition to having a good will) is that one does what one does because it is one's *duty* to do so. Duty is such an integral part of Kantian moral philosophy that his framework for moral philosophy is often referred to as *Deontological Ethics*. The Greek word for duty is *deon*. Thus, deontological ethics has to do with seeing or emphasizing the relationship between morality and the doing of one's duty. Morally speaking, to do the right thing is always one's duty, regardless of the circumstances. But what, exactly, does Kant mean by duty? He means doing the right thing simply because it is the right thing to do, not because one benefits in some way by doing the right thing. He uses the example of a grocery story owner to clarify his meaning.

> *It certainly accords with duty that a grocer should not overcharge his inexperienced customer;*

and where there is much competition a sensible shopkeeper refrains from doing so and keeps to a fixed and general price for everybody so that a child can buy from him just as well as anyone else. Thus people are served honestly; but this is not nearly enough to justify us in believing that the shopkeeper has acted in this way from duty or from principles of fair dealing; his interests required him to do so.[153]

Kant explains that the shopkeeper who deals honestly with his customers may look like one who is doing his duty (who is acting morally). But this may not the case. Duty, or morality, as Kant explains it, requires a response that is not rooted in self-interest. If one's actions are to qualify as dutiful or moral, they must be done without regard to one's self interest. One can run an honest business out of duty or out of self-interest. Kant's point is that an observation of honesty does not equal an observation of dutiful morality because one may be acting entirely out of self-interested motives.

Morality and motive, then, are linked in a crucial way. Why one does what one does determines whether or not one has acted in a moral manner. Suppose, for example, person X returns a lost wallet (with a good amount of cash in it) simply because that is the right thing to do (duty), while person Y returns the wallet out of self-interest, hoping for a reward. According to Kant, person X acted morally while person Y did not. Person Y did a right thing, a good thing, but his actions were not moral because his motive was not one of duty but of self-interest. So for Kant, an action can be socially appropriate and acceptable but not necessarily moral because morality depends on motive. Clearly, Kant is setting a very high standard of morality.

---

[153] Kant, *Groundwork*, 1: 397,9.

As morality and motive are crucially linked, so are morality and freewill. Kant was a scientist who enthusiastically embraced the idea of a Newtonian mechanistic cosmos. The problem with embracing that paradigm is that it does not appear to leave room for freedom of choice. The parts of a mechanism do not choose what to do, they do what they are designed to do. If humans are part of a mechanistic cosmos, how can they have free will? Kant believed that human autonomy stood apart from the mechanistic nature of the material cosmos.[154] Humans, as thinking beings are dualistic in nature—embodied minds. The material body may be part of the mechanistic cosmos, but the immaterial mind (the will) is not. Since it is not material in nature, it is not subject to mechanistic determinations. The mind is free to choose. Humans have freewill.[155] For Kant, this is an essential feature of human morality. There can be no morality or immorality without freewill. To be moral or immoral, we must be free to choose.

What is it, then, for Kant that connects all of these threads: intention, motive, and freewill? It is rationality. Where animals are guided by instinct (even "thinking" animals) humans are guided by rationality. The human being is a rational-moral being. Rationality and morality co-exist and are interdependent. If the only thing that is intrinsically good is a good will, then goodness or morality exists in relation to what we rationally *will* (determine) to do. For Kant, rationality and morality co-exist. Where you find one you find the other, and where you do not find both you do

---

[154] O'Neill, "Kantian Ethics," in *A Companion to Ethics*, 176.
[155] This is my own Cartesian explanation of human nature as it applies to the issue of freewill. And while I am not suggesting that Kant would have explained things in this way, I do believe he held the same basic opinion—that the human will (the mind) is autonomous, that it is free to choose (self-determined) and not subject to mechanistic determinations.

not find either. So when Kant says *the only thing that is itself good is a good will,* he is saying a lot.

Kant has laid a foundation to build on. He has said that a good will is the only intrinsic good. He has linked morality and motive, and he believes that rational, autonomous (self-determined) beings are capable of determining moral standards.[156] But how do they do so? What does Kant suggest as a framework for moral thinking and acting? He suggests what he calls the *categorical imperative.* Kant believes that *moral claims* result in *moral imperatives.* What are moral claims, and what are moral imperatives? A moral claim is a moral statement. You ought to do this or that, or you ought not do this or that. The statement, *murder is wrong,* is a moral claim. The statement, *a merchant ought to run an honest business,* is a moral claim.[157] Moral claims contain an implicit imperative, that is, a specific statement about what one ought or ought not do. These implicit imperatives can and must become explicit. They must be articulated utilizing what Kant calls a *maxim* and will result in either a *hypothetical* or a *categorical* imperative (which is reflective of *the* Categorical Imperative).

What is a maxim? A maxim has to do with "the intentional aspect of one's will."[158] It is a statement that describes an act one intends to perform. An example of a maxim would be: *Whenever I make a promise, I will keep my promise.* Or another might be: *Whenever I can benefit in some way by lying, I will lie.* A maxim has to do with one's intention, one's goal. Kant would say with one's *end,* meaning the end result one intends to accomplish. The *end* of the maxim, *Whenever I make a promise, I will keep my*

---

156 I would enjoy (if it was possible) visiting with Dr. Kant about the idea of the rational autonomous humans *discovering* morality instead of *determining* it. I would to think he would be open to the idea.
157 Glasgow, "Kant's Principle of Universal Law," in *Conduct and Character: Readings in Moral Theory,* 154.
158 Glasgow, 153.

promise, is that I will be a promise keeper and not a promise breaker. Notice that maxims do not suggest what should be done but what one intends to do. That raises an important question for Kant: How does one determine whether or not what one intends to do is moral? That is where *imperatives* come into play. Kant identifies two kinds of imperatives: *hypothetical* and *categorical.*

An imperative is a command. *"Close the door,"* is an example of an imperative. A *hypothetical imperative* is an imperative that applies to you given your subjective end, your personal intention or goal. For instance, the statement, *"If you want to lose weight, you must eat healthy food and exercise,"* is an example of a hypothetical imperative for a person who wants to lose weight. However, it does not apply to everyone. If one does not have the goal of losing weight, the imperative does not apply. Thus it is hypothetical. It may or may not apply to you, depending on your subjective end or goal.

A *categorical imperative,* however, is one that expresses what ought to be done because it is the right thing to do. A categorical imperative carries with it a moral obligation, obligating everyone, not just those who have corresponding subjective goals. A categorical imperative is a universal law, applying to everyone, all the time. Personal maxims must be weighed against categorical imperatives to determine whether or not the personal maxim is moral.

As Glasgow points out, Kant believed that there was one Categorical Imperative (with a capital C and a capital I) that represented the *supreme principle of morality* he was identifying in *Groundwork*.[159] But he also believed that there were other categorical imperatives (small c and i) that could be derived from *the* Categorical Imperative. Those derivative

---

[159] Kant's supreme principle of morality was, I believe, the moral law that says, in effect, there is a right and there is a wrong. That is the supreme principle of morality. The goal is to use categorical imperatives to discover *the* Categorical Imperative, i.e., the moral law.

imperatives are also binding on us regardless of our personal aims or intentions. [160] His main concern, however, in *Groundwork* is to identify, what he called the supreme principle of morality, which he also called the Categorical Imperative (with a capital C and a capital I).

While Kant believed there was only one Categorical Imperative, he believed it could be expressed in more than one way. This has caused significant confusion over the years, since what Kant considers as different expressions of the same idea sound to many like completely different imperatives. The issue will become clear as we consider two of Kant's formulations of the Categorical Imperative.

As Paton outlines Kant's material, he identifies Kant's first explanation of the Categorical Imperative as the Universal Law Formulation. [161] Kant's first formulation of the Categorical Imperative is: *"Act only on that maxim through which you can at the same time will that it should become a universal law."* [162]

Notice that the Categorical Imperative functions along with one's personal maxims. Utilizing the Categorical Imperative is a process. One begins with one's maxim (whatever it happens to be about) and then asks himself if he can truly say that he would like to see the action he is contemplating become a universal law, an action that all people will be required to carry out. For instance, utilizing my maxim above, *"whenever I make a promise, I will keep my promise,"* I must ask myself, am I willing that this maxim become a universal law? Would I want it to be the case, would I want it to be universal law, that everyone would have to keep their promises? I can honestly say yes to that question. I would be happy living in a society of promise-keepers. Kant would say, then, that my maxim is moral and I

---

160 Glasgow, 156.
161 Paton, 29, (in his presentation of Kant's *Groundwork*)
162 Kant, *Groundwork*, 2:421, 52

may proceed in carrying it out. If, however, I consider my other maxim, *"whenever I can benefit in some way by lying, I will lie,"* would I be comfortable having that maxim become universal law? I would have to say, no. I would not want to live in a society where everyone lied every time they thought it was to their advantage. Kant would say that my maxim regarding lying was not moral and that I should not act on it.

Why would Paton refer to this as the Universal Law formulation of the Categorical Imperative? Because in Kant's view, this basic Categorical Imperative (the supreme principle of morality) amounts to a Universal Law. Every person, every autonomous rational agent, ought to form a maxim for each proposed act or behavior and test it against the Categorical Imperative to know whether or not their maxims are moral. For Kant, this is not a hypothetical that depends on the subjective end one has chosen. It is an obligation the moral law places on every person.

The Universal Law formulation (as Paton calls it) is only one way to express the idea of the Categorical Imperative, the supreme principle of morality. Another way to express it, according to Kant, is: *"Act in such a way that you always treat humanity, whether in your own person or in the person of any other, never simply as a means, but always at the same time as an end."*[163] As noted earlier, this alternative expression of the Categorical Imperative has caused a good deal of concern. Why does Kant think he has said the same basic thing in this second expression of the Categorical Imperative as he did in the first when it sounds to many people like he has said something very different? I've no idea. But somewhere in his massive intellect Kant connected the two expressions so that they generated the same supreme principle of morality—the Categorical Imperative, the Moral Law.

---

[163] Kant, *Groundwork*, 2:429, 67.

Whether or not we agree with Kant that each expression of the Categorical Imperative says the same thing in different ways, we can accept and appreciate what he intends in this specific formulation (which Paton identifies as The End in Itself formulation of the Categorical Imperative). It is this: that people have intrinsic moral value and, because they do, they must be treated accordingly. People, Kant insists, cannot be treated as a means to our own ends but must be treated as an end in themselves. What does that mean? Suppose that a guy named Bill, a recent retiree, knows an older woman, Betty, who can't drive, has no family nearby, is lonely, and is also rich. Suppose Bill befriends and spends time with Betty (even though he does not really care to be around her), doing nice things to ingratiate himself to her, including driving her to the doctor and other important appointments. Suppose also that after a time Bill mentions that his old car is breaking down a lot and is no longer dependable. Suppose that Betty offers to buy Bill, her helpful friend, a new car (since he drives her to so many places). Bill accepts and she writes Bill a check for the amount of the car he wants. What has Bill done? Bill has used Betty as a means to an end—to get a new car.

Kant would say that this was an immoral act because Betty was used as a means to Bill's end rather than being valued as an end in herself. But why is this immoral? Do we not use other people as a means all the time? Yes. When I go to Walmart to shop and go to the checkout line, the clerk scanning my items becomes a means to my end—buying the things I need at Walmart. And I become a means to the clerk's end—having the job of helping customers buy the things they need. I am a means for the clerk and the clerk is a means for me. Why is this wrong? In this scenario it is not wrong. Why not? Because each of us is aware of the situation and freely chooses, as an autonomous self-determined person, to participate in the process. We each make an informed decision to be involved. But in Betty's case, she was not aware that she was merely being used as a means to an end. She assumed Bill's friendship was genuine. It wasn't. It was self-serving. That is why Bill's actions were immoral, according to Kant.

How would one recognize another person as an end in him or herself? By acknowledging each individual's intrinsic moral worth and treating that person accordingly; by respecting his or her right to be informed and aware of all aspects of a situation so that he or she can make an informed decision regarding participation. For instance, if Lori needs $50 and she knows that Ed has the $50 she needs, if Lori asks Ed to *loan* her $50 even though she knows she will not be able to pay it back, Lori is using Ed as a means to her end—getting $50. If, however, she asks for a *gift* of $50, perhaps even explaining that she will not be able to pay it back, Ed is being treated as an end in himself, because he is being given the opportunity to make an informed decision as to whether or not to participate in Lori's project—getting $50. According to Kant, one approach is immoral; the other is moral.

Consider how often this kind of a scenario occurs. Each time a politician makes a promise he (or she) knows he can't keep, but makes the promise in order to achieve his goal, to get elected, he is using the voting public as a means to his end. Each time a presidential candidate says he is going to reform Washington, knowing full well he can't, he is violating this formulation of the Categorical Imperative. He is engaging in an immoral act. And so are we each time we fail to treat an individual as an end in him or herself.

There are actually a couple more formulations of the Categorical Imperative, but these two are sufficient for us to get Kant's point: that there is a supreme principle of morality, a moral law, that is accessible to us through rational analysis using the Categorical Imperative. Because a moral law exists, the normal rational person can discover what is moral and what is immoral.

As Kant developed his moral theory, the idea that a moral law exists was not new. What was new was the idea that in order for it to be rational it must be free of specific content. It must not be (cannot be) a list of specific rules (laws). As Schneewind explains, "The moral law itself, Kant holds, can only be the form of lawfulness itself."[164] *The moral law is the idea that lawfulness exists, that moral absolutes exist.* As rational autonomous agents, humans use reason to discover what is moral. An autonomous agent cannot, in Kant's view, be told what is moral or immoral, but must determine that reality for himself. As noted earlier (in footnote 156), I believe Kant would have been comfortable with replacing the word *determine* with the word *discover.* Rational autonomous agents must discover what is moral, for otherwise they are not autonomous. Thus, the moral law cannot contain specific content (this act is right, this act is wrong) but must be a basic concept that a rational autonomous agent can use to discover specific moral realities. Thus, the moral law, the supreme moral principle, is exemplified as the basic Categorical Imperative: *"Act only on that maxim through which you can at the same time will that it should become a universal law."*

It is important that this not be understood as some form of relativity. Kant was not suggesting that morality is relative. He believed that when the rational will (mind) engaged the Categorical Imperative, it would discover a fundamental moral reality, things that are right and things that are wrong—moral absolutes, if you will. Kant believed in the existence of moral absolutes. Rational agents have to discover them. Moral absolutes exist and are discoverable. One such absolute (whether he referred to it as such or not) would be his second formulation of the Categorical Imperative: *"Act in such a way that you always treat humanity, whether in your own person or in the person of*

---

164 Schneewind, 320.

another, never simply as a means, but always at the same time as an end." That is a moral statement, and it is an absolute statement, a statement of a moral absolute. Kant embraced the idea of moral absolutes.

Kant's moral system is widely embraced today as a moral theory that works well in contemporary society. How does it compare to Virtue Ethics? Which of the two appears more useful or helpful to you?

Utilitarianism[165]

Utilitarianism is a moral theory proposed by Jeremy Bentham in his book entitled, *An Introduction to the Principles of Morals and Legislation,* first printed in 1780 and formally published in 1789. Social conditions in England at that time left a lot to be desired. Slavery was considered to be an economic necessity by many, women had few if any rights, there was a huge gap between the wealthy and the poor, and the legal system was not so much designed to solve legal problems or administer justice as it was to make lawyers rich. For the average working person in that new Industrial Age (many of whom were women and children), wages were low, hours were long, working conditions were deplorable and advocates concerned with social justice and change were few. One of the few advocates of social reform in late 18th and early 19th century England was Jeremy Bentham.

Generally speaking, Bentham proposed a system of moral decision-making and acting based on the anticipated consequences of a number of possible courses of action. *The right thing to do,* Bentham argued, *in any situation is that*

---

[165] Borrowed (with slight editing) from Rogers, *21st Century Ethics,* 120-129.

which brings the greatest amount of happiness to the greatest
number of people.

One of the ideas that set Bentham's theory apart from others is that he specifically wanted a moral framework that made no reference to God or religious concerns.[166] The morality or immorality of any act would be determined, not by reference to a list of rules, but solely on the basis of the consequences of the act. If an act resulted in good consequences, it was moral; if it resulted in bad consequences, it was immoral. How did Bentham justify this approach to moral philosophy? He argued that:

> *Nature has placed mankind under the governance of two sovereign masters, pain and pleasure. It is for them alone to point out what we ought to do, as well as determine what we shall do. On the one hand the standard of right and wrong, on the other the chain of causes and effects, are fastened to their throne... They govern us in all we do... The principle of utility recognizes this subjection, and assumes it for the foundation of that system...*
>
> *By the principle of utility is meant that principle which approves or disapproves of every action whatsoever, according to the tendency which it appears to have to augment or diminish the happiness of the party whose interest is in question; or what is the same thing in other words, to promote or to oppose that happiness... By utility is meant that property in any object, whereby it tends to produce benefit, advantage, pleasure, good, or happiness... or... to prevent the happening of mischief, pain, evil, or unhappiness to the party*

---

166 Bentham, *An Introduction to the Principles of Morals and Legislation*, Chapter 2.

423

whose interest is considered... A thing is said to promote the interest, or to be for the interest of an individual, when it tends to add to the sum total of his pleasure or, what comes to the same thing, to diminish the some total of his pains...

An action then may be said to be conformable to the principle of utility, or, for shortness sake, to utility, (meaning with respect to the community at large) when the tendency it has to augment the happiness of the community is greater than it has to diminish it... of an action that is conformable to the principle of utility one may always say either that it is one that ought to be done, or at least that it is not one that ought to be done. One may say also, that it is right and should be done, that it is a right action, at least that it is not a wrong action. When thus interpreted, the words ought, and right, and wrong, and others of that stamp, have a meaning, when otherwise, they have none.[167]

Bentham's belief is that people are ruled by their quest to experience pleasure or happiness and avoid pain or unpleasantness as far as possible. From one point of view, he is right. People prefer to have pleasant experiences rather than unpleasant ones. And we usually make decisions and behave in ways that will enhance the possibility of pleasure and diminish the possibility of pain. This is generally referred to as *psychological egoism*: the view that people are motivated by self-interest.[168] But Bentham is not merely observing that people are very self-interested. He is advocating that the desire to experience pleasure and avoid pain ought to be the basis for determining what is moral or

---

[167] Bentham, Chapter 1.
[168] Technically, psychological egoism says that people "only" act is self-interested ways, which is, I believe, untrue, making the theory false from a technical point of view.

424

immoral. Instead of the words pleasure and pain, he prefers the words happiness and unhappiness, but he means pleasure and pain. And his point is that which generates happiness, or the greatest amount of happiness, is to be judged as moral. That which results in unhappiness is immoral, or at least not the right thing to do. He refers to this is the *principle of utility*.

The idea that the purpose of life is the pursuit of happiness was not a new idea when Bentham proposed it. Socrates, Plato and Aristotle had embraced the idea of *eudaimonia* as the appropriate goal of life. And while *eudaimonia* can be translated happiness, Socrates, Plato and Aristotle meant something very different than Bentham meant. *Eudaimonia* (thriving or flourishing are better translations than happiness) is rooted in and grows out of *arête*, excellence or virtue. The excellent person will be the one who thrives or flourishes and will, therefore, be happy. Bentham's idea of happiness is more closely aligned with the hedonistic perspective of Epicurus—the absence of pain and the satisfaction of one's needs and desires, including intellectual enjoyment. Bentham is proposing that whatever results in that kind of happiness is moral.

Bentham's younger disciple and associate was John Stuart Mill (1806-1873). Mill, also a British philosopher, is considered one of the leading thinkers of the 19th century. His book, *Utilitarianism* (published in 1863), is a defense of Utilitarianism as a viable moral theory. Almost immediately after Bentham published his theory, it came under attack. Eventually, Mill, the leading Utilitarian of the next generation, attempted to address the challenges.

His defense of Utilitarianism (in chapter one of his book) begins with three interesting affirmations: 1) that Socrates advocated Utilitarianism (a questionable claim at best), 2) that moral philosophers who claim that the principles of morality are clearly evident have failed to produce a list of these clearly evident principles (a claim that

425

is again questionable—depending on which moral philosophers he has in mind), and 3) that Kant's Categorical Imperative can lead to all sorts of "outrageous" immorality. To this last charge I would reply that it is theoretically possible for a person who is morally bankrupt to misuse the Categorical Imperative. For instance, a person could conceivably say that his or her maxim, *"Whenever it is to my advantage I should lie, steal, and kill,"* should be adopted as a universal law. Kant is assuming, however, that most people are not morally bankrupt and are looking for a simple way to determine moral behavior. Mill's accusation against Kant's moral theory is unrealistic and without merit.

In Chapter Two of *Utilitarianism*, Mill begins his actual explanation/defense of the theory. He begins by noting that:

> *Every writer, from Epicurus to Bentham, who maintained the theory of utility, meant by it, not something to be contradistinguished from pleasure, but pleasure itself, together with exemption from pain... The creed which accepts as the foundation of morals, or the Greatest Happiness Principle, holds that actions are right in proportion as they tend to promote happiness, wrong as they tend to produce the reverse of happiness. By happiness is intended pleasure, and the absence of pain; by unhappiness, pain, and the privation of pleasure... pleasure, and freedom from pain, are the only things desirable as ends; and that all desirable things (which are as numerous in the utilitarian as in any other scheme) are desirable either for the pleasure inherent in themselves, or as means to the promotion of pleasure and the prevention of pain.*[169]

---

[169] Mill, *Utilitarianism*, Chapter Two.

Mill is very clear—the Utilitarian focus is the same as the Epicurean focus: to avoid pain and experience pleasure. Opponents of Utilitarianism argued that to make pleasure the foundational idea of a moral system was to cater to animalistic nature. It had been said, evidently, that Utilitarianism was a "doctrine worthy only of swine." Mill's response is, in effect, that such an accusation is an insult to human nature. Humans have not only the physical appetites that need satisfying, but higher level appetites, intellectual pleasures, that must also be satisfied. Mill explained:

> *There is no known Epicurean theory of life which does not assign to the pleasures of the intellect, of the feelings and imagination, and of the moral sentiments, a much higher value as pleasure than to those of mere sensation... It is quite compatible with the principle of utility to recognize the fact, that some kinds of pleasure are more desirable and more valuable than others. It would be absurd that while, in estimating all other things, quality is considered as well as quantity, the estimation of pleasure should be supposed to depend on quantity alone. Now it is an unquestionable fact that those who are equally acquainted with, and equally capable of appreciating and enjoying, both [physical and intellectual pleasures], do give a most marked preference to the manner of existence which employs their higher faculties.*[170]

Mill is affirming that in calculating pleasure one must calculate the qualities of pleasures not just the quantities. Some pleasures generate more happiness because they generate more pleasure, or result in pleasure that is

---

[170] Ibid.

qualitatively different—better, more pleasurable. Epicurus had made a similar argument.

It is important to be fair to Bentham and Mill, and remember that the focus of Utilitarianism was originally social reform. In making laws that will govern a society, one of the questions politicians and lawmakers ought to ask is, *What will make the greatest number of people happy?* Common sense would dictate that such a question be asked. Good leaders will ask questions of that sort. But will they not also ask, *What is the right thing to do?* The answer Utilitarianism provides when that question is asked is, *the right thing to do is whatever makes the greatest number of people happy.* The right thing to do, from a Utilitarian point of view, is whatever minimizes unhappiness and maximizes happiness—which is Epicurean in nature. Can Epicurean hedonistic happiness really be the foundation of morality?

That question bothered Mill, and his response to it is not a good one. Mill cites a Mr. Carlyle who had evidently argued that true happiness was unattainable and perhaps even beyond the right of human expectation. In response, Mill argues that humans have every right to desire and pursue happiness. And while he does again differentiate between mere physical gratification and the higher kinds of pleasures, he is still advocating a hedonistic kind of happiness and equates it with the *eudaimonistic* kind of thriving (flourishing) the classical philosophers advocated.[171] That, of course, is simply an unrealistic comparison. Epicurus was talking about a different kind of happiness than Socrates, Plato and Aristotle had discussed.

In Chapter Three of *Utilitarianism*, Mill argues, essentially, that happiness is the appropriate foundation for morality because God wants people to be happy. If we think metaphorically (analogically) of God as a parent, then it is

---

[171] While Mill does not actually use the world *eudaimonia* in his argument, it is clear that is what he has in mind.

not unwarranted to say that God wants his children (human beings) to be happy. What parent wants his or her children to be unhappy? But that does not add up to happiness being the determining factor in what is moral or immoral. Happiness is only one desire (goal) parents have for children. We also want them to be healthy, kind, strong, compassionate, just, and so forth. Sometimes that which leads to strength and justice, for example, does not generate happiness (at least in that moment). If there are considerations other than hedonistic happiness for biological parents, then certainly for God there must be other considerations as well. Mill seems to have missed this point.

Another feature of Utilitarianism that is crucial to the goal Bentham envisioned for it is that each person must be considered equally. No one can receive special consideration. Here is how Mill explained it:

> The happiness which forms the utilitarian standard of what is right in conduct, is not the agent's own happiness, but that of all concerned. As between his own happiness and that of others, utilitarianism requires him to be as strictly impartial as a disinterested and benevolent spectator. In the golden rule of Jesus of Nazareth, we read the complete spirit of the ethics of utility. To do as one would be done by, and to love one's neighbor as oneself, constitute the ideal perfection of utilitarian morality. As the means of making the nearest approach to this ideal, utility would enjoin, first, that laws and social arrangements should place the happiness, or (as speaking practically it may be called) the interest, of every individual, as nearly as possible in harmony with the interest of the whole.[172]

---

[172] Mill, *Utilitarianism*, Chapter Two.

Complete equality; no impartiality allowed. On the surface this sounds not only acceptable but commendable as well. Mill denies an egoistical approach (which is without a doubt commendable) by suggesting that according to Utilitarianism, it is not one's own happiness that is considered but the happiness of all concerned. It seems apparent that he is thinking in terms of utilizing the principle of utility in terms of a social collective rather than individual personal ethical decision-making. Social policy, for instance, ought to be considered and enacted from this impartial perspective. But as appropriate as this may sound on the surface, is it really a viable option? We will consider it more closely in the next section.

A final consideration in this section is Mill's assertion of what is ultimately behind (or underlying) Utilitarianism as a moral theory. He says:

> *The ultimate sanction, therefore, of all morality (external motive apart) being a subjective feeling in our own minds, I see nothing embarrassing to those whose standard is utility, in the question, what is the sanction of that particular standard? We may answer, the same as of all other moral standards— the conscientious feelings of mankind.*[173]

Mill is saying that not only is Utilitarianism subjective in nature, but all morality is subjective in nature. In Mill's view, humans decide what is and what is not moral. Notice how different this is from Kant's view that an objective moral law exists, which also means that moral absolutes exist, a morality that is discoverable by individuals utilizing one of the formulations of the Categorical Imperative. From Mill's subjective point of view, however, the mechanism people use to determine what is and what is

---

[173] Mill, *Utilitarianism*, Chapter Three.

not moral is a happiness calculation: whatever action generates the greatest amount of happiness for the greatest number of people is moral.

Are Bentham and Mill correct? Does the principle of utility provide a satisfactory foundation for moral thinking and acting? A number of ethicists are adamant that it does not. What do you think? Can morality be determined simply on the basis of what makes people happy? At one time in this country the vast majority of people were happy with the practice of slavery. Did that make it right? At another time in our history, the vast majority of people were happy with white people having rights and privileges that were not extended to people of other races. Did that make it right? At one time in our nation's history the majority of people were happy with the fact that women did not enjoy equality with men (equal rights, equal access, equal opportunity). Did that make it right? Of course not. Happiness simply cannot be the measure of morality.

Critical Ethical Eclecticism

My purpose in this section is to introduce and explain a new framework for moral thinking and acting. It is a framework of my own design. The foundational premise of the framework is what I refer to as the Principle of Essential Humanness. The idea[174] is that humanness has intrinsic value and that morality (what is or is not moral) grows out of the nature of humanness. The larger framework, then, called Critical Ethical Eclecticism, identifies and selectively utilizes features of other ethical theories that will prove beneficial in enhancing humanness as people interact with each other.

Based on the principle of essential humanness, I define morality as follows:

---

[174] Explained in detail in Rogers, *21st Century Ethics*, 181-186.

Morality involves recognizing the intrinsic value of humanness (one's own and that of others), along with actions, reactions, and interactions that reflect an appreciation of human value. Immorality involves a failure to recognize the intrinsic value of humanness (one's own and that of others), along with a subsequent failure to act, react and interact in ways that reflect an appreciation of human value. Thus, an act is moral if it recognizes and or enhances human value, and is immoral if it fails to recognize or in some way diminishes the value of humanness.

With this definition of morality in place, we need to discuss a framework in which it can be used for effective moral thinking and acting. That framework is Critical Ethical Eclecticism.

What is Critical Ethical Eclecticism? Critical Ethical Eclecticism (CEE) is an ethical theory or moral framework that makes use of a number of other ethical theories to create a new composite theory that (hopefully) will not suffer from the shortcomings of the other individual systems. By combining the best features of other theories, along with a definition of morality that links it to humanness, CEE will (hopefully) offer a more balanced framework for moral thinking and acting.

The word *ethical* in the name CEE is present for obvious reasons—it is an ethical theory. The word *eclectic* is also obvious—the theory borrows from and is composed of different aspects of other theories. But why include the word *critical* in CEE? By *critical* I refer not to criticizing other theories, although that is sometimes necessary, but rather to a critical, careful, and thoughtful analysis of: 1) what contemporary society needs in a moral theory (what features must be included in a functional moral theory), and 2) what features of already existing moral theories can be borrowed to create a composite theory that will work well in contemporary society.

How does CEE work? The paragraph above offers a brief explanation, but some additional clarification may be helpful. Perhaps it might be best to consider CEE in light of the five essential features of a functional moral theory discussed earlier. CEE is a functional moral theory because:

1. *CEE includes a thorough and effective definition/explanation of morality.* As discussed earlier, morality involves recognizing the intrinsic value of humanness (one's own and that of others), along with actions, reactions, and interactions that reflect an appreciation of human value. Immorality involves a failure to recognize the intrinsic value of humanness (one's own and that of others), along with a subsequent failure to act, react and interact in ways that reflect an appreciation of human value. Thus, an act is moral if it recognizes and or enhances human value, and is immoral if it fails to recognize or in some way diminishes the value of humanness.

The key here is that this is not merely a definition that says morality has to do with the concepts of right and wrong, which tells us nothing very helpful about morality, but one that equates morality with humanness in a way that allows for the specific identification of that which is moral or immoral based on how an act values and enhances or devalues and diminishes humanness.

2. *CEE includes a proper focus on the development of moral character.* Ancient moral philosophers were on to something important with their focus on becoming a person who lived an effective life because one lived according to the dictates of wisdom (which is what the ancient Hebrews believed), or because one became an excellent person, thereby flourishing and thriving (which is what the ancient Greeks believed), or being a loving person who treats others the way one would like to be treated (as in the moral philosophy of Jesus). The idea that one who is a person of high moral character who

433

habitually does the right kinds of things will be one who is likely to act morally when confronted with a moral dilemma is, I believe, a valid and useful idea. The kinds of things one does grows out of (is correlated to) the kind of a person one is. A good person is likely to do good things. If we, as a society, are concerned about people doing the right thing, the moral thing in any given situation, then we need to be concerned about the development of individual moral character.

How does moral character develop? Socrates asked this same question. The answer is, it must be taught. The development of moral character is part of an effective enculturation or socialization process. The kind of moral character needed in contemporary society is one that stresses the linkage between morality and humanness. Moral character must: 1) be rooted in and related to our essential humanness, 2) reflect the interrelational and interdependent nature of our essential humanness, and 3) be rooted in an appreciation of the intrinsic value of each human being, reflected in the way we interact with others. Insights regarding the moral character of individuals must be associated with the linkage between morality and humanness.

CEE stresses the need for a foundational moral character built on the linkage between morality and humanness, emphasizing the need for the further development of specific character traits. CEE borrows from Aristotle's Virtue Ethics, stressing the importance of moral character as a foundational feature of a functional moral theory. One of the key components of Critical Ethical Eclecticism is Virtue Ethics.

3. *CEE includes a mechanism for discovering the moral thing to do in a given situation.* Being the kind of person one ought to be has a lot to do with doing the right thing, the moral thing, in any given situation. But without some mechanism for analyzing specific situations and the options involved, one is left without clear guidance as to what to do

or not do in situations where the moral thing to do is not obvious. This is one of the complaints against Virtue Ethics—it contains no mechanism for making specific determinations of right and wrong. CEE avoids this weakness by including a mechanism for making specific determinations.

The mechanism CEE uses is the definition/explanation of morality described in number 1 above: *morality involves recognizing the intrinsic value of humanness (one's own and that of others), along with actions, reactions, and interactions that reflect an appreciation of human value. Immorality involves a failure to recognize the intrinsic value of humanness (one's own and that of others), along with a subsequent failure to act, react and interact in ways that reflect an appreciation of human value. Thus, an act is moral if it recognizes and or enhances human value, and is immoral if it fails to recognize or in some way diminishes the value of humanness.* This explanation of morality, the *Principle of Essential Humanness*, allows one to analyze a behavior (or potential behavior) and determine whether it is moral or immoral depending on whether it values and enhances or devalues and diminishes humanness.

At this point it might be appropriate to address the difference between a *rule-oriented process* for discovering what is moral and not moral, and an *analysis-oriented process*. A rule-oriented process is one that involves a list of rules—do this, don't do that. It does not involve any kind of critical thinking. It is a simple process. A child can determine what to do or not do if right and wrong is contained in a list of rules. The problem with rule-oriented morality is that the list of rules has to be continually updated if it is to remain relevant to evolving needs. For instance, consider the Ten Commandments of the Old Testament. It is a good list, as far as it goes. But what does it have to say regarding euthanasia, animal rights, environmental issues, human cloning and other contemporary ethical concerns? Nothing. If one is asking about adultery or stealing, the Ten Commandments have something to say. If one is asking about human cloning, they have nothing to say. In that regard the list is outdated and inadequate. For many contemporary ethical concerns the list is irrelevant. All rule-oriented approaches to moral philosophy are subject to this weakness.

What CEE offers is a mechanism for discovering what is and is not moral. It is an analysis-oriented process. It is a process that requires rational people to engage in critical thinking to discover (not determine but *discover*—the difference is crucial) [175] what is moral. Both Kant and Bentham offered something similar. Kant's Categorical Imperative, (either formulation) *"Act only on that maxim through which you can at the same time will that it should become a universal law,"*[176] or *"Act in such a way that you always treat humanity, whether in your own person or in the person of another, never simply as a means, but always at the same time as an end,"*[177] is an analysis-oriented process for discovering moral or immoral behavior. Bentham's Principle of Utility, *"that principle which approves or disapproves of every action whatsoever, according to the tendency which it appears to have to augment or diminish the happiness of the party whose interest is in question,"*[178] is also an analysis-oriented process for discovering moral or immoral behavior. Where Kant offered the Categorical Imperative and Bentham offered the Principle of Utility, CEE offers the Principle of Essential Humanness.

---

[175] Morality is not subjective, not relative. It is objective. Moral absolutes exist. That which is moral is inexorably connected to and associated with the intrinsic value of humanness. Those things that enhance rather than diminish humanness in any given situation must be "discovered" through the rational process.

[176] Kant, *Groundwork*, 2:421, 52.

[177] Kant, *Groundwork*, 2:429, 67.

[178] Bentham, *An Introduction to the Principles of Morals and Legislation*, Chapter 1.

If the goal of CEE in this regard is similar to Kant's or Bentham's (offering a mechanism for discovering morality), why not use those frameworks instead of offering a third alternative? Because neither Kantianism nor Utilitarianism are helpful in every case. And Utilitarianism has serious problems associated with it. Utilitarianism as proposed by Bentham is based on hedonistic happiness and is in my view unacceptable as a framework for moral thinking and acting. As for Kantianism, while I hold Kant's system in very high regard, it does not appear to be helpful in all cases. Also, Kant believed that only intention was important, that consequences were beyond one's control and thus unimportant. I disagree. While consequences cannot be the sole determinate of morality, they cannot be ignored.

For these reasons, then, instead of using Kant's Categorical Imperative (either version of it) or Bentham's Principle of Utility, CEE offers a third alternative. CEE utilizes one universal principle (the Principle of Essential Humanness) articulated in a precise manner, which allows one to utilize an analysis-oriented process to discover moral and immoral behavior. In this regard CEE follows the lead of Kant and Bentham.

4. *CEE involves a proper focus on motive and intention.* As noted earlier, what people do is important. Equally important is why they do it. Motive matters. Intention matters. In this regard Kant and Bentham disagreed. Kant believed that motive and intention were important and that consequences, since they are beyond our control, are not important in differentiating between moral and immoral. Bentham, however, believed consequences were all that mattered. Intentions are not important, but only results. Here all I can say is that I think Bentham was simply wrong. And I believe that thoughtful reflection on day-to-day experience will support that contention. How often do we ask people, why did you do that? Quite often, actually. Why do we ask? Because we want to know what their reason was for acting as

437

they did. We want to understand their motive. We want to understand their intention. Why? Because often, in day-to-day life, a person's motive or intention for what they do makes their action either acceptable or unacceptable. Consider the inept husband who is attempting to compliment his wife on her outfit. He might say, "I like that outfit. It doesn't make you look fat." At first his wife may be annoyed, but she might then realize that he was trying to compliment her, even though he did it badly. Because he was trying to say something nice, she will not (hopefully) become angry with him. Why not? Because of his motive, his intention. He did not mean to insult but to compliment. Because of his intention, his blunder will be overlooked. In the everyday world, intention and motive matter. And so, too, in the realm of ethics, intention and motive matter.

Kant believed that because we cannot control what happens we cannot be held accountable for what happens. But we are fully capable of managing our motives and intentions. Therefore, Kant argued that we are responsible for our intentions and must be sure that they are morally appropriate. To a degree, I agree with Kant. A functional moral theory will involve an appropriate focus on motives and intentions. Why we do what we do matters, especially when it come to determining morality.

Suppose, for instance, that one evening while my wife and I are watching our favorite TV show, someone knocks on our door. It is our neighbor, Betty, and she is in a panic. I bring her into the house. On the verge of hysteria, Betty explains that she just witnessed a murder a few blocks across town, and the killers are aware that she witnessed what they did. They are after her. One of them looked familiar to her, and she is worried that they know where she lives. She wants us to hide her. I agree and tell my wife to take Betty down into the basement and try to calm her while I call the police. A little unsettled myself, I sit down to think for a moment before I call the police. Before I can call, there is another knock at the door. Two rough-looking men are there, and one of them explains that they are Betty's cousins from out of town and have come to visit her. She isn't home and she's not answering her cell phone. They want to know if I know where she is. I hesitate a moment, shake my head and say, "No, I haven't seen Betty all day." They hesitate a moment before thanking me for my help. They turn to leave, and I close the door. I call the police, and when they arrive, Betty tells them her story and goes with them to the police station.

Later, as I'm reflecting on the event, I realize that I lied to the killers. I lied, telling them I had not seen Betty. But I'm an honest man. I don't lie. Lying is wrong—morally unacceptable. But surely in this case and others like it, lying is acceptable because I lied to save a life. Those men would have killed Betty if they had found her. By hiding her and lying to the killers, I saved her life. Surely that made the lie justifiable. Valuing Betty's humanness took precedent over (was more important than) the need to be honest with those who would devalue Betty's humanness by depriving her of life.

Most people, I think, would agree that in such cases that kind of a lie is justifiable. But Kant did not. He even told the same basic story and arrived at the conclusion that to lie to the killers would be morally wrong. I disagree with Kant. Why? Because my motive for lying, my intention, was to save a life. I was not deceiving them for any personal gain. I was concerned for the life of another. My motive justified my behavior. Because of why I lied, my lying was not immoral. Motive matters.

CEE includes a proper focus on motive and intention. This feature is borrowed from Kant, even though I apply it differently than Kant did.

5. *CEE involves a proper focus on consequences.* Motive and intention are important. But so are consequences. Kant's point about our not being able to control outcomes and

therefore not being responsible for outcomes is valid. But because we cannot control outcomes all the time does not mean that we should not be concerned about outcomes or that consequences have nothing to do with the rightness or wrongness of an act. Of course they do. Consider the example offered above, where Betty is being pursued by killers, and I lie to them about knowing where she was. I lied. But my lie is justifiable. Why? Because my intention was to save her life. Intention matters. But one can view the same situation from the perspective of consequences. My lying to the killers saved Betty's life. The result (consequences) of my lie was that Betty's life was saved. Consequences, in some cases, determine the rightness or wrongness of an act.

The role of consequences in determining morality (at least in some instances) demonstrates the value and preferability of an analysis-oriented mechanism for discovering morality over a rule-oriented mechanism. A list of rules is static, inflexible. If lying is on the list as an immoral act, then lying is wrong, all the time—even in cases such as the Betty dilemma. But can that possibly be the case? Was I wrong to deceive the killers to save Betty's life? A functional moral theory must be one that is appropriately flexible so that issues such as intention and consequences can be factored into an analysis of the morality of an act.

Considering the consequences of an act may be more subtle than it might first appear. Consider, for instance, Kant's first formulation of the Categorical Imperative—*Act only on that maxim through which you can at the same time will that it should become a universal law.* What is Kant really asking us to do here (whether he realized it or not)? He is saying that when one is anticipating an action and asking whether such an act would be moral or immoral, we must ask if we would be happy (comfortable) if the proposed action was required of everyone. For instance, if I am considering committing a robbery because I am short of cash, I should ask myself, would I want everyone to commit robbery whenever they were short of cash? If my answer is no, I would not want everyone committing robbery whenever they were short of cash, then I should not commit a robbery either. But why not? What is Kant's point? It grows out of a consequentialist perspective. He is asking, what would the world be like if people committed robbery every time they were short of cash? He is asking, what would the consequences be of everyone robbing each other all the time?

Consider Kant's second formulation of the Categorical Imperative—*Act in such a way that you always treat humanity, whether in your own person or in the person of another, never simply as a means, but always at the same time as an end.* Why does Kant think treating people merely as a means to an end is wrong? Because of what it does to the person who gets used. They are hurt. Their humanness is diminished. Kant does not specifically say this, but this is clearly his intent. His concern has to do with the consequences of treating others as a means instead of giving them the respect they deserve. Consequences matter.

If consequences are so important, why not use Bentham's system of Utilitarianism? Because Utilitarianism is hedonistic consequentialism. It is rooted in absolute relativity and does not give appropriate attention to intent and motive. Additionally, Utilitarianism is also rooted in a hedonistic form of happiness that, for many ethicists, makes it unacceptable as a functional moral theory. However, Utilitarianism is only one expression of consequentialism. A moral theory, such as CEE, can include a proper focus on consequences without embracing Utilitarianism. One of the important features of CEE is a healthy dose of consequentialism.

It is obvious that because of the eclectic nature of CEE, individuals using the model have the freedom to select the theories they believe will provide the most valuable insights in a given situation. One person wrestling with a particular moral concern might feel that Kantian theory will be helpful while another might think in terms of Virtue Ethics and another in terms of consequentialism. Sometimes a person may utilize Kant's Categorical Imperative in combination with Jesus' Golden Rule. The whole point of CEE being eclectic is that it allows for the utilization of one theory by itself or in combination with others. CEE's foundational concept (morality rooted in the value of humanness) working in combination with the various aspects of other moral theories gives CEE a flexibility that other theories lack. CEE's flexibility is its strength.[179]

Does CEE provide a viable framework for moral thinking and acting in our society? Whether we realize it or not, each of us has some system in place for making moral judgments. The system we have may be helpful in some regards and not so helpful in others. The basic question, how should humans live, is an important philosophical question that cannot be properly considered without thinking about the different moral theories that have been suggested over the centuries.

Summary

Philosophical questions about how life ought to be lived come under the heading of moral philosophy. How life ought to be lived was a topic of concern for the ancient

---

[179] Some, no doubt, will object that the eclectic nature of CEE is not a strength but a weakness, that the theory provides little in the way of moral guidance. Obviously, I would disagree. CEE's focus on morality being rooted in the value of humanness along with its mechanism for determining what is and what is not moral provides a great deal of moral guidance. In conjunction with those features, its flexibility allows it to be utilized in a wider variety of circumstances than would otherwise be the case. The most important feature of is eclectic nature is that the strengths of multiple theories can be utilized interdependently to address issues that might not otherwise be effectively addressed.

Hebrews as well as for the Greeks. The Hebrews had an entire genre of literature, called *wisdom literature*, which focused on advice for living a life of wisdom. The Greeks, of course, set the standards for rational reflection on how life ought to be lived, on what constituted living a good life. Socrates is known as the Father of Moral Philosophy. His student, Plato, believed that absolute knowledge about morality was available, and his student, Aristotle, produced the most detailed analysis of moral philosophy in the ancient world—*Nicomachean Ethics*.

What makes human beings moral beings? The same things that make us human beings make us moral beings. To be a human being is to be a moral being. So what makes human beings moral beings? In a nutshell it is this: humans are rational and enjoy second level awareness (not just being aware, but being aware of being aware). Thus, we are self-determined. And because we are self-determined we are moral beings.

I exist, and I know it. I am rational, and I can contemplate my existence, my reality, my meaning. I have a life to live. Should I live it this way or that way? Should I live as if I am the only one who matters, or should I consider other people's needs and feelings? Should I live as if my view of right and wrong, of good and evil, is all that matters, or should I consider that morality may depend on something other than my own personal or cultural perspective? In other words, I have choices to make. What choices should I make?

To think clearly about moral thinking and acting requires that we reflect on some of the moral theories philosophers have suggested over the centuries: Virtue Ethics, Kantian Ethics, Utilitarianism, and Critical Ethical Eclecticism.

Thought and Discussion Questions

1. Discuss the strengths and weaknesses of Virtue Ethics
2. Discuss the strengths and weaknesses of Kantian Ethics
3. Discuss the strengths and weaknesses of Utilitarianism
4. Discuss the strengths and weaknesses of Critical Ethical Eclecticism
5. Explain which of the four theories you find most helpful and why.

Conclusion

We have asked and at least attempted to answer a number of very important questions, the kinds of questions philosophers have contemplated for centuries. There are lots of additional questions we could have considered. I selected the specific questions we considered because I think they are interesting and can serve to introduce students to the study of philosophy. If you understand the kinds of questions philosophers deal with and how they go about reflecting on them, you have a good basic grasp of what philosophy is all about. And that, more than anything else, is what an introduction to philosophy ought to do—introduce you to the subject matter and process of philosophy. I hope that is what I have accomplished.

I also hope some of what you have read has sparked an interest in you and that you will take additional philosophy courses. The contemplation of philosophical concerns can enrich your life. And who knows, maybe there is another Socrates out there somewhere, or another Descartes, or another Kant who will change the world with his or her thinking.

445

Works Cited

Anselm. *St. Anselm's Proslogion*. Translated by M. J. Charlesworth. Notre Dame: Notre Dame, 1979.

Aristotle. "Metaphysics," in *The Basic Works of Aristotle*. Richard McKeon, Editor. New York: The Modern Library, 2001.

Bentham, Jeremy. *An Introduction to the Principles of Morals and Legislation*. Oxford: Clarendon, 1907. (A Bibliolife Network reprint).

Berryman, Sylvia, "Democritus", *The Stanford Encyclopedia of Philosophy (Fall 2010 Edition)*, Edward N. Zalta (ed.) URL = http://plato.stanford.edu/archives/fall2010/entries/democritus/

Brickhouse, Thomas and Nicholas D. Smith. "Plato," in *Internet Encyclopedia of Philosophy*. James Fieser and Bradley Dowden, Editors. 2013. URL= http://www.iep.utm.edu/plato/

Chalmers, David J. *The Conscious Mind: In Search of a Fundamental Theory*. Oxford: Oxford University Press, 1996.

Childhelp. *National Child Abuse Statistics*. URL= http://www.childhelp.org/pages/statistics?gclid=CLmD_5vW6LQCFeuPPAodvXcAdg

CNN. *Sandy Hook shooting: What Happened?*

URL =
http://www.cnn.com/interactive/2012/12/us/sandy-
hook-timeline/index.html

Connolly, Tim. "Plato's Phaedo," in *Internet Encyclopedia of Philosophy*. James Fieser and Bradley Dowden, Editors. 2013. URL= http://www.iep.utm.edu/phaedo/#SH3b

Cornford, F.M. *Before and After Socrates*. Cambridge: Cambridge University Press, 1932.

Couprie, Dirk L. "Anaximander (c.610—546 BCE)," *Internet Encyclopedia of Philosophy*. James Fieser and Bradley Dowden, Editors. URL= http://www.iep.utm.edu/anaximan/

Dancy, Jonathan. "Epistemology, Problems of," in *The Oxford Companion To Philosophy*. Second Edition. Ted Honderich, Editor. Oxford: Oxford University Press, 2005.

Descartes, René. *Discourse on Method*. Nashville: BN Publishing, 2007. (Originally Published 1637).

Duke, George. "The Sophists (Ancient Greek)." *Internet Encyclopedia of Philosophy*. James Fieser and Bradley Dowden, Editors. URL= http://www.iep.utm.edu/sophist/

Feser, Edward. *Philosophy of Mind: A Short Introduction*. Oxford: Oneworld, 2005.

Flew, Anthony. "Empiricism," in *The Dictionary of Philosophy*. 2nd Edition. New York: Gramercy Books, 1999.

Fisher, Alec. *Critical Thinking: An Introduction.* 2ⁿᵈ
    Edition. Cambridge: Cambridge University Press,
    2011.

Gallup. *"More Than 9 in 10 Americans Continue to Believe
    in God."* ULR=
    http://www.gallup.com/poll/147887/americans-
    continue-believe-god.aspx

Glasgow, Joshua. "Kant's Principle of Universal Law," in
    Conduct and Character: Readings in Moral Theory.
    6ᵗʰ Edition. Mark Timmons, Editor. Boston:
    Wadsworth, 2012.

Gonzalez, Guillermo and Jay W. Richards. *The Privileged
    Planet: How Our Place In The Cosmos Is Designed
    For Discovery.* Washington D.C.: Regnery, 2004.

Graham, Daniel W. "Heraclitus (fl. c.500 BCE)" *Internet
    Encyclopedia of Philosophy.* James Fieser and
    Bradley Dowden, Editors. URL=
    http://www.iep.utm.edu/heraclit/

Guthrie, W.K.C. *The Greek Philosophers From Thales to
    Aristotle.* New York: Harper & Row, 1975.

Huffman, Carl, "Pythagoras", *The Stanford Encyclopedia of
    Philosophy (Fall 2011 Edition)*, Edward N. Zalta
    (ed.) URL=
    http://plato.stanford.edu/archives/fall2011/entries/pyt
    hagoras/

Huffington Post. *Superstorm Sandy Deaths, Damage And
    Magnitude: What We Know One Month Later.* URL=
    http://www.huffingtonpost.com/2012/11/29/superstor
    m-hurricane-sandy-deaths-2012_n_2209217.html

Hume, David. *An Essay Concerning Human Understanding.* Stilwell: Digireads.com, 2005. (Originally Published 1748).

Kant, Immanuel. *Critique of Pure Reason.* London: Penguin Classics, 2007.

---. "Critique of Practical Reason," *Great Books of the Western World, Kant.* Robert M. Hutchins, Editor. Chicago: Encyclopedia Britannica, 1952.

---. *Groundwork of the Metaphysics of Morals.* Translated by H.J. Patton. New York: Harperperennial Modern Thought, 2009.

Kenny, Anthony. *An Illustrated Brief History of Western Philosophy.* Oxford: Blackwell, 2006.

Lesher, James, "Xenophanes", *The Stanford Encyclopedia of Philosophy (Fall 2011 Edition),* Edward N. Zalta (ed.) URL = http://plato.stanford.edu/archives/fall2011/entries/xenophanes/

Leibniz, Wilhelm Gottfried. "Monadology," in *Leibniz Philosophical Writings.* London: J. M. Dent & Sons, 1973.

Mackie, J. L. *The Miracle of Theism: Arguments for and against the existence of God.* Oxford: Clarendon Press, 1982.

---. "Evil and Omnipotence," in *Mind Association,* Vol. 64, No. 254, (1955).

Marias, Julian. *History of Philosophy*. New York: Dover, 1967.

Mcphee, Isaac. *Physics: Everyday Science at the Speed of Light*. New York: Metro Books, 2010.

Melchert, Norman. *Philosophical Conversations: A Concise Historical Introduction*. Oxford: Oxford University Press, 2009.

Mill, John Stuart. *Utilitarianism*. Reprint from original 1863 publication.

Moreland, J. P. *Consciousness and the Existence of God: A Theistic Argument*. New York: Routledge, 2008.

Moreland, J. P. and William Lane Craig. *Philosophical Foundations for a Christian Worldview*. Downers Grove: InterVarsity Press, 2003.

Murray, Michael, "Leibniz on the Problem of Evil", *The Stanford Encyclopedia of Philosophy (Spring 2011 Edition)*, Edward N. Zalta (ed.) URL = http://plato.stanford.edu/archives/spr2011/entries/leibniz-evil/.

O'Grady, Patricia. "Thales of Miletus (c. 620 BCE—c. 546 BCE)," The *Internet Encyclopedia of Philosophy*. James Fieser and Bradley Dowden, Editors. URL= http://www.iep.utm.edu/thales/

O'Neill, Onora, "Kantian Ethics," in *A Companion to Ethics*. Peter Singer, Editor. Malden: Blackwell, 1993.

Plato. "Protagoras," in *Plato: Complete Works*. John Cooper, Editor. Indianapolis: Hackett Publishing Company, 1997.

---. "Republic," in *Plato: Complete Works*. John Cooper, Editor. Indianapolis: Hackett Publishing Company, 1997.

---. "Republic," in *The Complete Works of Plato*, Editor and Translator, Benjamin Jowett. Kindle Edition, 2011.

---. "Euthyphro," in *Plato: Complete Works*. John Cooper, Editor. Indianapolis: Hackett Publishing Company, 1997.

---. "Apology," in *Plato: Complete Works*. John Cooper, Editor. Indianapolis: Hackett Publishing Company, 1997.

---. *Timaeus*. Translated by Benjamin Jowett. URL= http://classics.mit.edu/Plato/timaeus.html

---. "Timaeus," in *Plato: Complete Works*. John Cooper, Editor. Indianapolis: Hackett Publishing Company, 1997.

---. *Phaedo*. Translated by Benjamin Jowett. URL= http://pinkmonkey.com/dl/library1/phaedo.pdf

Rachels, James. "The Ethics of Virtue," in *Ethics: History, Theory, and Contemporary Issues*. Steven Cahn and Peter Markie, Editors. Oxford: Oxford University Press, 2006.

Robinson, Howard, "Dualism", *The Stanford Encyclopedia of Philosophy (Winter 2012 Edition)*, Edward N. Zalta (ed.) URL = http://plato.stanford.edu/archives/win2012/entries/dualism/.

Rogers, Glenn. *21st Century Ethics: An Introduction to Moral Philosophy*. Estherville: Simpson and Brook, Publishers, 2012.

---. *Proof of God: Inquiries into the Philosophy of Religion, A Concise Introduction*. Estherville: Simpson and Brook, Publishers, 2012.

---. *Becoming: A Philosophical Treatise on Human Potential*. Bedford: Simpson and Brook, Publishers, 2010.

Rosenberg, Jennifer. *Rwanda Genocide: A Short History of the Rwanda Genocide.* URL = http://history1900s.about.com/od/rwandangenocide/a/Rwanda-Genocide.htm

Rowe, William L. *Philosophy of Religion: An Introduction*. Belmont: Wadsworth, 2001.

Schneewind, J. B. "Autonomy, Obligation, and Virtue: An Overview of Kant's Moral Philosophy," in *The Cambridge Companion to Kant*. Paul Guyer, Editor. Cambridge: Cambridge, 1992.

Simpson, Peter. "Contemporary Virtue Ethics and Aristotle," in *The Review of Metaphysics*. Vol. 45, No. 3 (Mar., 1992), pp. 503-524.

Skirry, Justin. "René Descartes (1596-1650): Overview," The *Internet Encyclopedia of Philosophy*. James Fieser and Bradley Dowden, Editors. URL= http://www.iep.utm.edu/descarte/

Stack George J. "Materialism," in *The Shorter Routledge Encyclopedia of Philosophy*. Edward Craig, Editor. London: Routledge, 2005.

Strawson, Galen. "Free Will," in *The Shorter Routledge Encyclopedia of Philosophy*. Edward Craig, Editor. London: Routledge, 2005.

Thucydides. *Pericles's Funeral Oration*. Online copy located at URL= http://www.sammustafa.com/Resources/Thucydides.pdf

Truncellito, David. "Epistemology," The *Internet Encyclopedia of Philosophy*. James Fieser and Bradley Dowden, Editors. URL= http://www.iep.utm.edu/epistemo/

Van Inwagen, Peter. *An Essay on Free Will*. Oxford: Oxford University Press, 1986.

Weatherford, Roy C. "Freedom and Determinism," in *The Oxford Companion to Philosophy*, New Edition. Ted Honderich, Editor. Oxford: Oxford University Press, 2005.

Whitehead, Alfred North. *Process and Reality: An Essay in Cosmology*. Corrected Edition New York: Free Press, 1978.

Printed in the USA
CPSIA information can be obtained
at www.ICGtesting.com
LVHW04205328O823
756492LV00002B/60